DRAGON AGE THE VEILGUARD

GAME GUIDE

I0465341

Richard S. Pence

INTRODUCTION

Whether you're a newcomer to the world of Thedas or a seasoned hero returning to the battlefront, this guide was crafted with you in mind. *The Veilguard* expansion invites players into a realm darker and more complex than ever before, with mysteries that run deeper than the Fade itself. Here, choices echo across nations, friendships are tested, and enemies lie not only in plain sight but hidden behind every veil.

In writing this guide, I wanted to offer you more than a walkthrough. This is a companion for your journey, from the moment you step foot into Thedas as a fresh recruit to the final, climactic showdown. You'll find practical advice for building your character, tried-and-true combat strategies, and tips for making the most of each interaction and exploration. But more than that, I've included insights, lore, and hidden details to enrich your experience, whether you're navigating Veilguard's new lands or trying to solve its most tantalizing puzzles.

One thing that has always set the *Dragon Age* series apart is its depth—not just in gameplay, but in its storytelling. In *Veilguard,* every decision you make will shape not only your path but the world around you. This guide will help you understand these consequences, so you can play with both confidence and curiosity, knowing how each choice might unfold.

As you hold this guide in your hands, think of it as a friend by your side. It's here to share secrets, keep you safe, and make sure you don't miss a single detail on this unforgettable journey. So go ahead—choose your class, gather your allies, and prepare yourself. The Veil awaits, and adventure is just one step away.

CHAPTER 1

Introduction to Dragon Age: The Veilguard

In this chapter, we'll explore what makes *Dragon Age: The Veilguard* a unique addition to the beloved *Dragon Age* series. You'll get an overview of the storyline, the key themes, and how this expansion builds on the rich lore of Thedas. We'll walk through the game's background, introducing you to the new mechanics, characters, and places that set Veilguard apart. This chapter sets the stage for your journey, giving you everything you need to understand the stakes, the mysteries, and the role you're about to play in a world on the brink of change.

Overview of the Game

Welcome to *Dragon Age: The Veilguard*, where the familiar world of Thedas opens up in ways players never thought possible. This expansion doesn't just continue the story—it immerses you deeper into the lore, the conflicts, and the endless mysteries that define the *Dragon Age* universe. In *Veilguard*, the boundaries between the physical world and the Fade—the mystical realm of spirits and dreams—are dangerously thin. This isn't just another quest; it's a chance to make history in a world where every decision has rippling consequences.

From the moment you step into the game, you're given the freedom to choose a path that feels truly yours. Whether you're a seasoned *Dragon Age* fan or new to the series, *Veilguard* offers something for everyone. It combines rich storytelling, intense combat, and a deep exploration of the Veil—the invisible barrier between our world and the Fade. If you've ever wondered what truly lies beyond that barrier, this expansion gives you the chance to find out.

The game's intuitive mechanics, immersive environments, and compelling storyline promise an adventure that's as challenging as it is rewarding. Every character interaction, every choice, and every fight bring you closer to the heart of what makes *Dragon Age* unforgettable.

History of the Veilguard Expansion

The journey of *Veilguard* began with a desire to answer some of the *Dragon Age* universe's most tantalizing questions. Over the years, fans have speculated about the Veil's origins, its creators, and what might happen if it were to break down. The development team behind *Veilguard* wanted to dig into these mysteries and give players an experience that was both thrilling and thought-provoking.

The expansion was conceived to be more than just a new chapter. It was designed to uncover secrets that have lingered since the first *Dragon Age* game. Why was the Veil created, and who truly benefits from its existence? These questions sparked a storyline that would not only explore the world's past but also impact its future. As the *Dragon Age* team began to craft this narrative, they decided to introduce a group known as the Veilguard, an elite team with the task of protecting Thedas from the dangers of a weakened Veil.

In the storyline, the Veil begins to weaken in specific areas of Thedas, allowing creatures from the Fade to slip through. These events mark the beginning of an exploration into a hidden world—one where ancient spirits, forgotten gods, and long-lost secrets of magic come to light. The development team also wanted to introduce a darker, more nuanced side of magic, one that questions whether the Veil is a protective shield or a prison for something far more sinister.

The result is an expansion that blends new gameplay elements with deep lore and rich storytelling. It's not just a continuation of the *Dragon Age* series—it's an invitation to step into the unknown and confront the forces that shape the world of Thedas.

Lore of the Dragon Age Universe

The lore of *Dragon Age* has always been one of its most beloved elements. At its heart, *Dragon Age* is a world shaped by magic, politics, and ancient secrets. The story is set in Thedas, a land rich with different cultures, religions, and power struggles. The Fade, a mystical realm beyond human sight, holds spirits, demons, and the memories of ancient gods. The Veil, created to separate Thedas from the Fade, is one of the most mysterious and significant aspects of the world's lore.

In *Veilguard*, we're invited to question the Veil's true purpose. According to ancient legends, the Veil was created by the elven gods to protect Thedas from creatures that once roamed freely. But this expansion suggests there may be more to the story. Was the Veil truly created for protection, or was it a way to imprison something unspeakable? As players explore the world of *Veilguard*, they encounter spirits who remember a time before the Veil and uncover hidden knowledge that challenges everything they thought they knew.

This lore-rich expansion also provides a new perspective on magic. Mages, once feared for their connection to the Fade, find themselves grappling with new powers and dangers. The line between magic and reality blurs as the Veil weakens, and players must navigate a world where the rules are constantly shifting.

For longtime fans of *Dragon Age*, *Veilguard* is a thrilling chance to connect the dots between past stories and unanswered questions. For new players, it's an introduction to the complex history, moral ambiguities, and wonders that make Thedas so unforgettable.

Key Features and New Mechanics in Veilguard

Dragon Age: The Veilguard isn't just about story; it introduces a wealth of new features and mechanics designed to keep gameplay fresh and engaging. Here's what you can expect:

1. **Veilguard Class**: A unique addition to the character classes, the Veilguard class is specifically trained to handle creatures and phenomena associated with the Fade. They bring new skills and abilities tailored to combat supernatural threats and manipulate the Veil's energy. Players who choose this class gain access to abilities that affect both enemies and allies in surprising ways.

2. **Veil Zones**: As the Veil weakens, certain areas of Thedas become known as Veil Zones. These are special zones where the boundary between the physical world and the Fade is fragile, creating an unpredictable mix of threats and rewards. In these zones, you may encounter rare creatures, unexpected allies, or ancient relics with mysterious powers. However, the risk is high, as these areas are known for strange magic that can affect even the most seasoned heroes.

3. **New Companion System**: The expansion enhances the companion system, allowing for deeper relationships with party members. Companions now have personal quests tied to the Veilguard storyline, revealing secrets about their pasts and their views on the Fade. Players can influence these relationships by making choices that align with or challenge their companions' beliefs, potentially leading to new romance options or conflict.

4. **Enhanced Combat Mechanics**: *Veilguard* brings refined combat mechanics, allowing for smoother and more strategic fighting. New abilities for each class make combat more dynamic and tailored to supernatural threats. Players now have access to "Veil Powers," special moves that temporarily alter the rules of combat, such as phasing into the Fade to avoid attacks or summoning a spirit ally for support.

5. **Exploration and Puzzle Elements**: The expansion encourages exploration and introduces puzzle-solving as a core mechanic. Players will encounter Veilguard Seals—ancient relics that protect certain areas of the Veil. Unlocking these seals requires solving intricate puzzles, often combining environmental clues with knowledge of the game's lore. These puzzles add depth to exploration and reward players with powerful items and insights into the Veil's history.

6. **Moral Choices with Far-Reaching Consequences**: True to *Dragon Age* style, *Veilguard* emphasizes player choice. Every decision, from how you treat a spirit ally to whether you accept knowledge from an ancient demon, shapes the game's outcome. These choices affect not only the immediate storyline but

also the world around you, as NPCs react and factions respond to your actions. Players may find themselves grappling with ethical questions, especially as they learn more about the Veil's purpose.

7. **Multiplayer Co-op in Veilguard Zones**: For the first time, players can enter Veil Zones with friends. Multiplayer co-op allows for tactical teamwork in these high-stakes areas, where players can share abilities and take on challenging missions together. This mode emphasizes strategy and rewards groups that work in sync.

CHAPTER 2

Getting Started

In this chapter, we'll walk you through everything you need to begin your adventure in *Dragon Age: The Veilguard*. From setting up the game and customizing your character to learning the basic controls and navigating the interface, this section covers all the essentials. You'll also find tips on choosing a class that suits your playstyle, understanding the game's mechanics, and getting comfortable with your surroundings before you set out into the world. This guide is here to make sure your journey starts on the right foot, fully equipped and ready for the challenges ahead.

Game Installation and Setup

Setting up *Dragon Age: The Veilguard* is your first step into an epic adventure, and we're here to make it as simple as possible. Whether you're on PC, PlayStation, or Xbox, here's a clear, step-by-step guide to get you ready to play.

1. Purchasing and Downloading the Game

- **PC (Steam or Origin)**: Start by heading to your preferred game launcher, either Steam or Origin.
    - If you're using Steam, open the app, search for *Dragon Age: The Veilguard* in the search bar, and click on the game title. You'll see an "Add to Cart" button—click it, proceed to checkout, and follow the prompts to complete your purchase.
    - On Origin, open the launcher, search for *Dragon Age: The Veilguard*, click on the game, and then hit "Buy Now." Follow the steps for payment to finalize your purchase.
- **PlayStation**: On your console's home screen, open the PlayStation Store. Use the search bar at the top to look up *Dragon Age: The Veilguard*. Select the game, then press "Add to Cart." Go to your cart, press "Proceed to Checkout," and complete the purchase.
- **Xbox**: From your Xbox dashboard, open the Microsoft Store. Navigate to the search function, type in *Dragon Age: The Veilguard*, and choose the game. Select "Buy" and follow the prompts to complete the transaction.

2. Starting the Download and Installation

- **PC**: Once you've purchased the game, go to your library on Steam or Origin.

- In Steam, find *Dragon Age: The Veilguard* in your library list on the left, click on it, and hit "Install." Choose the destination folder if prompted, and press "Next" to begin the download.
- On Origin, go to your "My Game Library" section, locate *Dragon Age: The Veilguard*, and click "Download." Follow any prompts to confirm the location and start downloading.

- **PlayStation**: After purchasing, you'll see an option to "Download" or "Download to Console." Select this option to start downloading immediately. You can track the progress from your home screen; the game icon will show a download bar.
- **Xbox**: Post-purchase, you'll see a "Download" option on the game's store page. Click it to begin the download. Alternatively, you can go to "My Games & Apps" to view download progress.

3. Adjusting Settings

Once the game is installed, it's time to configure the settings to match your preferences.

- **Launching the Game**: Open *Dragon Age: The Veilguard* from your game library. After the title screen, you'll land on the main menu.
- **Adjusting Video and Audio**:
  - From the main menu, select "Settings."
  - Under "Video," you can adjust the resolution, brightness, and graphics quality. If you're on PC, choose settings that match your hardware capabilities—higher settings give better visuals but can impact performance.
  - Go to "Audio" to manage volume for music, dialogue, and sound effects. Balance these levels to ensure you don't miss out on important dialogue or sound cues.
- **Gameplay Settings**: In the "Gameplay" section, you'll find options for difficulty, controller preferences, and accessibility.
  - **Difficulty**: New players might want to start on "Normal," while seasoned *Dragon Age* players may opt for "Hard" or "Nightmare" for a real challenge.
  - **Controller Options**: If you're on PC and prefer a controller, make sure "Controller" is selected. Otherwise, keyboard and mouse will be the default.
  - **Accessibility**: Look into options like subtitle size, colorblind mode, and other accessibility features to make sure you're comfortable.

4. Creating Your Save File

After your settings are configured, the game will prompt you to create a new save file.

- **Save File Creation**: Select "New Game" from the main menu, which will automatically begin your character setup and create a save file. This file will store your progress, and you'll be able to save manually throughout the game.

- **Manual Saves and Auto-Saves**: *Dragon Age: The Veilguard* offers both. The game auto-saves frequently, but for extra security, create manual saves at key points by going to "Menu" and selecting "Save Game." This is especially helpful before making major decisions.

5. Network Settings (for Multiplayer)

If you plan on using any online features, make sure your console or PC is connected to the internet.

- **PC**: Open your system settings, go to "Network & Internet," and confirm you're connected. Steam and Origin will handle any additional network requirements for multiplayer.
- **PlayStation**: From your home screen, go to "Settings," then "Network." Select "Test Internet Connection" to verify.
- **Xbox**: Go to "Settings," then "Network Settings," and choose "Test Network Connection."

6. Preparing to Play

After everything is set up, it's time to start your journey in *The Veilguard*.

- **Launch Your First Session**: Head back to the main menu, select "New Game" (or "Continue" if you've already started), and immerse yourself in the world of Thedas. The game will guide you through character creation and a brief tutorial to introduce you to basic controls.

Navigating the Game Interface

Navigating the game interface in *Dragon Age: The Veilguard* is essential for making the most of your journey. Here's a detailed guide on how to use each part of the interface, where to find key features, and which buttons to press to access them. Whether you're exploring the map, managing your inventory, or setting up your party, this guide will walk you through it step-by-step.

1. Main Menu Navigation

Once you launch the game, you'll start on the main menu, where you'll find essential options:

- **New Game**: To start a fresh adventure, highlight and select "New Game." This takes you to character creation and starts your journey.
- **Load Game**: If you've already begun, select "Load Game" to continue from your last save point. Use the D-pad (console) or arrow keys (PC) to scroll through save files and press "A" (Xbox), "X" (PlayStation), or "Enter" (PC) to load the game.
- **Settings**: Access game options like graphics, audio, and gameplay settings. Use this menu to adjust preferences before starting or during gameplay.

- **Extras**: This section might include achievements, bonus content, or downloadable content (DLC) information if you've purchased any.

2. In-Game HUD (Heads-Up Display)

Once you're in the game, your HUD displays essential information. Here's what you'll see and how to interact with it:

- **Health and Mana/Stamina Bars**: Located in the top-left corner, these bars show your character's health (red bar) and mana/stamina (blue bar for mages, green for warriors and rogues). Keep an eye on these during combat.
- **Compass**: The compass, found at the top-center, guides you to your objectives and shows key points of interest around you. Follow the direction markers to reach your current quest location.
- **Quick Slots**: At the bottom of the screen, you'll see quick slots for abilities and items. Press the corresponding button to use each item or ability—these are typically mapped to the D-pad (console) or number keys (PC).

3. The Map

The map is your key to navigating *The Veilguard* world and tracking your objectives.

- **Accessing the Map**: Press "M" on PC, the touchpad on PlayStation, or "View" on Xbox to open the map.
- **Using the Map**: On the map screen, you'll see icons for quests, important characters, and other points of interest.
    - Use the left stick (console) or mouse (PC) to move around the map.
    - Zoom in and out by pressing R2/L2 on PlayStation, RT/LT on Xbox, or the scroll wheel on PC. This helps you get a better view of the surrounding area.
- **Setting Waypoints**: Highlight any location on the map and press "X" (PlayStation), "A" (Xbox), or right-click (PC) to set a waypoint. Your compass will now direct you to this spot.

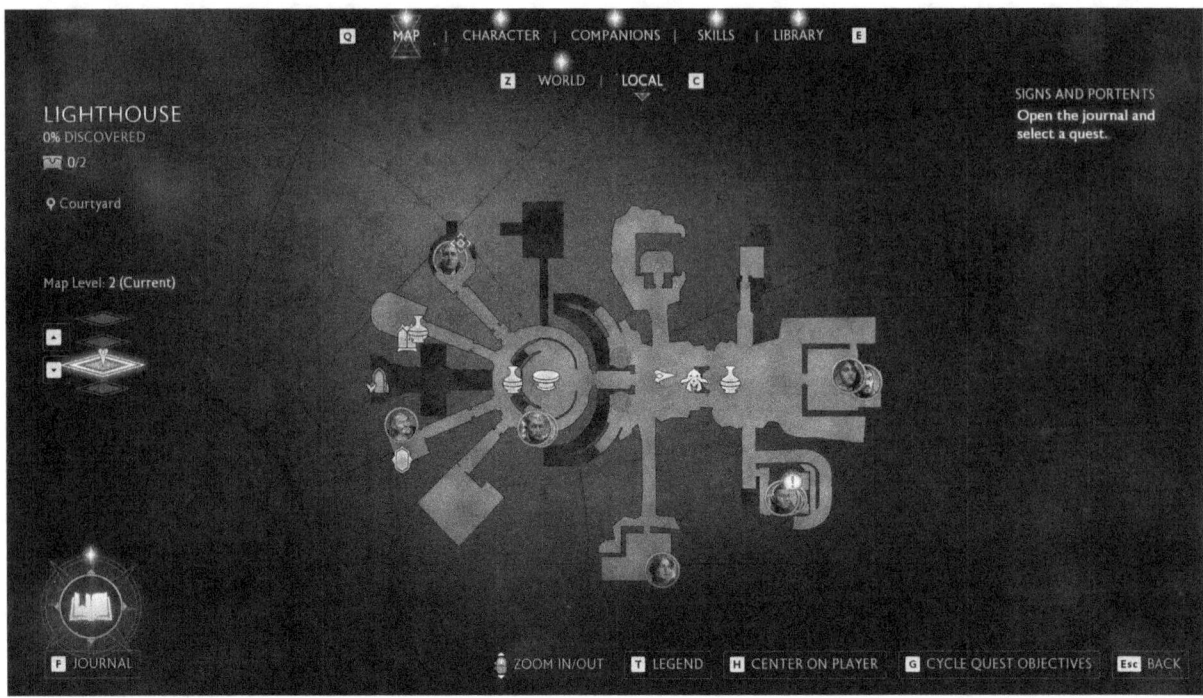

4. Quest Log and Journal

Your quest log keeps track of your active missions and provides details about each objective.

- **Accessing the Journal**: Press "J" on PC, the touchpad on PlayStation, or "View" on Xbox to open your journal.
- **Navigating Quests**: Use the D-pad (console) or arrow keys (PC) to scroll through main quests, side quests, and companion quests.
- **Quest Details**: Select any quest to view more details, including objectives, rewards, and any important notes. This is helpful for tracking your progress and knowing what's next.

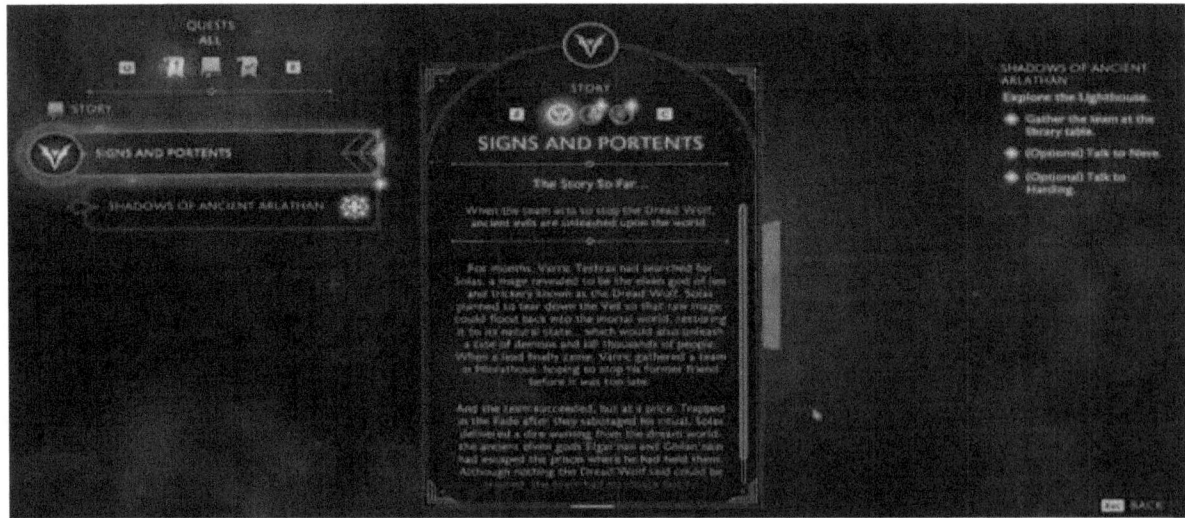

5. Inventory and Equipment

Your inventory is where you manage weapons, armor, potions, and other items.

- **Accessing the Inventory**: Press "I" on PC, "Options" on PlayStation, or "Menu" on Xbox.
- **Viewing and Equipping Items**: Use the left stick (console) or mouse (PC) to scroll through different inventory categories (weapons, armor, accessories, potions, etc.).
    - To equip an item, highlight it and press "X" (PlayStation), "A" (Xbox), or left-click (PC). Equipped items will show on your character's model.
- **Organizing Inventory**: Use R2/L2 (PlayStation), RT/LT (Xbox), or the tab keys (PC) to switch between item categories. Organizing your inventory regularly can help you quickly find what you need during battles.

6. Abilities and Skill Tree

This is where you unlock and upgrade abilities for your character.

- **Accessing the Skill Tree**: Press "K" on PC, "Options" on PlayStation, or "Menu" on Xbox.
- **Navigating the Skill Tree**: Use the left stick (console) or mouse (PC) to move between skill branches (e.g., combat, defense, special abilities).
- **Unlocking Skills**: Highlight a skill you want to unlock, and press "X" (PlayStation), "A" (Xbox), or left-click (PC) to confirm. You'll need skill points, which are earned by leveling up.
- **Assigning Abilities to Quick Slots**: After unlocking an ability, assign it to a quick slot by selecting it, then pressing the corresponding button for each slot (e.g., R1/RB, Triangle/Y).

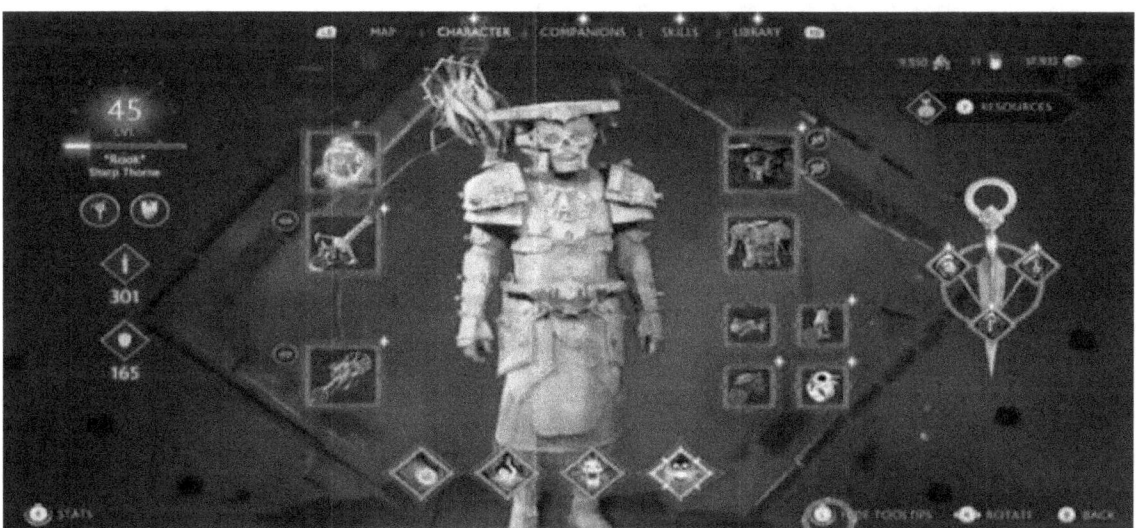

7. Party Management

In *The Veilguard*, you'll recruit companions who can join you in battle.

- **Accessing Party Menu**: Press "P" on PC, "Options" on PlayStation, or "Menu" on Xbox, then select "Party Management."
- **Swapping Companions**: Highlight the companion you want to swap and press "X" (PlayStation), "A" (Xbox), or left-click (PC). Choose the new companion and confirm to switch them in.
- **Customizing Companion Gear**: You can equip weapons and armor for your companions the same way as for your main character. Navigate to a companion, select their equipment slot, and choose the desired item.

8. In-Game Menu and Saving Progress

The in-game menu gives you quick access to settings, saves, and the option to quit.

- **Opening the Menu**: Press "Esc" on PC, "Options" on PlayStation, or "Menu" on Xbox.
- **Saving the Game**: To manually save, select "Save Game" from the menu. Creating manual saves regularly is useful if you want to try different choices or strategies.
- **Loading and Quitting**: From this menu, you can also load a previous save or exit the game if you're done for the session.

9. Tips for Easy Navigation

- **Use Quick Access Buttons**: Learn the shortcuts (like "M" for the map or "I" for inventory on PC) to quickly access each part of the interface. On consoles, keep the "Options" button handy to pull up the main menu when you need to adjust something.
- **Stay Organized**: Managing your inventory, skill tree, and quest log can make a big difference in your gameplay experience. Spend a few minutes each time you play to organize these, and you'll find it easier to focus on the adventure itself.

Character Creation Guide

Creating your character in *Dragon Age: The Veilguard* is one of the most exciting parts of starting your journey. This is where you decide who you want to be in Thedas: your background, strengths, weaknesses, and even the way you'll approach challenges. Here's a step-by-step guide to help you create a character that feels just right for you.

1. Choosing Your Race

- After selecting "New Game" from the main menu, you'll be taken to the character creation screen, where the first decision is choosing your race. Each race—Human, Elf, Dwarf, or Qunari—comes with its own unique storylines, dialogue options, and advantages.
- **Human**: Balanced stats and more respect among the nobility. Choose Humans if you want a flexible starting experience.
- **Elf**: High Dexterity, making them ideal for stealthy or agile roles like rogues. Elves often have a mysterious backstory and unique interactions with other characters.
- **Dwarf**: High resilience and combat skills, especially effective as warriors or rogues. However, they cannot use magic, which can affect certain aspects of gameplay.
- **Qunari**: Known for their strength and imposing presence, Qunari make powerful warriors and mages with a unique cultural background.
- **Selecting Your Race**: Use the D-pad (console) or arrow keys (PC) to highlight each race, and press "X" (PlayStation), "A" (Xbox), or left-click (PC) to confirm. Take your time to read the descriptions; each choice will shape how characters in the game world react to you.

2. Selecting Your Class

- Next up, you'll choose your class, which defines your combat style and abilities. This is a crucial step, as it determines how you'll handle challenges in the game.

- **Warrior**: Warriors are the tanks of *Veilguard*, capable of wielding heavy weapons and taking a lot of damage. Ideal for those who like a straightforward, head-on combat style.
- **Mage**: Mages can use powerful spells to heal allies, deal massive damage, and control the battlefield. They're more fragile than other classes, but they make up for it with versatility.
- **Rogue**: Quick, stealthy, and agile, Rogues specialize in critical hits and taking down enemies swiftly. They work well with ranged or melee weapons and excel in areas where stealth and agility matter.
- **Veil Warden** (new class): Exclusive to *Veilguard*, the Veil Warden specializes in abilities related to the Fade and has unique powers that make them effective against supernatural threats.
- **Selecting Your Class**: Use the left stick (console) or mouse (PC) to highlight your choice and press "X" (PlayStation), "A" (Xbox), or left-click (PC) to confirm. Think about how you like to play games—do you enjoy close combat, casting spells from a distance, or striking from the shadows? There's a class to fit each style.

3. Customizing Appearance

- Now comes the fun part: customizing your character's appearance. You'll find options for facial structure, hair, skin tone, and much more. Here's a quick rundown of the key sections:

- ○ **Face Shape**: Choose from several face shapes to set the base look of your character. Use the D-pad (console) or arrows (PC) to scroll and select.
- ○ **Hair Style and Color**: Pick a hairstyle that matches your character's vibe. You'll have multiple options, from sleek to rugged. Select "Hair Color" to open a palette of colors.
- ○ **Eye Color and Shape**: Fine-tune your character's gaze by selecting an eye shape and color.
- ○ **Scars and Tattoos**: If you want to add some story to your character's look, go to the "Scars and Tattoos" section. You can choose facial scars, body tattoos, and other features that hint at a life of adventure.
- ○ **Confirming Appearance**: Once you're happy with the look, select "Confirm" to lock in your character's appearance. Remember, this is how you'll look for the entire game, so make it feel like someone you'll enjoy playing!

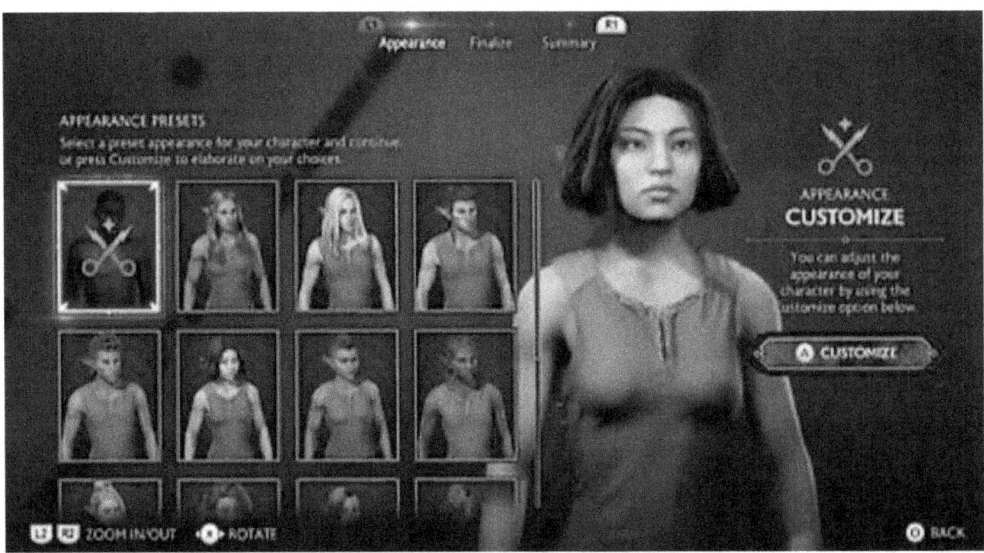

4. Choosing a Background

- Depending on your race and class, you'll have a selection of backgrounds to choose from. These backgrounds add depth to your character and can affect how NPCs interact with you.
  - ○ **Noble Backgrounds**: Often available to Human characters, giving you more influence among the nobility.
  - ○ **Mage Background**: Offers unique dialogue options and relationships with other magic-users.
  - ○ **Commoner Background**: Provides a more down-to-earth perspective and can lead to stronger connections with the general populace.
- Each background comes with a brief description, so read these carefully—they'll play into your interactions, story options, and even some quests.
- **Selecting Background**: Highlight your chosen background with the D-pad (console) or mouse (PC), and press "X" (PlayStation), "A" (Xbox), or left-click (PC) to confirm.

5. Assigning Starting Attributes

- Now, you'll distribute a few points into your starting attributes: Strength, Dexterity, Constitution, Magic, and Willpower. These points help define your character's skills right from the start.
    - **Strength**: Improves melee damage and is essential for Warriors.
    - **Dexterity**: Boosts accuracy and critical hits, making it a must for Rogues.
    - **Constitution**: Increases health and stamina, which is helpful for all classes.
    - **Magic**: Determines spell power and mana, essential for Mages.
    - **Willpower**: Affects stamina and mental resilience, useful for all characters.
- **Assigning Points**: Highlight an attribute, press "X" (PlayStation), "A" (Xbox), or left-click (PC) to add a point. You can also remove points by selecting the attribute and pressing the corresponding button.

6. Selecting Starting Abilities

- Each class begins with a few basic abilities that set the tone for how you'll handle combat. You'll have a couple of points to invest in abilities from the start, so choose wisely based on how you plan to play.
    - For example, a **Warrior** might start with a basic attack boost and a defense skill, while a **Mage** might have access to a healing spell and an offensive spell.
    - **Veil Warden** characters will find unique abilities that involve interacting with the Fade, like summoning spirit allies or weakening supernatural enemies.
- **Choosing Abilities**: Highlight the ability you want, then press "X" (PlayStation), "A" (Xbox), or left-click (PC) to select it. Check the descriptions to get a sense of what each skill does and how it will affect your early combat encounters.

7. Finalizing Your Character

- After setting everything up, review your choices. This is your last chance to make adjustments before you begin the game. Take a moment to make sure you're happy with your race, class, appearance, and attributes.
- **Confirming Character**: Once you're ready, press "Start" (console) or "Enter" (PC) to confirm and officially start your journey.

Creating a character in *The Veilguard* is all about bringing your vision to life. Choose a race and class that resonate with you, and don't be afraid to put your personality into every detail, from scars to spell choices. This character will become your guide and hero in a world full of wonders, challenges, and unforgettable experiences. So take your time, get creative, and make someone you'll enjoy exploring Thedas with—because this is your story to tell.

Choosing Your Class: Warrior, Mage, Rogue, or Veil Warden

In *Dragon Age: The Veilguard*, choosing your class is one of the most crucial decisions you'll make. Your class determines your abilities, combat style, and how you approach challenges in the game. Here's an in-depth guide to help you select the class that best fits your playstyle, including where to press to make your selection.

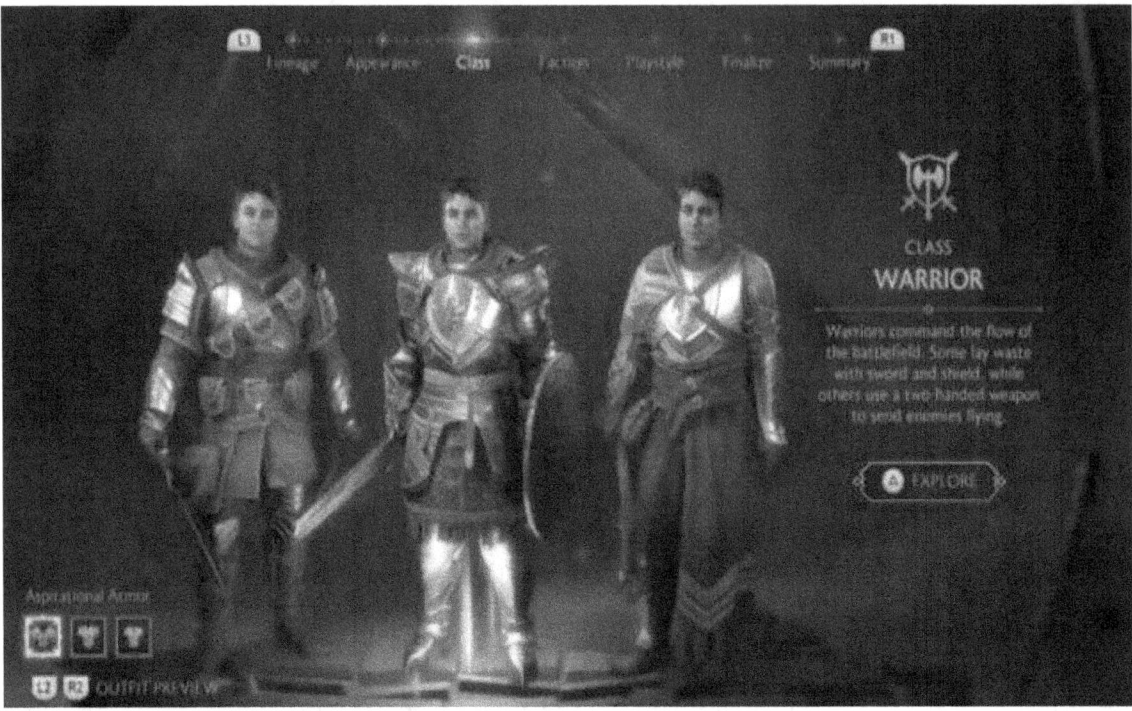

1. Navigating to the Class Selection Screen

- After selecting "New Game" from the main menu, you'll start creating your character. The first options will be race and background, but shortly after, you'll arrive at the class selection screen.
- Here, you'll see the four available classes: **Warrior**, **Mage**, **Rogue**, and the new **Veil Warden**.
- **Selecting a Class**: Use the D-pad (console) or arrow keys (PC) to navigate through each class option. To confirm your selection, press "X" (PlayStation), "A" (Xbox), or left-click (PC).

2. Warrior Class

- **Overview**: Warriors are the heavy hitters and protectors on the battlefield. They wield powerful melee weapons, like swords, axes, and hammers, and can take a lot of damage, making them ideal for front-line combat.
- **Playstyle**: If you enjoy direct combat, tanking, and taking the lead in battles, the Warrior is a great choice. They have high health and armor, allowing them to withstand attacks while dealing solid damage.
- **Specializations**:

- **Champion**: Focuses on defense, with abilities that protect both the Warrior and their allies.
- **Reaver**: Gains power from taking damage, making them incredibly deadly at low health.
- **Templar**: Ideal for countering magic-users, with abilities to disrupt and nullify spells.
- **Selecting Warrior**: Once you're on the Warrior class option, press "X" (PlayStation), "A" (Xbox), or left-click (PC) to select. You'll have the option to confirm your choice if you're certain.

3. Mage Class

- **Overview**: Mages are spellcasters, capable of powerful offensive, defensive, and support abilities. They can wield staffs and harness magical energy to cast spells, making them versatile and dangerous in combat.
- **Playstyle**: Mages work best from a distance, casting spells to control the battlefield, heal allies, or inflict heavy damage on enemies. If you enjoy strategic combat and have an interest in the magical aspects of *Dragon Age*, the Mage is perfect for you.
- **Specializations**:
    - **Knight-Enchanter**: Uses magic in close combat with a spirit blade, allowing the Mage to engage in melee without sacrificing spell power.
    - **Necromancer**: Focuses on death and decay, with abilities that weaken enemies and summon spirits.
    - **Rift Mage**: Specializes in manipulating the Veil itself, creating powerful area-of-effect spells that control groups of enemies.
- **Selecting Mage**: Highlight the Mage class, then press "X" (PlayStation), "A" (Xbox), or left-click (PC) to choose. Confirm your selection when you're ready.

4. Rogue Class

- **Overview**: Rogues are agile and precise, specializing in critical hits, traps, and stealth. They can wield daggers for close-range combat or bows for ranged attacks, allowing them to adapt to various scenarios.
- **Playstyle**: Rogues are best for players who enjoy a stealthier, tactical approach. They excel in positioning and timing, striking when enemies least expect it. Rogues can sneak behind enemies for critical hits or use traps and ranged attacks to control the battlefield.
- **Specializations**:
    - **Assassin**: Focuses on stealth and critical hits, with abilities that deal massive damage from behind.
    - **Tempest**: Uses alchemical abilities to enhance attacks and create chaotic effects on the battlefield.
    - **Artificer**: Skilled in traps and gadgets, allowing them to set up ambushes and control enemy movement.
- **Selecting Rogue**: Scroll to the Rogue option, then press "X" (PlayStation), "A" (Xbox), or left-click (PC) to select. Confirm your choice to lock in the Rogue as your class.

5. Veil Warden Class (Exclusive to Veilguard)

- **Overview**: The Veil Warden is a unique class introduced in *The Veilguard* expansion. These warriors have a deep connection to the Fade and wield abilities that allow them to manipulate the Veil, offering a blend of offensive and support abilities that are especially effective against supernatural foes.
- **Playstyle**: Veil Wardens are best suited for players who want a mix of magic and melee, with abilities that let them weaken or control enemies, especially spirits and demons. Their unique connection to the Fade also allows them to perform special actions unavailable to other classes, making them invaluable in certain quests and battles.
- **Specializations**:
  - **Spirit Guardian**: Focuses on protective abilities, creating barriers and healing allies with Fade energy.
  - **Fade Weaver**: Uses the power of the Fade to weaken and drain enemies, making them vulnerable to attacks.
  - **Shadow Walker**: Specializes in stealth and phasing abilities, allowing them to temporarily disappear and surprise enemies.
- **Selecting Veil Warden**: Highlight the Veil Warden class, then press "X" (PlayStation), "A" (Xbox), or left-click (PC) to choose it. You'll have an option to confirm, as this choice is final.

6. Making Your Final Choice

- Choosing a class is one of the biggest decisions you'll make in *The Veilguard*, so take your time to read through each description, think about your preferred playstyle, and consider how you want to approach combat.
- Once you're happy with your choice, press "Start" (console) or "Enter" (PC) to confirm your class and move to the next phase of character creation. Remember, each class offers a unique way to experience the game, so whatever you choose will bring its own strengths and challenges.

Selecting a class is more than just picking a fighting style—it's about choosing how you want to interact with the world of *Dragon Age*. Whether you're charging into battle as a Warrior, wielding powerful spells as a Mage, striking from the shadows as a Rogue, or harnessing the Fade as a Veil Warden, each class opens up new ways to explore, engage, and make an impact. Once you've made your choice, you're one step closer to beginning an unforgettable adventure.

Customizing Your Character: Races, Backgrounds, and Attributes

Customizing your character in *Dragon Age: The Veilguard* is where you bring your unique hero to life. From choosing your race and background to distributing key attributes, every choice will shape your character's story, abilities, and the way other characters in Thedas react to you. Here's a comprehensive guide to help you craft a character that feels personal and engaging.

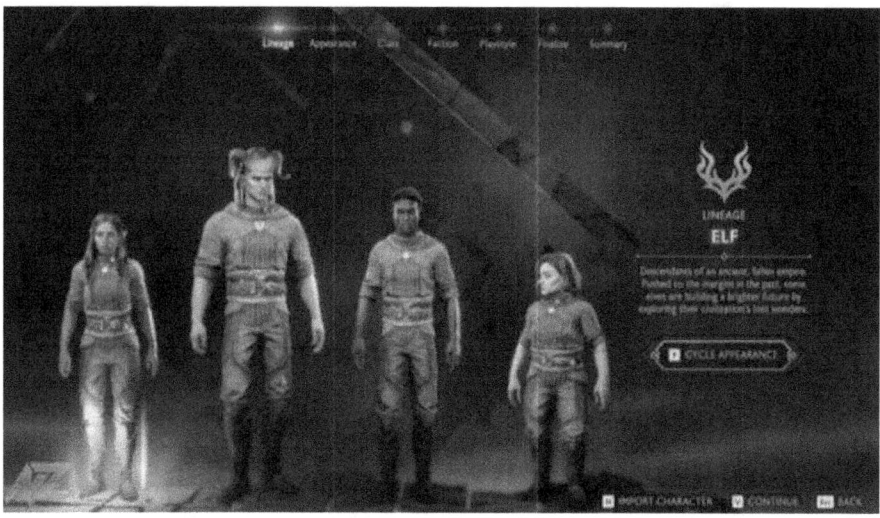

1. Selecting Your Race

- After choosing your class, the next screen will prompt you to select your character's race. Each race offers unique advantages and can affect your interactions with NPCs.
- **Races Available**:
    - **Human**: Humans are the most versatile, with balanced stats and more favorable treatment from nobility and authority figures.
    - **Elf**: Elves have higher Dexterity, making them agile and ideal for stealthy or ranged roles. They often face prejudice in human societies, but they gain special interactions with elven characters.
    - **Dwarf**: Known for their resilience and toughness, Dwarves are especially strong as warriors or rogues. However, they cannot use magic, which limits certain role options.
    - **Qunari**: The Qunari are physically powerful and make effective warriors or mages. Their size and culture often lead to unique interactions with others in Thedas.
- **Selecting Your Race**: Use the D-pad (console) or arrow keys (PC) to highlight each race option, and read the descriptions carefully. When you're ready to make your selection, press "X" (PlayStation), "A" (Xbox), or left-click (PC) to confirm your choice.

2. Choosing Your Background

- Your background adds an extra layer to your character's identity, influencing their perspective and shaping their relationships in the story. Depending on your race and class, certain backgrounds will be available.
- **Common Backgrounds**:
    - **Noble** (Humans): Noble characters often have connections with powerful families and receive favorable treatment from other noble NPCs.

- o **Dalish Elf** (Elves): As a member of a nomadic elven clan, the Dalish background gives you unique insight into elven lore and cultural pride.
- o **Surface Dwarf** (Dwarves): Unlike their deep-dwelling kin, Surface Dwarves interact more with humans, giving them a broader perspective and mixed treatment from others.
- o **Vashoth** (Qunari): As a Qunari who left their strict cultural structure, the Vashoth background allows you to shape your own path but often leads to complex interactions with other Qunari.
- **Selecting Background**: Use the D-pad (console) or arrow keys (PC) to scroll through available backgrounds. Highlight your chosen background, and press "X" (PlayStation), "A" (Xbox), or left-click (PC) to confirm. Be sure to read each description; your background will shape dialogue options, quest availability, and unique story moments.

3. Customizing Your Appearance

- Next, you'll move into the appearance customization screen, where you can make your character look just the way you envision. You'll find options for facial features, hair, eyes, and more.
- **Key Customization Options**:
  - o **Face Shape**: Start by selecting a face shape that gives your character the basic look you want. Use the D-pad (console) or mouse (PC) to scroll through the presets.
  - o **Hair Style and Color**: Choose from various hairstyles, then select "Hair Color" to adjust the color. Scroll with the D-pad (console) or mouse (PC) and press "X" (PlayStation), "A" (Xbox), or left-click (PC) to confirm each choice.
  - o **Eye Color and Shape**: Adjust eye shape for expression, and pick an eye color that reflects your character's personality.
  - o **Scars and Tattoos**: Add scars or tattoos to give your character more story. These options are located under "Extras." Select "Scars" or "Tattoos" to browse and confirm.
- **Finalizing Appearance**: Once you're happy with your character's appearance, select "Confirm" to move to the next step. Make sure you're satisfied; this is how your character will appear throughout the game.

4. Assigning Attributes

- Attributes define your character's basic strengths and playstyle, from physical prowess to magical ability. When you start, you'll have a few attribute points to assign.
- **Key Attributes**:
  - o **Strength**: Increases melee damage and is critical for Warriors who engage in close combat.
  - o **Dexterity**: Enhances accuracy and critical hit rate, especially important for Rogues who rely on quick, agile attacks.
  - o **Constitution**: Boosts health and stamina, which benefits all classes by improving durability in fights.

- **Magic**: Increases spell power, a must-have for Mages who want to deal high magical damage or use complex spells.
- **Willpower**: Affects stamina and mental resilience, allowing your character to handle tough situations and cast more abilities without running out of resources.
- **Assigning Points**: Highlight each attribute and press "X" (PlayStation), "A" (Xbox), or left-click (PC) to add points. To remove points, select the attribute again and use the corresponding button. As you assign points, keep in mind your character's class and playstyle.

5. Selecting Starting Abilities

- Each class has a selection of abilities you can choose from, allowing you to specialize in certain skills right from the start. These abilities lay the foundation for your combat style and strategy.
- **Abilities by Class**:
    - **Warrior**: Select abilities that increase melee attack power or defensive skills. Look for abilities that allow you to manage crowds or resist damage, especially if you want to play a tank role.
    - **Mage**: Choose a balance of offensive and defensive spells. Healing spells or area-of-effect attacks are great options for starting out as a Mage.
    - **Rogue**: Pick abilities that enhance stealth, critical hits, or ranged attacks. Rogues benefit from mobility and high-damage attacks, so consider options that let you hit hard and disappear quickly.
    - **Veil Warden**: Unique to *Veilguard*, the Veil Warden has abilities that interact with the Fade. Choose abilities that weaken enemies or summon Fade creatures to assist in battle.
- **Choosing Abilities**: Highlight the ability you wish to unlock, and press "X" (PlayStation), "A" (Xbox), or left-click (PC) to confirm. The abilities you select here can be modified and expanded as you level up.

6. Finalizing Your Character Customization

- Once you've chosen your race, background, appearance, attributes, and starting abilities, it's time to review everything. This is your chance to make sure your character feels just right.
- **Confirming Your Choices**: When you're ready, press "Start" (console) or "Enter" (PC) to finalize your character and begin your journey in *The Veilguard*.

Character customization in *Dragon Age: The Veilguard* lets you create a hero that feels uniquely yours. From physical appearance to the very essence of your abilities, every choice shapes the story you're about to experience. So take your time, explore the options, and craft a character that you'll love guiding through the adventures and challenges that await in Thedas.

CHAPTER 3.

Exploring The World of Thedas and Veilguard

In this chapter, we'll walk through the vast, rich lands of Thedas and the mysterious new regions introduced in *Veilguard*. You'll learn how to navigate the map, discover hidden locations, and make the most of every journey. We'll also cover landmarks, Veil Zones, and key areas you won't want to miss. This guide is designed to make exploring feel as exciting and rewarding as possible, helping you uncover the secrets, challenges, and treasures that await in this incredible world.

Overview of Thedas: Main Regions

The world of *Dragon Age* takes place across the sprawling continent of Thedas, where ancient ruins, bustling cities, and wild lands await exploration. Each region has its own history, culture, and dangers, making the journey through Thedas an unforgettable experience. Here's a guide to the main regions you'll encounter in *The Veilguard*, with tips on what to look for and how to navigate these diverse landscapes.

1. Ferelden

- **Overview**: Ferelden is a rugged land known for its cold climate, strong warrior culture, and deep connection to the history of *Dragon Age*. Here, players will encounter historic castles, rolling hills, and war-torn villages, each reflecting the resilience of its people.
- **Key Locations**:
  - **Denerim**: The capital city, bustling with traders, quests, and political intrigue.
  - **Redcliffe Village**: Known for its beautiful lakeside views and as the site of critical events in *Dragon Age* history.
  - **Brecilian Forest**: A mysterious, dense forest said to be haunted by ancient magic and filled with secrets.
- **Navigating Ferelden**: To open the map, press "M" on PC, the touchpad on PlayStation, or "View" on Xbox. You'll see marked icons for each major location—select Denerim, Redcliffe, or other areas to set waypoints, which will help guide your path.

2. Orlais

- **Overview**: Known for its elegance, wealth, and sophisticated culture, Orlais is the seat of high fashion, power struggles, and grand architecture. It's also a land of masked nobles and intense political games.
- **Key Locations**:

- **Val Royeaux**: The capital city, where players can experience Orlesian culture, engage with traders, and encounter the Chantry's grand center.
- **The Exalted Plains**: A battlefield scarred by the Orlesian civil war, filled with historic relics and hidden treasures.
- **Emerald Graves**: A vast, beautiful forest, where you'll find abandoned elven ruins and rare resources.
- **Navigating Orlais**: Open your map, and use the D-pad (console) or mouse (PC) to navigate. Highlight Val Royeaux or other points of interest and press "X" (PlayStation), "A" (Xbox), or click to set waypoints for easier travel.

3. The Free Marches

- **Overview**: This region is known as the "City of Chains" due to its history of being a central trade hub. The Free Marches are a series of independent city-states that range from thriving merchant cities to ancient ruins.
- **Key Locations**:
  - **Kirkwall**: One of the most iconic cities in *Dragon Age*, famous for its dark history and complex political landscape.
  - **Starkhaven**: A wealthy city-state with a strong military presence and notable nobility.
  - **The Wounded Coast**: A rugged, dangerous area with winding coastal paths and hidden caverns.
- **Navigating the Free Marches**: Use your map to locate Kirkwall or other key cities. Once highlighted, press "X" (PlayStation), "A" (Xbox), or click (PC) to set your waypoints, guiding you toward quests and exploration spots.

4. Tevinter Imperium

- **Overview**: Known as a place of powerful mages and ancient structures, Tevinter is a land steeped in dark magic, where power and intrigue rule. The Imperium is an empire of contrasts, from its stunning architecture to its eerie, twisted rituals.
- **Key Locations**:
  - **Minrathous**: The capital, filled with towering mage towers, dark secrets, and mysterious artifacts.
  - **Qarinus**: A region known for its lush beauty and hidden magical dangers, teeming with rare creatures.
  - **Ventus**: Ancient ruins where powerful relics can be found, though they're guarded by powerful spirits and traps.
- **Navigating Tevinter**: Open your map, scroll to Tevinter locations, and press "X" (PlayStation), "A" (Xbox), or click (PC) to set waypoints for quests and points of interest. Pay close attention to warnings about powerful enemies in certain areas.

5. Antiva

- **Overview**: Known for its vibrant cities, skilled assassins, and complex political scene, Antiva is often called the "Land of the Crow." It's a region where beauty and danger coexist, thanks to the presence of the Antivan Crows, a famous guild of assassins.
- **Key Locations**:
  - **Antiva City**: A bustling city famous for its art, culture, and the Antivan Crows.
  - **Rialto Bay**: A scenic coastal area with a thriving port and plenty of trading opportunities.
  - **Port of Rialto**: Known for exotic goods and trade, it's an excellent location for gathering resources and meeting traders.
- **Navigating Antiva**: Open the map, select Antiva City or other locations, and press "X" (PlayStation), "A" (Xbox), or click (PC) to set your waypoints. Explore thoroughly; Antiva is filled with hidden treasures and quests tied to its history.

6. Nevarra

- **Overview**: A region rich in tombs and burial traditions, Nevarra is home to the Mortalitasi, a powerful order of necromancers. It's a land steeped in ancient rites, and players can expect encounters with spirits and rare magical artifacts.
- **Key Locations**:
  - **Nevarra City**: A place of grand tombs and towering monuments to the dead, filled with cultural lore and Mortalitasi influences.
  - **The Tombs of the Kings**: An ancient burial site known for powerful relics and rare encounters with spirits.
  - **Hunter Fell**: A forested area where players can gather rare resources and engage with wandering necromancers.
- **Navigating Nevarra**: Use the map to locate Nevarra City or The Tombs of the Kings, and press "X" (PlayStation), "A" (Xbox), or click (PC) to set waypoints. Nevarra's tombs are filled with mysteries and powerful loot for those willing to explore.

7. The Anderfels

- **Overview**: A desolate, windswept land known for its rough terrain and constant battles with darkspawn. The Anderfels is home to the legendary Grey Wardens, making it a place of danger and valor.
- **Key Locations**:
  - **Weisshaupt Fortress**: The Grey Wardens' headquarters, filled with ancient history and elite fighters.
  - **Anderfell Mountains**: Rugged landscapes filled with dangerous creatures and occasional darkspawn activity.

- The Silent Plains: Known for haunting silence and ancient battles, this area is rich with hidden artifacts.
- **Navigating the Anderfels**: Open your map, scroll to Weisshaupt or other major locations, and press "X" (PlayStation), "A" (Xbox), or click (PC) to set waypoints. Exploring this harsh region rewards you with unique insights into the Grey Wardens.
- **Overview**: Par Vollen is the mysterious homeland of the Qunari, while Seheron is a contested island with ongoing conflict between the Qunari and the Tevinter Imperium. These regions are steeped in Qunari culture and secrets.
- **Key Locations**:
  - **The Fortress of Saheron**: A stronghold of the Qunari with significant military and cultural importance.
  - **Sunset Cliffs**: A breathtaking area with dramatic coastal views and hidden passages.
  - **Jungle of Vashoth**: A wild, untamed jungle filled with rare creatures and Qunari outposts.
- **Navigating Par Vollen and Seheron**: Use the map to find Seheron's locations and set waypoints by pressing "X" (PlayStation), "A" (Xbox), or clicking (PC). The regions are challenging but rich in lore for players looking to understand the Qunari's world.

9. Hints for Exploring Thedas

- **Use Waypoints**: Setting waypoints is key to efficient exploration. Highlight any point of interest and press "X" (PlayStation), "A" (Xbox), or click (PC) to set one.
- **Track Quests on the Map**: Open your quest log by pressing "J" on PC, the touchpad on PlayStation, or "View" on Xbox. Track specific quests to see their locations on your map.
- **Collect Resources**: Each region offers unique resources. When you see glowing items or herbs, press "X" (PlayStation), "A" (Xbox), or "E" (PC) to pick them up.

Exploring Thedas is all about immersing yourself in its lore and landscapes. Each region brings its own culture, dangers, and secrets, offering a vast, dynamic world for you to uncover. As you travel through these lands, keep an eye out for hidden paths, resources, and encounters that make your journey truly unique. Happy exploring!

New Locations in Veilguard

The Veilguard expansion introduces a host of new locations that bring both beauty and mystery to the world of *Dragon Age*. Each new area has its own atmosphere, creatures, and secrets waiting to be uncovered. Here's a guide to these fresh, intriguing spots in *Veilguard*, with tips on navigating them and details on what to look out for as you explore.

1. The Veiled Shore

- **Overview**: A haunting coastal area where the Veil is particularly thin, the Veiled Shore is shrouded in mist and features abandoned fishing villages, ghostly shipwrecks, and strange, otherworldly lights. It's known for rare materials and dangerous creatures that have slipped through from the Fade.
- **Key Points of Interest**:
  - **The Lighthouse Ruins**: Said to hold ancient artifacts, but guarded by spirits who resent the living.
  - **The Foggy Caves**: Inside, players can gather rare resources and encounter mysterious Fade creatures.
- **Navigating the Veiled Shore**: Open the map by pressing "M" on PC, the touchpad on PlayStation, or "View" on Xbox. Locate the Veiled Shore, and set a waypoint by highlighting the location and pressing "X" (PlayStation), "A" (Xbox), or clicking (PC). Be sure to bring plenty of health potions—many creatures here are resistant to normal attacks.

2. The Shattered Vale

- **Overview**: The Shattered Vale is a dramatic landscape of broken cliffs, deep chasms, and remnants of ancient elven architecture. The Veil's instability has caused the land to fracture, creating deadly gaps filled with swirling Fade energy. It's a perfect area for players looking to uncover elven lore and lost history.
- **Key Points of Interest**:
  - **Elven Ruins**: Scattered across the cliffs, these ruins are filled with valuable artifacts and pieces of Veil lore.
  - **Echoing Falls**: A waterfall that conceals a hidden cave, where powerful magical relics can be found.
- **Navigating the Shattered Vale**: Open your map, select the Shattered Vale, and set a waypoint. As you explore, be cautious around cliff edges and look for magical bridges or pathways that can be activated with Veil powers. Use "R2" (PlayStation), "RT" (Xbox), or "Q" (PC) to interact with these hidden pathways.

3. The Fade-Worn Woods

- **Overview**: Known for its twisted, ancient trees and ever-present fog, the Fade-Worn Woods is an eerie forest where the Veil is barely holding. Spirits and demons roam freely, making it one of the most dangerous areas in *Veilguard*. However, it's also rich in rare resources and artifacts tied to the Veil.
- **Key Points of Interest**:
  - **The Tree of Echoes**: A large, mysterious tree that holds memories of past events. Interacting with it can reveal hidden lore and sometimes summon spirits.

- **Forgotten Shrine**: Deep within the woods, the shrine offers blessings to those who can solve its puzzles.
- **Navigating the Fade-Worn Woods**: Open the map and set a waypoint for the Fade-Worn Woods. Use "X" (PlayStation), "A" (Xbox), or "E" (PC) to interact with environmental clues or hidden objects, and keep an eye out for shimmering objects, which often indicate Veil-worn artifacts.

4. The Crystal Scar

- **Overview**: The Crystal Scar is a breathtaking landscape filled with massive, luminescent crystals that hum with Veil energy. These formations disrupt the Fade, making it a volatile and magical hotspot. The area is filled with unique Veilguard creatures and rare resources used in high-level crafting.
- **Key Points of Interest**:
    - **Veil Crystal Deposits**: Rare crystals that can be mined for powerful crafting materials.
    - **The Spirit Pools**: Pools of concentrated Veil energy where players can meditate to receive visions or boost magical power temporarily.
- **Navigating the Crystal Scar**: Open the map, select the Crystal Scar, and set a waypoint. While exploring, look for bright crystal nodes, which can be mined by pressing "X" (PlayStation), "A" (Xbox), or "E" (PC). Be prepared to face creatures that guard these deposits fiercely.

5. The Lost Hollow

- **Overview**: A sunken area with ruins of an ancient civilization, the Lost Hollow is a labyrinth of crumbling stone, thick vines, and scattered Veil rifts. The air is thick with mystery, and players can encounter unique Veil phenomena here, such as time echoes—visions of past events playing out like shadows in the present.
- **Key Points of Interest**:
    - **Echoing Chamber**: A room filled with ancient murals and Veil echoes, where players can witness the past and learn lore secrets.
    - **Veil Rifts**: Powerful rifts that summon hostile creatures, but can be closed to gain rewards.
- **Navigating the Lost Hollow**: Open the map, find the Lost Hollow, and set a waypoint. Use "L2" (PlayStation), "LB" (Xbox), or "Shift" (PC) to shield yourself from Veil energy in certain areas, as exposure can drain health over time.

6. The Silent City

- **Overview**: The Silent City is an abandoned metropolis hidden deep underground, where the air is filled with silence and magic. It's believed to be an ancient city that predates even the Elves, possibly linked to the creation of the Veil. Exploring the Silent City is dangerous but rewarding, with high-level loot and powerful artifacts for those who survive its traps and guardians.
- **Key Points of Interest**:

- **Hall of Whispers**: A hall filled with ghostly voices; interacting here can reveal valuable lore and quests.
- **The Golem Forge**: An ancient workshop where powerful golems can be activated—sometimes for better, sometimes for worse.
- **Navigating the Silent City**: To reach the Silent City, open your map and set a waypoint. Bring plenty of supplies, as the city's traps and enemies require a well-prepared party. To activate ancient mechanisms or open doors, press "X" (PlayStation), "A" (Xbox), or "E" (PC) when prompted.

7. The Obsidian Marsh

- **Overview**: The Obsidian Marsh is a dark, swampy landscape filled with murky water, thick fog, and dangerous creatures. Known for its rich resources, it's also home to hidden Veilguard camps and old battlefields, where the energies of the Veil have left their mark.
- **Key Points of Interest**:
  - **Fallen Obelisk**: A towering black stone that resonates with Veil energy, drawing supernatural creatures.
  - **Witch's Hut**: A secluded hut said to belong to a mysterious figure who trades rare items for Veil artifacts.
- **Navigating the Obsidian Marsh**: Open the map, locate the Obsidian Marsh, and set a waypoint. As you explore, keep an eye on your surroundings; quicksand pits and traps are common here. Interact with items by pressing "X" (PlayStation), "A" (Xbox), or "E" (PC) as you encounter them.

8. The Silvered Spire

- **Overview**: A towering structure that stretches into the sky, the Silvered Spire is a mix of ruins and magical wards. It's rumored to be a site of powerful Fade magic, and climbing it brings players closer to the Veil itself, with increasing challenges and powerful rewards at each level.
- **Key Points of Interest**:
  - **Mirror Chambers**: Rooms filled with enchanted mirrors that can transport players to different levels of the spire.
  - **Veil's Peak**: The summit, where players encounter the strongest Veilguard creatures and gain access to rare artifacts.
- **Navigating the Silvered Spire**: Open the map, select the Silvered Spire, and set a waypoint. Use elevators and enchanted mirrors to ascend each level, and press "X" (PlayStation), "A" (Xbox), or "E" (PC) to activate these magical objects.

9. Exploration Tips for Veilguard's New Locations

- **Setting Waypoints**: For any new location, open the map by pressing "M" on PC, the touchpad on PlayStation, or "View" on Xbox. Highlight a location, then press "X" (PlayStation), "A" (Xbox), or click (PC) to set a waypoint.

- **Prepare for Encounters**: Many areas in Veilguard have unique enemies and high-level threats. Make sure your party is well-equipped with potions, spells, and high-quality gear.
- **Watch for Veil Interactions**: Look for shimmering objects or faded symbols, as they often indicate Veil-related interactions or hidden paths. Use "L2" (PlayStation), "LB" (Xbox), or "Shift" (PC) to activate or shield yourself from these energies.

Exploring the new locations in *Veilguard* is a thrilling experience, with each area bringing a distinct atmosphere, challenges, and rewards. Keep your eyes open, your party prepared, and your curiosity ready—these new regions hold secrets

Important Landmarks and Exploration Tips

Dragon Age: The Veilguard is filled with breathtaking landmarks and hidden treasures that add depth to every journey. This guide covers some key landmarks and offers tips to help you explore efficiently, avoid common pitfalls, and get the most out of each new discovery. Here's where to go, what to look out for, and a few insider tips to make exploring both fun and rewarding.

1. The Tree of Echoes (Fade-Worn Woods)

- **Description**: The Tree of Echoes is a towering, twisted tree located in the Fade-Worn Woods, and it's rumored to carry the memories of countless souls. Interacting with the tree can reveal hidden lore, open side quests, and sometimes trigger visions that offer valuable insights.
- **Exploration Tips**:
    - **Approach Carefully**: The Tree of Echoes is often surrounded by spirits and creatures attracted to its power. Approach with caution and bring plenty of potions.
    - **Interacting**: Stand close to the tree and press "X" (PlayStation), "A" (Xbox), or "E" (PC) to interact. This may prompt dialogue or a vision sequence, so be ready to listen and take notes—some visions may hint at nearby treasures or hidden quests.

2. The Lighthouse Ruins (Veiled Shore)

- **Description**: This crumbling lighthouse is perched on a cliff overlooking the Veiled Shore, and it's said to hold artifacts from an ancient mage who once guarded the coast. It's a haunting spot with rich loot and occasional enemy ambushes.
- **Exploration Tips**:
    - **Climbing the Tower**: The lighthouse can be accessed by climbing a series of broken stairs and ladders. Press "X" (PlayStation), "A" (Xbox), or "E" (PC) to climb each section.

- **Finding Hidden Items**: Check each level for hidden loot crates or lore books, often tucked behind rubble. Hold the "R2" (PlayStation), "RT" (Xbox), or "Q" (PC) button to reveal interactable objects.

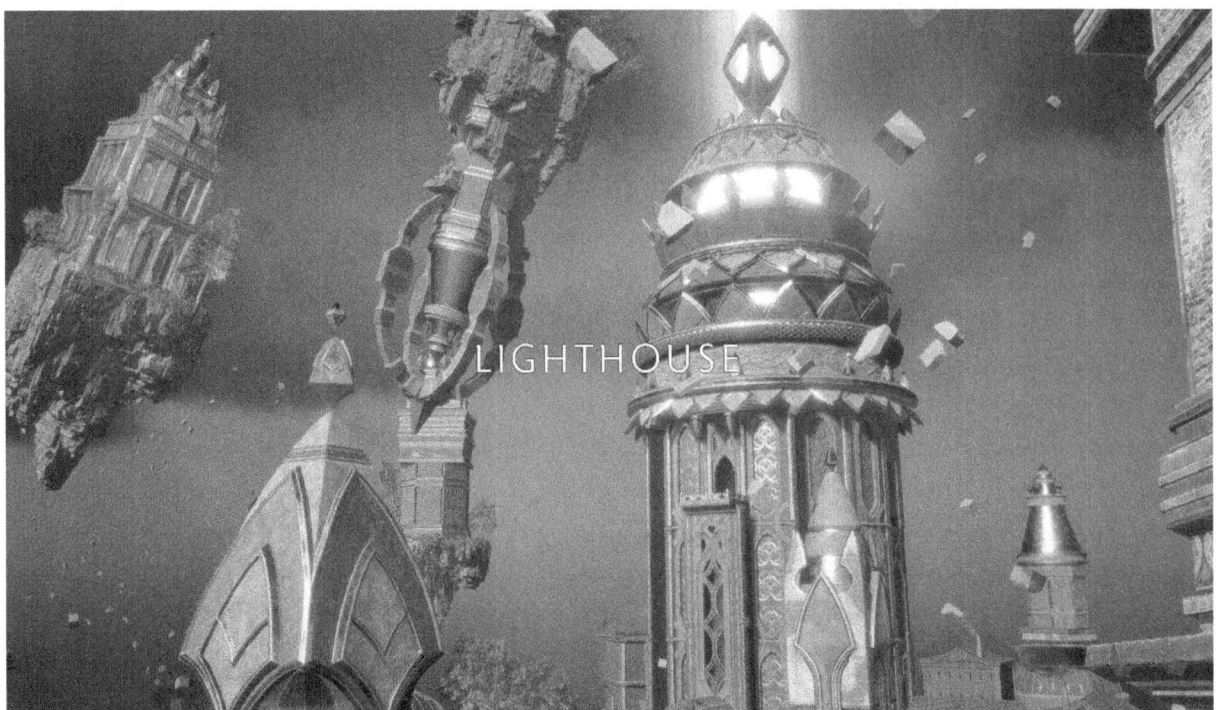

3. Hall of Whispers (Silent City)

- **Description**: Located in the Silent City, the Hall of Whispers is a large, echoing chamber where ghostly voices can be heard. Interacting with the hall's echoes reveals ancient lore and hidden pathways to deeper areas of the city.
- **Exploration Tips**:
  - **Listening to the Voices**: As you enter the Hall of Whispers, you'll hear faint voices. Stand still and press "X" (PlayStation), "A" (Xbox), or "E" (PC) to listen more closely. These voices often guide you to secrets or provide clues for puzzles.
  - **Activating Hidden Doors**: Some areas in the hall are hidden behind walls that can be opened by pressing "L2" (PlayStation), "LB" (Xbox), or "Shift" (PC) when standing near a faded symbol.

4. Veil Crystal Deposits (Crystal Scar)

- **Description**: The Crystal Scar is filled with rare, glowing Veil crystal deposits. These crystals are valuable resources for high-level crafting and can be harvested for materials that aren't found anywhere else in the game.
- **Exploration Tips**:

- ○ **Mining Crystals**: Approach a crystal node and press "X" (PlayStation), "A" (Xbox), or "E" (PC) to mine it. You may need a mining tool, which can be obtained from merchants in major cities.
- ○ **Avoiding Guardians**: Some crystal nodes are protected by powerful creatures. If you're not prepared for a fight, it's better to scout the area first and come back later when you're stronger.

5. Echoing Chamber (Lost Hollow)

- **Description**: Deep in the Lost Hollow, the Echoing Chamber contains murals and artifacts that reveal ancient secrets. It's a sacred place, but accessing its full potential requires solving puzzles related to the Veil.
- **Exploration Tips**:
  - ○ **Solving Puzzles**: Each mural represents part of a story. Stand in front of a mural and press "X" (PlayStation), "A" (Xbox), or "E" (PC) to inspect it. Some murals will activate a puzzle, where you'll need to use your Veil abilities to align symbols correctly.
  - ○ **Unlocking Lore and Rewards**: Successfully solving these puzzles can unlock lore entries and powerful artifacts, so it's worth taking your time with them.

6. The Obsidian Marsh Pits

- **Description**: The Obsidian Marsh is dotted with dangerous quicksand pits that can drain your health quickly if you're not careful. However, these pits often conceal hidden loot or passages.
- **Exploration Tips**:
  - ○ **Avoiding Quicksand**: Keep an eye out for darker patches in the ground. To avoid stepping into quicksand, use "R2" (PlayStation), "RT" (Xbox), or "Q" (PC) to scan the area. If you do step in, rapidly press "X" (PlayStation), "A" (Xbox), or "E" (PC) to escape.
  - ○ **Finding Hidden Paths**: Some quicksand pits contain tunnels beneath. Carefully navigate these pits and look for glowing markers indicating hidden paths.

7. The Golem Forge (Silent City)

- **Description**: This ancient forge, found in the Silent City, was once used to create powerful golems. You can activate the forge to summon a temporary golem companion or craft powerful items if you gather the right materials.
- **Exploration Tips**:
  - ○ **Activating the Forge**: Stand at the control panel and press "X" (PlayStation), "A" (Xbox), or "E" (PC) to interact. This may summon a golem, which will protect you for a limited time.
  - ○ **Gathering Materials**: The Golem Forge requires rare materials like Veil crystals and enchanted metals. These items can be found throughout the Silent City or traded with specific merchants.

8. Rialto Bay Dock Market (Antiva)

- **Description**: A lively market located by the water in Antiva's Rialto Bay, this dockside market offers unique items from around Thedas, including exotic crafting ingredients and powerful gear.
- **Exploration Tips**:
  - **Interacting with Merchants**: Walk up to a merchant stall and press "X" (PlayStation), "A" (Xbox), or "E" (PC) to open their inventory. Some merchants here specialize in rare goods, so check back often.
  - **Bartering for Discounts**: Occasionally, you can barter with merchants for better prices. Look for dialogue options that appear when interacting with vendors to negotiate.

9. The Tombs of the Kings (Nevarra)

- **Description**: This vast burial ground houses the remains of ancient rulers and is filled with treasures, traps, and powerful spirits. The Tombs of the Kings are guarded by the Mortalitasi, a secretive order of necromancers.
- **Exploration Tips**:
  - **Navigating Traps**: The tombs are filled with traps, so move slowly and watch for pressure plates. Use "L2" (PlayStation), "LB" (Xbox), or "Shift" (PC) to trigger traps at a distance or disable them if your character has the required skill.
  - **Engaging with Spirits**: Some spirits are friendly and may offer quests or clues. Approach them carefully and press "X" (PlayStation), "A" (Xbox), or "E" (PC) to interact.

10. Sunset Cliffs Hidden Cove (Seheron)

- **Description**: This hidden cove at the base of Seheron's Sunset Cliffs is accessible only at certain times when the tide is low. Inside, players can find rare treasure, unique enemies, and a view that's worth the visit.
- **Exploration Tips**:
  - **Timing Your Visit**: The cove entrance is submerged at high tide, so check your map and head there when the tide indicator shows low. Press "X" (PlayStation), "A" (Xbox), or "E" (PC) to interact with any clues that appear.
  - **Exploring the Cove**: Inside, look for hidden loot chests and be prepared for ambushes from Veil-touched creatures that guard the area.

Exploration Tips for Maximum Enjoyment

- **Use the Compass**: Keep an eye on your compass at the top of the screen, as it highlights nearby points of interest and quest markers, helping you find important landmarks without constantly checking the map.
- **Collect Resources**: Every region has unique resources that can be used for crafting and upgrades. When you see glowing plants or objects, press "X" (PlayStation), "A" (Xbox), or "E" (PC) to gather them.
- **Look for Interact Prompts**: Many hidden secrets are only accessible if you interact with specific objects. Watch for the "Press X/A/E" prompts to discover lore entries, hidden doors, and valuable loot.

With these landmarks and tips, you're set to explore *The Veilguard* like a seasoned adventurer. Keep your eyes open for rare items, listen to hints in the environment, and don't be afraid to take your

Map Guide with Detailed Points of Interest

The map in *Dragon Age: The Veilguard* is a crucial tool for exploring Thedas and its new Veilguard locations. This guide will help you get the most out of the map, from setting waypoints and tracking quests to identifying hidden points of interest that can make your adventure richer and more rewarding. Here's everything you need to know to navigate like a pro.

1. Opening and Navigating the Map

- **Accessing the Map**: To open the map, press "M" on PC, the touchpad on PlayStation, or the "View" button on Xbox. This will display the region you're in, along with icons marking important locations, quest objectives, and other points of interest.
- **Navigating the Map**: Use the left stick (console) or mouse (PC) to scroll through the map. You can zoom in and out by pressing R2/L2 on PlayStation, RT/LT on Xbox, or using the scroll wheel on PC. Zooming in provides more details about each area, while zooming out gives you a better sense of your overall location in the region.

2. Setting Waypoints

- **How to Set Waypoints**: To set a waypoint, highlight the location you want to navigate to and press "X" on PlayStation, "A" on Xbox, or right-click on PC. This will create a marker on your map, and a directional indicator will appear on your compass at the top of the screen, guiding you to the location.
- **Benefits of Waypoints**: Waypoints are helpful for keeping track of your destination, especially in areas with complex terrain or multiple paths. They make it easier to stay on track, whether you're heading to a quest objective, a resource node, or an important landmark.

3. Quest Markers and Objectives

- **Viewing Active Quests**: Open the quest log by pressing "J" on PC, the touchpad on PlayStation, or "View" on Xbox. This will show you all your current quests, which you can highlight to see specific objectives.

- **Tracking Quests on the Map**: Once you select a quest, its objective marker will appear on the map. Highlight the quest objective and set a waypoint (press "X" on PlayStation, "A" on Xbox, or right-click on PC) to make tracking easier as you move toward your goal.

- **Multiple Quest Objectives**: Some quests have multiple steps or objectives. Use the zoom function to view the entire region and locate all objectives before starting, which can help you plan the most efficient route.

4. Important Points of Interest

- **Landmarks**: Landmarks are marked with unique icons on the map and often represent key locations, such as ancient ruins, historic sites, or significant buildings. Visiting landmarks can unlock lore entries, provide quest clues, or grant experience.

- **Merchants and Camps**: Merchants are marked by bag icons, and campsites by tent icons. Campsites allow you to rest, heal, and manage your party, while merchants offer supplies and unique items.

- **Resource Nodes**: Resource nodes appear as small icons representing herbs, ores, or other materials. These icons only appear if you've already discovered a node in that area, so it's worth exploring thoroughly to reveal them on your map.

- **Veil Rifts**: Veil rifts, unique to *Veilguard*, are marked with a swirling icon. Closing these rifts rewards you with valuable items and experience. Approach carefully, as these areas are typically guarded by powerful creatures from the Fade.

5. Hidden Locations and Secrets

- **Fogged-Out Areas**: Some areas on the map will appear fogged-out until you explore them. Moving into these areas clears the fog, revealing any hidden locations, resources, or enemies. Make it a habit to explore fogged areas to ensure you're not missing valuable items or lore.

- **Secret Caves and Passageways**: Secret locations, such as caves or hidden paths, may not be marked on the map until you discover them. As you explore, look for environmental clues like unusual rock formations, footprints, or hidden doorways. Press "X" (PlayStation), "A" (Xbox), or "E" (PC) to interact with objects that could reveal secret areas.

- **Veil-Worn Symbols**: In certain Veilguard areas, you may encounter faded symbols on the ground or walls. Stand near these symbols and press "L2" (PlayStation), "LB" (Xbox), or "Shift" (PC) to reveal hidden paths or activate unique features.

6. Tips for Efficient Map Use

- **Frequently Update Waypoints**: As you progress, update your waypoint to match your next objective. This keeps your compass direction accurate and helps prevent backtracking.

- **Use Zoom for Better Planning**: Zooming out lets you see an entire region, while zooming in shows detailed terrain, which is helpful for navigating tricky paths or finding shortcuts.

- **Track Multiple Quests**: If you have several quests in one region, plan your route by marking the closest objectives first. Completing several quests in one area saves time and maximizes your efficiency.

- **Check for Respawned Resources**: Resources often respawn over time. If you're low on supplies, return to previously explored areas and check the map for resource nodes.

7. Exploring Specific Regions in Veilguard

- **Veiled Shore**: Known for its misty landscapes and dangerous cliffs, Veiled Shore is home to many hidden caves and cliffside paths. Use waypoints to mark these locations, as the area's dense fog can make navigation tricky.

- **Shattered Vale**: This fractured region is marked by cliffs and chasms. Look for markers that represent bridges and paths. Zoom in to see paths that may not be immediately obvious.

- **Crystal Scar**: In this crystal-rich landscape, resource icons mark crystal nodes that can be mined for rare materials. Zoom in for a clearer view, as the crystals often blend into the scenery.

- **Silent City**: This complex underground city has multiple levels. Use the map to mark stairways and elevators, as they're key to navigating between floors and finding hidden rooms.

8. Returning to Previous Regions

- **How to Access Region Maps**: To open the world map and switch to a different region, press "M" (PC), the touchpad (PlayStation), or "View" (Xbox). Scroll to find the region you wish to revisit, then zoom in to access its specific map.

- **Setting Waypoints Across Regions**: If you have a quest that spans multiple regions, set waypoints in the current region, then open the next region's map and set waypoints there as well. This allows you to transition smoothly between objectives as you travel.

9. Tracking Lore and Collectibles

- **Lore Entries**: Many regions contain lore entries that provide background on Thedas's history, cultures, and magical traditions. These entries are marked with a scroll icon. Approach them and press "X" (PlayStation), "A" (Xbox), or "E" (PC) to add them to your codex.

- **Collectibles**: Some regions have collectibles, such as Veil artifacts or unique plants. Check your map for special markers and use waypoints to locate them. Completing collectible sets may unlock unique rewards or achievements.

10. Map Guide Summary

- **Setting Waypoints**: Press "X" (PlayStation), "A" (Xbox), or right-click (PC) on the map to set waypoints for quests or points of interest.
- **Tracking Objectives**: Open the quest log ("J" on PC, touchpad on PlayStation, or "View" on Xbox) to select and track active quests, then view their markers on the map.
- **Zoom and Pan**: Use R2/L2 (PlayStation), RT/LT (Xbox), or the scroll wheel (PC) to zoom in and out on the map for better visibility and planning.
- **Exploring Secret Areas**: Pay attention to environmental clues on the map and interact with faded symbols by pressing "L2" (PlayStation), "LB" (Xbox), or "Shift" (PC) to reveal hidden paths or items.

The map is your best friend in *The Veilguard*, guiding you through quests, secrets, and unexplored areas. With these tips, you'll be ready to navigate like a pro, making each journey across Thedas both smooth and rewarding. Enjoy the adventure, and let the map lead you to the hidden wonders waiting in *The Veilguard*!

Hidden Areas and Secrets

Exploring hidden areas and uncovering secrets is one of the most exciting aspects of *Dragon Age: The Veilguard*. These areas are often filled with powerful artifacts, rare resources, and lore that deepens your understanding of the world. Many secrets require a keen eye and some puzzle-solving skills, so here's a guide to help you discover the game's most rewarding hidden spots.

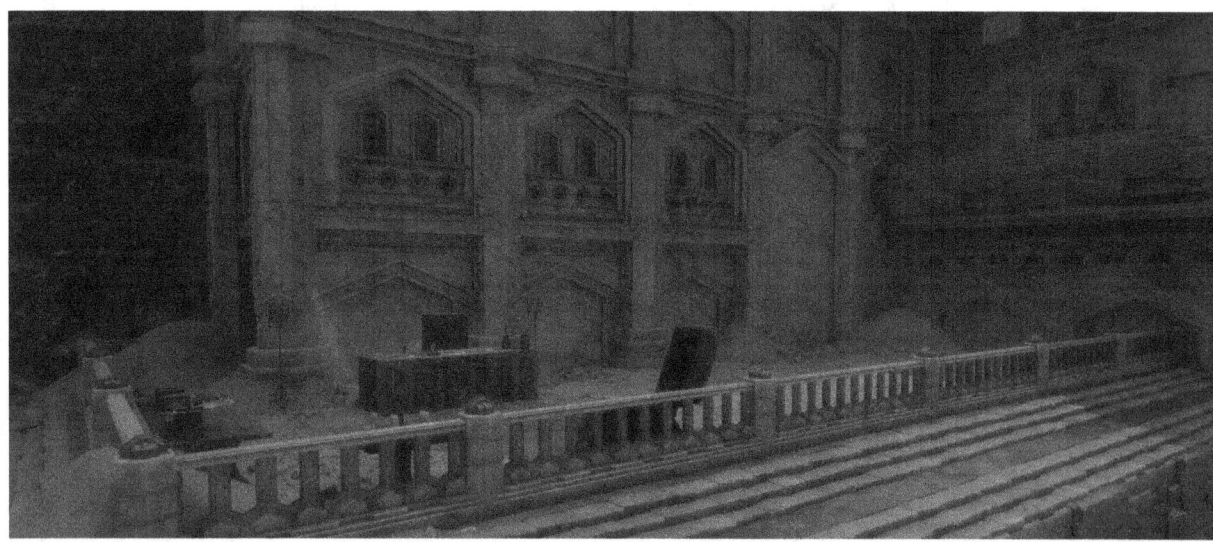

1. Veil-Worn Symbols

- **Description**: In certain areas, you may notice faded, mystical symbols on walls or the ground. These symbols mark places where the Veil is especially thin, creating hidden paths and secret chambers accessible only with Veil-based abilities.
- **How to Access**: Stand near a symbol and press "L2" (PlayStation), "LB" (Xbox), or "Shift" (PC) to activate your Veil power. This will often reveal hidden doorways or passageways that lead to secret areas filled with treasures or lore entries.
- **Tip**: Keep an eye out for these symbols in areas like the Fade-Worn Woods, Crystal Scar, and Lost Hollow, where Veil disturbances are common.

2. Veil Rifts

- **Description**: Veil rifts are portals to the Fade that occasionally open up in specific locations. These rifts are often guarded by powerful creatures from the Fade, but closing them can yield valuable loot and rare crafting materials.
- **How to Access**: Approach the rift and be prepared for a battle. Press "X" (PlayStation), "A" (Xbox), or "E" (PC) to interact with the rift, which will summon creatures to defend it. After defeating the enemies, you'll be able to close the rift and collect your rewards.
- **Tip**: Some Veil rifts only appear at certain times of day or after completing specific quests, so revisit areas to check for new rift openings.

3. Hidden Caves and Tunnels

- **Description**: Throughout Thedas and Veilguard's new regions, hidden caves and tunnels contain rare resources, lore entries, and sometimes even secret quests. These caves are usually concealed behind rock formations, vines, or other natural features.
- **How to Access**: Look for slight differences in the environment—such as rocks that seem out of place or large vines that can be parted. Approach and press "X" (PlayStation), "A" (Xbox), or "E" (PC) to interact, opening up a hidden path.
- **Tip**: Some caves are marked on your map as fogged-out areas, so make it a habit to explore these sections and unlock potential treasures.

4. Echoing Walls (Lost Hollow)

- **Description**: In the Lost Hollow, there are walls that resonate with echoes of the past. Interacting with these walls can trigger visions that provide valuable lore or clues for nearby puzzles.

- **How to Access**: Stand near an echoing wall and press "X" (PlayStation), "A" (Xbox), or "E" (PC) to activate it. This may trigger a brief vision or a clue that points you toward a hidden item or secret.
- **Tip**: The visions sometimes reveal hidden switches or symbols that can unlock doors in other parts of the Lost Hollow, so pay close attention to details.

5. Treasure-Filled Cliffside Paths

- **Description**: In mountainous areas like the Shattered Vale and the Veiled Shore, narrow cliffside paths often lead to secluded spots with valuable loot. These paths can be difficult to spot and often require careful navigation.
- **How to Access**: Look for narrow ledges or rough paths along cliff edges. Move carefully and press "X" (PlayStation), "A" (Xbox), or "E" (PC) to climb or jump when needed. Once you reach the end, you'll often find a chest or rare item.
- **Tip**: If the path seems too dangerous, consider using a Veil Warden's Fade abilities to phase through certain obstacles or cliffs safely.

6. Puzzle Shrines (Fade-Worn Woods)

- **Description**: Scattered throughout the Fade-Worn Woods are hidden shrines that contain powerful rewards but require players to solve a puzzle to unlock them. These shrines are typically marked by runes or statues and offer a unique challenge.
- **How to Access**: Approach the shrine and press "X" (PlayStation), "A" (Xbox), or "E" (PC) to examine it. The shrine will present a puzzle, often involving symbols or patterns related to the Veil.
- **Tip**: Look for environmental clues around the shrine, such as markings on trees or stones, which may hint at the correct solution.

7. The Ancient Tombs (Nevarra)

- **Description**: The ancient tombs of Nevarra are filled with relics and guarded by spirits of the Mortalitasi, who protect their secrets fiercely. These tombs often have hidden chambers that require careful exploration to access.
- **How to Access**: As you explore the tombs, keep an eye out for faded symbols or unusual architecture. Some walls may look solid but can be phased through with Veil abilities. Press "L2" (PlayStation), "LB" (Xbox), or "Shift" (PC) near these walls to uncover hidden rooms.
- **Tip**: The spirits within the tombs may respond to certain relics. If you find a relic, try presenting it to a spirit or altar to unlock additional rewards.

8. The Enchanted Mirror Chambers (Silvered Spire)

- **Description**: Within the Silvered Spire, there are enchanted mirror chambers that act as portals to other parts of the spire. These mirrors are often hidden or require specific interactions to activate.

- **How to Access**: Enter the mirror chamber and look for mirrors with a faint glow. Stand in front of a glowing mirror and press "X" (PlayStation), "A" (Xbox), or "E" (PC) to activate it. This will transport you to a different level or hidden area of the spire.
- **Tip**: Each mirror can only be used once, so make sure to explore each new area thoroughly before returning.

9. Time-Locked Coves (Sunset Cliffs)

- **Description**: At Sunset Cliffs, there are coves that can only be accessed during low tide. These time-locked coves hold rare treasures and unique enemies, making them worth the wait.
- **How to Access**: Check your map for tide indicators. When the tide is low, return to Sunset Cliffs and press "X" (PlayStation), "A" (Xbox), or "E" (PC) to enter the cove. Inside, you'll often find rare loot or Veil-touched enemies.
- **Tip**: Time your visit for low tide to maximize exploration. The cove will remain inaccessible at high tide, so plan your trip accordingly.

10. Obsidian Marsh Alchemist's Hidden Hut

- **Description**: Deep within the Obsidian Marsh lies a hidden hut belonging to a mysterious alchemist. It's said that the alchemist trades rare potions and artifacts in exchange for Veil crystals or other magical items.
- **How to Access**: The hut is often concealed behind thick marsh vegetation. Look for subtle markers like unusual plants or glowing mushrooms that indicate a hidden path. Press "X" (PlayStation), "A" (Xbox), or "E" (PC) to interact with the hidden path to access the hut.
- **Tip**: Bring rare Veil items with you, as the alchemist may offer unique potions in exchange that aren't available anywhere else in the game.

Tips for Finding Hidden Areas and Secrets

- **Stay Observant**: Watch for subtle environmental clues, like faint glows, faded symbols, or unusual vegetation that can indicate hidden paths.
- **Experiment with Veil Powers**: Veil-worn areas often require the use of specific Veil abilities. Use "L2" (PlayStation), "LB" (Xbox), or "Shift" (PC) near faded symbols or walls to reveal hidden pathways.
- **Revisit Areas**: Some hidden areas only appear after completing certain quests or objectives, so it's worth revisiting places after making story progress.
- **Use the Compass**: Occasionally, your compass will flicker or show unmarked points when you're near a hidden area, so pay attention to any unusual activity on the compass.

Exploring hidden areas and secrets in *The Veilguard* is all about curiosity, observation, and sometimes a bit of puzzle-solving. Each secret adds depth to your journey, rewarding you with valuable loot, lore, and unique experiences that make your adventure across Thedas all the more exciting.

CHAPTER 4

Character Development and Progression

This chapter focuses on helping you grow and strengthen your character throughout your journey in *Dragon Age: The Veilguard*. We'll cover leveling up, skill trees, and specialization options, as well as how to find the best gear and manage attributes effectively. You'll also learn about building strong relationships with companions, which can unlock unique abilities and story moments. This guide is designed to make sure you're always moving forward with a character that feels powerful, balanced, and uniquely suited to your playstyle.

Leveling Up and Gaining Experience

Leveling up in *Dragon Age: The Veilguard* is key to strengthening your character, unlocking powerful abilities, and overcoming tougher challenges. This guide will walk you through everything you need to know about gaining experience, leveling up efficiently, and making the most of each level-up to customize your character's growth.

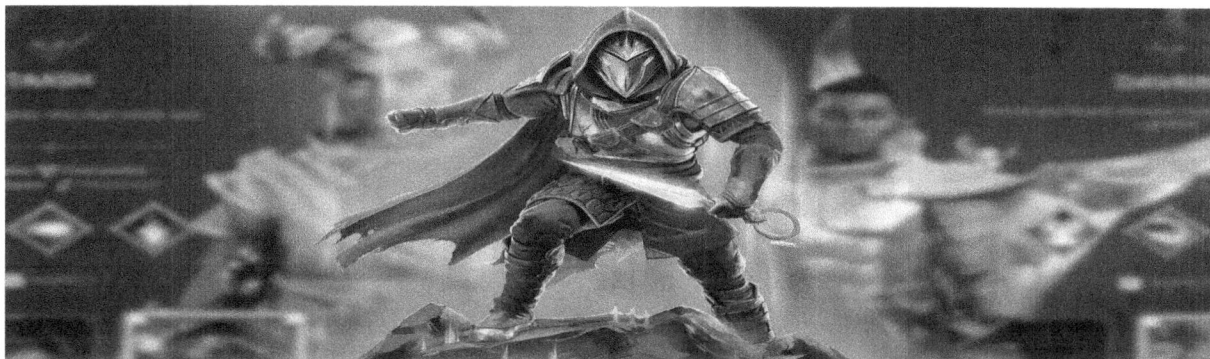

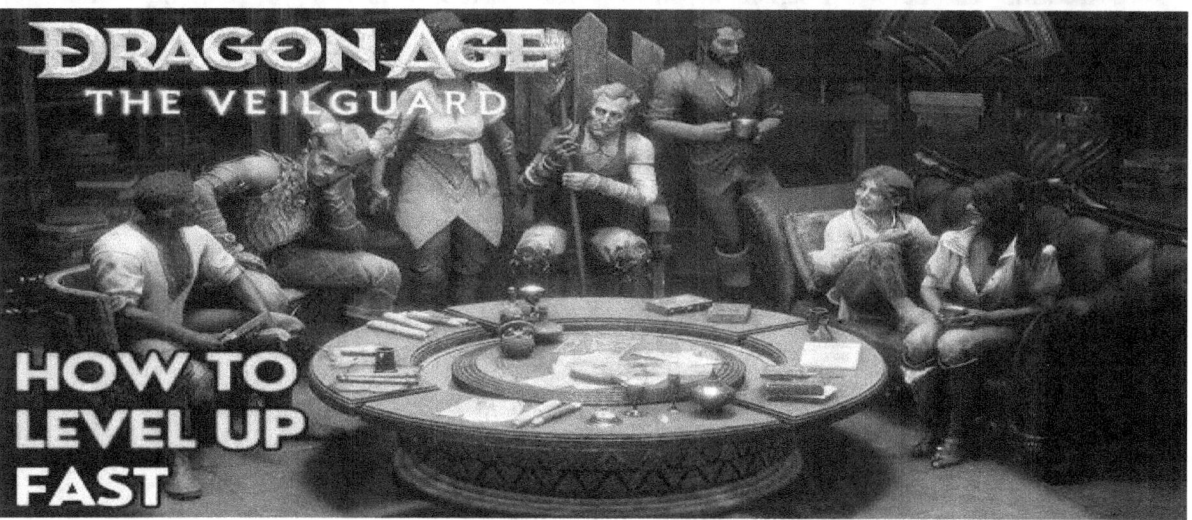

1. Gaining Experience Points (XP)

- **Defeating Enemies**: Most enemies you defeat will grant XP, with tougher foes giving more. Keep an eye on challenging areas for higher rewards.
- **Completing Quests**: Quests provide some of the largest XP rewards in the game, so prioritize finishing main story quests, side quests, and companion missions.
- **Exploring New Locations**: Discovering new areas, hidden landmarks, and Veilguard-specific locations often grants XP, rewarding you for curiosity and exploration.
- **Solving Puzzles and Closing Veil Rifts**: Engaging with puzzles, such as those found at shrines, and closing Veil rifts will also add to your XP. These activities often involve unique rewards, so they're well worth the effort.

2. Checking Your XP and Progress Toward the Next Level

- **Accessing the Character Screen**: To view your current XP and progress toward the next level, open the character screen by pressing "C" on PC, "Options" on PlayStation, or "Menu" on Xbox.
- **Viewing XP Bar**: On this screen, you'll see an XP bar showing your current progress. The bar will fill as you gain XP, and once it's full, you'll level up and receive points to spend on attributes and abilities.
- **Keeping Track**: It's helpful to regularly check your XP bar, especially if you're close to leveling up. That way, you can prepare for the next level and decide in advance where to allocate points.

3. Leveling Up and Spending Points

- **Level-Up Notification**: Once you've gained enough XP, a notification will appear on your screen letting you know you've leveled up. At this point, you'll be awarded attribute points and skill points, which can be spent on enhancing your character's abilities and stats.
- **Accessing the Level-Up Screen**: Open the level-up screen by pressing "C" on PC, "Options" on PlayStation, or "Menu" on Xbox. This will take you to your character development menu, where you can spend your points.

4. Allocating Attribute Points

- **Attributes Overview**: Each attribute boosts specific aspects of your character:
    - **Strength**: Increases melee damage—especially useful for Warriors.
    - **Dexterity**: Improves accuracy and critical hit rate, ideal for Rogues.
    - **Constitution**: Boosts health and stamina, essential for survivability.
    - **Magic**: Powers up spell damage for Mages, making spells more effective.
    - **Willpower**: Enhances stamina and mana regeneration, helpful for all classes.

- **Spending Attribute Points**: To assign points to an attribute, highlight the desired attribute, then press "X" (PlayStation), "A" (Xbox), or left-click (PC) to add a point. Make sure to distribute points based on your class and playstyle—focusing on Strength and Constitution for Warriors, for example, or Dexterity and Willpower for Rogues.

5. Choosing and Upgrading Abilities

- **Accessing the Skill Tree**: After allocating attribute points, navigate to your skill tree by selecting the "Abilities" tab. Here, you'll find different branches of skills related to your class (e.g., combat, defense, stealth, and magic).
- **Unlocking New Abilities**: Highlight an ability you want to unlock, and press "X" (PlayStation), "A" (Xbox), or left-click (PC) to confirm. Certain abilities have prerequisites, so check to see if other abilities need to be unlocked first.
- **Upgrading Existing Abilities**: Many abilities can be upgraded for enhanced effects, such as increased damage or reduced cooldown times. To upgrade, highlight the ability and press "X" (PlayStation), "A" (Xbox), or left-click (PC) to spend your skill point.

6. Specialization Options (After Reaching Higher Levels)

- **Unlocking Specializations**: As you progress, you'll eventually unlock specialization options, which allow you to take on advanced roles within your class. For instance, Mages may choose between Knight-Enchanter, Necromancer, or Rift Mage.
- **Choosing a Specialization**: Once specializations are available, you'll receive a quest or notification in the "Abilities" tab. Highlight your chosen specialization and press "X" (PlayStation), "A" (Xbox), or left-click (PC) to begin the quest to unlock it.
- **Gaining New Abilities in Your Specialization**: After completing the specialization quest, additional skill trees open up with unique abilities. These are specific to your specialization, and investing points here will enhance your combat effectiveness in specialized ways.

7. Using Companions to Support Your Progress

- **Companion Abilities**: Your companions level up alongside you, gaining attribute points and abilities. You can customize their growth based on their role in your party.
- **Accessing Companion Level-Up**: Open the character screen, switch to the companion tab, and level them up the same way as your main character. Press "X" (PlayStation), "A" (Xbox), or left-click (PC) to allocate points and select abilities for each companion.
- **Team Synergy**: Think about your companions' abilities in relation to your own—choosing skills that complement each other will make your team stronger and more effective in battle.

8. Planning for Advanced Levels and High-Level Enemies

- **Strategic Skill Point Allocation**: As you level up, you'll face tougher enemies, so plan your abilities around your preferred combat style. Mages might want to invest in area-of-effect spells for crowd control, while Warriors could focus on defensive skills to withstand powerful attacks.
- **Respec Options**: If you're not satisfied with your build, *The Veilguard* may provide an option to respec (reallocate skill points). Look for NPCs or merchants who offer respec services in major towns, often for a fee.

9. Experience Boosts and Tips for Fast Leveling

- **Use Experience Boost Potions**: Some merchants offer potions that grant temporary XP boosts. Stock up on these and use them before big battles or quest turn-ins.
- **Complete Daily Challenges**: If available, daily challenges often offer bonus XP, helping you level up faster.
- **Focus on High-Reward Quests**: Main story quests and certain side quests give the most XP. When aiming to level up quickly, prioritize quests with significant rewards listed in the quest log.

10. Leveling Up Summary

- **Earn XP**: Gain XP through combat, quests, exploration, and activities like solving puzzles and closing rifts.
- **Spend Points Wisely**: When leveling up, assign attribute points based on your class's needs and distribute skill points to build a well-rounded character.
- **Plan for Specialization**: As you level up, plan for specializations that match your playstyle to unlock powerful new abilities.
- **Utilize Companion Leveling**: Level up your companions strategically to create a balanced, powerful team.

Leveling up in *Dragon Age: The Veilguard* is more than just raising numbers—it's about shaping your character's strengths, adjusting your strategies, and preparing for tougher challenges. With this guide, you'll be ready to make every level count, building a character that's powerful, adaptable, and ready for the adventure ahead. Enjoy the journey, and may each level bring you closer to becoming a legend in Thedas!

Skill Trees and Specializations

Skill trees and specializations are crucial elements of character progression in *Dragon Age: The Veilguard*. They allow you to tailor your character's abilities, making them more effective in combat and specialized for unique situations. This guide will take you through the skill trees available to each class, how to unlock specializations, and how to make the most of these features to build a powerful character.

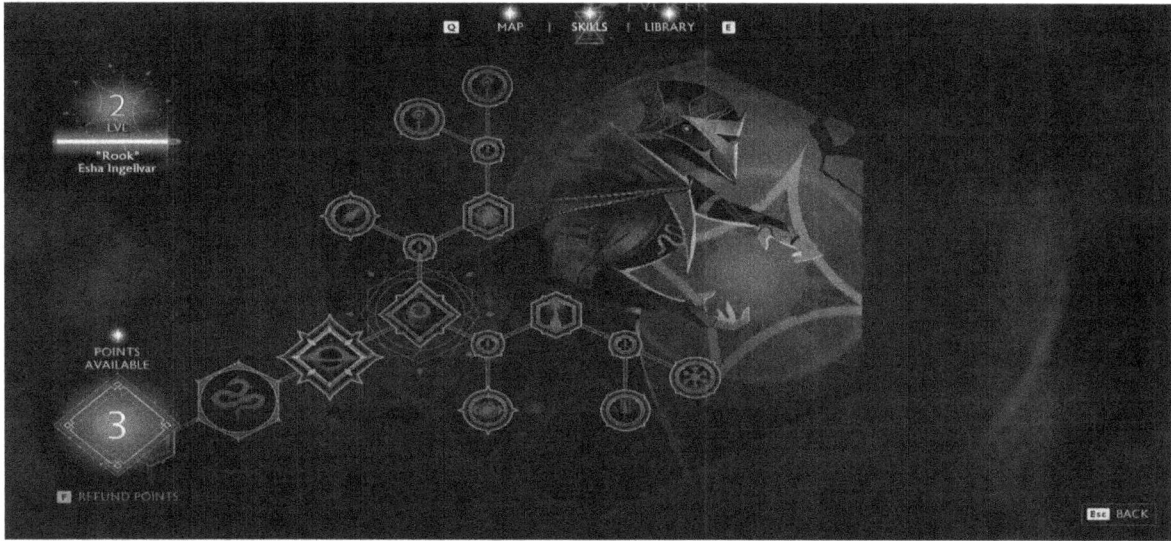

1. Accessing Skill Trees

- **Opening the Skill Tree**: To access your skill tree, press "K" on PC, "Options" on PlayStation, or "Menu" on Xbox. This will take you to the abilities tab, where you can view different branches of skills available for your class.
- **Navigating the Skill Tree**: Use the left stick (console) or mouse (PC) to scroll through the various skill branches. Each branch focuses on a different aspect of your character's abilities, allowing you to choose the path that fits your desired playstyle.

2. Skill Trees for Each Class

Each class has multiple skill trees, each dedicated to a different type of combat or utility. Let's take a look at what's available:

Warrior Skill Trees

- **Weapon and Shield**: Focuses on defensive abilities, allowing Warriors to block attacks and protect teammates.

- **How to Upgrade**: Highlight a skill and press "X" (PlayStation), "A" (Xbox), or left-click (PC) to unlock or upgrade it.
- **Two-Handed**: For those who like dealing heavy damage, this tree focuses on using two-handed weapons to unleash powerful attacks.
- **Battlemaster**: Provides support abilities, like war cries that bolster allies or debilitate enemies.
- **Vanguard**: Emphasizes threat management, allowing Warriors to attract enemy attention and protect the more vulnerable members of their party.

Mage Skill Trees

- **Spirit**: A skill tree focused on defensive spells, barriers, and healing abilities.
- **Storm**: Specializes in lightning-based attacks, offering area-of-effect spells that deal significant damage to multiple enemies.
- **Inferno**: Concentrates on fire magic, with high damage-over-time spells and abilities to set enemies ablaze.
- **Winter**: Features ice-based spells that can freeze enemies in place, providing crowd control and reducing incoming threats.

Rogue Skill Trees

- **Archery**: Ideal for ranged combat, this tree focuses on powerful bow attacks and abilities that can target enemies from afar.
- **Dual-Wield**: Emphasizes quick, dual-weapon attacks, perfect for players who prefer close-quarters, high-damage combat.
- **Sabotage**: Provides utility abilities, such as traps and poison, to weaken and outsmart enemies.
- **Subterfuge**: Focuses on stealth and evasion, allowing Rogues to vanish from sight, evade attacks, or sneak up on enemies for critical hits.

Veil Warden Skill Trees (Exclusive to *Veilguard*)

- **Veil Strike**: Focuses on abilities that manipulate the Veil to weaken enemies and create opportunities for powerful attacks.
- **Spirit Allies**: Allows you to summon spirits to fight alongside you, providing support in the form of damage or healing.
- **Fade Shroud**: Grants abilities related to phasing through obstacles or using the Veil to shield yourself from attacks.

3. Unlocking and Upgrading Skills

- **Unlocking New Skills**: As you level up, you'll earn skill points that you can spend in the skill tree. Highlight the skill you want to unlock and press "X" (PlayStation), "A" (Xbox), or left-click (PC). Make sure to read the skill descriptions to understand its effects.

- **Upgrading Existing Skills**: Many skills have upgrades that make them more effective, such as reducing cooldown times or adding bonus effects. To upgrade an existing skill, navigate to it and press "X" (PlayStation), "A" (Xbox), or left-click (PC). Upgrading is often just as important as unlocking new skills, as it can dramatically enhance your character's effectiveness in battle.

4. Skill Combinations and Synergies

- **Combining Skills**: To create a powerful character, think about how different skills can work together. For example, a Mage might use **Winter's Grasp** to freeze enemies, followed by a **Fireball** from the Inferno tree to shatter the frozen enemies for extra damage.

- **Building Synergies with Companions**: Your companions' skills can also complement yours. For instance, a Warrior with a taunt ability can draw enemy attention, allowing a Rogue to use backstab skills for critical damage. Coordinate your abilities to maximize your party's overall effectiveness.

5. Specializations Overview

Specializations are advanced branches of skill trees that allow you to focus your character on a unique role. Each class has three specializations that become available as you progress through the game.

Warrior Specializations

- **Champion**: Focused on defense, Champions are nearly impossible to kill, with skills that protect both themselves and allies.
    - **How to Unlock**: You'll receive a specialization quest during the story. Complete this quest to unlock the Champion tree.
- **Reaver**: Gains power from pain, dealing more damage the lower their health. Reavers are ideal for aggressive players who thrive in high-risk situations.
- **Templar**: Specializes in fighting mages and demons, with abilities to nullify magic and protect the party from spells.

Mage Specializations

- **Knight-Enchanter**: Uses magic to create a spectral blade, allowing Mages to fight up close without sacrificing their spellcasting.

- **Necromancer**: Focuses on death magic, with abilities to raise spirits, weaken enemies, and deal significant damage over time.
- **Rift Mage**: Manipulates the Veil itself, controlling enemies and dealing massive area-of-effect damage.

Rogue Specializations

- **Assassin**: Specializes in dealing massive critical damage from stealth, perfect for players who like to strike hard and fast.
- **Tempest**: Uses alchemical concoctions to enhance attacks, creating chaotic effects on the battlefield.
- **Artificer**: Skilled in gadgets and traps, Artificers excel at setting ambushes and controlling the flow of battle.

Veil Warden Specializations (Exclusive to *Veilguard*)

- **Spirit Guardian**: Focuses on protective abilities, creating powerful barriers and using Fade energy to heal.
- **Fade Weaver**: Draws on the power of the Fade to weaken and drain enemies, leaving them vulnerable to attacks.
- **Shadow Walker**: Blends stealth and Fade magic, allowing the Veil Warden to phase in and out of sight and strike from the shadows.

6. How to Unlock Specializations

- **Receiving Specialization Quests**: As you progress through the story, you'll eventually reach a point where specialization quests become available. You'll be prompted to visit a specific NPC to begin these quests.
- **Completing the Quest**: Specialization quests are tailored to the class you're playing. For example, Mages might need to collect rare magical items, while Warriors could face combat trials. Track the quest in your journal by pressing "J" (PC), the touchpad (PlayStation), or "View" (Xbox), then follow the objectives.
- **Unlocking the Specialization Skill Tree**: After completing the quest, your chosen specialization will become available in the skill tree. Navigate to the specialization tab and start unlocking new abilities with the skill points you earn as you level up.

7. Choosing the Right Specialization for Your Playstyle

- **Warrior Specializations**: Choose **Champion** if you prefer tanking and want to protect your allies. **Reaver** is for aggressive players who don't mind taking damage in exchange for powerful attacks. **Templar** is perfect if you're facing many magical enemies and want a strong anti-magic toolkit.
- **Mage Specializations**: **Knight-Enchanter** is ideal for Mages who want to engage in melee combat while still casting spells. **Necromancer** is best for those who enjoy dealing damage over time and

controlling the dead. **Rift Mage** is for players who like to control groups of enemies and deal area-of-effect damage.

- **Rogue Specializations**: Choose **Assassin** if you like high damage output from stealth attacks. **Tempest** is for chaotic players who want to enhance their attacks with unpredictable effects. **Artificer** is excellent for those who prefer a strategic approach using traps and gadgets.
- **Veil Warden Specializations**: **Spirit Guardian** is for those who prefer a support role, protecting and healing allies. **Fade Weaver** is perfect for players who want to debilitate enemies and drain their power. **Shadow Walker** is ideal if you enjoy stealth tactics mixed with magical abilities.

8. Specialization Skills and Combos

- **Combining Specialization Skills**: Each specialization comes with unique skills that can combine in powerful ways. For example, a **Knight-Enchanter Mage** can cast **Fade Shield** to protect themselves while engaging in melee combat with their spectral blade.
- **Party Combinations**: Mix and match specializations within your party for maximum effectiveness. A **Champion Warrior** can protect a **Necromancer Mage**, while an **Assassin Rogue** takes advantage of enemies distracted by the tank. Using specializations to complement each other can make challenging battles much more manageable.

9. Upgrading Specialization Abilities

- **Unlocking New Skills**: Once your specialization is unlocked, spend skill points to acquire new abilities. These are often more powerful than base class abilities, providing significant boosts in combat.
- **Customizing Your Playstyle**: Focus on abilities that match your playstyle. If you're a **Tempest Rogue**, you may want to invest in skills that allow you to enhance your attacks with fire or ice, making every strike unpredictable and powerful.

Summary: Mastering Skill Trees and Specializations

- **Open the Skill Tree**: Press "K" (PC), "Options" (PlayStation), or "Menu" (Xbox) to view and upgrade skills.
- **Unlock Specializations**: Progress through the story to receive specialization quests, complete them, and unlock your chosen specialization skill tree.
- **Spend Points Wisely**: Plan your skill and specialization points based on your desired combat role, whether it's tanking, dealing damage, supporting allies, or controlling enemies.
- **Synergize with Your Team**: Coordinate with your companions to create a balanced team, combining abilities and specializations for maximum effectiveness.

Gearing Up: Armor, Weapons, and Enchantments

In *Dragon Age: The Veilguard*, choosing the right gear is essential to building a strong, resilient, and powerful character. Armor, weapons, and enchantments each play a unique role in enhancing your abilities, providing protection, and letting you tackle tougher challenges. This guide will walk you through everything you need to know about finding, equipping, and upgrading gear, so you can make the most of your character's potential.

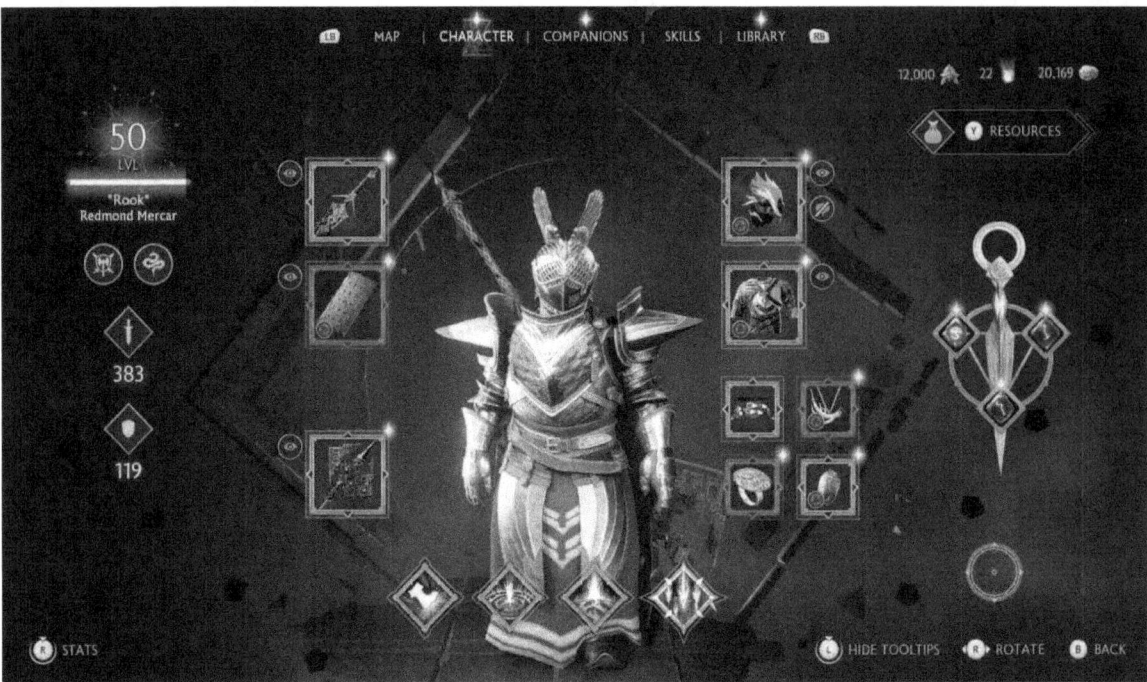

1. Accessing Your Inventory

- **Opening the Inventory Menu**: To view and manage your equipment, press "I" on PC, "Options" on PlayStation, or "Menu" on Xbox to open the inventory menu.
- **Navigating Inventory Categories**: Use the D-pad (console) or arrow keys (PC) to scroll through inventory categories, such as weapons, armor, accessories, and crafting materials. This will help you locate specific items quickly.

2. Equipping Armor

- **Selecting Armor**: In the inventory menu, go to the "Armor" tab to view all available armor pieces. You'll see options like helmets, chest plates, gloves, and boots, each providing unique stat boosts and effects.
- **Reviewing Stats and Bonuses**: Highlight an armor piece to see its stats, including protection, health bonuses, and any additional resistances (e.g., fire or cold resistance). Higher-tier armor will offer better protection and bonuses, so consider upgrading as you progress.

- **Equipping Armor**: To equip an armor piece, highlight it, then press "X" (PlayStation), "A" (Xbox), or left-click (PC). Equipped items will show up on your character immediately.
- **Tip**: Choose armor that suits your playstyle. Warriors benefit from heavy armor with high defense, Mages often prefer robes that boost magic, and Rogues excel with lightweight armor that enhances agility and stealth.

3. Choosing Weapons

- **Selecting a Weapon Type**: Go to the "Weapons" tab in your inventory to view available weapons. Each class has preferred weapon types—Warriors use swords, axes, and hammers; Mages wield staffs; and Rogues excel with daggers or bows.
- **Reviewing Weapon Stats**: Highlight a weapon to see its damage, critical chance, and any elemental effects (like fire or ice). Pay attention to bonuses that match your character's strengths, such as melee damage for Warriors or critical chance for Rogues.
- **Equipping Weapons**: To equip a weapon, highlight it and press "X" (PlayStation), "A" (Xbox), or left-click (PC). You can also equip dual weapons for classes like the Rogue, adding more versatility to your attacks.
- **Two-Handed vs. Dual-Wield**: Some classes, like Warriors, can choose between two-handed weapons and dual-wield setups. Two-handed weapons are slower but more powerful, while dual-wielding allows for faster attacks with additional effects. Pick what suits your combat style.

4. Finding and Crafting High-Quality Gear

- **Looting and Quest Rewards**: High-quality gear can be found as loot, bought from merchants, or earned as quest rewards. Always check chests, defeated enemies, and merchant inventories for upgraded items.
- **Using Crafting Stations**: Visit crafting stations, typically located in major towns or camps, to craft weapons and armor. Crafting requires specific materials like leather, metal, and rare ores, so gather resources from each region.
- **Crafting Process**:
  - Open the crafting station by pressing "X" (PlayStation), "A" (Xbox), or left-click (PC).
  - Choose the item type you want to craft (e.g., sword, chest plate) and view the required materials.
  - Once all materials are gathered, press "X" (PlayStation), "A" (Xbox), or left-click (PC) to craft the item. The crafted gear will automatically appear in your inventory.

5. Upgrading Gear with Runes and Enchantments

- **Runes and Enchantment Slots**: Some weapons and armor pieces have enchantment slots where you can add runes. Runes provide various bonuses, such as elemental damage or resistance. Check each item's description to see if it has rune slots.

- **Applying Runes**:
  - Go to a rune workbench, usually found in larger settlements or near crafting stations.
  - Open the rune menu by pressing "X" (PlayStation), "A" (Xbox), or left-click (PC).
  - Select a weapon or armor piece with an open slot, then choose a rune from your inventory. Press "X" (PlayStation), "A" (Xbox), or left-click (PC) to apply the rune.
- **Choosing the Right Rune**: Different enemies have specific weaknesses. Fire runes are great against ice creatures, while spirit runes deal extra damage to undead foes. Customize your equipment based on the area you're exploring.

6. Legendary and Unique Items

- **Finding Legendary Gear**: Legendary weapons and armor pieces, marked with a unique icon, are rare but incredibly powerful. They can be found by completing specific quests, defeating bosses, or exploring hidden areas.
- **Reviewing Special Effects**: Legendary items often come with unique effects, such as life-stealing or increased elemental resistance. When you acquire a legendary item, review its stats and bonuses carefully—these items can significantly enhance your character's power.
- **Equipping Legendary Gear**: To equip a legendary item, follow the same steps as with regular gear. Legendary items often require a certain level, so check that your character meets the requirements.

7. Gear for Companions

- **Managing Companion Gear**: Your companions can also benefit from upgraded weapons and armor. Open the inventory, switch to the companion tab by pressing R1/L1 (PlayStation), RB/LB (Xbox), or the tab key (PC), and choose items to equip on your companions.
- **Choosing Gear Based on Role**: Equip each companion according to their role. Give defensive items to tank companions, high-damage weapons to offensive companions, and magic-boosting gear to support characters.
- **Assigning Runes and Enchantments for Companions**: Companions can also have their gear enchanted with runes. Follow the same process at a rune workbench to add bonuses to their weapons and armor.

8. Repairing Gear (If Required)

- **Repairing Damaged Equipment**: Some high-tier gear may degrade over time, especially after tough battles. Visit a blacksmith or crafting station to repair your items.
- **How to Repair**: Approach the blacksmith or repair station and press "X" (PlayStation), "A" (Xbox), or left-click (PC). Select the item you want to repair and confirm to restore its durability.
- **Tip**: Regularly check for damaged equipment, as worn gear loses its effectiveness in combat.

9. Tips for Efficient Gear Management

- **Regularly Update Your Gear**: As you level up and progress through the story, continue to update your gear to keep up with tougher enemies.
- **Optimize for the Area You're In**: Equip gear and enchantments that counter specific enemies in your current area (e.g., fire resistance in lava zones, cold damage in icy regions).
- **Sell or Salvage Unused Gear**: If your inventory becomes cluttered, consider selling old gear to merchants or salvaging it for crafting materials at a crafting station.
- **Experiment with Different Loadouts**: Try different combinations of armor, weapons, and enchantments to find what works best for your playstyle and team composition.

10. Gearing Up Summary

- **Access Inventory**: Press "I" (PC), "Options" (PlayStation), or "Menu" (Xbox) to open your inventory and manage gear.
- **Equip and Upgrade**: Select weapons and armor that suit your character's strengths and use runes and enchantments for additional bonuses.
- **Find Legendary Items**: Explore hidden areas and defeat bosses to acquire powerful legendary items that provide unique benefits.
- **Update Companions' Gear**: Make sure your companions have gear that complements their roles in combat.

By mastering your armor, weapons, and enchantments, you'll be ready to face even the most challenging enemies in *The Veilguard*. Gear up wisely, adapt your loadout for different regions, and upgrade regularly to ensure your character is always at their strongest. Enjoy building a powerful, customized character that's ready to conquer every adventure in Thedas!

Attribute Management and Optimization

In *Dragon Age: The Veilguard*, managing and optimizing your character's attributes is essential for maximizing their potential and adapting to tougher challenges. Your attribute points—spent on core stats like Strength, Dexterity, Magic, Constitution, and Willpower—shape your character's strengths and define their playstyle. Here's a comprehensive guide to attribute management and optimization, including tips on where to allocate points based on your class and combat strategy.

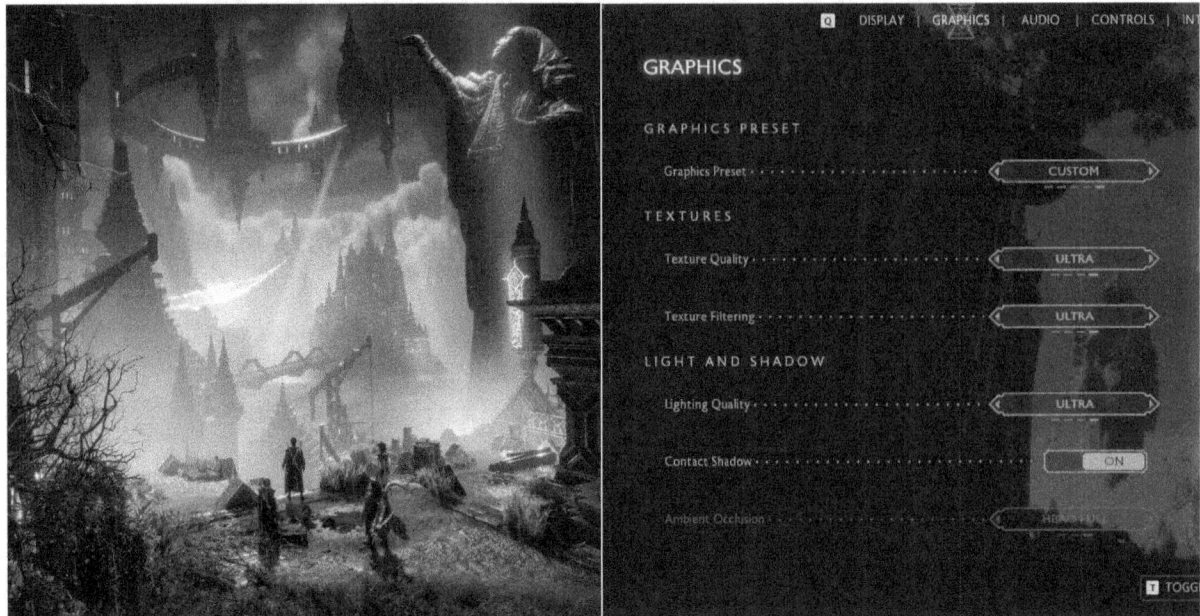

1. Accessing Attributes

- **Opening the Character Screen**: To view and manage your attributes, press "C" on PC, "Options" on PlayStation, or "Menu" on Xbox to open the character screen.
- **Navigating to Attributes**: In the character screen, switch to the "Attributes" tab to see your current stats and available attribute points.

2. Overview of Core Attributes

Each attribute in *The Veilguard* has a specific function that benefits certain classes and playstyles. Understanding what each attribute does will help you make smarter decisions when allocating points.

- **Strength**: Increases melee damage and is essential for Warriors. It enhances physical attacks and contributes to armor penetration, making it perfect for those who engage in close combat.
- **Dexterity**: Boosts accuracy, critical hit chance, and evasion. This attribute is ideal for Rogues, who rely on agility and critical strikes to excel in combat, especially when dual-wielding or using ranged weapons.
- **Magic**: Amplifies spell power and mana regeneration, making it a core attribute for Mages. More points in Magic allow Mages to cast more powerful spells and boost their elemental damage.
- **Constitution**: Increases health and stamina, which benefits all classes but is particularly crucial for Warriors who take on tank roles. Higher Constitution means better durability and the ability to withstand more damage in battles.
- **Willpower**: Affects stamina and mana regeneration, making it useful for all classes, especially those that rely on high energy consumption like Rogues and Mages. More Willpower means you can use abilities more frequently without exhausting resources.

3. Allocating Attribute Points

- **Receiving Attribute Points**: Every time you level up, you'll receive attribute points to spend on these core stats. This allows you to gradually customize your character's strengths to fit your preferred playstyle.
- **Spending Points**: Highlight an attribute in the "Attributes" tab, and press "X" (PlayStation), "A" (Xbox), or left-click (PC) to add a point. Each point you allocate immediately boosts that attribute, making your character stronger in specific areas.
- **Removing Points** (if available): Some versions may allow re-spec options where you can reset your points if you want to change your build. If this is available, you'll see an option to re-spec by pressing the corresponding button.

4. Optimizing Attributes by Class

Here's a breakdown of the ideal attribute focus for each class. While every class can benefit from a mix of attributes, certain stats are more advantageous for specific roles.

- **Warrior**:
  - **Primary Attributes**: Strength, Constitution
  - **Recommended Build**: Focus heavily on Strength to increase melee damage and armor penetration. Invest in Constitution to build up health, making your Warrior a more effective tank and allowing them to withstand heavy attacks.
  - **Additional Attribute**: A few points in Willpower can be useful for stamina regeneration, allowing for frequent use of abilities.
- **Mage**:
  - **Primary Attributes**: Magic, Willpower
  - **Recommended Build**: Magic should be your main focus, as it powers up your spells and boosts elemental damage. Invest in Willpower to enhance mana regeneration, letting you cast more spells without running out of resources.
  - **Additional Attribute**: Some points in Constitution can improve survivability since Mages are typically vulnerable in close combat.
- **Rogue**:
  - **Primary Attributes**: Dexterity, Willpower
  - **Recommended Build**: Dexterity increases critical hit chance and evasion, which are key to dealing high damage quickly and avoiding attacks. Willpower will help with stamina regeneration, so you can use Rogue abilities more frequently.

- **Additional Attribute**: A few points in Strength for close-combat Rogues can add some melee power. Constitution is also useful if you plan to take risks by staying in close quarters with enemies.
- **Veil Warden** (exclusive to *Veilguard*):
  - **Primary Attributes**: Magic, Dexterity (depending on build)
  - **Recommended Build**: If you're using abilities that rely heavily on the Fade, prioritize Magic for higher spell power. Dexterity is useful for evasive and stealth-based builds, giving you the flexibility to phase in and out of danger.
  - **Additional Attribute**: Constitution can provide much-needed health for survival, as Veil Wardens often face challenging enemies from the Fade. Willpower is also beneficial for maintaining stamina and mana for Fade abilities.

5. Balancing Offense and Defense

- **Offensive Builds**: Focus on primary damage stats (Strength for Warriors, Magic for Mages, Dexterity for Rogues) if you prefer dealing high damage and engaging in aggressive combat. These builds are effective in taking down enemies quickly but may require extra attention to positioning and defense.
- **Defensive Builds**: If you prioritize survivability, invest in Constitution for a higher health pool, which allows you to withstand more hits. This is especially useful for Warriors and Veil Wardens who spend time in close combat.
- **Hybrid Builds**: Many players benefit from a balanced approach, combining offense with some defensive attributes. For instance, a Mage might focus on Magic and Willpower while adding a few points to Constitution for durability.

6. Respec Options for Attribute Reallocation

- **Respec Availability**: Some versions of the game provide respec options, allowing you to reallocate attribute points if you want to change your character's build. This is particularly useful if you decide to try a different playstyle or encounter areas where a new attribute focus could be beneficial.
- **How to Respec**: Look for merchants or NPCs in major cities who offer respec services, often for a fee. You may also find respec items in the game that allow you to reset your attributes. Approach the NPC or open the respec item in your inventory, then press "X" (PlayStation), "A" (Xbox), or left-click (PC) to confirm the reset.

7. Tips for Effective Attribute Management

- **Plan for Future Levels**: Consider your long-term goals when allocating points. If you plan to unlock specific skills or specializations, ensure your attributes align with their requirements.

- **Adapt to Enemy Types**: Certain areas require specific builds (e.g., high Constitution for durability in boss fights). Adjust your attributes based on your location and the enemies you'll face.
- **Experiment with Builds**: If respec options are available, try different attribute combinations. Experimenting lets you find the build that best fits your playstyle and provides flexibility in various situations.

8. Attribute Optimization Summary

- **Access Attributes**: Open the character screen by pressing "C" on PC, "Options" on PlayStation, or "Menu" on Xbox, and navigate to the "Attributes" tab.
- **Allocate Points by Class**: Focus on primary attributes based on your class—Strength for Warriors, Magic for Mages, Dexterity for Rogues, and a combination for Veil Wardens.
- **Balance Offense and Defense**: Choose a balanced approach if you want both power and durability, or focus on either offense or defense based on your combat preference.
- **Use Respec Options**: If available, use respec options to reallocate points if you want to change your build.

Managing attributes effectively in *The Veilguard* allows you to create a character that feels truly powerful and uniquely suited to your playstyle. With thoughtful allocation and optimization, you'll be able to face any challenge that comes your way in Thedas with confidence.

Companions and Relationship Building

In *Dragon Age: The Veilguard*, your companions are more than just allies in battle—they're complex characters with unique personalities, skills, and storylines. Building strong relationships with your companions can lead to powerful team synergies, unlock special abilities, and even affect the storyline. Here's a detailed guide on how to make the most of your companions, foster meaningful relationships, and maximize their impact on your adventure.

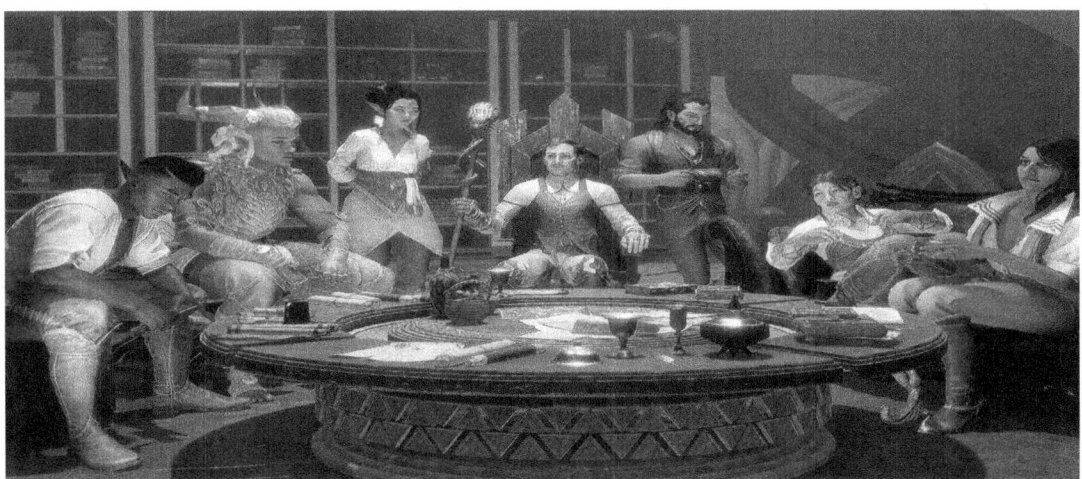

1. Recruiting Companions

- **Story-Driven Recruitment**: Companions join your team as you progress through the main storyline and complete certain side quests. Pay attention to dialogue choices and actions, as they can influence when and how companions decide to join you.
- **Optional Companions**: Some companions are optional and can be missed if you don't explore thoroughly or make specific choices. Keep an eye out for characters with unique skills who can offer additional benefits to your team.
- **Viewing Companion List**: To see all recruited companions, open the character menu by pressing "C" on PC, "Options" on PlayStation, or "Menu" on Xbox, and navigate to the "Party" or "Companions" tab.

2. Managing Your Party

- **Setting Up Your Party**: To add companions to your party, go to a campsite, your home base, or an in-game menu when selecting your team. Press "X" (PlayStation), "A" (Xbox), or left-click (PC) on each character to add them to your active party.
- **Switching Companions**: You can switch companions at camps or other key locations. This lets you tailor your team to the specific needs of each mission or battle, ensuring you have the right combination of skills.
- **Companion Roles**: Each companion has a designated role—some are strong tanks, others are skilled healers, damage dealers, or support characters. Choose companions based on their strengths and your current needs.

3. Understanding Companion Skills and Attributes

- **Viewing Companion Skills**: Open the character menu, navigate to the "Party" tab, and select each companion to view their attributes and skill trees.
- **Allocating Skill Points**: When your companions level up, they receive skill points. Highlight an attribute or skill and press "X" (PlayStation), "A" (Xbox), or left-click (PC) to allocate points. Aim to boost skills that enhance their primary role, such as strength and constitution for tanks, or dexterity and agility for damage-dealing Rogues.
- **Upgrading Companions' Gear**: Don't forget to equip companions with high-quality weapons and armor to improve their survivability and effectiveness in combat. You can manage their equipment the same way you manage your own by switching to the companion tab in the inventory menu.

4. Building Relationships with Companions

- **Dialogue Choices**: Your dialogue choices with companions greatly impact your relationships with them. Open dialogue by approaching a companion and pressing "X" (PlayStation), "A" (Xbox), or "E" (PC). Choose responses that align with their values to improve rapport.
- **Understanding Companion Preferences**: Each companion has their own beliefs, moral code, and personal goals. Some may value honor and bravery, while others appreciate wit, loyalty, or empathy. Tailor your responses to match their personalities.
- **Avoiding Negative Reactions**: Some actions or dialogue choices can lead to negative reactions from companions. If you disagree on a core value, be mindful of how that affects your relationship with them.

5. Gaining Approval and Unlocking Perks

- **Approval System**: As you make choices and complete quests, companions will gain or lose approval based on how your actions align with their values. A high approval rating can unlock special perks, unique dialogue, and even romance options.
- **Checking Approval Levels**: Open the character menu and select a companion to view their approval level. Higher levels mean stronger relationships, while low approval can lead to disagreements or even risk a companion leaving.
- **Unlocking Unique Perks**: With enough approval, some companions unlock unique perks, such as enhanced abilities or special buffs. These perks are often tied to the character's skills and provide benefits that can significantly improve your team's performance in combat.

6. Romancing Companions

- **Romance Options**: Certain companions are open to romantic relationships, depending on your character's gender, race, and the choices you make. These options usually become available as you build higher approval levels.
- **Flirtatious Dialogue**: To pursue a romance, choose flirtatious or warm dialogue options when speaking to the companion. These options will often be marked by heart icons or special phrases.
- **Progressing Romance**: As you continue interacting and gaining approval, romance dialogue choices will evolve. These choices can lead to more intimate moments and unlock unique storylines, scenes, and even special abilities.
- **Balancing Relationships**: Keep in mind that some companions may react negatively to seeing you build close relationships with others, so be mindful of how your actions impact the team dynamics.

7. Companion Quests and Storylines

- **Unlocking Companion Quests**: As your approval level with a companion increases, they may open up about their personal story and give you quests related to their background. Completing these quests strengthens your bond and provides deeper insight into their character.

- **Starting a Companion Quest**: If a companion has a quest available, they will often approach you at your camp or main base. Accept the quest by pressing "X" (PlayStation), "A" (Xbox), or "E" (PC) when prompted.

- **Completing Companion Quests**: Completing these quests boosts approval and can unlock powerful abilities or items for your companion. These quests also provide some of the most engaging and rewarding stories in the game, so prioritize them to make the most of your relationships.

8. Synergizing Abilities for Team Performance

- **Choosing Complementary Skills**: Select companions whose abilities complement your own. For example, if you play as a Mage, adding a tank companion can create a balanced team.

- **Using Team Abilities**: Some companions' abilities are designed to work well together, such as combinations that immobilize enemies for other teammates to attack. Experiment with different ability combos to find what works best for your team.

- **Positioning Companions in Battle**: During combat, keep your tank up front to absorb damage while allowing ranged companions to attack from a distance. Positioning can make a big difference in combat effectiveness and survival.

9. Regularly Checking In with Companions

- **Camp Conversations**: Visiting your camp or home base is a great opportunity to check in with your companions. Talk to them regularly to unlock new dialogue options and potentially trigger new quests or scenes.

- **Paying Attention to Companion Reactions**: Your companions will often react to the decisions you make in missions. If a companion has a strong reaction, this may be a sign that your relationship with them is about to change. Use these reactions as a way to guide your choices and manage relationships.

10. Companions and Relationship Building Summary

- **Recruit and Manage**: Set up your team by adding companions at camps or bases and choose companions who align with your needs.

- **Build Relationships Through Dialogue**: Improve rapport by choosing dialogue options that match each companion's personality, and avoid choices that could harm your relationship.

- **Gain Approval and Unlock Perks**: High approval ratings unlock unique perks and abilities. Keep track of approval levels to maximize benefits.

- **Pursue Companion Quests**: Complete companion-specific quests to strengthen bonds, unlock new abilities, and experience deep storytelling.

Your companions in *The Veilguard* bring depth, personality, and power to your journey in Thedas. By building strong relationships, pursuing companion quests, and carefully managing your team's strengths, you'll create a more cohesive and effective team ready to face the challenges that await. Invest time in understanding and bonding with each character, and you'll be rewarded with a richer, more immersive adventure.

CHAPTER 5

Combat System and Strategies

In this chapter, we cover everything you need to succeed in combat, from basic mechanics to advanced tactics for each class. You'll get tips on effectively using special abilities, creating powerful combos, and managing resources like health, mana, and stamina. We'll also share survival strategies for handling tough battles and provide guidance on adapting your approach based on the enemies you face. With these insights, you'll be ready to tackle any challenge and lead your team to victory in *Dragon Age: The Veilguard*.

Basics of Combat Mechanics

Understanding the fundamentals of combat in *Dragon Age: The Veilguard* is essential for surviving and thriving on the battlefield. Mastering basic mechanics like targeting, attack types, and using abilities will give you a strong foundation to build on as you progress through the game. Here's a comprehensive guide to help you make the most of each encounter, including where to press for different actions.

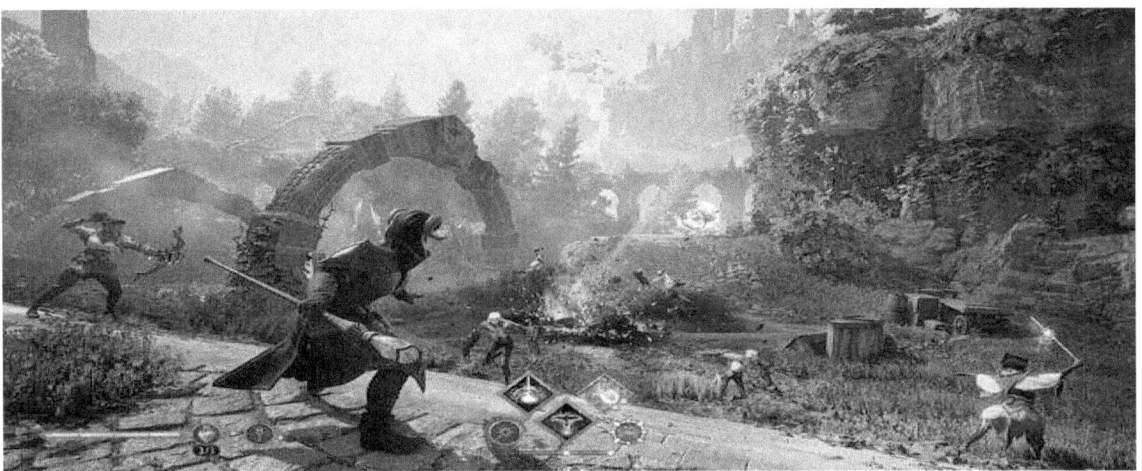

1. Targeting and Locking Onto Enemies

- **Locking On**: In combat, it's important to focus on a specific target. To lock onto an enemy, press "R3" (push down the right stick) on consoles or "Tab" on PC. Locking on allows you to keep the camera focused on your target, making it easier to aim attacks and abilities.

- **Switching Targets**: To switch between enemies while locked on, flick the right stick left or right (console) or press "Tab" again (PC). This is helpful when dealing with multiple foes, as you can quickly adjust your focus.

2. Basic Attacks and Combos

- **Melee and Ranged Attacks**:
  - **Melee Attacks**: For close-range characters (Warriors, Rogues with dual-wield), press "R1" (PlayStation), "RB" (Xbox), or left-click (PC) to perform a basic attack. Melee attacks are your primary source of damage in close quarters and can be chained together for simple combos.
  - **Ranged Attacks**: For characters with ranged weapons (Rogues with bows, Mages with staffs), press the same button to launch a basic ranged attack. Ranged attacks are excellent for keeping distance from enemies while dealing consistent damage.
- **Combos**: Chaining multiple basic attacks can trigger small combos. For example, pressing "R1/RB" or left-clicking three times in a row may result in a stronger finishing hit. Practice chaining basic attacks to maximize your damage output.

3. Using Abilities and Skills

- **Opening the Ability Wheel**: During combat, open the ability wheel by holding "L2" (PlayStation), "LT" (Xbox), or pressing "Q" (PC). The ability wheel displays all assigned abilities, allowing you to select the right skill for the moment.
- **Activating Abilities**: Once the ability wheel is open, highlight the ability you want to use and press "X" (PlayStation), "A" (Xbox), or click on it (PC) to activate. Abilities have cooldown times, so plan accordingly.
- **Assigning Abilities to Quick Slots**: For quick access, assign frequently used abilities to quick slots by opening the character menu and navigating to the ability customization tab. Highlight an ability and press "X" (PlayStation), "A" (Xbox), or left-click (PC) to assign it to a quick slot. This lets you activate abilities instantly with designated controller buttons or number keys (PC).

4. Dodging and Blocking

- **Dodging**: Dodging is key to avoiding incoming attacks. For Rogues and Veil Wardens, press "Circle" (PlayStation), "B" (Xbox), or "Space" (PC) to perform a dodge roll, allowing you to quickly evade attacks. Dodging is useful when fighting heavy-hitting enemies or when surrounded.
- **Blocking and Parrying**: Warriors equipped with a shield can block or parry incoming attacks. To block, press and hold "L1" (PlayStation), "LB" (Xbox), or "Shift" (PC). Blocking reduces incoming damage and, if timed correctly, can negate it entirely. Parrying with a well-timed block also opens opportunities for counterattacks.

5. Managing Positioning

- **Staying Mobile**: Movement is critical in combat, especially for ranged classes and mages who need to avoid close-range attacks. Use the left stick (console) or "WASD" keys (PC) to stay on the move, keeping a safe distance from enemies.
- **Using Terrain**: Position yourself advantageously by using natural cover or high ground. Mages and ranged Rogues, for example, can benefit from elevated positions, where they can attack enemies from a distance with reduced risk of being hit.

6. Using Tactical Pause (if available)

- **Pausing Combat**: In some modes, *The Veilguard* allows you to pause combat to plan your moves, especially helpful in challenging encounters. Press the touchpad (PlayStation), "View" (Xbox), or "Space" (PC) to pause the action.
- **Issuing Commands**: While in tactical pause, highlight each character and choose abilities, movement, or target assignments. This allows you to control the entire team, issuing orders and setting up combos without time pressure.
- **Resuming Combat**: Once commands are set, press the same button to resume combat and watch your strategy unfold. Tactical pause is especially useful for players who enjoy a more strategic approach to battle.

7. Understanding Cooldowns and Resource Management

- **Cooldowns**: Abilities have cooldown times, which means they can't be used repeatedly without a short wait. Pay attention to cooldown timers to know when an ability will be ready again.
- **Resource Management**:
  - **Mana**: Used by Mages, mana regenerates slowly over time or can be restored by using certain items. Keep an eye on your mana pool to avoid running out mid-battle.
  - **Stamina**: Used by Warriors and Rogues, stamina is spent with each special attack or ability. Stamina also regenerates over time, but you can accelerate it by using items or abilities.
  - **Managing Resources**: Use basic attacks while waiting for resources to replenish, and avoid spamming abilities to conserve mana or stamina for critical moments.

8. Using Companion Abilities

- **Switching to Companions**: To directly control a companion, press "Up" or "Down" on the D-pad (console) or the F1-F4 keys (PC). This can be useful if you need to position a companion, activate a specific ability, or handle a particular enemy.

- **Issuing Commands to Companions**: You can also command companions without switching to them directly. Open the tactical pause menu, highlight a companion, and select their target or ability. Press "X" (PlayStation), "A" (Xbox), or left-click (PC) to confirm the command.
- **Synergizing Abilities**: Coordinate abilities between your character and companions to create powerful combos. For example, a Mage's freezing spell followed by a Warrior's shattering attack can deal significant damage to enemies.

9. Enemy Targeting and Weakness Exploitation

- **Analyzing Enemy Types**: Each enemy type has specific strengths and weaknesses. For example, fire spells work well against ice creatures, while blunt weapons are effective against armored enemies.
- **Exploiting Weaknesses**: Use abilities that target enemy vulnerabilities to maximize damage. Pay attention to status effects, as some abilities can stun, freeze, or immobilize enemies, making them easier to defeat.
- **Switching Targets Based on Priority**: In encounters with mixed enemy types, prioritize high-damage or healing enemies first. Use the target-switching feature to quickly adjust your focus and take out the most dangerous foes.

10. Basic Combat Strategy Summary

- **Lock Onto Targets**: Use "R3" (console) or "Tab" (PC) to lock onto enemies, making it easier to focus your attacks.
- **Chain Basic Attacks**: Press "R1" (PlayStation), "RB" (Xbox), or left-click (PC) to perform basic attacks and combos.
- **Activate Abilities**: Open the ability wheel with "L2" (PlayStation), "LT" (Xbox), or "Q" (PC) and select an ability.
- **Dodge and Block**: Use "Circle" (PlayStation), "B" (Xbox), or "Space" (PC) to dodge, and "L1" (PlayStation), "LB" (Xbox), or "Shift" (PC) to block.
- **Use Tactical Pause for Strategy**: Press the touchpad (PlayStation), "View" (Xbox), or "Space" (PC) to pause and issue commands in tough encounters.

Mastering the basics of combat in *The Veilguard* gives you a solid foundation for the more advanced tactics and strategies you'll develop as you progress. By learning these mechanics and refining your timing, positioning, and resource management, you'll be prepared to take on any challenge Thedas throws your way. Enjoy the thrill of battle and watch your skills grow as you become a powerful force in the game.

Advanced Tactics for Each Class

As you progress in *Dragon Age: The Veilguard*, developing advanced tactics tailored to your character's class is essential to mastering combat and defeating tougher enemies. Each class—Warrior, Mage, Rogue, and Veil

Warden—has unique skills, strengths, and playstyles that can be further enhanced with strategic planning and a deep understanding of their abilities. This guide covers advanced tactics for each class, including specific tips to help you maximize your effectiveness and where to press to execute key actions.

1. Warrior: Advanced Tactics

Warriors are the backbone of any team, with abilities to tank, deal high melee damage, and control the battlefield. Here's how to make the most of a Warrior's potential:

- **Tank Positioning and Threat Management**:
    - **Holding the Front Line**: Warriors are best positioned at the front, drawing enemy attention and protecting squishier teammates. To keep enemies focused on you, use taunting abilities like **Challenge** by pressing "X" (PlayStation), "A" (Xbox), or left-click (PC).
    - **Area Control**: Abilities like **War Cry** help increase threat generation, pulling enemies towards you. Use it by selecting from your ability wheel ("L2" on PlayStation, "LT" on Xbox, or "Q" on PC) and selecting the ability to activate.
- **Managing Crowd Control Abilities**:
    - **Stunning and Knocking Down**: Abilities like **Shield Bash** and **Mighty Blow** deal high damage while also knocking down or stunning enemies. Use these abilities strategically to interrupt enemies preparing powerful attacks.
    - **Using AoE Abilities**: Abilities such as **Earthshaker** or **Whirlwind** are ideal for crowd control, hitting multiple targets. Position yourself in the middle of enemy groups and activate these skills to maximize damage output. Open the ability wheel, select the skill, and press "X" (PlayStation), "A" (Xbox), or left-click (PC) to activate.
- **Advanced Defense Tactics**:
    - **Timing Blocks and Parries**: When equipped with a shield, press and hold "L1" (PlayStation), "LB" (Xbox), or "Shift" (PC) to block incoming attacks. Mastering the timing for parries can negate incoming damage and open up enemies for counterattacks.
    - **Health Recovery**: Warriors can sustain more damage than other classes but should monitor health closely. Keep health potions on standby by pressing "D-Pad Down" (console) or the assigned key (PC) for quick healing.

2. Mage: Advanced Tactics

Mages are versatile spellcasters with abilities for crowd control, elemental damage, and healing. Advanced tactics help Mages control the battlefield while keeping a safe distance.

- **Elemental Damage and Enemy Weaknesses**:
    - **Switching Elements**: Mages have access to fire, ice, and lightning spells, each suited for specific enemy types. Use **Fire spells** against ice creatures and **Ice spells** to slow or freeze

fast-moving enemies. Open the ability wheel ("L2" on PlayStation, "LT" on Xbox, or "Q" on PC) to quickly switch between spells as needed.

- **Area Control with AoE Spells**: Spells like **Firestorm** or **Blizzard** cover large areas and are ideal for controlling enemy groups. Position yourself at a safe distance and cast AoE spells by selecting the ability from the wheel and pressing "X" (PlayStation), "A" (Xbox), or left-click (PC).

- **Using Defensive Barriers and Healing**:
  - **Casting Barriers**: Mages can protect teammates with barrier spells. Use **Barrier** by selecting it in the ability wheel and pressing "X" (PlayStation), "A" (Xbox), or left-click (PC). Apply barriers when you or a companion are low on health to absorb incoming damage.
  - **Healing Spells and Potions**: Some Mages specialize in healing abilities or have passive abilities that enhance health regeneration. Equip healing spells in your quick slots for easy access, and remind teammates to use health potions in critical situations.

- **Maximizing Combos with Status Effects**:
  - **Freezing and Shattering**: Use **Winter's Grasp** to freeze enemies and follow up with a high-damage attack (like **Stonefist**) to shatter them, dealing massive damage. Practice combo timing to pull off these powerful attacks effectively.
  - **Paralyzing and Burning**: Use **Paralyze** to immobilize enemies, then cast a **Fire spell** to deal burn damage while they're trapped. This combination is particularly effective against higher-level enemies that deal strong melee damage.

3. Rogue: Advanced Tactics

Rogues are experts at dealing high burst damage, using stealth, and exploiting critical hits. Advanced tactics for Rogues involve strategic positioning, quick attacks, and precise combos.

- **Stealth and Backstabbing**:
  - **Entering Stealth**: Press "Circle" (PlayStation), "B" (Xbox), or "Space" (PC) to enter stealth. Position yourself behind enemies for backstab opportunities, which grant extra critical damage.
  - **Using Shadow Strike**: **Shadow Strike** deals increased damage from behind and has a high critical hit rate. Sneak up on enemies and press "X" (PlayStation), "A" (Xbox), or left-click (PC) to unleash powerful attacks.

- **Critical Hits and High Burst Damage**:
  - **Maximizing Crit with Twin Fangs**: **Twin Fangs** is an ideal skill for maximizing burst damage, especially against single targets. Get close to the enemy, activate **Twin Fangs** from the ability wheel, and press "X" (PlayStation), "A" (Xbox), or left-click (PC) to attack.

o   **Poison and Trap Synergy**: Set traps in strategic locations, then lure enemies into them. Poison abilities, such as **Toxic Cloud**, allow you to deal continuous damage over time, adding to the Rogue's high DPS.

- **Ranged Tactics (for Archery Rogues)**:
  o   **Maintaining Distance**: Archery Rogues are best when keeping a safe distance from enemies. Use **Leaping Shot** to create distance by jumping back while firing arrows. Open the ability wheel, select **Leaping Shot**, and press "X" (PlayStation), "A" (Xbox), or left-click (PC).
  o   **Pinning Shots for Control**: Use **Pinning Shot** to immobilize distant enemies, stopping them in their tracks. Activate **Pinning Shot** from the ability wheel, allowing you to control the battlefield and prioritize targets safely.

4. Veil Warden: Advanced Tactics

The Veil Warden, exclusive to *The Veilguard*, uses Fade powers to disrupt enemies and protect allies. This class thrives on evasion, spectral allies, and manipulating the Veil.

- **Using Fade-Based Powers**:
  o   **Phasing Through Attacks**: Veil Wardens can use abilities like **Phase Shift** to become temporarily immune to attacks. Press "X" (PlayStation), "A" (Xbox), or left-click (PC) to activate **Phase Shift** and reposition yourself or avoid dangerous attacks.
  o   **Unleashing Spectral Allies**: Summon allies from the Fade to support you in battle. Use **Spectral Summon** from the ability wheel by pressing "L2" (PlayStation), "LT" (Xbox), or "Q" (PC), selecting the ability, and pressing "X" (PlayStation), "A" (Xbox), or left-click (PC) to activate. Spectral allies can distract enemies or provide temporary buffs.

- **Defensive and Offensive Veil Manipulation**:
  o   **Using Fade Shields**: Cast **Fade Shield** to protect yourself or allies, reducing incoming damage. This is especially useful when facing groups of enemies. Activate **Fade Shield** by selecting it in the ability wheel and pressing "X" (PlayStation), "A" (Xbox), or left-click (PC).
  o   **Veil Storms for Area Control**: **Veil Storm** is a powerful area-of-effect ability that disrupts enemies within a radius, dealing damage over time. Position yourself strategically, open the ability wheel, select **Veil Storm**, and press "X" (PlayStation), "A" (Xbox), or left-click (PC) to cast it.

- **Evasive and Stealth Tactics**:
  o   **Using Shadow Cloak**: **Shadow Cloak** allows the Veil Warden to temporarily become invisible, ideal for repositioning or escaping tough situations. Activate **Shadow Cloak** by pressing "X" (PlayStation), "A" (Xbox), or left-click (PC) to enter stealth and evade enemies.
  o   **Teleportation and Repositioning**: **Veil Step** lets Veil Wardens teleport short distances, helping you escape crowds or reach vantage points. Use it by selecting **Veil Step** in the ability wheel and pressing "X" (PlayStation), "A" (Xbox), or left-click (PC) to teleport instantly.

Advanced Class Tactics Summary

- **Warriors**: Master threat management and area control with crowd-control abilities like **War Cry** and **Earthshaker**. Use shield blocks and taunts to protect your team.
- **Mages**: Use elemental spells strategically to exploit enemy weaknesses. Maximize control with AoE spells and defensive barriers.
- **Rogues**: Utilize stealth and critical-hit abilities like **Shadow Strike** for high burst damage. Place traps and poisons to control the battlefield.
- **Veil Wardens**: Use Fade-based abilities to phase through attacks, summon spectral allies, and manipulate the battlefield. Master evasion and teleports for survival.

Each class in *The Veilguard* offers a unique style of combat, allowing for a variety of tactics to handle any encounter. By mastering these advanced techniques, you'll enhance your team's performance, dominate challenging battles, and tailor each class to your personal playstyle. Enjoy developing these powerful tactics and become a formidable force in Thedas!

Special Abilities and Combos

Special abilities and combos are essential for mastering combat in *Dragon Age: The Veilguard*. By combining abilities from different skill trees and classes, you can create powerful effects that maximize damage, control the battlefield, or support your team. This guide covers how to use special abilities, set up combos, and unleash devastating attacks that turn the tide in any battle.

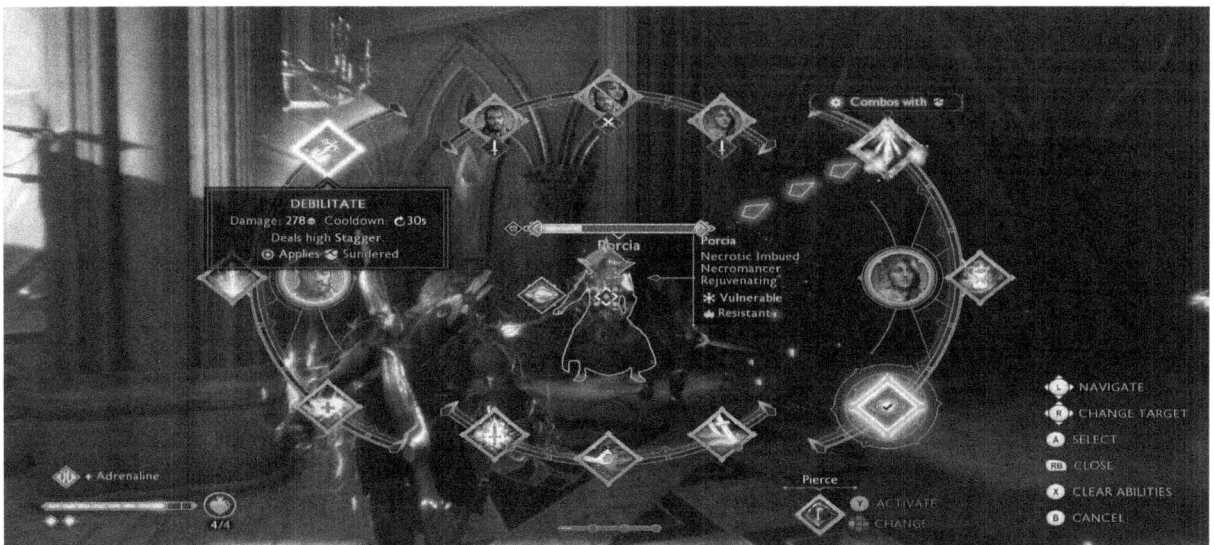

1. Understanding Special Abilities

- **What Are Special Abilities?**: Special abilities are skills unique to each class that can deal extra damage, control groups of enemies, or provide support to allies. These abilities often have cooldowns, so using them strategically is key.
- **Accessing Your Abilities**: You can view and equip abilities from the skill tree by pressing "K" on PC, "Options" on PlayStation, or "Menu" on Xbox. Once unlocked, assign them to your quick slots to access them easily during combat.
- **Using Abilities in Combat**: Press the corresponding quick slot button (such as R2 on PlayStation, RT on Xbox, or numbers 1-4 on PC) to activate each ability. Timing and order are important, especially when setting up combos.

2. Basic Combo System

- **Primer and Detonator**: The combo system in *The Veilguard* relies on "primers" and "detonators." A primer is an ability that sets up an enemy for a combo, while a detonator is an ability that "triggers" the combo, dealing extra damage or causing additional effects.
- **Identifying Primer and Detonator Abilities**: Abilities that act as primers are marked with an icon (often a circle or symbol) in the skill description. Detonators have a different icon, usually an explosion or burst symbol.
- **Example**: A Mage might cast **Winter's Grasp** (a freezing primer) on an enemy, then follow up with **Stonefist** (a detonator) to create a shatter effect, dealing massive damage.

3. Class-Specific Combos

Each class has unique abilities that can be combined to create devastating effects. Let's break down some of the most effective combos for each class:

Warrior Combos

- **Challenge and Mighty Blow**:
  - **Combo**: Use **Challenge** to taunt enemies, drawing them into one area, and follow up with **Mighty Blow** to deal area damage.
  - **How to Execute**: Press the quick slot button for **Challenge** (like R2 on PlayStation, RT on Xbox, or 1-4 on PC) to taunt, then activate **Mighty Blow** immediately after to strike multiple enemies.
- **Earthshaking Strike and Block & Slash**:
  - **Combo**: Use **Earthshaking Strike** to knock down enemies, then follow up with **Block & Slash** to deal powerful strikes while they're vulnerable.
  - **How to Execute**: Trigger **Earthshaking Strike** first, then press the quick slot for **Block & Slash** to capitalize on the knockdown effect.

Mage Combos

- **Winter's Grasp and Stonefist**:
    - **Combo**: **Winter's Grasp** freezes the enemy, and **Stonefist** shatters them for extra damage.
    - **How to Execute**: Activate **Winter's Grasp** by pressing its quick slot button, followed by **Stonefist** while the enemy is frozen.
- **Static Cage and Chain Lightning**:
    - **Combo**: **Static Cage** traps multiple enemies, then **Chain Lightning** deals area damage within the cage, bouncing between trapped targets.
    - **How to Execute**: Use **Static Cage** to trap enemies, then trigger **Chain Lightning** for a devastating area-of-effect attack.

Rogue Combos

- **Caltrops and Leaping Shot**:
    - **Combo**: **Caltrops** slows enemies, making them vulnerable to follow-up attacks. Use **Leaping Shot** to deal a barrage of critical hits.
    - **How to Execute**: Drop **Caltrops** in an enemy's path, then use **Leaping Shot** from a distance to take advantage of their slowed movement.
- **Stealth and Twin Fangs**:
    - **Combo**: Go into **Stealth** to approach an enemy unseen, then use **Twin Fangs** for a surprise critical hit.
    - **How to Execute**: Activate **Stealth**, approach the target, and trigger **Twin Fangs** to unleash a powerful attack from behind.

Veil Warden Combos (Exclusive to *Veilguard*)

- **Veil Strike and Spirit Rend**:
    - **Combo**: **Veil Strike** weakens an enemy's defenses, then **Spirit Rend** deals extra Fade-based damage.
    - **How to Execute**: Start with **Veil Strike** to soften up the enemy, then press the quick slot for **Spirit Rend** to maximize damage.
- **Fade Shroud and Phantom Blade**:
    - **Combo**: **Fade Shroud** allows the Veil Warden to phase through attacks, setting up for **Phantom Blade** to deal a high-damage strike while in Fade form.
    - **How to Execute**: Activate **Fade Shroud** to avoid enemy attacks, then use **Phantom Blade** while phased to surprise the enemy with a powerful hit.

4. Cross-Class Combos with Companions

Working with your companions allows for even more powerful combo opportunities. Each companion's abilities can synergize with your own, creating combos that cover the battlefield.

- **Warrior and Mage Combo: Taunt and Firestorm**:
  - **Combo**: Have a Warrior taunt enemies with **Challenge** to gather them in one area, then have a Mage cast **Firestorm** for massive area damage.
  - **How to Execute**: Use **Challenge** (Warrior) to group enemies, then trigger **Firestorm** (Mage) to strike while they're gathered.
- **Rogue and Mage Combo: Poison Cloud and Chain Lightning**:
  - **Combo**: The Rogue drops **Poison Cloud** to weaken enemies, and the Mage follows up with **Chain Lightning** to hit them all at once.
  - **How to Execute**: The Rogue uses **Poison Cloud**, then the Mage casts **Chain Lightning** for extra impact.

5. Using Area-of-Effect (AoE) Combos

Area-of-Effect combos are especially effective against groups of enemies. By layering abilities that affect an area, you can maximize your damage output.

- **Static Cage and Fire Mine (Mage)**:
  - **Combo**: **Static Cage** traps enemies, and **Fire Mine** adds explosive damage to the area.
  - **How to Execute**: Cast **Static Cage** first, trapping the enemies, then place **Fire Mine** within the cage to cause a fiery blast.
- **War Cry and Whirlwind (Warrior)**:
  - **Combo**: **War Cry** taunts enemies into a tight formation, then **Whirlwind** deals spinning damage to all surrounding foes.
  - **How to Execute**: Activate **War Cry** to draw enemies in, then trigger **Whirlwind** to spin and hit all nearby enemies.

6. Timing Combos for Maximum Damage

- **Cooldown Awareness**: Many abilities have cooldowns, so be aware of which skills are ready and plan your combos accordingly. Waiting a few seconds for a key ability to be ready can make a big difference in executing the perfect combo.
- **Using Primers and Detonators Efficiently**: Start battles by applying primer abilities to enemies, then follow up with detonators to trigger combos. This sequence is crucial to getting the full effect and maximizing damage.

7. Specialization-Specific Combos

Once you unlock specializations, you'll gain access to powerful new abilities that open up even more combo possibilities.

- **Champion Warrior**: Use **To the Death** to focus an enemy's attention, then **Counter Strike** for a powerful retaliation combo.
- **Necromancer Mage**: Apply **Horror** to cause enemies to flee in fear, then cast **Walking Bomb** on a fleeing enemy. If the enemy dies, **the Walking Bomb** will spread to nearby enemies, creating a chain reaction.
- **Assassin Rogue**: Use **Mark of Death** to mark an enemy for extra damage, then unleash **Twin Fangs** or **Hidden Blades** for a massive burst.

8. Managing Stamina and Mana for Combos

- **Watch Your Resources**: Special abilities use stamina (Warriors and Rogues) or mana (Mages). Managing these resources is key to chaining combos effectively.
- **Using Potions**: Keep potions or elixirs handy to restore stamina or mana when needed. Press "D-Pad Up" (console) or the assigned number (PC) to use a potion and get back into the fight.

9. Advanced Tips for Combo Mastery

- **Experiment with New Combos**: Try different ability combinations to discover what works best for your playstyle and enemies. Some combos are especially effective against certain enemy types, like undead or demons.
- **Use the Environment**: In some areas, you can knock enemies off ledges or into traps by combining knockback abilities with environmental features. For example, use a Warrior's **Mighty Blow** to knock an enemy into a trap set by your Rogue.

Mastering special abilities and combos in *Dragon Age: The Veilguard* is key to becoming a powerful force in Thedas. With practice, you'll be able to unleash devastating attacks, control the battlefield, and support your team in every battle. Enjoy experimenting, stay strategic, and watch as your combos make you an unstoppable hero!

Managing Health, Mana, and Stamina

Health, mana, and stamina are essential resources in *Dragon Age: The Veilguard*, and managing them effectively is crucial for success in combat. This guide will walk you through how to monitor and replenish each resource, as well as strategies to help you get the most out of your abilities while staying alive and ready for battle.

1. Understanding Health, Mana, and Stamina

- **Health**: Health represents your character's vitality. When it reaches zero, your character is downed, and you'll need to either use a revival item or rely on a teammate to bring you back.
- **Mana (Mages)**: Mana is the energy resource used by Mages to cast spells. Without mana, you can't perform magic abilities.
- **Stamina (Warriors and Rogues)**: Stamina is used by Warriors and Rogues to perform special attacks and combat maneuvers. Running out of stamina limits your ability to use powerful skills.

2. Monitoring Your Health, Mana, and Stamina

- **Resource Bars**: Health, mana, and stamina are displayed as bars on your HUD. The health bar is usually red, while mana (for Mages) is blue, and stamina (for Warriors and Rogues) is green.
- **Checking During Combat**: Keep an eye on these bars, especially during intense fights. If you notice them dropping quickly, it's a signal to adjust your tactics, use a potion, or fall back briefly to recover.
- **Accessing Detailed Stats**: To view more information about your resources, open the character menu by pressing "C" on PC, "Options" on PlayStation, or "Menu" on Xbox. This will display your maximum health, mana, and stamina, as well as any buffs or effects currently active.

3. Healing and Restoring Health

- **Using Health Potions**: Health potions are the primary way to restore health during combat. To use a potion, press "D-Pad Up" on consoles or the assigned number key (such as "1" or "4") on PC.
- **Setting Up Potions in the Quick Slot**: Open the inventory menu and assign health potions to your quick slot for easy access. Make sure you're stocked up on health potions before heading into tough areas—most camps or merchants sell them.
- **Resting at Camps**: When not in combat, you can rest at camps to fully restore your health. Camps also automatically replenish potions, so use them strategically as checkpoints during long quests.

4. Managing Mana (for Mages)

- **Understanding Mana Costs**: Every spell costs mana, and powerful spells use more of it. Monitor your mana bar to ensure you don't run out during critical moments.
- **Mana Regeneration**: Mana regenerates slowly over time, but certain abilities and potions can speed up this process.
  - **Mana Potions**: To replenish mana quickly, use a mana potion. Set it in your quick slot and press "D-Pad Up" on consoles or the assigned number key (like "2" or "3") on PC to use it.
- **Using Lower-Cost Spells**: Rotate between high-cost and low-cost spells to manage your mana efficiently. This keeps you from running out of mana quickly, allowing you to maintain a steady output of spells during combat.

- **Energy Surge Abilities**: Some Mage abilities, like **Energy Surge** or **Focus**, temporarily boost mana regeneration. Use these abilities in longer battles to maintain your mana pool.

5. Managing Stamina (for Warriors and Rogues)

- **Stamina Usage in Abilities**: Stamina is used for most Warrior and Rogue abilities, from heavy attacks to stealth maneuvers. Running out of stamina restricts your ability to perform these actions, so keep an eye on the green bar.
- **Stamina Regeneration**: Stamina also regenerates over time, but using certain skills can slow the process. Abilities with high stamina costs are best saved for critical moments.
- **Stamina Potions**: Some potions can restore stamina. Add stamina potions to your quick slot by accessing the inventory menu and press "D-Pad Up" on consoles or the assigned number key (like "2" or "3") on PC to drink one when needed.
- **Mixing Light and Heavy Attacks**: Alternate between basic and stamina-consuming abilities to maintain a balanced stamina pool. Warriors, for example, can use **Shield Bash** sparingly while relying on regular attacks in between.

6. Effective Potion Management

- **Stocking Up on Potions**: Potions can be restocked at camps, merchants, or supply caches. Health, mana, and stamina potions are essential, so ensure you're carrying enough before venturing into challenging areas.
- **Using Potions Strategically**: Try not to use potions at the start of a battle—wait until your health, mana, or stamina is low to maximize the potion's effect. Avoid using multiple potions in quick succession to conserve resources.
- **Upgrade Potions at Alchemy Stations**: Certain camps and towns have alchemy stations where you can improve your potions' effectiveness, making them restore more health, mana, or stamina with each use.

7. Companion Resource Management

- **Monitoring Companion Health**: Your companions' health bars appear next to yours. If one of them is losing health quickly, consider using a health potion on them, especially if they're essential to your strategy.
- **Assigning Potions to Companions**: In the inventory menu, assign potions to your companions' quick slots so they can access health or stamina boosts when needed. They'll use them automatically if they run low during battle.
- **Reviving Downed Companions**: If a companion's health reaches zero, they'll be downed. To revive them, stand close to their location and press "X" on PlayStation, "A" on Xbox, or "E" on PC to bring them back into the fight.

8. Special Abilities and Resource Management

- **Abilities That Restore Resources**: Some abilities can restore health, mana, or stamina. For example:
  - **Warriors** may have abilities that increase health regeneration or absorb damage temporarily.
  - **Mages** can unlock spells like **Barrier** to protect themselves and allies, reducing the need for health potions.
  - **Rogues** with certain skills can regenerate stamina through critical hits or successful dodges.
- **Using Regenerative Abilities Wisely**: These abilities usually have cooldowns, so use them strategically when you're low on resources or facing multiple enemies.

9. Resting and Regrouping

- **Setting Up Camps**: Camps serve as safe zones where you can rest, heal, and restock potions. Press "X" (PlayStation), "A" (Xbox), or "E" (PC) at a camp to fully restore health, mana, and stamina.
- **Retreating from Combat**: If you're low on resources and near a camp, it may be wise to retreat temporarily, recover, and return with full health and stamina. Avoid engaging in combat immediately after using all your resources.

10. Advanced Tips for Health, Mana, and Stamina Management

- **Use Buffs and Debuffs**: Certain abilities allow you to apply buffs that reduce mana or stamina costs or increase health regeneration temporarily. These are particularly useful in long battles.
- **Monitor Debuffs**: Some enemies can apply debuffs that drain mana or stamina faster. Watch for status effects on your HUD and use potions or specific abilities to counter them.
- **Prioritize Targets**: Focus on enemies that drain your resources quickly, such as spellcasters who use mana-draining abilities or enemies that use stamina-sapping attacks.

Summary of Managing Health, Mana, and Stamina

- **Use Potions Wisely**: Set up potions in your quick slot and only use them when necessary to avoid running out too quickly.
- **Balance Abilities and Regular Attacks**: Alternate between resource-heavy abilities and basic attacks to conserve stamina and mana.
- **Regenerate at Camps**: Set up camps and use them as checkpoints to rest, recover, and restock potions.
- **Keep an Eye on Companions**: Make sure your companions have access to health potions and manage their health in longer battles.

Managing health, mana, and stamina effectively will ensure that you're always ready to face whatever Thedas throws at you. By staying aware of your resources and planning ahead, you can tackle challenging fights with confidence, knowing that you're fully prepared for every encounter.

Survival Tips for Difficult Battles

In *Dragon Age: The Veilguard*, some battles will test your strategy, resource management, and timing. These challenging encounters are where survival tips can make all the difference. This guide provides essential survival techniques to help you navigate difficult battles, manage resources, and come out victorious.

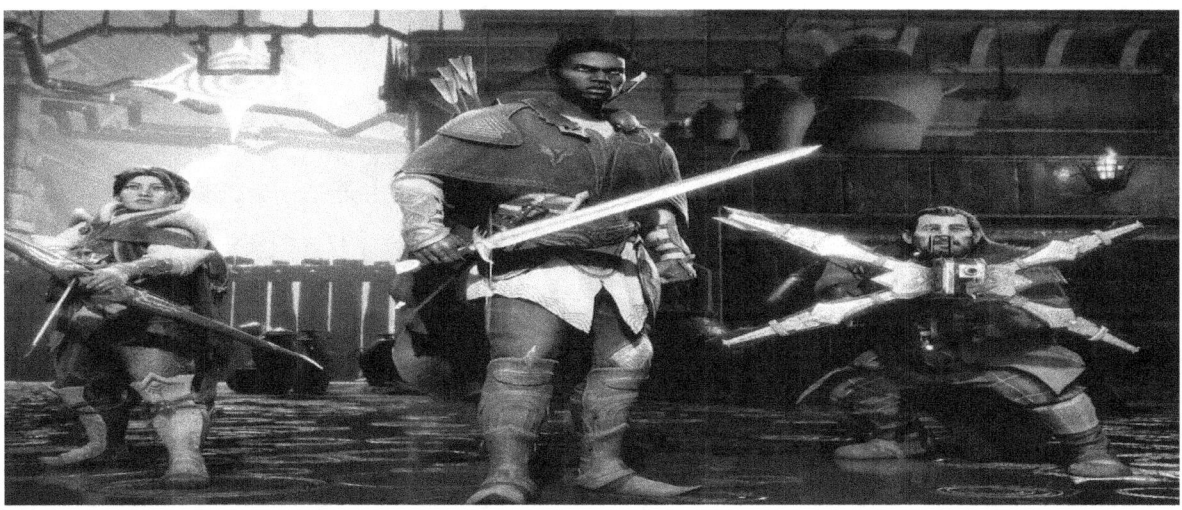

1. Prepare Before the Battle

- **Stock Up on Potions**: Before any major fight, ensure you have enough health, mana, and stamina potions. Visit merchants or camps to restock.
  - **How to Stock Up**: Open the inventory menu and check potion levels. Purchase additional potions from a merchant, then equip them in the quick slot for easy access.
- **Adjust Your Team's Equipment**: Equip your characters with the best weapons and armor available. You may need high resistance gear or special items for tougher enemies.
  - **Equipping Gear**: Access the inventory by pressing "I" on PC, "Options" on PlayStation, or "Menu" on Xbox, then equip items by highlighting them and pressing "X" (PlayStation), "A" (Xbox), or clicking on PC.
- **Save Before Entering**: For tough battles, save your game before entering. This way, you can reload if the fight doesn't go as planned.

2. Analyze Your Enemy

- **Check Enemy Types and Weaknesses**: Before charging in, identify what types of enemies you're facing and their potential weaknesses. This helps you choose the right abilities and tactics.
  - **How to Analyze**: Hold the target lock button—R3 on PlayStation, RS on Xbox, or Tab on PC—to examine enemies. Pay attention to any elemental weaknesses, resistances, or attack patterns.

- **Focus on Priority Targets**: Take down high-damage enemies, spellcasters, or healers first, as these can quickly turn the tide of battle against you. Mark them for priority if needed.
  - **Marking Enemies**: To focus your party on a specific enemy, use the target lock or tactical view.

3. Positioning and Movement

- **Keep Moving**: Constant movement can help you avoid attacks and make it harder for enemies to lock onto you. Circle around enemies, especially those with heavy attacks, to strike from behind.
  - **Dodging**: Use the dodge button (Circle on PlayStation, B on Xbox, or Spacebar on PC) to quickly sidestep attacks and get into better positions.
- **Use Terrain to Your Advantage**: Higher ground, obstacles, and choke points can give you a tactical edge. Ranged attackers, for example, can stay on elevated terrain to avoid melee enemies.
  - **How to Move to High Ground**: Look for ledges, rocks, or natural barriers, and position your ranged characters on them by moving the left stick or mouse.
- **Spread Out Your Team**: Avoid clustering, as this makes your team more vulnerable to area-of-effect attacks. Position each character with space between them.

4. Use Tactical Mode for Control

- **Activate Tactical Mode**: Tactical mode slows down time, allowing you to position and command each character individually. This is essential for coordinating complex battles.
  - **How to Activate**: Press the touchpad on PlayStation, "View" on Xbox, or "T" on PC to enter tactical mode.
- **Plan Your Moves**: While in tactical mode, select each character and position them strategically. Set up combos, place traps, or have your tank draw enemy attention while others flank.
- **Setting Attack Orders**: Use tactical mode to assign specific targets for each party member, ensuring they focus on the most dangerous enemies first.

5. Effective Use of Abilities

- **Prioritize Crowd Control Abilities**: Stun, freeze, or immobilize large groups of enemies with abilities like **Static Cage** (Mage) or **Challenge** (Warrior) to keep them contained.
  - **Activating Abilities**: Press the corresponding quick slot button to activate these abilities during combat.
- **Use Buffs and Debuffs**: Abilities that buff allies or debuff enemies are invaluable in difficult fights. Buffs can increase resistance or damage, while debuffs weaken the enemy's attacks.
  - **Example**: Use a Warrior's **War Cry** to increase defense, or a Mage's **Weaken** to lower enemy damage output.
- **Chain Combos with Primers and Detonators**: Set up combos with abilities that prime enemies for extra damage, followed by a detonator ability. For instance, **Winter's Grasp** (Mage) followed by **Stonefist** creates a powerful shatter effect.

6. Managing Health and Resources

- **Use Potions Wisely**: Don't wait until health is critically low to use a health potion. If your health falls below half, take a potion to stay in the fight longer.
  - **Using Potions**: Press "D-Pad Up" on consoles or the assigned quick slot number on PC.
- **Save High-Cost Abilities for Critical Moments**: Mana and stamina are limited, so save high-cost abilities for when you're facing multiple enemies or a dangerous foe.
- **Activate Health Regeneration Skills**: If your character has health regeneration abilities (like **Second Wind** for Warriors), use them when health is low to avoid relying solely on potions.

7. Teamwork and Companion Commands

- **Direct Companions to Cover Roles**: Assign each character to their specific role—tanks draw attention, rogues flank for high damage, and mages control the battlefield.
  - **Commanding Companions**: In tactical mode, select each character and assign them a position or target.
- **Use Revive and Heal Abilities**: Some companions may have revive or heal spells. Make sure these abilities are mapped to their quick slots for easy access.
- **Rotate Defensive Roles**: If your tank is taking heavy damage, rotate them out temporarily or assign a companion to provide cover until they recover.

8. Escape Strategies

- **Retreat if Necessary**: If the fight becomes overwhelming, fall back to a safe distance. Use the terrain to shield yourself from attacks and regroup.
  - **How to Retreat**: Use the dodge button or sprint (if available) to create space between you and the enemy. Move your team away using tactical mode if they're in danger.
- **Use Temporary Shields or Barriers**: If you have a Mage in your party, cast **Barrier** to shield allies while you reposition or escape.
- **Disengage from High-Health Enemies First**: If a large, powerful enemy is proving too challenging, consider focusing on weaker enemies first to reduce the overall number of threats before returning to the stronger foe.

9. Boosts and Temporary Enhancements

- **Use Tonics and Elixirs**: Some items provide temporary buffs, such as increased resistance, critical hit rate, or stamina regeneration. Use these at the start of a difficult battle to boost your team's stats.
  - **How to Use Boost Items**: Equip tonics in the quick slot, then press "D-Pad Up" (console) or the assigned number key (PC) to activate.
- **Apply Resistance Buffs for Specific Enemies**: If facing fire-wielding enemies, for instance, use fire resistance tonics to minimize damage from those attacks.

10. Reviving Downed Companions

- **Reviving in Battle**: If a companion is downed, go to their position, and press "X" on PlayStation, "A" on Xbox, or "E" on PC to revive them.
- **Wait for the Right Moment**: Don't rush to revive a companion if it puts you in danger. Wait until the enemy's attention is diverted, then move in for a safe revival.
- **Use a Mage with Revival Skills**: If you have a Mage with a resurrection ability, they can revive companions from a distance, keeping you out of harm's way.

11. Advanced Tactics for Boss Fights

- **Watch for Boss Patterns**: Bosses often have attack patterns that can be anticipated. Observe their moves to learn when they're vulnerable and when to dodge.
- **Attack Between Phases**: Many bosses have phases where they're more vulnerable, such as after a powerful attack. Save your strongest abilities for these moments to deal maximum damage.
- **Avoid Damage Over Time (DOT) Zones**: Some bosses create dangerous zones that deal continuous damage. Use dodge or movement abilities to stay clear of these areas.

Summary of Survival Tips

- **Prepare**: Stock up on potions, equip your best gear, and save before tough encounters.
- **Stay Mobile**: Keep moving, use terrain, and avoid clustering your party.
- **Use Tactical Mode**: Slow down time to assign specific commands and position each character.
- **Manage Resources**: Use potions strategically and save high-cost abilities for critical moments.
- **Revive Carefully**: Wait for a safe time to revive downed companions.

CHAPTER 6

Quests and Missions

This chapter is your guide to the quests and missions that define your journey in *Dragon Age: The Veilguard*. From the main storyline walkthrough to exploring side quests and unique rewards, we cover each aspect in detail. You'll also find insights on loyalty missions to strengthen bonds with companions, as well as Veilguard-exclusive questlines with hidden lore and treasures. Additionally, we'll explore how choices you make during quests impact the world, offering a unique experience shaped by your decisions.

Main Storyline Walkthrough

The main storyline in *Dragon Age: The Veilguard* is filled with intrigue, battles, and tough choices that shape the world around you. This guide provides a step-by-step walkthrough of key moments in the main storyline, offering tips on navigating quests, handling challenges, and making impactful decisions. Let's jump into your epic journey through Thedas and beyond.

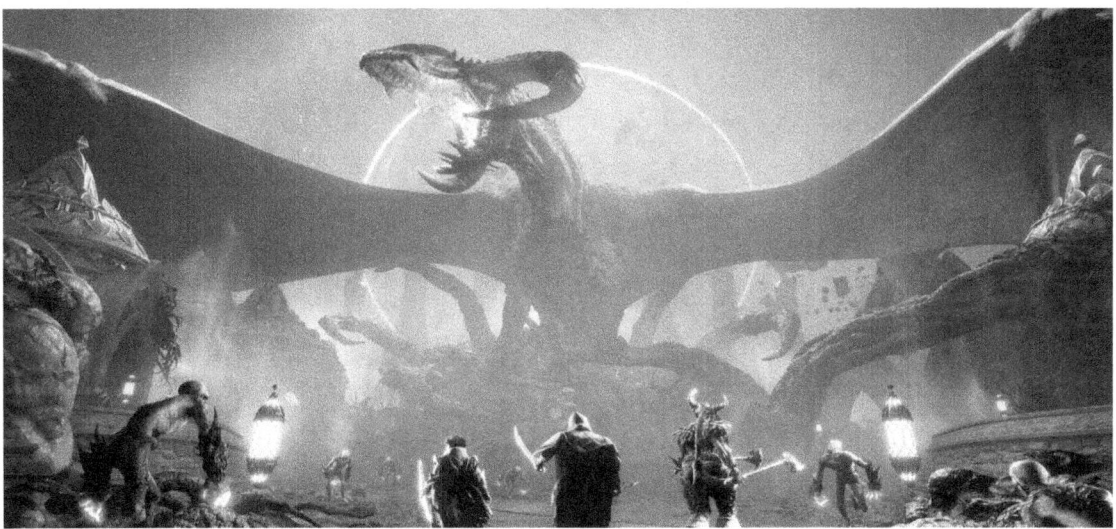

1. Starting Your Journey

- **Introduction and Character Creation**: When you begin, you'll create your character and choose your race, class, and background. Each choice impacts the storyline, so take your time to set up the hero you'll guide through the game.
    - **Where to Begin**: Select "New Game" from the main menu, then follow the prompts for character creation. Use the D-pad (console) or mouse (PC) to scroll through options, and press "X" (PlayStation), "A" (Xbox), or click to confirm each choice.

- **Initial Quest - Gathering Allies**: Your first quest involves gathering allies to face a rising threat. Follow the quest markers on your map to meet potential allies and complete introductory tasks that build your reputation.
  - **Navigating the Map**: Open the map by pressing "M" on PC, the touchpad on PlayStation, or "View" on Xbox. Follow the marked icons to locate each ally and set a waypoint by pressing "X" (PlayStation), "A" (Xbox), or right-clicking on PC.

2. The First Major Decision: Choosing Your Path

- **Quest Description**: Early in the storyline, you'll face a major choice that sets the course for your journey. Each path offers unique challenges, quests, and alliances, so consider the impact of your decision.
  - **Making Your Choice**: During the dialogue, use the dialogue wheel to select your response. Choices on the left are neutral, while options on the right and bottom indicate different paths. Press "X" (PlayStation), "A" (Xbox), or left-click to select.
- **Consequences of the Choice**: This decision will shape your allies, enemies, and the quests you'll face. Be sure to consider the strengths of each path as well as the kind of hero you want to become.

3. Navigating Key Locations and Completing Main Objectives

- **Key Location: The Sacred Grove**: In this early mission, you'll travel to the Sacred Grove to recover an artifact. The grove is guarded by spirits, so prepare for battle.
  - **Entering Combat**: Use your equipped weapon by pressing "R2" (PlayStation), "RT" (Xbox), or left-click (PC) for basic attacks. Use abilities assigned to quick slots for special moves.
- **Main Objective - Securing the Artifact**: Once you reach the artifact, interact with it by pressing "X" (PlayStation), "A" (Xbox), or "E" (PC). Prepare for an ambush after claiming it, as this often triggers enemy encounters.
- **Tip**: Use the terrain to your advantage, and be prepared to use potions by pressing "D-Pad Up" (console) or the assigned number key on PC.

4. Recruiting Key Allies

- **Recruitment Missions**: Throughout the storyline, you'll encounter potential allies with their own backstories and unique skills. Completing their recruitment missions will add them to your party.
  - **Finding Allies**: Follow the quest markers on your map to locate allies. Each ally has specific requirements for recruitment, so be sure to fulfill their requests.
  - **Companion Dialogue Choices**: Building trust with companions is important, as certain dialogue choices will improve your relationship. Select supportive responses during conversations, which can be done using the dialogue wheel and pressing "X" (PlayStation), "A" (Xbox), or left-click on PC.

5. The Veilguard Invasion

- **Quest Description**: A major turning point in the storyline involves the appearance of powerful creatures from the Veil. You'll need to investigate the invasion, close rifts, and protect villages from attacks.
  - **Closing Rifts**: When you reach a rift location, press "X" (PlayStation), "A" (Xbox), or "E" (PC) to interact with the rift. This will summon creatures from the Veil. Defeat all enemies to close the rift and receive rewards.
- **Defending Villages**: Some missions require you to protect villages from Veil creatures. Keep your companions positioned around the area by using tactical mode (touchpad on PlayStation, "View" on Xbox, or "T" on PC) to direct them to key locations.
- **Tip**: Use area-of-effect spells and abilities to control groups of enemies, which helps protect civilians in the village.

6. The Mid-Game Choice: Allies or Personal Power?

- **Description**: In the middle of the storyline, you'll face a choice between strengthening your alliances or pursuing personal power. Each choice will unlock different abilities, resources, and companion reactions.
  - **Making Your Decision**: Choose your path in dialogue. Alliances will grant you additional support in battles, while personal power provides unique abilities but can strain relationships with allies.
- **Consequences**: This choice affects your standing with certain factions, so choose based on your long-term goals. Your choice will also influence the final battle, as allies may come to your aid or hold back depending on your decision.

7. Late-Game Questline: The Hidden Enemy

- **Uncovering the Plot**: As you approach the final stages of the main storyline, you'll discover a hidden enemy working against you. Gather clues from various locations to piece together their identity and motives.
  - **Finding Clues**: Investigate locations marked on your map by pressing "X" (PlayStation), "A" (Xbox), or "E" (PC) to search for clues. These clues will often be guarded, so prepare for combat encounters.
- **Choosing How to Confront the Enemy**: When you identify the hidden enemy, you'll be given choices on how to confront them—either with force, diplomacy, or strategy.
  - **Making Your Choice**: Use the dialogue wheel to select your approach. Each option leads to different outcomes, and allies may respond differently based on your decision.

8. Final Battle Preparation

- **Gathering Resources and Allies**: Before the final battle, you'll have the chance to gather resources, equip your party with the best gear, and rally any allies you've gained throughout your journey.
  - **Where to Find Resources**: Return to previous areas, visit merchants, and collect rare resources for crafting. Use camps to stock up on potions and prepare for the fight ahead.
- **Dialogue with Companions**: Speak to each companion before the final battle. Use supportive dialogue choices to strengthen bonds and boost morale.
  - **How to Talk with Companions**: Approach each companion, initiate dialogue by pressing "X" (PlayStation), "A" (Xbox), or "E" (PC), and select responses that show loyalty or encouragement.

9. The Final Confrontation

- **Quest Description**: The final battle involves multiple stages, each with unique challenges and difficult enemies. You'll face your greatest foes and confront the main antagonist in a climactic showdown.
  - **Navigating the Battlefield**: Use tactical mode to position your team, and be prepared to heal and revive frequently. Keep your high-damage companions focused on the main boss while tanks hold off other enemies.
  - **Using Special Abilities**: Save your most powerful abilities for the final stages of the battle. Abilities like **Barrier** (Mage) and **Taunt** (Warrior) can help protect your team, while high-damage spells and attacks should be used when the enemy's defenses are down.
- **Making Final Choices**: As the battle progresses, you'll face choices that shape the ending of the story. These choices impact your character's legacy and the fate of Thedas.
  - **Making Your Final Decision**: Use the dialogue wheel to choose how to finish the fight. Select your ending carefully, as each option has unique consequences for you and your allies.

10. After the Battle: Epilogue and Reflections

- **Epilogue**: After the final battle, you'll experience an epilogue that reflects the consequences of your choices throughout the game. Your actions in the main storyline will have lasting impacts on Thedas, your allies, and your legacy.
- **Celebration or Mourning**: Depending on your choices and alliances, the epilogue will reveal whether your character is celebrated as a hero or remembered with mixed feelings.
- **Reconnecting with Companions**: In the epilogue, you can have final conversations with your companions, reflecting on your journey together. Approach each companion by pressing "X" (PlayStation), "A" (Xbox), or "E" (PC) to initiate dialogue.

Summary of the Main Storyline Walkthrough

- **Gather Allies and Complete Key Missions**: Recruit allies and complete each mission as marked on the map.
- **Make Major Choices with Impact**: Carefully consider choices that impact the story and relationships with companions.
- **Prepare for the Final Battle**: Equip your team, gather resources, and speak to companions before facing the final antagonist.
- **Reflect in the Epilogue**: Your choices will shape the epilogue, creating a unique ending that reflects your character's journey.

Side Quests and Their Rewards

In *Dragon Age: The Veilguard*, side quests offer not only additional XP but also unique rewards that enhance your journey. Side quests can reveal hidden lore, unlock rare items, and improve your relationships with companions. Here's a guide to help you make the most of side quests and understand the valuable rewards they offer.

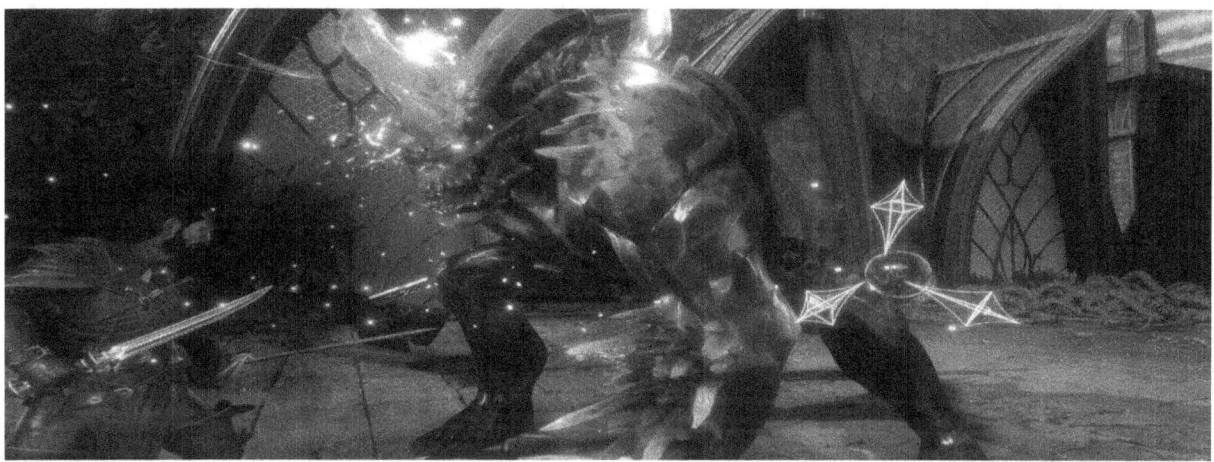

1. Locating Side Quests

- **Quest Givers and Locations**: Side quests are often given by NPCs in towns, camps, or other key locations. Look for characters with quest markers over their heads, usually indicated by a "!" or a quest icon on your map.
  - **Initiating a Side Quest**: Approach the quest giver and press "X" (PlayStation), "A" (Xbox), or "E" (PC) to begin the conversation and accept the quest.
- **Exploring the Map**: Many side quests are also revealed as you explore the map. Discover new areas or interact with objects to trigger hidden quests.
  - **Opening the Map**: Press "M" on PC, the touchpad on PlayStation, or "View" on Xbox to open the map and locate quest icons.

2. Tracking Side Quests in Your Quest Log

- **Accessing the Quest Log**: To track your side quests, open the quest log by pressing "J" on PC, the touchpad on PlayStation, or "View" on Xbox. This log provides details on each quest's objective, location, and rewards.

- **Setting Waypoints for Side Quests**: Highlight the side quest you wish to pursue, then set a waypoint by pressing "X" (PlayStation), "A" (Xbox), or right-click on PC. This will display a directional marker on your HUD, guiding you to the quest location.

3. Types of Side Quests and Their Benefits

Exploration Quests

- **Description**: Exploration quests reward players for discovering hidden locations, collecting rare resources, and finding lore pieces. These quests are ideal for uncovering secrets about the world of Thedas.

- **Rewards**: Completing exploration quests often provides XP, unique gear, and sometimes valuable crafting materials.

- **Example**: The "Lost Relics" quest involves finding relics scattered around ancient ruins. Each relic collected grants lore entries and a piece of powerful armor once all are gathered.

Resource Collection Quests

- **Description**: These quests task you with gathering herbs, minerals, or other resources for crafting or trading. They're great for stocking up on supplies and earning additional rewards.

- **Rewards**: Rewards include crafting materials, gold, and sometimes potions or elixirs.

- **Example**: In the "Healer's Request" quest, you gather rare herbs for a healer in a nearby village. Completing this quest unlocks a unique healing potion recipe that can be used during tougher battles.

Combat Challenges

- **Description**: Combat-based side quests pit you against specific enemies or groups of creatures. These challenges are designed to test your skills and can provide substantial rewards for completion.

- **Rewards**: Often reward high XP, rare weapons, and accessories with special bonuses.

- **Example**: In the "Champion's Gauntlet" quest, you face a series of powerful enemies. Each victory grants a new weapon, and completing the entire gauntlet rewards you with a rare sword and a significant XP boost.

Companion-Specific Quests

- **Description**: These side quests allow you to learn more about your companions' backstories and build stronger relationships with them.

- **Rewards**: Completing these quests can unlock unique abilities for your companions, deepen your bond with them, and provide special items.
- **Example**: In the "Shadow of the Past" quest for a Rogue companion, you assist them in settling an old score. Upon completion, you unlock a skill upgrade exclusive to that companion.

Puzzle and Lore Quests

- **Description**: These quests involve solving puzzles or uncovering ancient lore, adding depth to the world's history.
- **Rewards**: Often grant lore entries, special artifacts, or stat-boosting items.
- **Example**: In the "Ancient Riddles" quest, you solve riddles in a ruined library, with each solution providing a lore entry and a piece of a powerful amulet.

4. Maximizing Rewards from Side Quests

- **Prioritize High-Reward Quests**: Quests with unique items, high XP, or companion abilities can make your character stronger, so prioritize these when possible.
- **Complete Quest Chains**: Some side quests are part of a series. Completing an entire quest chain often unlocks additional rewards, so make sure to finish each quest in sequence.
- **Track Multiple Quests**: If several side quests are in the same area, track them together to complete them efficiently. This allows you to gather multiple rewards while minimizing backtracking.

5. Using Rewards to Improve Your Character

- **Equipping Special Items**: Many side quests provide powerful weapons, armor, or accessories that enhance your character's abilities.
  - **Equipping Items**: Open the inventory by pressing "I" on PC, "Options" on PlayStation, or "Menu" on Xbox. Highlight the item and press "X" (PlayStation), "A" (Xbox), or click to equip it.
- **Unlocking Skills and Abilities**: Completing certain quests grants new skills or upgrades. These abilities can make a big difference in combat, so check your skill tree to equip them.
  - **Equipping New Skills**: Go to the skill tree menu and assign new skills to your quick slots for easy access in battle.
- **Crafting and Upgrading Gear**: Resource collection quests provide materials that can be used at crafting stations. Use these materials to upgrade gear and improve your combat effectiveness.
  - **Crafting**: Access crafting stations at camps or towns, then select an item to craft or upgrade using your collected resources.

6. Companion Reactions to Side Quests

- **Building Relationships**: Completing certain side quests, especially those tied to companion interests, can strengthen your relationships. Dialogue choices during these quests can also impact how companions feel about you.
    - **Dialogue Choices**: When talking to companions during a quest, use supportive or agreeable responses by selecting from the dialogue wheel. This can improve their loyalty and unlock additional abilities.
- **Unlocking Companion Perks**: By completing quests that matter to your companions, you can unlock unique perks or skills exclusive to them, making them more effective in battle.

7. Unique Veilguard Side Quests and Rewards

- **Veilguard-Exclusive Quests**: Some side quests are unique to *The Veilguard* expansion, offering access to Veil-specific lore and rare Fade-based items.
- **Rewards**: These quests often grant powerful Veil abilities, unique artifacts, or access to hidden areas.
- **Example**: In "Echoes of the Fade," you help a mysterious character close Veil rifts. Completing the quest unlocks a Veil ability that lets you temporarily phase through enemies, offering a tactical advantage in battle.

8. Collecting and Managing Rewards

- **Storing Items**: High-level items from side quests can take up inventory space. Use storage chests at camps or your main base to keep items you're not currently using.
- **Selling or Trading Unused Items**: For items that don't fit your playstyle, consider selling or trading them with merchants to earn gold. This will help you buy more potions, upgrades, and gear.
    - **Selling Items**: Visit a merchant, select the item in your inventory, and press "X" (PlayStation), "A" (Xbox), or click (PC) to sell.

9. Tips for Efficiently Completing Side Quests

- **Track Multiple Quests in Each Area**: Check your map and quest log to identify multiple quests in the same region. This will save time and allow you to gather more rewards at once.
- **Use Fast Travel**: When available, use fast travel to return to previously visited locations and turn in completed quests. This allows you to complete more quests and quickly collect rewards.
    - **How to Fast Travel**: Open the map, highlight a fast travel point, and press "X" (PlayStation), "A" (Xbox), or right-click (PC) to travel instantly.
- **Check Quest Log for Expiring Quests**: Some side quests may be time-sensitive or have a limited window to complete. Make sure to prioritize these to avoid missing out on rewards.

Summary of Side Quests and Their Rewards

- **Locate and Track Side Quests**: Find quests from NPCs, objects, or exploration and track them in your quest log.
- **Understand Reward Types**: Complete quests for items, XP, crafting materials, companion abilities, and unique lore.
- **Equip and Upgrade**: Use the rewards to strengthen your character and companions, equipping items and unlocking skills.
- **Maximize Efficiency**: Complete quests in the same area, use fast travel, and manage your inventory to optimize your progress.

Side quests in *The Veilguard* add depth to the storyline and give you opportunities to gain unique rewards and experience. By exploring each quest type, building relationships, and strategically managing your items, you'll create a richer, more powerful character and enjoy a more immersive journey through Thedas. Embrace the adventure, and enjoy discovering the hidden treasures within each side quest!

Loyalty Missions for Companions

Loyalty missions are special quests focused on your companions, allowing you to deepen your bond with them and learn more about their backstories. Completing these missions not only strengthens your relationship but also unlocks unique abilities, exclusive items, and story moments that make your journey more rewarding. Here's a guide to completing loyalty missions in *Dragon Age: The Veilguard* and getting the most out of your companions.

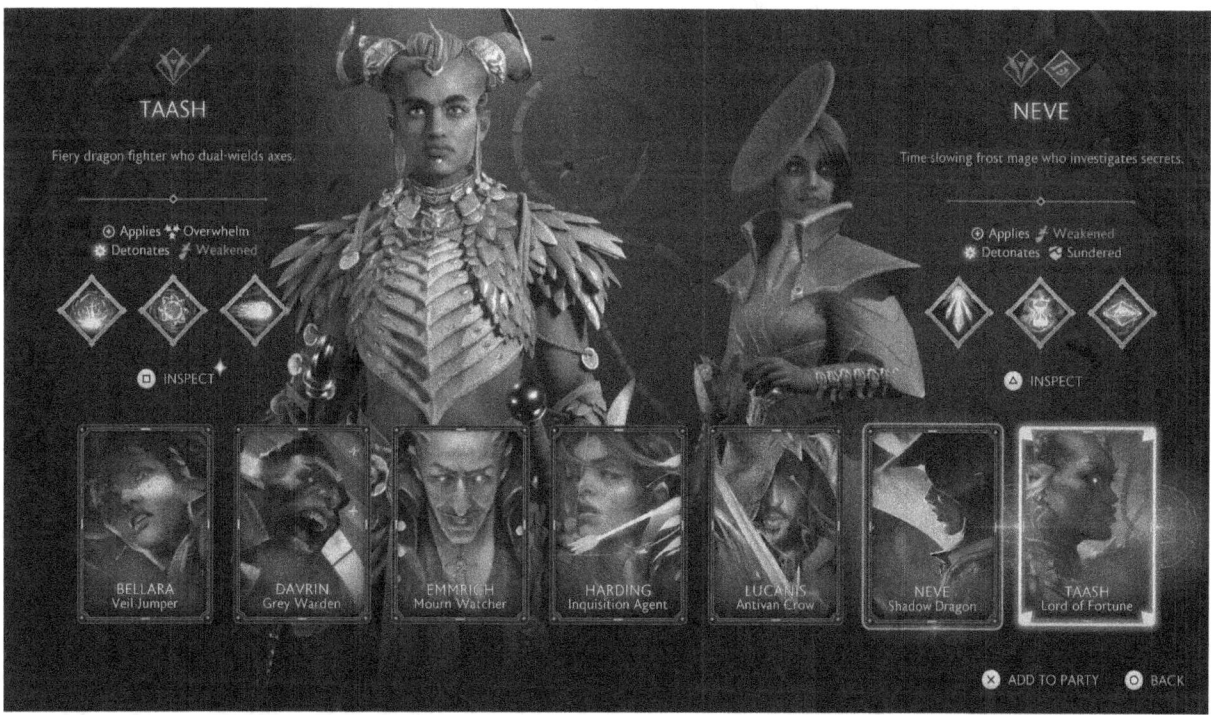

1. Unlocking Loyalty Missions

- **Building Trust with Companions**: To unlock loyalty missions, you need to build trust with each companion by engaging in positive dialogue, making decisions they support, and completing general quests with them in your party.
    - **Increasing Approval**: Choose dialogue options that align with a companion's values and personality. Use the dialogue wheel and press "X" (PlayStation), "A" (Xbox), or click (PC) to select responses.
- **Checking Companion Status**: To see each companion's approval level, access the character menu by pressing "C" on PC, "Options" on PlayStation, or "Menu" on Xbox. Higher approval levels will lead to conversations that eventually unlock their loyalty missions.
- **Triggering Loyalty Mission Conversations**: When a companion's approval is high enough, they'll initiate a conversation at your base or camp. Speak with them by pressing "X" (PlayStation), "A" (Xbox), or "E" (PC) to start the loyalty mission.

2. Starting a Loyalty Mission

- **Accepting the Mission**: Once a companion brings up a personal issue or past event, you'll have the option to support them and accept the loyalty mission.
    - **How to Accept**: Use the dialogue wheel to agree to help them, then check your quest log for the mission details. Press "J" on PC, the touchpad on PlayStation, or "View" on Xbox to open the quest log.
- **Setting a Waypoint**: Highlight the loyalty mission in your quest log, then set a waypoint by pressing "X" (PlayStation), "A" (Xbox), or right-click (PC). This will help guide you to the mission location on your map.

3. Types of Loyalty Missions and Challenges

- **Personal Vendettas**: Some companions seek revenge or closure for past events. These missions often involve intense combat against specific enemies or rival groups.
    - **Example**: For a Rogue companion with a shady past, the mission might involve tracking down an old rival in a dangerous area. Expect combat-heavy encounters with waves of enemies.
    - **Reward**: Completing these missions may unlock powerful weapons or exclusive combat abilities tailored to the companion's strengths.
- **Family Matters**: Many companions have unresolved issues with family members or loved ones. These missions often focus on exploration and diplomacy.
    - **Example**: A Mage companion might ask you to accompany them on a journey to reconcile with estranged family members. You'll encounter dialogue-heavy choices that impact the mission's outcome.

- **Reward**: Successfully navigating these missions can improve the companion's loyalty, granting unique stat bonuses or special items from their family.
- **Mysterious Artifacts and Curses**: Some companions may be affected by or drawn to mysterious objects or magical forces, leading you to locations filled with traps and puzzles.
  - **Example**: A Veil Warden companion might feel compelled to investigate an ancient artifact connected to the Fade. This mission involves solving puzzles and confronting dangerous spirits.
  - **Reward**: Completing these missions may unlock unique Veil-based abilities or items that enhance your companion's magical abilities.

4. Companion Dialogue Choices During Missions

- **Navigating Companion Reactions**: During loyalty missions, your responses to events and dialogue can impact your relationship with the companion. Pay attention to their personality and values when making choices.
  - **Selecting Responses**: Use the dialogue wheel to select options that show support or empathy. Choosing supportive responses strengthens bonds, while conflicting choices may lower approval.
- **Understanding Mission-Specific Choices**: Some loyalty missions present moral dilemmas or high-stakes decisions that reflect on your companion's backstory. The choices you make can lead to different rewards or endings for the mission.

5. Strategies for Completing Loyalty Missions Successfully

- **Bring a Balanced Team**: Loyalty missions often have varied challenges, from combat to puzzles, so bring a well-rounded party with different abilities. Your companion may have unique skills suited for the mission, but backup from other party members is essential.
- **Equip the Companion with Suitable Gear**: Since loyalty missions often highlight a companion's abilities, make sure they're equipped with the best gear that complements their strengths.
  - **Equipping Gear**: Access the inventory by pressing "I" on PC, "Options" on PlayStation, or "Menu" on Xbox. Select the companion's equipment and upgrade their weapons or armor as needed.
- **Use Tactical Mode**: Some loyalty missions involve complex encounters with multiple enemies or environmental hazards. Use tactical mode (touchpad on PlayStation, "View" on Xbox, or "T" on PC) to position your team strategically and control the flow of battle.

6. Loyalty Mission Rewards

- **Unlocking Unique Abilities**: Completing loyalty missions often unlocks a powerful skill or ability exclusive to that companion, enhancing their effectiveness in battle.
  - **How to Equip**: After the mission, access the companion's skill tree and assign the new ability to their quick slots.

- **Receiving Exclusive Gear**: Loyalty missions frequently reward unique weapons, armor, or accessories that are either rare or exclusive to the companion's storyline.
  - **Example**: A Warrior companion may receive a legendary sword, or a Mage companion could obtain a magical staff with enhanced effects.
- **Increasing Approval and Bonding**: Loyalty missions boost approval ratings, deepening your bond with the companion and potentially unlocking future dialogue or special interactions.

7. Companion-Specific Rewards and Perks

- **Passive Buffs**: Some loyalty missions grant passive bonuses that apply to the entire team when the companion is in your party. These buffs could include increased health, damage resistance, or stamina regeneration.
- **Story-Based Perks**: Completing a loyalty mission may also grant perks that impact future story events. For example, a companion's loyalty may lead to special dialogue options or influence other characters' reactions.
- **Improved Combat Skills**: Loyalty mission rewards can include enhancements to existing skills, making the companion more powerful. Check their skill tree after the mission to allocate new points or upgrades.

8. Veilguard-Specific Loyalty Missions

- **Fade-Related Quests**: Veilguard introduces loyalty missions that delve into the mysterious connections between certain companions and the Fade. These missions often require specialized tactics or magical abilities to complete.
  - **Example**: A Veil Warden companion might have a loyalty mission in a haunted location where spirits from the Fade are drawn. This mission involves navigating dangerous rifts and confronting powerful Fade-based enemies.
- **Rewards for Veilguard Loyalty Missions**: Rewards include powerful artifacts that boost Veil-based abilities or grant temporary immunity to certain types of magic. Completing these quests also provides additional lore related to the Fade and its influence on Thedas.

9. Making Critical Choices in Loyalty Missions

- **Balancing Morality and Loyalty**: Many loyalty missions involve tough choices that affect not only the mission's outcome but also your relationship with the companion. Make decisions that align with your values and the companion's personality.
  - **Example**: A companion may seek revenge against an enemy, and you'll have to decide whether to support their choice or encourage mercy.
- **Replaying Loyalty Missions**: If you're unsatisfied with the outcome, consider replaying the mission to explore alternative choices and see how they impact rewards and approval.

10. Follow-Up Conversations and Future Interactions

- **Engage in Post-Mission Dialogue**: After completing a loyalty mission, speak with the companion at your base or camp to reflect on the mission and discuss its outcomes.
  - **Initiating Conversation**: Approach the companion and press "X" (PlayStation), "A" (Xbox), or "E" (PC) to initiate dialogue. This conversation can reveal new insights and strengthen your bond further.
- **Unlocking Future Interactions**: Completing loyalty missions may unlock special scenes, dialogue, or follow-up quests. Keep an eye out for future interactions that build upon your choices and experiences from the mission.

Summary of Loyalty Missions for Companions

- **Unlock Loyalty Missions by Building Trust**: Engage in positive dialogue and make supportive choices to unlock each companion's loyalty mission.
- **Choose Responses that Strengthen Bonds**: Make decisions in line with the companion's values to build loyalty and gain exclusive rewards.
- **Equip Companions for Success**: Prepare companions with the best gear and bring a balanced party for challenging loyalty missions.
- **Reap the Rewards**: Completing loyalty missions grants unique abilities, gear, and story-based perks, improving your team and adding depth to each character's story.

Loyalty missions offer some of the most rewarding and personal moments in *The Veilguard*. By supporting your companions, you deepen your relationships, gain powerful rewards, and enrich the storyline. Enjoy discovering each companion's backstory and unlocking their potential as trusted allies on your epic journey through Thedas!

Veilguard Exclusive Questlines

The *Veilguard* expansion introduces exclusive questlines that delve into the mysteries of the Veil, the Fade, and new, otherworldly forces at play in Thedas. These quests are essential for players looking to unlock powerful Veil-based abilities, unique artifacts, and a deeper understanding of the magic influencing the world. Here's a guide to navigating these unique questlines, managing their challenges, and claiming the exclusive rewards they offer.

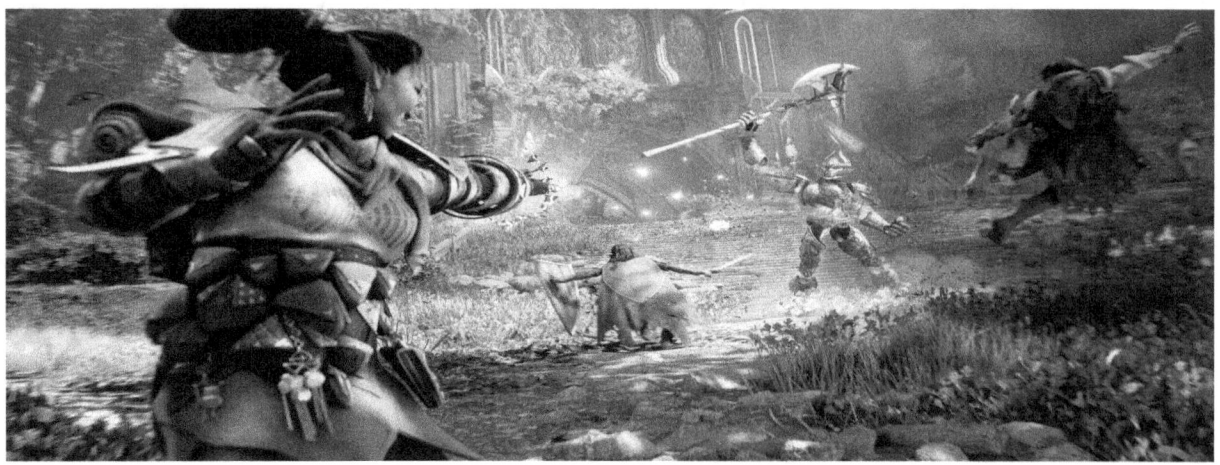

1. Introduction to Veilguard Questlines

- **Accessing Veilguard Content**: To start these exclusive quests, you'll need to progress in the main storyline to a certain point where the Veilguard content is introduced. You'll be notified in-game once you reach this phase.
    - **How to Begin**: Follow the main storyline until you unlock access to Veilguard-exclusive areas. Look for notifications or prompts that introduce new Veilguard quests.
- **Identifying Veilguard Quests**: Veilguard-exclusive quests are often marked with a unique symbol (such as a Fade-like swirl or icon) in your quest log and on the map.
    - **Quest Log**: Access your quest log by pressing "J" on PC, the touchpad on PlayStation, or "View" on Xbox to track these exclusive quests.

2. Key Themes of Veilguard Questlines

- **Exploring the Veil and the Fade**: These quests delve into the mysteries of the Veil, a boundary between the physical world and the Fade. Expect to encounter dangerous spirits, Veil rifts, and areas where reality itself warps.
- **Uncovering Veilguard Lore**: Many quests center around ancient artifacts, lost magic, and individuals deeply connected to the Fade. Completing these quests provides insights into the origins and power of the Veil.
- **Challenging Enemies and Bosses**: The Veilguard questlines include some of the toughest enemies in the game, from high-level demons to Fade-enhanced creatures that require strategic approaches.

3. Key Veilguard Questline Locations

The Veiled Shore

- **Quest Description**: This eerie coastal region is where the Veil is thin, and strange phenomena occur. Here, you'll begin your journey into the secrets of the Veil.

- **Objective**: Investigate reports of mysterious lights and sounds, uncover hidden rifts, and confront creatures that have slipped through the Veil.
- **How to Navigate**: Open your map by pressing "M" on PC, the touchpad on PlayStation, or "View" on Xbox. Set a waypoint for the Veiled Shore to begin the quest.
- **Reward**: Completing this quest unlocks Veil-based abilities and the Veil Warden's Cloak, an item that enhances Fade-related magic.

Fade-Worn Woods

- **Quest Description**: In the heart of the Fade-Worn Woods, you'll encounter a series of puzzles and encounters with spirits that hold valuable Veil lore.
- **Objective**: Solve magical puzzles tied to ancient elven relics and free spirits trapped by the weakening of the Veil.
- **Solving Puzzles**: Use your Veil-based abilities to interact with objects by pressing "X" (PlayStation), "A" (Xbox), or "E" (PC). Some puzzles require you to align symbols or activate multiple runes in the correct order.
- **Reward**: Completing this quest grants the *Elven Amulet of the Fade*, which increases mana regeneration and spell resistance.

The Silvered Spire

- **Quest Description**: This towering structure is rumored to hold secrets of the Fade and is guarded by powerful Fade-touched golems.
- **Objective**: Ascend the spire, defeating golems and solving Veil-based challenges along the way. Each floor holds clues to the ancient magic powering the spire.
- **Climbing the Spire**: To move to different levels, interact with enchanted mirrors by pressing "X" (PlayStation), "A" (Xbox), or "E" (PC). These mirrors teleport you to hidden chambers.
- **Reward**: Reaching the top grants the *Heart of the Fade*, an artifact that temporarily boosts your Veil abilities and grants powerful buffs during combat.

4. Navigating Veil Rifts and Spirit Realms

- **Encountering Veil Rifts**: Throughout Veilguard-exclusive questlines, you'll encounter Veil rifts that summon creatures from the Fade. Closing these rifts requires defeating all summoned enemies and interacting with the rift itself.
    - **How to Close Rifts**: Approach the rift and press "X" (PlayStation), "A" (Xbox), or "E" (PC) to begin closing it. Be prepared to fight off waves of enemies during this process.
- **Spirit Realms**: Some areas within the Veilguard questlines allow you to temporarily enter spirit realms, revealing hidden objects and pathways.
    - **Activating Spirit Sight**: Use a Veil Warden ability like **Spirit Sight** to enter these realms. Press "L2" (PlayStation), "LB" (Xbox), or "Shift" (PC) to activate.

- **Rewards**: Closing Veil rifts grants powerful items, and exploring spirit realms reveals hidden treasures and lore entries.

5. Special Abilities and Powers Unlocked through Veilguard Quests

- **Fade Shroud**: An ability that lets you temporarily phase through enemies, avoiding damage and setting up surprise attacks. Perfect for Veil Wardens, this power is unlocked early in the Veilguard questline.
  - **How to Activate**: Once unlocked, assign **Fade Shroud** to a quick slot and press the corresponding button during combat.
- **Veil Strike**: A powerful melee attack enhanced by Fade energy, dealing bonus damage to Veil-touched enemies and demons.
  - **How to Unlock**: Complete the Fade-Worn Woods questline to unlock this ability, which is especially effective in Veilguard quests with high demon encounters.
- **Veil Shroud**: A defensive ability that reduces incoming magic damage by 50% for a short time, ideal for battles against Fade creatures.
  - **Unlocking the Ability**: This ability becomes available after completing the Silvered Spire quest.

6. Veilguard Exclusive Enemies and Bosses

- **The Veilborn**: These shadowy creatures emerge from rifts and attack with Fade energy. They're vulnerable to Veil-based attacks and holy magic.
- **Wraith Lords**: Elite spirits that guard Veil artifacts. They have high resistance to physical attacks and can summon Fade creatures to assist them.
  - **Defeating Wraith Lords**: Use magic-based attacks or Fade-enhanced abilities like **Veil Strike**. Press tactical mode (touchpad on PlayStation, "View" on Xbox, or "T" on PC) to control your party's positioning during these tough battles.
- **Final Boss: The Veil Reaper**: This powerful entity is the last challenge in the Veilguard questlines, using devastating Fade-based attacks and summoning spirits.
  - **Tactics for the Veil Reaper**: Use all your Veil-based abilities, stay on the move, and avoid its area-of-effect spells by dodging (Circle on PlayStation, B on Xbox, or Spacebar on PC).

7. Exclusive Veilguard Artifacts and Items

- **Amulet of the Veil**: Grants a 20% boost to Veil-based abilities and increases resistance to spirit attacks.
  - **How to Obtain**: Complete the Veiled Shore quest and defeat the Wraith Lord guarding the artifact.
- **Ring of Fade Immunity**: This ring protects the wearer from certain Fade-based damage, making it essential for battles against Veil creatures.
  - **How to Obtain**: Found as a reward after completing the Silvered Spire quest.

- **Veilguard Sigil**: Enhances Veilguard-exclusive abilities and unlocks a special passive skill that regenerates mana during combat.
  - **Obtained from**: Completing all Veilguard quests and defeating the final boss, the Veil Reaper.

8. Tips for Success in Veilguard Quests

- **Equip Fade-Resistant Gear**: Many enemies in these quests deal Fade-based damage, so equip armor and accessories that provide resistance to magic or spirit attacks.
- **Manage Resources Carefully**: The Veilguard quests are challenging, with limited opportunities for rest and resupply. Stock up on potions and make use of abilities that restore health or mana over time.
- **Use Tactical Mode for Positioning**: Since Veilguard quests involve complex enemy patterns and traps, use tactical mode to position your party and control the flow of battle.

9. Story Impact and Epilogue of Veilguard Questlines

- **Final Choices in Veilguard Quests**: The choices you make during Veilguard quests—such as how you interact with spirits, whether you close certain rifts, and which allies you recruit—will affect the epilogue.
- **Epilogue Outcomes**: Depending on your actions, the Veilguard questlines may end with significant changes to the Veil and its influence on Thedas. Allies may remember your decisions, and certain factions could react differently to your character in the future.

Summary of Veilguard Exclusive Questlines

- **Begin the Veilguard Quests**: Unlock these quests by progressing in the main storyline, then track them in your quest log.
- **Explore Key Locations**: Discover the Veiled Shore, Fade-Worn Woods, and Silvered Spire for special challenges and rewards.
- **Unlock Unique Abilities and Items**: Complete quests to gain Veil-based powers, powerful artifacts, and exclusive Veilguard gear.
- **Face Powerful Enemies and Bosses**: Defeat challenging foes using strategic positioning, Veil-enhanced abilities, and Fade-resistant equipment.

Veilguard's exclusive questlines add depth, mystery, and incredible rewards to your *Dragon Age* experience. Embrace these powerful quests, make meaningful choices, and uncover the hidden magic of the Veil as you shape your character's legacy in Thedas!

Choices and Consequences in Quest Outcomes

Dragon Age: The Veilguard places significant weight on player decisions, with choices that shape your journey, influence relationships, and impact the world of Thedas. Each choice in a quest can lead to different rewards, consequences, and story outcomes, making every decision meaningful. This guide will help you understand how to approach these choices, anticipate their impacts, and make decisions that align with your character's goals.

1. Understanding the Types of Choices in Quests

- **Moral Choices**: Many quests present ethical dilemmas, such as deciding the fate of a captured enemy or choosing between personal power and helping an ally.
  - **Making the Choice**: Use the dialogue wheel to select your decision. Press "X" (PlayStation), "A" (Xbox), or left-click (PC) to confirm your choice.
- **Faction-Related Choices**: Certain choices impact your standing with factions in Thedas, such as the Templars, the Mages, or regional rulers. Faction decisions can affect future interactions, allies, and quest availability.
- **Companion-Influenced Choices**: Decisions that align or conflict with a companion's values will impact your relationship. High approval unlocks loyalty missions and unique interactions, while low approval can lead to tension or even departure.
  - **Dialogue Options**: Pay attention to companions' reactions in dialogue, choosing responses that respect their beliefs to build approval.

2. How Choices Affect Quest Outcomes

- **Multiple Endings for Quests**: Many quests have several possible outcomes, from peaceful resolutions to violent confrontations. Each outcome has unique rewards and may impact future events.
- **Influencing Future Story Events**: Some choices have far-reaching consequences that affect the main storyline or trigger new quests. For example, sparing a defeated enemy might lead them to return later as an ally or a betrayer.
- **Impact on The World**: Choices in certain quests may affect the state of Thedas itself. You may save or doom a village, strengthen or weaken a faction, or alter the balance of power.

3. Key Decisions in Main Story Quests

- **Alliance Decisions**: Early in the main storyline, you'll be asked to align with certain factions. Your choice of alliance affects the support you receive, the allies in your camp, and the quests available.
  - **How to Choose**: During dialogue, select the faction you wish to align with by pressing "X" (PlayStation), "A" (Xbox), or left-click (PC).
  - **Consequences**: Allied factions will back you in battle and provide unique abilities or resources. However, factions you reject may oppose you later.
- **Critical Storyline Decisions**: Certain main story quests include pivotal choices that define your character's legacy. These decisions will impact the game's epilogue and can affect which companions or allies survive until the end.
  - **Example**: Choosing whether to accept a powerful artifact for personal gain or to use it to help others. This choice will shape how NPCs and companions view you.

4. Choices in Side Quests and Their Rewards

- **Moral Outcomes in Side Quests**: Many side quests allow you to decide the fate of NPCs or creatures, leading to rewards that reflect your decision.
  - **Example**: In the quest "Trial of the Wicked," you capture a rogue mage who's terrorized a village. You can choose to spare the mage, gaining his knowledge, or turn him in for a monetary reward. Sparing him may lead to a future encounter where he assists you.
- **Rewards Based on Choices**: Side quests frequently reward you differently depending on your actions. Choosing a diplomatic approach might grant an alliance, while a combative approach could yield valuable items.
  - **How to Decide**: Review the dialogue options carefully and think about your goals—whether you prioritize relationships, resources, or reputation.

5. Companion Reactions to Major Choices

- **Building Approval with Companions**: Each companion has personal values, and choices you make during quests will either increase or decrease their approval. Higher approval unlocks unique abilities and loyalty missions.
  - **How to Choose Companion-Friendly Options**: Look for dialogue choices that align with your companion's values and press "X" (PlayStation), "A" (Xbox), or left-click (PC) to select them.
- **Low Approval and Consequences**: Repeatedly making choices that clash with a companion's values may lead to negative interactions, and in extreme cases, companions may leave your party.
- **Unique Companion Endings**: High approval ratings can unlock unique epilogues for your companions, showing how their journey with you influenced their future.

6. Faction Choices and World Impacts

- **Choosing Sides in Faction Conflicts**: Throughout *The Veilguard*, you'll encounter factional disputes, such as those between mages and templars or local lords. Siding with one group often alienates the other but provides unique allies, items, or skills.
  - **How to Decide**: During faction-related quests, select your stance in dialogue or by taking actions that favor one side. Each choice can affect future quests and your standing with the chosen faction.
- **Consequences for Thedas**: Supporting or opposing certain factions may shift the power balance in Thedas. For example, aiding a powerful noble might increase their control over a region, affecting later quests or interactions with NPCs.

7. Veilguard-Specific Choices and Their Consequences

- **Decisions Involving the Veil**: In Veilguard-exclusive quests, you'll often have the option to manipulate the Veil for personal power or choose to protect it. Each choice affects the Veilguard storyline and can unlock or prevent certain abilities.

- **Moral Dilemmas with Spirits**: Veilguard quests involve encounters with spirits, who may ask for aid or attempt to trick you. Helping them could lead to valuable Fade-based abilities, while refusing might close off certain quests but reduce risks.
  - **Example**: In the "Spirit of the Lost" quest, a trapped spirit asks you to release it. Freeing the spirit could grant you a new ability but risks releasing a dangerous entity. Refusing might result in a different reward and a safer outcome.

8. Endgame Choices and Final Outcomes

- **Choosing How to Approach the Final Confrontation**: In the last stages of the game, you'll make choices that impact the endgame's difficulty and the legacy your character leaves behind.
  - **Example**: You may be given the option to recruit powerful allies but risk alienating your companions, or you might decide to face the final enemy alone, maintaining your honor but making the battle more challenging.

- **Final Decision in the Epilogue**: Your final choices during the last questlines affect the epilogue, determining the fate of Thedas, your companions, and your own legacy.
  - **Making the Final Choice**: Select your final dialogue and actions carefully, as these decisions will shape your character's ending and can unlock different epilogues for each companion and faction.

9. Tips for Making Impactful Choices

- **Review Quest Objectives**: Before making a major decision, check your quest log to ensure you understand the objectives and possible consequences. Press "J" (PC), the touchpad (PlayStation), or "View" (Xbox) to access the quest log.

- **Consider Companion Reactions**: Keep track of your companions' preferences and aim for choices that align with their values to maintain high approval ratings.

- **Weigh Immediate vs. Long-Term Rewards**: Some choices offer immediate rewards, while others have delayed benefits. Consider the potential for future alliances, lore, and unique abilities when making decisions.

10. Summary of Choices and Consequences in Quest Outcomes

- **Types of Choices**: Understand the various choice types, from moral decisions to faction-based and companion-related choices.

- **Impact on Quests and Rewards**: Each choice can lead to unique quest endings, special items, or influence your reputation in Thedas.
- **Companion Reactions and Approval**: Make choices that align with companion values to build relationships and unlock loyalty missions.
- **Endgame and Legacy**: Your choices culminate in a powerful endgame that reflects your decisions throughout the storyline, creating a personalized legacy.

Navigating the choices in *The Veilguard* requires careful thought and an understanding of your character's goals, values, and relationships. With each decision you make, you'll be shaping the world, building alliances, and crafting a legacy unique to your journey. Enjoy the power of your choices, and see how your path through Thedas unfolds!

CHAPTER 7

Companion Guide

This chapter provides an in-depth look at each companion you'll meet in *Dragon Age: The Veilguard*. You'll find introductions to each companion, highlighting their unique abilities, skills, and personalities. Learn how to build trust and explore romance options, as well as how to navigate their personal questlines and understand the impact these quests have on the story. Finally, we'll cover strategies for choosing the right companions to create a balanced, powerful team that supports your playstyle and helps you succeed on your journey through Thedas.

Introduction to Each Companion

In *Dragon Age: The Veilguard*, companions are more than just allies; they are complex individuals with distinct personalities, abilities, and backstories. Each companion adds a unique dynamic to your team, offering support in battle and adding depth to your journey. This guide introduces each companion, covering their strengths, weaknesses, and how to recruit them, so you can build a powerful and well-balanced team.

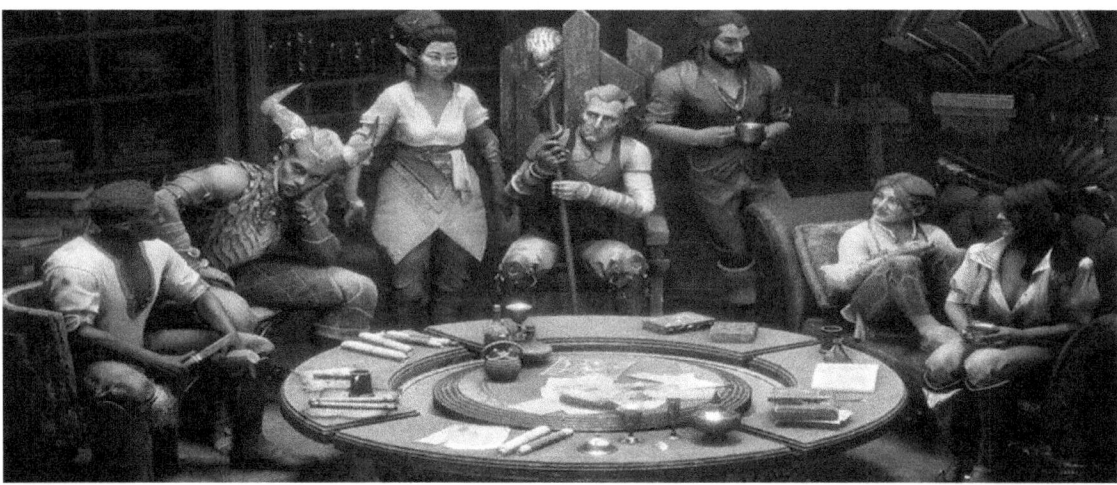

1. Lorian - The Stoic Warrior

- **Background**: Lorian is a seasoned warrior who has fought in many battles, known for his calm demeanor and unwavering loyalty. His focus on honor and duty makes him a reliable and steadfast companion.

- **Role in Team**: As a frontline tank, Lorian excels in absorbing damage and drawing enemy attention, making him ideal for players who need a strong defensive presence.
- **How to Recruit**: Lorian can be found at the **Stormguard Keep** during an early quest. After helping him fend off bandits, speak with him and select supportive dialogue options to gain his trust.
  - **Dialogue Selection**: Use the dialogue wheel to show respect for his values, and press "X" (PlayStation), "A" (Xbox), or left-click (PC) to confirm.
- **Strengths**: High defense and threat generation; capable of keeping enemies away from weaker teammates.
- **Weaknesses**: Limited ranged capabilities, so pair him with ranged companions for balance.

2. Elara - The Elven Mage

- **Background**: A powerful mage with deep ties to the Fade, Elara is both curious and cautious. Her knowledge of the Veil and Fade-based magic makes her invaluable in quests related to the supernatural.
- **Role in Team**: Elara is a spellcaster with a wide range of offensive and defensive spells, specializing in crowd control and elemental magic.
- **How to Recruit**: Elara is encountered at the **Veiled Shore** during a Veilguard-exclusive quest. Help her investigate strange Fade anomalies, and she'll offer to join your team afterward.
  - **Accepting Her Offer**: When she offers to join, press "X" (PlayStation), "A" (Xbox), or "E" (PC) to confirm her recruitment.
- **Strengths**: Powerful area-of-effect spells and high mana pool; excellent for dealing with groups of enemies.
- **Weaknesses**: Low defense; vulnerable to close-range attacks, so position her carefully.

3. Rylan - The Rogue Archer

- **Background**: Rylan is a resourceful rogue with a sharp wit and a hidden past. Known for his agility and marksmanship, he's motivated by personal freedom and a disdain for authority.
- **Role in Team**: Rylan is a ranged damage dealer, focusing on precision attacks and critical hits, making him ideal for taking down high-priority targets from a distance.
- **How to Recruit**: Rylan can be found in **Westport** during a side quest. Help him escape from a group of bounty hunters, and he'll agree to join you.
  - **Dialogue Selection**: Choose supportive or humorous dialogue options to gain his trust. Press "X" (PlayStation), "A" (Xbox), or left-click (PC) to interact.
- **Strengths**: High critical hit rate and agility; excellent for sniping and controlling the battlefield from afar.
- **Weaknesses**: Fragile in close combat; needs to keep distance from melee enemies.

4. Mira - The Compassionate Healer

- **Background**: Mira is a healer with a kind heart, dedicated to helping others. She has a strong sense of empathy and is motivated by a desire to alleviate suffering wherever she finds it.
- **Role in Team**: As a healer, Mira specializes in restorative spells and protective barriers, making her essential for keeping your team alive during difficult battles.
- **How to Recruit**: Mira can be recruited at **Brightfall Village** after helping her tend to the wounded during a side quest. Speak with her afterward to discuss joining forces.
  - **Recruitment Dialogue**: Show compassion during your interactions. Select empathetic dialogue options and press "X" (PlayStation), "A" (Xbox), or left-click (PC) to accept her offer.
- **Strengths**: Strong healing abilities and crowd control support; essential for longer battles and tougher encounters.
- **Weaknesses**: Limited offensive capabilities; best used in a supportive role rather than direct combat.

5. Kailen - The Fearless Duelist

- **Background**: A thrill-seeking duelist with a knack for adventure, Kailen is quick to laugh and quicker to fight. He loves challenges and lives by his own set of rules, often bringing humor and spontaneity to the team.
- **Role in Team**: Kailen is a melee-focused rogue who excels at dealing high burst damage up close. His agility and reflexes make him hard to hit, while his damage output is impressive.
- **How to Recruit**: Kailen appears in **Darkspire Caverns**, where he's trapped in a duel with a powerful creature. Help him defeat the enemy, and he'll join your team as a show of gratitude.
  - **Dialogue Selection**: Engage with his adventurous spirit by selecting humorous or bold dialogue options. Press "X" (PlayStation), "A" (Xbox), or left-click (PC) to invite him to the team.
- **Strengths**: High damage output and evasion; perfect for players who prefer aggressive, up-close tactics.
- **Weaknesses**: Low health; vulnerable if surrounded, so ensure he has support nearby.

6. Lyra - The Mysterious Veil Warden

- **Background**: Lyra is a Veil Warden with extensive knowledge of the Fade. Her motivations are enigmatic, but her insights into the Veil make her an essential ally in Veilguard-exclusive quests.
- **Role in Team**: Lyra's abilities revolve around manipulating the Veil, including phasing through enemies and summoning spirits for support.
- **How to Recruit**: Lyra can be found in the **Shattered Vale**. Assist her with a ritual involving a Veil rift, and she'll agree to join you to learn more about the Veil disturbances.
  - **Recruitment Process**: Help complete the ritual by interacting with the Veil rift (press "X" on PlayStation, "A" on Xbox, or "E" on PC). Afterward, speak with her to finalize her recruitment.

- **Strengths**: Unique Veil-based abilities that disrupt enemies and provide tactical support; highly effective in Veilguard areas.
- **Weaknesses**: Low stamina; her abilities can quickly drain her resources, so manage her actions carefully.

7. Taryn - The Former Templar

- **Background**: Taryn is a former Templar who left his order after questioning their methods. Strong and disciplined, he provides stability and wisdom to the team, often acting as a voice of reason.
- **Role in Team**: Taryn is a hybrid fighter who balances offensive and defensive abilities. He can use holy magic to deal damage to magical foes, making him valuable in battles against Fade creatures.
- **How to Recruit**: Taryn can be recruited in **Ironwood Outpost** during a quest involving a group of rogue mages. Help him bring the mages to justice, and he'll offer to join you.
  - **Dialogue Choices**: Select dialogue options that show support for justice and order. Press "X" (PlayStation), "A" (Xbox), or left-click (PC) to accept his offer to join.
- **Strengths**: Versatile skills and high magic resistance; particularly effective against supernatural enemies.
- **Weaknesses**: Jack-of-all-trades; lacks specialization, so pair him with more focused companions.

8. Tips for Recruiting and Choosing Companions

- **Check Each Companion's Compatibility**: Consider how each companion's skills complement your playstyle and other team members. For example, pairing a strong melee character with a healer provides a balanced approach.
- **Use Dialogue to Build Relationships**: Conversations with companions strengthen your bond and may unlock loyalty missions. Engage with companions after each major quest to build trust.
  - **Initiate Conversations**: Speak with companions at camp by pressing "X" (PlayStation), "A" (Xbox), or "E" (PC) and choosing dialogue options that reflect their values.
- **Reassess Team Composition as You Progress**: As you gain new companions, adjust your team based on the enemies and quests ahead. Veilguard-exclusive areas, for example, may benefit from Lyra's Veil-based abilities.

Summary of Companion Introductions

- **Lorian**: Stoic warrior, ideal for defense and tanking.
- **Elara**: Knowledgeable mage, excellent for crowd control and spellcasting.
- **Rylan**: Skilled archer, excels in ranged damage and critical hits.
- **Mira**: Compassionate healer, provides vital support and healing.
- **Kailen**: Fearless duelist, high burst damage and agility.
- **Lyra**: Mysterious Veil Warden, specializes in Fade manipulation.
- **Taryn**: Former Templar, balanced fighter with holy magic.

Each companion in *The Veilguard* brings something unique to your team, enriching your journey with their strengths and personal stories. Take time to understand their roles and personalities, and you'll build a well-rounded team capable of tackling any challenge Thedas throws your way. Enjoy building bonds and exploring the world with these unforgettable allies!

Companion Abilities and Skills

Each companion in *Dragon Age: The Veilguard* comes equipped with a unique set of abilities and skills, tailored to their strengths, backgrounds, and combat roles. Understanding and effectively utilizing each companion's abilities can significantly enhance your team's overall performance. This guide provides an overview of each companion's core abilities, skill progression, and tips on how to maximize their impact in battle.

1. Lorian - The Stoic Warrior

- **Core Abilities**:
  - **Shield Wall**: Lorian raises his shield to block incoming attacks, reducing damage taken by himself and nearby allies.
    - **How to Use**: Press the assigned quick slot button for **Shield Wall** (e.g., R2 on PlayStation, RT on Xbox, or 1-4 on PC) when Lorian is under attack to protect himself and allies.
  - **Taunt**: Lorian taunts enemies, forcing them to target him. This ability is ideal for keeping enemies away from vulnerable teammates.
    - **Activation**: Use **Taunt** by selecting the quick slot. Ideal for initiating combat or controlling enemy focus.
  - **Mighty Blow**: A powerful overhead strike that deals heavy damage to a single target, particularly effective against armored foes.
    - **Execution**: Activate **Mighty Blow** when facing tougher enemies to maximize Lorian's damage output.
- **Skill Progression**:
  - **Focus on Defensive Skills**: Invest points in skills that increase Lorian's defense, health regeneration, and stamina, ensuring he can remain on the frontlines.

- **Suggested Upgrades**: Upgrades like **Fortified Shield** and **Iron Will** enhance Lorian's durability and stamina recovery.

2. Elara - The Elven Mage

- **Core Abilities**:
  - **Fireball**: Elara casts a fireball that deals area damage, burning enemies within range. Great for crowd control.
    - **How to Cast**: Assign **Fireball** to a quick slot and activate by pressing the corresponding button. Best used on clustered enemies.
  - **Barrier**: Creates a magical shield that absorbs damage for Elara and nearby allies, providing crucial protection in tough battles.
    - **Activation**: Use **Barrier** before engaging in battle or when teammates are at low health. Assign it to a quick slot for quick access.
  - **Freeze**: A single-target spell that freezes an enemy in place, immobilizing them and setting them up for shatter combos.
    - **Using Freeze**: Activate **Freeze** on high-threat enemies to neutralize them temporarily.
- **Skill Progression**:
  - **Invest in Elemental Magic**: Upgrades to **Fireball** and **Freeze** increase their effectiveness. Skills like **Blazing Storm** improve area damage, while **Icy Touch** boosts her freezing abilities.
  - **Mana Regeneration Upgrades**: Consider upgrades that reduce mana costs or increase Elara's mana regeneration, allowing her to cast spells more frequently.

3. Rylan - The Rogue Archer

- **Core Abilities**:
  - **Leaping Shot**: Rylan fires a series of quick shots while jumping backward, dealing damage and creating space between him and his enemies.
    - **How to Use**: Activate **Leaping Shot** when enemies are closing in on Rylan. Assign it to a quick slot for ease of access.
  - **Poisoned Arrows**: Coats arrows with poison, dealing damage over time to targets hit. This is useful for weakening enemies from a distance.
    - **Activation**: Toggle **Poisoned Arrows** on by selecting it in the quick slot. Effective against stronger enemies over longer fights.
  - **Critical Shot**: Fires a precise, high-damage arrow aimed at a vulnerable point on the enemy, perfect for dealing heavy damage.
    - **Execution**: Use **Critical Shot** against single high-priority targets for maximum impact.

- **Skill Progression**:
  - **Enhance Critical Hit Rate**: Invest in skills that boost Rylan's critical hit rate and damage, such as **Keen Eye** and **Deadly Precision**.
  - **Improve Poisoned Abilities**: Upgrading **Poisoned Arrows** and related skills allows Rylan to deal more damage over time, making him highly effective against tough enemies.

4. Mira - The Compassionate Healer

- **Core Abilities**:
  - **Healing Aura**: Mira generates a healing aura that gradually restores health to nearby allies. A must-have for longer battles.
    - **Activation**: Use **Healing Aura** when party health is low or during difficult encounters. Activate by selecting the quick slot.
  - **Revitalize**: A powerful spell that revives downed teammates with a portion of their health restored, crucial for high-stakes battles.
    - **How to Cast**: Activate **Revitalize** by selecting it from the quick slot when a companion is downed.
  - **Protective Ward**: Mira casts a barrier that reduces incoming damage, helping allies stay in the fight longer.
    - **How to Use**: Select **Protective Ward** when facing heavy enemy fire. Assign it to a quick slot for quick access.
- **Skill Progression**:
  - **Invest in Healing Abilities**: Upgrades to **Healing Aura** increase its effectiveness, and skills like **Lifeblood** improve Mira's healing output.
  - **Supportive Buffs**: Skills like **Guardian's Blessing** enhance Mira's protective abilities, making her an invaluable support character in extended battles.

5. Kailen - The Fearless Duelist

- **Core Abilities**:
  - **Shadow Strike**: Kailen disappears momentarily, then reappears behind an enemy to deliver a critical backstab. Perfect for quick, high-damage attacks.
    - **How to Use**: Activate **Shadow Strike** by selecting the quick slot and targeting a nearby enemy.
  - **Flurry of Blades**: Kailen unleashes a rapid series of strikes, dealing heavy damage in a short burst.
    - **Execution**: Use **Flurry of Blades** in close-range combat against high-health enemies to maximize damage output.
  - **Evasion**: Increases Kailen's chance to dodge attacks, making him harder to hit in close combat.

- **Activation**: Toggle **Evasion** on during battle to reduce damage taken. Select it in the quick slot to activate.
- **Skill Progression**:
  - **Boost Attack Speed and Damage**: Skills like **Duelist's Precision** and **Razor Edge** enhance Kailen's burst damage potential, making him an excellent damage dealer.
  - **Focus on Evasion**: Upgrades like **Shadow Dance** further increase Kailen's agility, helping him survive longer in the heat of battle.

6. Lyra - The Mysterious Veil Warden

- **Core Abilities**:
  - **Veil Strike**: A melee attack enhanced by Veil magic that disrupts enemies, causing them to stagger and become vulnerable to follow-up attacks.
    - **How to Use**: Assign **Veil Strike** to a quick slot, and activate it on enemies in close range.
  - **Fade Shroud**: Lyra can temporarily phase into the Veil, becoming invulnerable to physical attacks while regenerating stamina.
    - **Activation**: Use **Fade Shroud** by selecting the quick slot when Lyra is under heavy fire.
  - **Spirit Summon**: Summons a spectral ally from the Veil to assist in battle. The spirit fights alongside Lyra, dealing damage and absorbing hits.
    - **Summoning**: Activate **Spirit Summon** by pressing the quick slot button. Ideal for fights against multiple enemies.
- **Skill Progression**:
  - **Enhance Veil Abilities**: Skills like **Spectral Edge** and **Veil's Reach** improve the range and power of Lyra's Veil-based attacks.
  - **Increase Stamina Regeneration**: Stamina-boosting upgrades allow Lyra to use her abilities more frequently, ensuring she's always ready to phase or strike.

7. Taryn - The Former Templar

- **Core Abilities**:
  - **Smite**: Taryn channels holy energy to strike down magical foes, dealing extra damage to demons and Fade creatures.
    - **How to Use**: Assign **Smite** to a quick slot, and use it on enemies with magical abilities.
  - **Holy Shield**: Creates a shield of holy energy that reduces magic damage taken by Taryn and nearby allies.
    - **Activation**: Use **Holy Shield** in encounters with magical enemies. Assign it to a quick slot for ease of access.

- **Purify**: Removes harmful effects from allies and weakens nearby magical enemies, reducing their effectiveness.
    - **Execution**: Activate **Purify** when allies are affected by debuffs. Select it in the quick slot to remove effects.
- **Skill Progression**:
    - **Invest in Anti-Magic Skills**: Upgrades like **Divine Resolve** boost Taryn's damage against magic-users, making him more effective against Fade creatures.
    - **Increase Supportive Buffs**: Skills like **Holy Strength** enhance his support abilities, making him a balanced addition to any team.

Tips for Using Companion Abilities Effectively

- **Assign Abilities to Quick Slots**: Open the abilities menu, assign each companion's key abilities to quick slots, and access them easily during combat.
- **Use Tactical Mode for Precision**: Activate tactical mode (touchpad on PlayStation, "View" on Xbox, or "T" on PC) to position companions and use abilities strategically, especially during complex fights.
- **Balance Abilities Across the Team**: Choose companions with complementary abilities, balancing defense, offense, and support for a well-rounded team.

Mastering companion abilities in *The Veilguard* allows you to tackle challenges more effectively and creates synergy in combat. With this guide, you'll know how to make the most of each companion's unique skills, ensuring your team is ready for any challenge Thedas throws at you. Enjoy building a powerful, coordinated team and experiencing all the game has to offer!

Building Trust and Romance Options

In *Dragon Age: The Veilguard*, developing trust with companions is crucial for unlocking their full potential, gaining loyalty missions, and, for certain characters, exploring romance options. Trust-building opens up new storylines and abilities, while romance adds depth and emotional connection to your journey. This guide provides tips on how to build trust, initiate romance, and deepen bonds with each companion.

1. Understanding Trust-Building with Companions

- **Approval System**: Companions have an approval system that reflects their reactions to your choices. Making decisions they agree with will increase approval, while actions that clash with their values can lower it.
- **Engage in Conversations**: Talk to companions regularly at camp or key locations to learn about their past, motivations, and thoughts on recent events. These conversations often contain hints about their values, making it easier to understand how to build trust.

- **How to Talk to Companions**: Approach a companion at camp or in safe zones, press "X" (PlayStation), "A" (Xbox), or "E" (PC) to initiate dialogue, and explore all available conversation options.

---

2. Increasing Approval with Companions

- **Responding to Personal Beliefs**: Each companion has their own beliefs, ideals, and attitudes. Pay attention to how they react to certain decisions, and adjust your choices accordingly to match their preferences.
  - **Example**: If a companion values compassion, showing mercy to enemies or helping NPCs in need will likely increase their approval.
- **Completing Companion Quests**: Many companions have personal quests tied to their backstory. Completing these quests not only increases approval but may also unlock exclusive abilities and story elements.
  - **How to Accept Companion Quests**: Companions will often bring up their quests after you reach a certain approval level. When they request your help, accept by pressing "X" (PlayStation), "A" (Xbox), or "E" (PC).
- **Selecting Positive Dialogue Options**: When speaking with a companion, choose supportive or empathetic responses to increase approval. Certain responses will show a positive reaction, indicating you're strengthening the bond.
  - **Using the Dialogue Wheel**: During conversations, select options on the wheel that align with the companion's beliefs. Press "X" (PlayStation), "A" (Xbox), or left-click (PC) to confirm.

3. Companion-Specific Trust-Building Tips

- **Lorian**: Lorian respects duty, loyalty, and honor. Show respect for tradition and make choices that emphasize loyalty to allies. Avoid actions that seem reckless or disrespectful.
  - **Example**: Lorian approves of helping villages defend against threats and opposing corrupt leaders.
- **Elara**: Elara is fascinated by magic and the mysteries of the Veil. She values curiosity and knowledge but dislikes cruelty or manipulation of magical beings.
  - **Example**: Engage in quests involving the Veil, and choose dialogue options that express curiosity and respect for the Fade.
- **Rylan**: Rylan values independence and freedom and has a playful, rebellious streak. He appreciates witty banter, humor, and choices that emphasize personal freedom.
  - **Example**: Use humorous responses in conversations with him and support actions that oppose authoritarian figures.

- **Mira**: Mira is compassionate and values kindness. She approves of actions that help others, especially the vulnerable, and dislikes violence unless it's absolutely necessary.
  - **Example**: Help villagers in need, choose peaceful solutions when possible, and express empathy in dialogue with her.
- **Kailen**: Kailen is drawn to thrill and adventure. He admires courage and despises cowardice. Bold, risk-taking actions appeal to him, especially if they involve fighting formidable foes.
  - **Example**: Embrace challenging fights and select bold or daring dialogue options when speaking with him.
- **Lyra**: Lyra values knowledge of the Veil and seeks to maintain balance between the Fade and the physical world. She approves of careful, balanced decisions regarding magic and the Veil.
  - **Example**: Approach magical issues thoughtfully and be cautious with Veil-related powers.
- **Taryn**: Taryn values justice and order. He respects those who are honorable and dislikes decisions that seem reckless or chaotic.
  - **Example**: Support lawful decisions, show respect for discipline, and assist people in maintaining peace and stability.

4. Romance Options and How to Initiate Romance

- **Understanding Romance Triggers**: Each romanceable companion has specific approval thresholds and story moments that must be reached to initiate romance. High approval is essential for unlocking romantic dialogue options.
- **Look for Romance Cues in Dialogue**: Once your approval with a companion is high enough, you'll notice new, flirtatious dialogue options during conversations. Selecting these options will initiate romantic storylines.
  - **Activating Romance Dialogue**: When you see a heart symbol or flirtatious response on the dialogue wheel, press "X" (PlayStation), "A" (Xbox), or left-click (PC) to select it.
- **Continue Building Approval After Initial Romance**: Romance doesn't end after one interaction. Continue choosing supportive and affectionate dialogue options to deepen the relationship and trigger special romance scenes.

5. Romanceable Companions and Romance Tips

Lorian

- **Romance Requirements**: Lorian values loyalty and honor. To romance him, show respect for his ideals and focus on choices that reflect courage and integrity.
- **Romantic Dialogue**: Use respectful and sincere dialogue options, expressing admiration for his strength and honor. As approval grows, he'll eventually open up about his past and feelings.

Elara

- **Romance Requirements**: Elara is interested in those who share her curiosity and respect for magic. Build trust by showing appreciation for her knowledge and making thoughtful decisions.
- **Romantic Dialogue**: Use options that reveal fascination with the Veil and the mysteries of magic. When approval is high, she'll share deeper insights into her connection to the Fade.

Rylan

- **Romance Requirements**: Rylan is drawn to humor and freedom. Flirt with him during lighthearted conversations, and make choices that emphasize independence and personal strength.
- **Romantic Dialogue**: Use playful and teasing options. If his approval is high enough, he'll start reciprocating your affection with humorous banter and eventually open up emotionally.

Mira

- **Romance Requirements**: Mira appreciates kindness and compassion. Show empathy in your choices and assist others whenever possible to earn her trust and admiration.
- **Romantic Dialogue**: Select gentle, understanding options that express support and empathy. High approval unlocks tender, thoughtful dialogue where she confides in you.

Kailen

- **Romance Requirements**: Kailen respects courage and enjoys spontaneity. Impress him with bold choices and a willingness to take risks, especially in challenging situations.
- **Romantic Dialogue**: Choose daring and adventurous responses. As approval increases, he'll start to reveal his own vulnerabilities and admiration for your bravery.

6. Navigating Romance Scenes and Interactions

- **Private Moments**: Certain high-approval scenes will lead to private conversations where companions share their feelings more openly. These moments allow you to deepen the romance.
- **End-of-Quest Conversations**: After completing major quests or loyalty missions, speak with romanceable companions at camp for additional romantic dialogue. These moments often show their gratitude or admiration.
    - **How to Initiate**: After a quest, approach the companion and press "X" (PlayStation), "A" (Xbox), or "E" (PC) to begin a conversation.

7. Consequences of Romance Choices

- **Impact on Story and Dialogue**: Romance can affect how certain story events unfold and may unlock unique dialogue during key moments. Companions in a relationship with the protagonist may show greater concern or even offer unique support in challenging situations.
- **Potential for Jealousy**: If you begin flirting with another romanceable companion, some companions may express jealousy or disappointment. Once you commit to one romance, avoid flirting with others to maintain trust.

8. Tips for Balancing Trust and Romance

- **Stay Consistent with Choices**: Choose actions that align with your companion's values throughout the game, not just during romantic dialogue. Consistency builds a deeper bond and prevents approval loss.
- **Communicate Regularly**: Talk to your companions often to check on their approval level and ensure you're on the right track for romance or loyalty missions.
- **Watch for Companion Cues**: Pay attention to subtle hints in dialogue that reveal what your companions value. This can help you make choices that resonate with them.

Summary of Building Trust and Romance Options

- **Increase Approval**: Make choices that align with each companion's values and complete their personal quests.
- **Use Romantic Dialogue**: Select flirtatious or affectionate options when available to initiate romance.
- **Balance Trust with Romantic Interests**: Build trust with all companions, but once you commit to a romance, avoid interactions that may upset them.

Building trust and exploring romance in *The Veilguard* creates a rich, immersive experience that brings emotional depth to your journey. As you strengthen bonds and unlock romance options, you'll discover more about each character and create lasting memories that add to the adventure. Enjoy connecting with your companions and making your story truly unforgettable!

Companion Questlines and Their Impact

Companion questlines in *Dragon Age: The Veilguard* provide unique insights into each character's backstory, motivations, and personal struggles. Completing these quests not only strengthens your bond with each companion but also impacts the storyline, unlocks exclusive rewards, and can influence the game's ending. Here's an in-depth guide on how to navigate companion questlines and maximize their impact on your journey.

1. Unlocking Companion Questlines

- **Building Trust**: Companion quests become available as you build trust with each companion. To unlock these quests, engage with them regularly, make choices that align with their values, and choose supportive dialogue options.
  - **Initiating Conversations**: Approach companions at camp or designated safe zones, then press "X" (PlayStation), "A" (Xbox), or "E" (PC) to begin dialogue. Ask about their background and goals to increase approval and potentially trigger their personal quests.
- **Approval Thresholds**: Each companion's questline is typically unlocked after reaching a high enough approval level. Make sure to monitor your interactions and maintain positive relationships to ensure their quests become available.

2. Starting a Companion Quest

- **Triggered by Conversations**: Companions will often bring up their quests during camp or key story moments. They'll hint at unresolved issues or past events that need closure. Responding positively and offering your help will initiate the quest.
  - **Accepting the Quest**: When a companion asks for help, select the supportive dialogue option to accept their quest. Press "X" (PlayStation), "A" (Xbox), or left-click (PC) to confirm your decision.
- **Tracking the Quest**: Once accepted, the quest will appear in your quest log. Open the log by pressing "J" on PC, the touchpad on PlayStation, or "View" on Xbox, and set a waypoint for easy navigation.

3. Companion Questline Summaries and Tips

Lorian - Honor's Legacy

- **Quest Description**: Lorian's quest focuses on reclaiming an heirloom weapon stolen from his family. The journey involves tracking down bandits who have been terrorizing nearby villages.
- **Impact of the Quest**: Completing this quest grants Lorian a unique weapon and increases his loyalty, making him more effective in battle. It also cements his respect for you as a leader.
- **Tips for Success**: Keep Lorian in your party during this quest for unique dialogue options that reveal his family's history. Choose responses that support his sense of honor and duty to maximize approval.

Elara - Whispers of the Fade

- **Quest Description**: Elara's questline explores her mysterious connection to the Fade. She seeks to uncover the source of disturbing dreams and encounters powerful spirits tied to her past.
- **Impact of the Quest**: Successfully completing this quest unlocks a Fade-based ability for Elara, enhancing her magic capabilities. It also deepens her understanding of the Fade, affecting future interactions in Veilguard-related content.

- **Tips for Success**: During the quest, take a thoughtful approach in conversations with Elara. Avoid reckless decisions with Fade entities, as she values a respectful attitude toward magic.

Rylan - Shadows of the Past

- **Quest Description**: Rylan is being hunted by a group of mercenaries he once crossed. His quest involves confronting his past and resolving a dangerous vendetta.
- **Impact of the Quest**: Completing Rylan's quest unlocks a special weapon upgrade, boosts his agility, and brings closure to his past, improving his attitude and loyalty.
- **Tips for Success**: Take a balanced approach between strength and wit when dealing with his enemies. Choose dialogue options that show you support his independence and resourcefulness.

Mira - Light in the Dark

- **Quest Description**: Mira's quest revolves around an illness spreading in a small village. She is determined to help, but the cause of the illness is tied to dark magic.
- **Impact of the Quest**: Finishing this quest unlocks a powerful healing ability for Mira, increasing her effectiveness as a support character. The quest also strengthens her compassion and dedication, impacting her loyalty and future interactions.
- **Tips for Success**: Use empathetic and supportive responses when talking with Mira during the quest. She appreciates efforts to protect others and will respond well to choices that prioritize helping the villagers.

Kailen - Duelist's Challenge

- **Quest Description**: Kailen is drawn to a duelist's guild where fighters compete for glory and fame. His quest involves participating in the tournament and facing off against skilled opponents.
- **Impact of the Quest**: Completing Kailen's quest grants him a unique duelist ability and boosts his damage output. It also deepens his bond with you, as he respects those who support his passion for combat.
- **Tips for Success**: Encourage Kailen's adventurous spirit and choose dialogue options that show enthusiasm for the competition. This will increase his approval and reinforce his loyalty to you.

Lyra - Bound by the Veil

- **Quest Description**: Lyra's quest centers around a powerful Veil rift threatening to destabilize the area. She needs your help to close it and protect nearby villages from the Fade's influence.
- **Impact of the Quest**: Completing Lyra's quest unlocks a Veil-related ability for her, making her even more effective in Veilguard encounters. It also reveals secrets about her connection to the Veil, impacting the Veilguard storyline.

- **Tips for Success**: Approach the quest with caution and respect for the Veil. Lyra appreciates a balanced approach, so avoid reckless decisions when dealing with rifts and spirits.

Taryn - Shadows of the Order

- **Quest Description**: Taryn's quest explores his complicated past with the Templars. He uncovers corruption within the order and seeks justice for the people affected.
- **Impact of the Quest**: Completing Taryn's quest grants him a holy magic ability and strengthens his sense of justice. His loyalty to you increases, and he becomes a valuable ally against magical threats.
- **Tips for Success**: Take a disciplined, justice-oriented approach to conversations and decisions. Taryn respects order and will appreciate choices that reflect fairness and integrity.

4. Navigating Key Moments and Choices in Companion Questlines

- **Dialogue Decisions**: Throughout each quest, you'll have dialogue choices that shape the story and impact your bond with the companion. Choose responses that align with their values to increase approval and reveal unique insights.
  - **Example**: When a companion faces a moral dilemma, supporting their stance or showing empathy will strengthen your relationship.
- **Combat Strategies**: Certain questlines involve tough battles or encounters. Use tactical mode (touchpad on PlayStation, "View" on Xbox, or "T" on PC) to position companions advantageously and make the most of their unique abilities.
- **Moral Choices**: Many companion quests present ethical decisions, such as sparing or punishing enemies. These choices can impact the companion's loyalty and affect how they view you as a leader.

5. Impact of Completed Companion Questlines

- **New Abilities and Skills**: Completing a companion's questline often unlocks exclusive abilities or skill upgrades, making them stronger and more useful in battle. Check their skill tree after the quest to equip new abilities.
- **Improved Loyalty and Approval**: Successfully completing a companion quest boosts approval and strengthens your bond, leading to unique dialogue options, story moments, and potential romance.
- **Story and Epilogue Changes**: Some companion quests have lasting effects on the storyline, especially if they involve choices with far-reaching consequences. Companions with completed questlines may show up in the game's epilogue with unique endings reflecting their journey with you.

6. Tips for Maximizing the Impact of Companion Questlines

- **Focus on High-Approval Companions**: Prioritize quests for companions with whom you have a strong relationship. This ensures that you'll achieve the best possible outcome and unlock the most impactful rewards.
- **Engage in Follow-Up Conversations**: After completing a companion quest, speak with them at camp. These post-quest dialogues often reveal how the quest impacted them personally, strengthening your connection.
- **Prepare for Unique Combat Scenarios**: Many companion quests feature specific enemies or environmental challenges. Equip companions with relevant gear, like fire-resistant armor or anti-magic items, to maximize their effectiveness.

Summary of Companion Questlines and Their Impact

- **Unlock by Building Trust**: Gain access to companion quests by increasing approval and engaging in regular conversations.
- **Complete for Unique Rewards**: Finish each questline to unlock exclusive abilities, items, and story insights.
- **Make Meaningful Choices**: Choose responses and actions that align with each companion's values for maximum impact.
- **Influence the Story and Epilogue**: Companion quests can shape the storyline and epilogue, adding depth to your character's legacy.

Companion questlines in *The Veilguard* are rich in storytelling, character development, and gameplay rewards. By completing these quests thoughtfully, you'll not only strengthen your team but also uncover powerful connections and shape the course of your adventure. Enjoy each companion's journey and the lasting impact they bring to your story!

Choosing the Right Companions for Your Team

Building a strong, balanced team in *Dragon Age: The Veilguard* is essential for tackling various challenges and maximizing each companion's unique abilities. Your team composition depends on your playstyle, the mission requirements, and the types of enemies you expect to face. Here's a guide to help you choose the right companions, create effective synergies, and position them optimally in combat.

1. Assessing Your Own Role and Playstyle

- **Identify Your Character's Strengths**: Start by evaluating your character's primary role. Are you a warrior on the frontlines, a mage casting spells from afar, or a rogue attacking from the shadows? Your companions should complement your abilities to create a well-rounded team.
- **Choose Complementary Roles**: If you play a tanky character, consider adding a healer and ranged DPS to balance your team. If you're a mage, a tank and a melee damage dealer can help protect you while you focus on spellcasting.
  - **Example**: If you're a damage-focused rogue, select a tank like Lorian and a healer like Mira to balance out your offensive capabilities with defense and support.

2. Understanding Companion Roles and Synergies

- **Tank**: Characters like Lorian excel at drawing enemy focus, absorbing damage, and keeping weaker companions safe.
- **Damage Dealer (DPS)**: Companions like Rylan and Kailen focus on high damage output, either at range (Rylan) or up close (Kailen).
- **Support and Healer**: Mira provides healing and protective spells that keep your team sustained during tough battles.
- **Crowd Control and Spellcaster**: Elara's abilities focus on controlling the battlefield with powerful spells, while Lyra's Veil-based magic adds utility and unique control effects.

3. Building Your Team Based on Mission Requirements

- **Combat-Heavy Missions**: For quests involving numerous enemies or tough bosses, a balanced team with a tank, DPS, and healer is ideal.
  - **Suggested Team**: Lorian (tank), Mira (healer), and Rylan (ranged DPS). Lorian holds enemy focus, Mira heals, and Rylan deals damage from a distance.
- **Stealth or Infiltration Missions**: Missions that require subtlety or speed benefit from stealthy, agile companions.
  - **Suggested Team**: Rylan (rogue archer), Kailen (melee rogue), and Elara (spellcaster). This team provides high burst damage and agility, ideal for quick, controlled engagements.
- **Veil-Heavy Areas**: In areas with Veil rifts and Fade creatures, bring companions skilled in dealing with magical threats.
  - **Suggested Team**: Lyra (Veil Warden), Taryn (anti-magic Templar), and Mira (healer). Lyra's Veil abilities, Taryn's holy magic, and Mira's support make a strong team against supernatural foes.

4. Creating Synergies Between Companions

- **Combining Crowd Control and Burst Damage**: Pair a crowd-control specialist like Elara with a high-damage companion like Kailen to maximize the effect of immobilizing enemies.

- **Example Combo**: Use Elara's **Freeze** to immobilize a group, then activate Kailen's **Flurry of Blades** to deal massive damage while enemies are unable to fight back.
- **Healing and Tanking**: Combining a tank like Lorian with Mira's healing abilities allows for a durable frontline that can withstand heavy damage.
  - **Example Combo**: Position Lorian to taunt enemies, while Mira's **Healing Aura** keeps him sustained. This combination ensures Lorian stays active on the frontlines, protecting the rest of the team.
- **Ranged Support and High DPS**: Use Rylan's critical hit abilities with Lyra's spirit summoning to support him with additional allies on the battlefield.
  - **Example Combo**: Rylan focuses on taking down high-priority targets, while Lyra's **Spirit Summon** adds extra firepower and distracts enemies.

5. Maximizing Companion Abilities for Different Enemy Types

- **Fighting Armored Foes**: Bring companions with abilities that penetrate or break armor, such as Lorian's **Mighty Blow** or Kailen's **Shadow Strike**.
- **Facing Magic-Using Enemies**: For enemies that cast spells or summon Fade creatures, companions like Taryn (holy magic) and Lyra (Veil-based powers) provide effective countermeasures.
- **Battling High-Mobility Enemies**: Quick enemies that evade attacks are best handled with crowd control. Elara's **Freeze** or Mira's **Protective Ward** can slow them down, allowing high-DPS companions like Rylan to land critical hits.

6. Positioning Companions in Combat

- **Frontline Positioning**: Place your tank (Lorian or Taryn) at the front to draw enemy attacks, keeping squishier teammates safe.
  - **How to Position**: Use tactical mode (touchpad on PlayStation, "View" on Xbox, or "T" on PC) to move Lorian or Taryn ahead of the group and set them to taunt nearby enemies.
- **Ranged and Support Positioning**: Position ranged companions like Rylan and spellcasters like Elara at the back to keep them safe and give them a clear line of sight for attacks.
  - **How to Position**: In tactical mode, set Rylan and Elara at a distance from the main conflict, where they can attack without drawing aggro.
- **Healer Positioning**: Keep Mira near the center of the team, allowing her to move between allies and heal or buff as needed.
  - **How to Position**: Place Mira centrally on the battlefield so she can reach the tank, DPS, or any other ally in need of healing quickly.

7. Companion-Specific Team Compositions

Balanced Team Composition

- **Companions**: Lorian (tank), Mira (healer), Rylan (ranged DPS)
- **Strengths**: This setup covers defense, healing, and long-range damage, making it effective in most situations.
- **Best For**: General combat and exploration, where balanced abilities provide versatility.

High-DPS Team Composition

- **Companions**: Kailen (melee DPS), Rylan (ranged DPS), Elara (spellcaster)
- **Strengths**: High burst damage with strong single-target and area-of-effect abilities, ideal for taking down powerful enemies quickly.
- **Best For**: Missions with lower enemy count but higher difficulty, where quick takedowns are crucial.

Anti-Magic Team Composition

- **Companions**: Taryn (anti-magic), Lyra (Veil Warden), Mira (healer)
- **Strengths**: Excellent against magic-using enemies and supernatural threats, with high resistance to magic damage and strong counter-attacks.
- **Best For**: Veilguard-exclusive missions and battles against Fade creatures or mages.

Crowd Control Team Composition

- **Companions**: Elara (mage), Lorian (tank), Mira (healer)
- **Strengths**: Strong crowd control with defensive capabilities, allowing you to immobilize and debuff enemies while staying protected.
- **Best For**: Missions with multiple groups of enemies, where controlling the battlefield is essential.

8. Adjusting Companions Based on Difficulty Level

- **Harder Difficulty Levels**: At higher difficulties, focus on durability and healing. Choose companions with defensive or support abilities, such as Lorian (tank), Mira (healer), and Taryn (anti-magic).
- **Normal or Easy Difficulty Levels**: For lower difficulty settings, you can afford to focus on high damage output. Consider a team of Kailen (DPS), Rylan (DPS), and Elara (spellcaster) for quick and aggressive strategies.

9. Quick Tips for Choosing Companions on the Fly

- **Check Your Quest Requirements**: Before starting a mission, review the quest details and enemy types to adjust your team accordingly.
- **Balance Roles When Uncertain**: If you're unsure of what to expect, bring a tank, a healer, and a high-DPS companion for a versatile setup.
- **Equip Appropriate Gear**: Make sure companions have relevant gear equipped, such as fire resistance for missions involving dragons or magical protection for Fade-heavy areas.

○ **How to Equip Gear**: Open the inventory by pressing "I" (PC), "Options" (PlayStation), or "Menu" (Xbox). Select a companion and equip gear that suits their role and the mission.

Summary of Choosing the Right Companions for Your Team

- **Consider Your Role and Playstyle**: Choose companions who complement your character's strengths and weaknesses.
- **Build for Mission Requirements**: Adjust your team composition based on the mission's expected challenges, such as high enemy counts or magical threats.
- **Use Positioning and Tactical Mode**: Place companions strategically in combat to protect weaker members and maximize damage output.
- **Balance Durability and Damage**: For harder missions, lean on a balanced team with defensive and healing abilities, while focusing on DPS for easier challenges.

With a solid understanding of companion roles, synergies, and strategic positioning, you're ready to assemble a team that's prepared for any challenge *The Veilguard* throws your way. Experiment with different setups, adapt to each mission's needs, and enjoy the dynamic, engaging combat that comes with a well-chosen team!

CHAPTER 8

Exploring the Veil

In this chapter, you'll uncover the secrets of the Veil and the Fade, learning how these mystical forces shape the world of *Dragon Age: The Veilguard*. Discover tips for navigating Veilguard zones, where reality blurs with magic, and find guidance on interacting with spirits and demons. This chapter also covers hidden Veilguard relics and artifacts, offering powerful items that enhance your journey. Finally, explore the Veilguard-exclusive abilities and enhancements that grant you unique powers, transforming the way you engage with the magical forces in Thedas.

Understanding the Veil and Fade

The Veil and the Fade are central to the magic and lore of *Dragon Age: The Veilguard*. They are forces that influence everything from the nature of magic to the spirits and demons that interact with the physical world. Understanding these mystical elements can enhance your experience in the game, helping you navigate Veilguard zones, interact safely with spirits, and make the most of Veil-related powers.

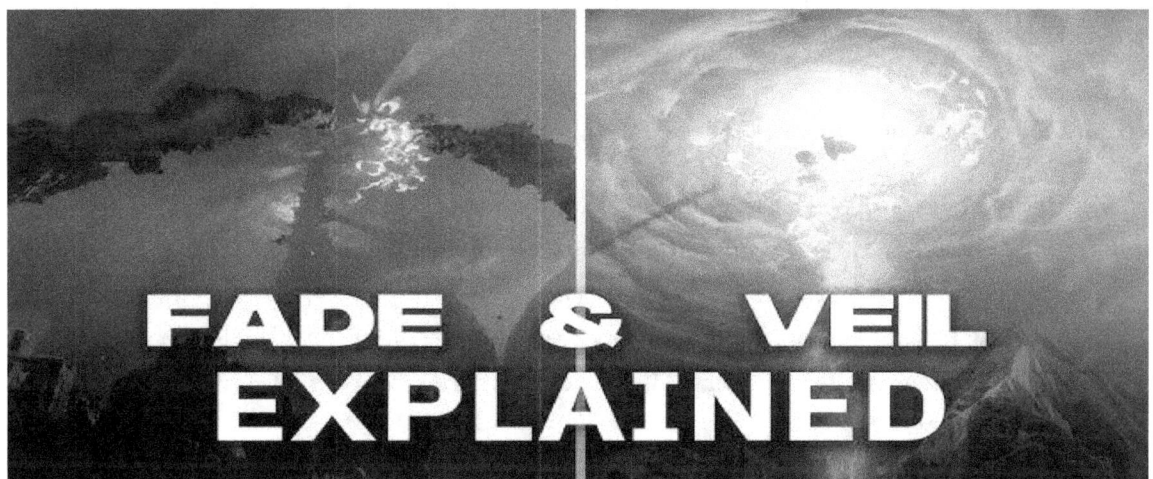

1. What is the Veil?

- **Definition**: The Veil is a metaphysical barrier that separates the physical world of Thedas from the Fade, a realm of dreams, magic, and spiritual beings. It prevents most spirits and demons from crossing into the physical realm, but the Veil can be weakened or breached, allowing these entities to interact with humans.
- **Why It Matters**: In certain areas, the Veil is thin, making it easier for magical forces and creatures to seep into the world. Veilguard quests often take place in these weakened areas, leading to unique challenges and encounters.

2. What is the Fade?

- **Definition**: The Fade is an ethereal realm inhabited by spirits and demons. It's the source of all magic and a place where dreams take form. Mages often access the Fade to channel magical energy, but doing so is risky, as it opens them to potential danger from Fade entities.
- **Exploring the Fade in Veilguard**: Certain Veilguard missions involve stepping into or interacting with the Fade, making it crucial to understand its dangers and rewards. The Fade is unpredictable; while it offers powerful magic, it also harbors hostile entities.

3. The Role of Spirits and Demons in the Fade

- **Spirits**: Spirits are beings in the Fade that represent ideals like justice, wisdom, compassion, and curiosity. They are usually harmless unless threatened, and some can even offer assistance to mages or travelers who treat them with respect.
- **Demons**: Unlike spirits, demons are entities in the Fade that represent negative emotions and desires, such as rage, desire, and pride. They are dangerous and will often attempt to harm or manipulate those who enter the Fade.
- **Recognizing Friend from Foe**: During Veilguard missions, pay attention to the nature of spirits and demons. Spirits may appear in calm or neutral colors, while demons often emit ominous, dark energy. Use caution when approaching any Fade being.

4. Veilguard Zones: Areas of Weakened Veil

- **Identifying Veilguard Zones**: Veilguard zones are areas where the Veil is thin, resulting in visible rifts or disturbances in reality. These zones are often marked on your map and can be visually identified by a distortion in the environment or unusual magical energy.
  - **How to Locate Veilguard Zones**: Open your map by pressing "M" on PC, the touchpad on PlayStation, or "View" on Xbox. Veilguard zones are marked with a special icon that resembles a rift or swirl.
- **Navigating Safely**: Entering a Veilguard zone puts you at higher risk of encountering demons and other Fade creatures. Bring companions skilled in dealing with magic, such as Lyra or Taryn, to give yourself an advantage.
- **Benefits of Veilguard Zones**: These areas often contain valuable relics, powerful artifacts, and sources of magical knowledge that can enhance your abilities. Approach each zone prepared for both danger and reward.

5. Understanding Veil Rifts and How to Close Them

- **Veil Rifts Explained**: Veil rifts are breaches where the Veil is thinnest, allowing creatures from the Fade to pass into the physical world. These rifts are dangerous, as they continually summon hostile Fade creatures until they are closed.
- **How to Close Rifts**: To close a Veil rift, approach it and press "X" (PlayStation), "A" (Xbox), or "E" (PC). Closing a rift typically requires defeating waves of summoned enemies first.

- **Using Veil Abilities**: Certain Veilguard-exclusive abilities, such as **Veil Strike** or **Spirit Ward**, can weaken or control rift creatures, making it easier to close the rift. Equip these abilities in your quick slots for immediate access.
- **Rewards for Closing Rifts**: Successfully closing a rift can grant unique items, experience points, and sometimes Veilguard relics that boost your abilities in the Fade.

6. Veilguard Relics and Artifacts: Tools to Control the Veil

- **Finding Relics**: Veilguard relics are often hidden in Veilguard zones or close to Veil rifts. They appear as shimmering objects or ancient statues that pulse with magical energy.
  - **How to Collect Relics**: Approach a Veilguard relic and press "X" (PlayStation), "A" (Xbox), or "E" (PC) to collect it. Relics typically add permanent enhancements to Veil-related abilities or provide temporary buffs against Fade creatures.
- **Using Artifacts to Strengthen the Veil**: Some artifacts allow you to repair weakened parts of the Veil, reducing the chance of rift-related encounters in an area. This can be useful if you want to clear Veilguard zones without engaging in constant battles.
  - **Activating Artifacts**: After collecting an artifact, access your inventory by pressing "I" (PC), "Options" (PlayStation), or "Menu" (Xbox) and select the artifact to activate its powers.

7. Veilguard-Exclusive Abilities and Enhancements

- **Understanding Veil Abilities**: Veil abilities are unique powers that allow you to interact directly with the Veil and Fade entities. These abilities can only be unlocked through Veilguard quests and often have powerful effects in Veilguard zones.
- **Examples of Veil Abilities**:
  - **Veil Strike**: A melee attack that disrupts rift creatures, making them more vulnerable to physical attacks.
    - **How to Equip**: Assign **Veil Strike** to a quick slot by opening the abilities menu and selecting it. Press the quick slot button to activate in combat.
  - **Spirit Ward**: A defensive ability that protects you from Fade creatures, reducing damage from demons and spirits.
    - **How to Activate**: Equip **Spirit Ward** in your quick slot, then activate when near hostile Fade creatures.
  - **Fade Shroud**: Temporarily allows you to phase into the Veil, avoiding physical attacks and regenerating mana or stamina.
    - **How to Use**: Select **Fade Shroud** from your quick slot during combat to evade attacks. It's especially useful for avoiding heavy-hitting enemies or repositioning.

8. Interacting with Spirits and Demons

- **Dialogue with Spirits**: Spirits in the Fade are often willing to communicate with respectful visitors. They may offer valuable insights, guidance, or even rewards if you interact carefully.
  - **How to Initiate Dialogue**: Approach a spirit and press "X" (PlayStation), "A" (Xbox), or "E" (PC) to initiate conversation. Choose dialogue options that reflect curiosity or respect to maintain positive interactions.
- **Dealing with Demons**: Unlike spirits, demons are usually hostile and won't engage in peaceful dialogue. They represent dangerous emotions and will often attempt to manipulate or harm anyone who approaches.
  - **Combat Tips**: Use Veilguard abilities to weaken demons, as they are particularly vulnerable to Veil-based attacks like **Veil Strike** or **Spirit Ward**.

9. Recognizing the Risks of Interacting with the Veil

- **Corruption and Fade Exposure**: Prolonged exposure to Veilguard zones or repeated interactions with demons can lead to Fade corruption. This effect weakens characters' stamina or mana over time.
- **Using Veil Wards**: Some Veilguard quests provide Veil wards that protect against corruption. To use a ward, activate it from your inventory when entering a Veil-heavy area.
- **Monitoring Your Character's Condition**: Keep an eye on your stamina and mana when exploring Veilguard zones. If they start depleting faster, consider leaving the area to recover or using Veil protection items to reduce the effects.

Summary of Understanding the Veil and Fade

- **The Veil and Fade Explained**: The Veil separates the physical world from the Fade, a realm of magic, dreams, and spirits. Weakened areas of the Veil can lead to encounters with spirits and demons.
- **Navigating Veilguard Zones**: Approach Veilguard zones cautiously, as these areas contain rifts and relics that can both aid and challenge you.
- **Using Veilguard Abilities**: Veilguard-exclusive abilities help control and protect against Fade creatures, making them valuable tools in Veil-heavy missions.
- **Interacting with Spirits and Demons**: Spirits may offer guidance or rewards, while demons generally attack on sight. Use respect and caution when dealing with Fade entities.

Understanding the Veil and Fade in *Dragon Age: The Veilguard* equips you with the knowledge to navigate magical encounters, close dangerous rifts, and harness Veil powers. With these insights, you'll be prepared to explore the mysteries of the Fade and use its energy to strengthen your journey through Thedas. Enjoy unlocking the power of the Veil and discovering what lies beyond!

Navigating the Veilguard Zones

Veilguard zones are areas in *Dragon Age: The Veilguard* where the Veil—the barrier between the physical world and the Fade—is thin, making it easier for magical phenomena and dangerous Fade creatures to spill into Thedas. These zones are both challenging and rewarding, filled with powerful relics, unique Veilguard-exclusive abilities, and encounters with spirits and demons. Here's a comprehensive guide to safely navigating these zones and making the most of the opportunities they offer.

1. Identifying Veilguard Zones on the Map

- **Finding Veilguard Zones**: Veilguard zones are marked with a distinct icon on your map—usually a swirling or rift-like symbol. These areas are accessible only after completing certain main storyline quests that unlock Veilguard content.
  - **How to Access the Map**: Open your map by pressing "M" on PC, the touchpad on PlayStation, or "View" on Xbox. Look for the Veilguard icon to locate these zones.
- **Planning Your Route**: Veilguard zones are often remote or require traveling through dangerous areas. Use the map to set a waypoint by pressing "X" (PlayStation), "A" (Xbox), or right-clicking on PC, guiding you safely to the zone's entrance.

2. Preparing for Veilguard Zone Exploration

- **Equip Veilguard-Specific Gear**: Gear that resists magic or Fade corruption is essential in Veilguard zones. Use armor or accessories that boost your magical defenses or equip items that reduce corruption effects.
  - **How to Equip Gear**: Access your inventory by pressing "I" (PC), "Options" (PlayStation), or "Menu" (Xbox). Select and equip gear with protective enchantments to prepare for magic-heavy encounters.
- **Bringing the Right Companions**: Certain companions, like Lyra (Veil Warden) and Taryn (anti-magic Templar), are highly effective in Veilguard zones. Their abilities counteract Fade creatures and Veil rifts, making these allies invaluable for these missions.
  - **How to Change Companions**: At camp, interact with the party selection area and press "X" (PlayStation), "A" (Xbox), or "E" (PC) to switch out companions.

3. Entering a Veilguard Zone and Spotting Key Features

- **Recognizing Veilguard Characteristics**: Veilguard zones often exhibit environmental distortions, such as floating particles, shimmering air, or faintly glowing rifts. These visuals indicate weakened areas of the Veil.
- **Key Features to Watch For**:

- Veil Rifts: Breaches that allow creatures from the Fade to enter the physical world. These rifts emit an eerie glow and are surrounded by ghostly figures or distortions.
- **Veilguard Relics and Artifacts**: Often hidden or protected by spirits, these relics appear as glowing objects or ancient carvings. They grant unique powers when collected, adding strength or skills useful in Fade-heavy zones.

4. Closing Veil Rifts and Handling Fade Creatures

- **Initiating Rift Closures**: To close a Veil rift, approach it and press "X" (PlayStation), "A" (Xbox), or "E" (PC). This action triggers waves of Fade creatures that must be defeated before the rift can fully close.
- **Defeating Fade Creatures**: Veil rifts summon hostile spirits and demons that vary in strength. These creatures are weak to Veilguard abilities and magic-focused attacks.
  - **Using Veilguard Abilities**: Equip abilities like **Veil Strike** or **Spirit Ward** to weaken and control Fade creatures. Assign these abilities to quick slots for quick access during combat.
- **Tips for Effective Rift Closures**:
  - **Use Area-of-Effect Spells**: Abilities like **Fireball** (Elara) or **Barrier** (Mira) help manage multiple enemies.
  - **Target Summoning Points**: Some rifts have summoning points that, if disrupted, slow down or weaken the waves of creatures. Position your companions near these points for quicker control.

5. Finding and Collecting Veilguard Relics

- **Locating Relics in Veilguard Zones**: Relics are often hidden in corners, behind magical barriers, or near Veil rifts. Watch for objects that glow or emit a faint pulse, as these indicate powerful relics.
  - **How to Collect Relics**: Approach a relic and press "X" (PlayStation), "A" (Xbox), or "E" (PC) to interact and collect it. Collecting relics often grants temporary or permanent boosts to Veil abilities.
- **Using Collected Relics**: Relics can grant Veil-related abilities, such as increased magic resistance or enhanced Fade stamina. These are useful in combat against Fade creatures and bosses.
  - **Activating Relic Effects**: After collecting a relic, check your abilities or passive bonuses in the character menu to see the effect. Relics usually activate automatically once collected.

6. Avoiding or Managing Veil Corruption

- **Understanding Veil Corruption**: Veilguard zones contain corrupting magic that drains stamina or mana, weakening you the longer you stay in the zone.
- **Using Veil Wards**: Certain items, called Veil Wards, protect against corruption. These are often found during Veilguard missions or can be crafted from rare materials.

- **How to Use Veil Wards**: Open your inventory and select the Veil Ward to activate it. Press "X" (PlayStation), "A" (Xbox), or left-click (PC) to apply the protection.
- **Monitoring Corruption Effects**: Check the status bar for indicators of corruption, usually marked by a darkened or ghostly icon. If corruption starts affecting your abilities, consider exiting the zone temporarily to recover.

7. Navigating Veilguard Puzzles and Riddles

- **Magical Puzzles and Barriers**: Some Veilguard zones contain puzzles that need to be solved to access relics or continue the mission. These may involve aligning symbols, activating runes, or solving riddles provided by spirits.
    - **How to Interact with Puzzles**: Approach the puzzle element and press "X" (PlayStation), "A" (Xbox), or "E" (PC) to examine it. Look for clues in the environment or dialogue with spirits nearby.
- **Using Fade Sight**: Certain puzzles require Fade Sight, a Veilguard ability that reveals hidden clues or paths.
    - **Activating Fade Sight**: Assign Fade Sight to a quick slot, then press the assigned button to activate. This ability temporarily reveals hidden symbols, pathways, or objects tied to the Veil.

8. Interacting with Spirits and Demons

- **Identifying Friendly Spirits**: Some spirits in Veilguard zones may be neutral or helpful, offering hints or rewards if you approach them respectfully. They often appear calm and may emit a gentle light.
    - **How to Talk to Spirits**: Approach the spirit and press "X" (PlayStation), "A" (Xbox), or "E" (PC) to initiate conversation. Choose dialogue options that reflect curiosity and respect to avoid provoking them.
- **Handling Hostile Demons**: Demons are typically aggressive and attack on sight. They tend to cluster around Veil rifts and relics.
    - **Combat Tips**: Use anti-magic abilities or powerful spells to defeat demons quickly. Pair offensive companions like Rylan or Kailen with support characters like Mira to maximize your team's effectiveness against them.

9. Unlocking and Using Veilguard-Exclusive Abilities

- **Acquiring Veil Abilities**: Certain abilities can only be unlocked by interacting with Veilguard relics or completing specific Veilguard missions.

- - **Equipping New Abilities**: Access the abilities menu by pressing "I" (PC), "Options" (PlayStation), or "Menu" (Xbox). Assign Veil abilities like **Fade Shroud** or **Veil Strike** to quick slots for use in combat.
  - **Recommended Veil Abilities**:
    - **Fade Shroud**: Grants temporary invisibility and reduces incoming magic damage.
    - **Veil Strike**: A melee attack that disrupts Fade creatures, making them more vulnerable to follow-up attacks.
    - **Spirit Ward**: A defensive ability that reduces damage from Fade entities, perfect for encounters in Veilguard zones.

10. Exiting Veilguard Zones Safely

- **Monitoring Health and Resources**: Veilguard zones can drain health, stamina, and mana over time. Keep an eye on these resources and exit the zone if they drop too low.
- **Setting Waypoints to Find the Exit**: Open your map, locate the nearest exit, and set a waypoint to guide you out. Use tactical mode to move companions away from fights if necessary.
- **Avoiding Last-Minute Encounters**: Fade creatures may respawn in Veilguard zones, so leave the area quickly once you've collected relics and closed rifts. Avoid lingering to minimize the risk of new encounters.

Summary of Navigating the Veilguard Zones

- **Identify and Plan**: Locate Veilguard zones on your map and prepare with gear and companions suited for magical encounters.
- **Collect Relics and Close Rifts**: Gather relics for Veil powers and close rifts to stop Fade creature invasions.
- **Handle Corruption and Demons**: Protect yourself against Veil corruption and use anti-magic tactics for fighting demons.
- **Use Veilguard Abilities**: Unlock and equip exclusive Veil abilities for added strength and control in these zones.

Navigating Veilguard zones successfully requires preparation, caution, and a solid understanding of Veil-based magic. With this guide, you'll be ready to face the challenges of these unique areas, harness powerful relics, and close rifts to protect Thedas from the forces of the Fade. Embrace the magic of the Veil and enjoy the mysteries that lie within!

Interacting with Spirits and Demons

In *Dragon Age: The Veilguard*, spirits and demons from the Fade play a major role in the game's lore and present unique interactions and challenges in Veilguard zones. Spirits often represent positive concepts like compassion or wisdom, while demons embody darker forces such as rage, desire, or pride. Knowing how to interact with these beings—whether through diplomacy or combat—is crucial for survival and maximizing the rewards available in the Fade.

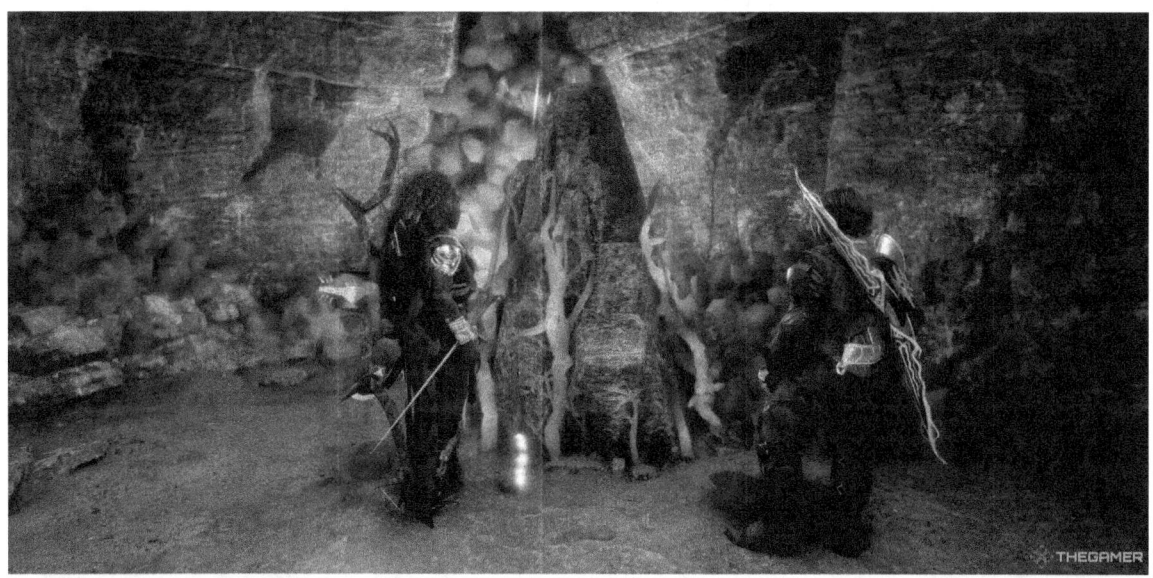

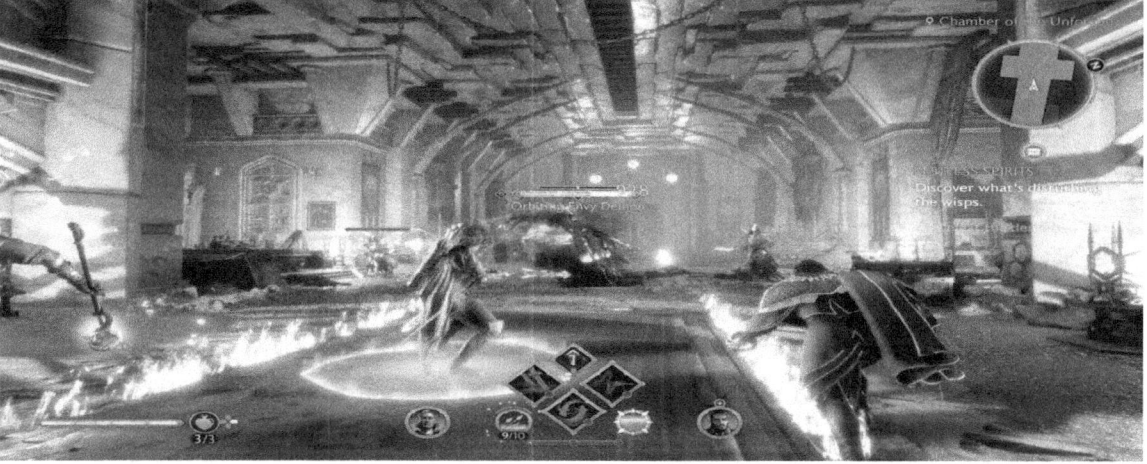

1. Understanding the Difference Between Spirits and Demons

- **Spirits**: Spirits are generally neutral or benevolent beings that represent abstract concepts like justice, curiosity, and empathy. They are usually harmless unless provoked or corrupted by a negative influence from the Veil.
- **Demons**: Demons represent destructive emotions, including anger, envy, and despair. They are almost always hostile and may try to manipulate or attack those who enter their domain.
- **Identifying Spirits and Demons**: Spirits typically appear with calm, soft glows and neutral or warm auras, while demons often have dark, ominous energy and aggressive postures.

2. Approaching Spirits: Gaining Guidance and Rewards

- **Finding Spirits**: Spirits are often found near relics, magical sites, or within Veilguard zones. They may offer guidance, provide lore, or even grant protective blessings to respectful visitors.
  - **How to Initiate Interaction**: Approach a spirit slowly and press "X" (PlayStation), "A" (Xbox), or "E" (PC) to begin conversation.
- **Choosing Respectful Dialogue Options**: Spirits respond well to respectful dialogue that shows curiosity, empathy, or a desire to understand their perspective. Avoid aggressive or dismissive responses.
  - **Selecting Dialogue**: Use dialogue options that indicate understanding or support. Select these options on the dialogue wheel, then press "X" (PlayStation), "A" (Xbox), or left-click (PC) to confirm.
- **Gaining Spirit Blessings**: Some spirits may bless your character with temporary buffs or provide Veilguard relics. Accept these gifts politely, as they often improve your performance in Veilguard zones.

3. Dealing with Demons: Combat Tactics and Survival Tips

- **Recognizing Hostile Demons**: Demons typically appear near Veil rifts, often guarding relics or corrupting areas. They will attack on sight, using magic and Fade-based powers.
  - **How to Prepare for Combat**: Equip anti-magic abilities or items that protect against corruption before entering a Veilguard zone. Check your inventory by pressing "I" (PC), "Options" (PlayStation), or "Menu" (Xbox).
- **Using Veilguard Abilities**: Demons are especially vulnerable to Veilguard abilities, such as **Veil Strike** or **Spirit Ward**, which weaken or disrupt their powers.
  - **Equipping Abilities**: Open the abilities menu and assign Veil abilities to quick slots. Activate them during combat by pressing the corresponding quick slot button.
- **Exploiting Weaknesses**:
  - **Rage Demons** are weak to cold-based attacks. Use abilities like Elara's **Freeze** to slow them down and deal extra damage.
  - **Desire Demons** can charm characters, so try to engage from a distance with Rylan's arrows or Lyra's Veil powers to minimize risk.
  - **Pride Demons** have strong defenses but are vulnerable to high-damage burst attacks. Kailen's **Flurry of Blades** or Rylan's **Critical Shot** can be effective in breaking through their defenses.

4. Using Tactical Mode to Control Demon Encounters

- **Activating Tactical Mode**: When facing multiple demons, use tactical mode to position your companions strategically. Press the touchpad on PlayStation, "View" on Xbox, or "T" on PC to activate tactical mode.
- **Positioning Companions**:
  - **Place your tank (Lorian or Taryn)** at the frontline to draw demon attention and absorb damage.

- ○ **Position ranged attackers (Rylan or Elara)** at a distance to maximize damage output while staying safe.
  - ○ **Use Mira to support** by healing allies and casting protective spells.
- **Coordinating Abilities**: In tactical mode, direct each companion's abilities to focus on demon vulnerabilities. For example, assign Elara's **Freeze** to slow down a Rage Demon or Taryn's **Smite** to weaken a Desire Demon.

5. Handling Possessed Spirits and Corrupted Entities

- **Understanding Possession**: Some spirits may become corrupted or possessed, turning them hostile. These entities retain some of their spirit-like qualities but have been twisted by a demonic force, making them dangerous.
- **Signs of Corruption**: Possessed spirits have an unstable, flickering appearance, often shifting between calm and aggressive forms.
- **Combat Tactics for Possessed Spirits**:
  - ○ **Use Anti-Corruption Abilities**: Abilities like **Spirit Ward** reduce the damage received from corrupted entities, making them essential when fighting possessed spirits.
  - ○ **Attack During Vulnerable Phases**: Possessed spirits may reveal weaker points when shifting forms. Time your attacks during these moments to maximize damage.

6. Engaging in Conversations with Neutral or Benevolent Spirits

- **Recognizing Benevolent Spirits**: Neutral or benevolent spirits may offer valuable information, request aid, or ask questions that test your character's values.
- **Responding to Spirit Questions**: These spirits may ask about your intentions or motivations. Choose responses that reflect honesty and curiosity to gain their trust.
  - ○ **Selecting Dialogue**: Choose thoughtful or compassionate dialogue options, then press "X" (PlayStation), "A" (Xbox), or left-click (PC) to respond.
- **Potential Rewards from Spirits**: Helpful spirits sometimes reward players with Veilguard relics, temporary buffs, or rare lore entries that enrich the game's story.

7. Managing Fade Corruption from Demon Encounters

- **Understanding Fade Corruption**: Prolonged exposure to demon encounters or lingering in Veilguard zones can lead to Fade corruption, which drains stamina or mana over time and weakens your defenses.
- **Using Veil Wards to Counter Corruption**: Veil Wards are items that reduce or negate the effects of Fade corruption for a limited time.
  - ○ **Activating a Veil Ward**: Open your inventory, select a Veil Ward, and press "X" (PlayStation), "A" (Xbox), or left-click (PC) to use it before entering a corrupted area or engaging with demons.

- **Monitoring Corruption Levels**: Watch your stamina and mana bars during demon encounters. If they start depleting rapidly, consider using additional protection items or retreating from the zone temporarily.

8. Special Abilities for Interacting with Spirits and Demons

- **Veil Strike**: A melee ability that disrupts demon magic, making it ideal for fighting Fade creatures.
    - **How to Use**: Assign **Veil Strike** to a quick slot and activate it during close-range combat with demons.
- **Spirit Ward**: A defensive ability that reduces incoming damage from spirits and demons, providing essential protection in Fade-heavy areas.
    - **How to Equip**: Open the abilities menu, assign **Spirit Ward** to a quick slot, and activate it when facing multiple Fade creatures.
- **Fade Shroud**: Allows you to phase temporarily, avoiding demon attacks while regenerating mana or stamina.
    - **How to Activate**: Equip **Fade Shroud** in a quick slot and press the corresponding button during battle. Use it to reposition or avoid powerful attacks from demons.

9. Tips for Avoiding Demon Manipulation

- **Beware of Desire and Envy Demons**: Some demons may try to manipulate you through promises or threats. Desire demons, for example, might offer knowledge or power in exchange for allowing them to remain in the world.
- **Choosing Dialogue Carefully**: When engaging with these manipulative demons, avoid dialogue options that express curiosity or willingness to bargain. Instead, select responses that affirm your character's resolve to banish them.
    - **Confirming Dialogue Choices**: Use the dialogue wheel to select resolute responses, then press "X" (PlayStation), "A" (Xbox), or left-click (PC) to confirm.
- **Using Companions for Insight**: Companions like Lyra and Taryn have experience with the Fade and may provide insights or warnings about certain demons. Speak with them after encountering a demon to gain additional perspective.

10. Rewards for Successfully Banishing Demons

- **Veilguard Relics and Items**: Many demons guard Veilguard relics or powerful artifacts that can enhance your Veil-based abilities or grant temporary boosts in Veilguard zones.
    - **Collecting Relics**: After defeating a demon, approach the relic or item they were guarding and press "X" (PlayStation), "A" (Xbox), or "E" (PC) to collect it.
- **Experience and Skill Progression**: Banishing demons grants experience points, which help level up your character and unlock new abilities. Regularly check your skill tree after demon encounters to see if any new Veil abilities or upgrades are available.

○ **How to Check Skill Tree**: Access your character menu by pressing "C" (PC), "Options" (PlayStation), or "Menu" (Xbox), then navigate to the skills tab to upgrade abilities.

Summary of Interacting with Spirits and Demons

- **Approach Spirits with Respect**: Spirits may offer lore, blessings, or assistance if you show empathy and curiosity.
- **Prepare for Demons**: Equip Veilguard abilities, use tactical positioning, and exploit demon weaknesses to gain an advantage.
- **Manage Corruption and Protect Yourself**: Use Veil Wards and watch your stamina and mana levels to minimize the effects of Fade corruption.
- **Claim Rewards and Progress**: Defeating demons and interacting with spirits can yield valuable relics, experience points, and insights into the Fade.

Interacting with spirits and demons in *The Veilguard* provides valuable insights, powerful rewards, and thrilling challenges. By understanding the nature of these entities and using the right strategies, you'll be able to navigate Veilguard zones confidently, harness the magic of the Veil, and protect yourself from the dangers of the Fade. Enjoy the depth and mystery these interactions bring to your journey in Thedas!

Hidden Veilguard Relics and Artifacts

In *Dragon Age: The Veilguard*, hidden relics and artifacts within Veilguard zones offer powerful enhancements and insights into the magic and mysteries of the Veil. These valuable items provide boosts to your abilities, unlock exclusive Veilguard powers, and strengthen your defenses against Fade creatures. Finding and using these relics and artifacts can greatly impact your journey through the game. Here's an in-depth guide on locating, collecting, and utilizing these hidden treasures.

1. Identifying Veilguard Relics and Artifacts

- **What They Look Like**: Veilguard relics and artifacts often emit a distinct glow, sometimes with swirling energy patterns or faint, shimmering light. They may also be surrounded by protective barriers or guarded by spirits or demons.
- **Common Locations**: Relics and artifacts are frequently found near Veil rifts, hidden paths, or ancient ruins within Veilguard zones.
- **How to Spot Them on the Map**: Some Veilguard relics are marked with icons on your map, resembling a small rune or star symbol. Press "M" on PC, the touchpad on PlayStation, or "View" on Xbox to access your map and identify relic locations if they're highlighted.

2. Types of Veilguard Relics and Artifacts

- **Empowering Relics**: These relics enhance your Veilguard abilities, such as increasing the duration of **Fade Shroud** or boosting the damage of **Veil Strike**.
- **Protective Artifacts**: Protective artifacts reduce the effects of Fade corruption or grant temporary immunity to certain types of magic. These are ideal for exploring corruption-heavy areas.
- **Lore Artifacts**: Some artifacts contain lore or historical records about the Veil, the Fade, and the Veilguard. Collecting these can reveal unique backstories or unlock special dialogue options.
- **Temporary Buff Relics**: Certain relics provide temporary buffs, such as increased stamina, mana regeneration, or enhanced resistance to spirit attacks. These effects last until you leave the Veilguard zone or are defeated in battle.

3. Finding and Collecting Relics

- **Exploring Hidden Paths**: Many relics are tucked away along hidden paths or behind environmental puzzles. These paths may be obscured by illusions or camouflaged by the surroundings.
  - **How to Access Hidden Paths**: Use **Fade Sight** to reveal hidden paths. Equip this ability in your quick slot, and activate it by pressing the assigned button. Fade Sight will reveal hidden symbols, doors, or pathways that lead to relics.
- **Solving Environmental Puzzles**: Some relics are locked behind Veil puzzles that require activating runes, aligning symbols, or interacting with objects in a specific sequence.
  - **Solving Runes and Symbols**: Approach each rune or symbol and press "X" (PlayStation), "A" (Xbox), or "E" (PC) to interact. Follow clues found nearby to complete the puzzle, which often involves examining markings on walls or the ground.

4. Guarded Relics: Overcoming Spirit and Demon Defenders

- **Encountering Guardians**: Certain powerful relics are protected by spirits or demons. These entities guard the relic fiercely and will attack anyone attempting to claim it.
- **Defeating Guardians**: Use Veil-based abilities, such as **Veil Strike** to disrupt the guardians' powers or **Spirit Ward** to reduce the damage they inflict.
  - **Using Tactical Mode**: When facing multiple guardians, activate tactical mode by pressing the touchpad (PlayStation), "View" (Xbox), or "T" (PC) to position your companions and manage abilities. Position your tank, like Lorian, to draw attention while Elara or Rylan attack from a distance.
- **Claiming the Relic**: Once the guardians are defeated, approach the relic and press "X" (PlayStation), "A" (Xbox), or "E" (PC) to collect it. Some relics may also require a specific ability to interact with, such as **Fade Shroud** for passing through barriers.

5. Using Collected Relics and Artifacts

- **Accessing Relic Effects**: After collecting a relic, its effects will automatically apply or become accessible in your abilities menu. Relic bonuses can include enhanced Veil abilities, increased resistance to Fade damage, or temporary boosts.
- **Equipping Artifacts**: Some artifacts, like protective amulets or Veilguard rings, must be equipped to provide benefits.
  - **How to Equip**: Open your inventory by pressing "I" (PC), "Options" (PlayStation), or "Menu" (Xbox). Select the artifact from your inventory and press "X" (PlayStation), "A" (Xbox), or click (PC) to equip it.
- **Using Lore Artifacts**: If you collect an artifact containing lore, you may notice new journal entries or dialogue options with certain NPCs. These entries deepen your understanding of the Veil and the Fade and sometimes open up new quests.

6. Temporary Buffs and Strategic Use

- **Understanding Buff Duration**: Some relics grant temporary buffs, such as increased mana regeneration or enhanced spell resistance. These effects remain active until you leave the Veilguard zone or until they are overridden by another relic's buff.
- **Choosing the Right Time**: Activate these relics before facing a tough encounter or entering a Veil-heavy area.
  - **Activating Buffs**: Temporary buffs automatically activate upon collecting the relic. To check active buffs, view your status menu, accessed by pressing "C" (PC), "Options" (PlayStation), or "Menu" (Xbox).

7. Relic-Triggered Veil Abilities

- **Unlocking Veil-Specific Powers**: Some relics grant Veilguard-exclusive abilities, like **Fade Shroud** or **Veil Strike**. These abilities are particularly powerful in Veilguard zones, providing both offensive and defensive benefits against Fade creatures.
  - **Equipping and Using New Abilities**: Open the abilities menu and assign newly unlocked Veil abilities to a quick slot. Activate these abilities by pressing the corresponding button in combat.
- **Examples of Veil-Exclusive Abilities**:
  - **Fade Shroud**: Allows temporary invisibility and protection from Fade creatures.
  - **Veil Strike**: A powerful attack that disrupts magical enemies, ideal for battling demons and corrupted spirits.
  - **Spirit Ward**: Reduces incoming damage from Fade creatures and is especially useful when fighting multiple enemies.

8. Locating Rare Veilguard Relics

- **Special Relic Locations**: Rare Veilguard relics are usually hidden in hard-to-reach areas, such as the deepest parts of Veilguard zones or behind advanced puzzles. Some are also tied to specific quests.
- **Unlocking Relic-Exclusive Quests**: Certain rare relics can only be accessed by completing related quests. For example, a relic guarded by an ancient spirit might require you to complete a test of wisdom or courage.
  - **Triggering Quests**: Approach key NPCs or spirits to initiate relic-related quests. Press "X" (PlayStation), "A" (Xbox), or "E" (PC) to begin the conversation and accept the quest.
- **Benefits of Rare Relics**: These powerful items offer significant bonuses, such as permanently reducing corruption effects or increasing your resistance to demon magic by a large margin.

9. Interacting with Relic-Granting Spirits

- **Conversing with Benevolent Spirits**: Certain benevolent spirits grant relics or artifacts if you engage them respectfully and show understanding. They may offer clues or ask questions that test your knowledge of the Fade.
  - **Initiating Conversation**: Approach the spirit and press "X" (PlayStation), "A" (Xbox), or "E" (PC) to start a conversation. Choose dialogue options that reflect empathy or curiosity.
- **Gaining Relics as Rewards**: If you successfully answer a spirit's questions or assist them, they may reward you with a relic or artifact without a fight.

10. Tracking Collected Relics and Artifacts

- **Viewing Collected Relics**: You can review all collected relics and their effects in your inventory or journal.
  - **How to Check Inventory**: Open your inventory by pressing "I" (PC), "Options" (PlayStation), or "Menu" (Xbox). Relics and artifacts will be stored under the "Special Items" tab.
- **Checking Relic Buffs and Passive Effects**: Passive relic effects, such as increased Veil resistance or enhanced Fade abilities, are listed in your character's status menu.
  - **How to View Status Effects**: Press "C" (PC), "Options" (PlayStation), or "Menu" (Xbox) to open your character menu, where all active relic effects and buffs will be displayed.

Summary of Hidden Veilguard Relics and Artifacts

- **Recognize and Find Relics**: Identify relics by their glowing or swirling appearance, and locate them in Veilguard zones marked on your map.
- **Overcome Challenges to Collect Relics**: Use Fade Sight for hidden paths, solve puzzles, and defeat spirit or demon guardians to access relics.
- **Equip and Activate Effects**: Some relics grant passive benefits, while others unlock Veilguard abilities you can equip in combat.

- **Utilize Temporary Buffs Strategically**: Collect relics that provide temporary boosts before tough encounters or Veil-heavy areas.

By mastering the art of finding and using Veilguard relics and artifacts, you'll gain powerful enhancements, exclusive abilities, and valuable lore that enhance your journey through *The Veilguard*. Enjoy uncovering the secrets hidden in these mystical zones and strengthening your character with the magic of the Veil!

Veilguard-Exclusive Abilities and Enhancements

Dragon Age: The Veilguard introduces a range of Veilguard-exclusive abilities and enhancements that empower players to manipulate the Veil, protect themselves from Fade corruption, and combat Fade creatures with specialized skills. These abilities unlock new tactical options, providing unique offensive and defensive advantages in Veilguard zones. Here's an in-depth guide on acquiring, equipping, and using these powerful abilities and enhancements to their fullest potential.

1. Unlocking Veilguard-Exclusive Abilities

- **Completing Veilguard Quests**: Veilguard-exclusive abilities are often unlocked by progressing through specific Veilguard quests. As you close Veil rifts, interact with Veilguard relics, and complete main story events, you'll gradually acquire these special powers.
  - **Tracking Quest Progress**: To monitor your progress, access your quest log by pressing "J" on PC, the touchpad on PlayStation, or "View" on Xbox. Veilguard quests that unlock abilities are typically marked with a Veil symbol.
- **Collecting Veilguard Relics**: Certain abilities are tied to powerful relics hidden within Veilguard zones. Finding these relics and interacting with them grants access to exclusive powers.
  - **Collecting Relics**: Approach the relic and press "X" (PlayStation), "A" (Xbox), or "E" (PC) to activate it. The relic will either unlock a new ability directly or add it to your skill tree.

2. Core Veilguard Abilities and Their Uses

- **Veil Strike**
  - **Description**: Veil Strike is a melee ability that disrupts enemies with Fade-based energy, causing them to stagger and weakening their defenses. This attack is particularly effective against demons and corrupted spirits.
  - **How to Use**: Equip Veil Strike by opening your abilities menu. Assign it to a quick slot, then activate it by pressing the corresponding quick slot button. Use this ability on close-range enemies to stagger them, opening them up for follow-up attacks.
- **Fade Shroud**

- **Description**: Fade Shroud allows you to briefly phase into the Fade, becoming invisible and invulnerable to physical attacks. This ability regenerates mana or stamina while active, making it a valuable tool for repositioning or avoiding heavy attacks.
  - **How to Activate**: Equip Fade Shroud in your quick slot. During combat, press the quick slot button to activate it. You'll gain temporary invisibility, allowing you to move safely or regain resources.
- **Spirit Ward**
  - **Description**: Spirit Ward is a defensive ability that reduces incoming damage from Fade creatures. It creates a protective barrier around you and your allies, making it particularly useful in Veilguard zones filled with spirits and demons.
  - **How to Equip and Use**: Assign Spirit Ward to a quick slot, then press the corresponding button to activate it. Use this ability when surrounded by Fade creatures to reduce their damage output and keep your party safe.

3. Supportive Veil Abilities for Enhanced Survival

- **Fade Sight**
  - **Description**: Fade Sight reveals hidden pathways, symbols, and objects that are otherwise invisible to the naked eye. This ability is essential for uncovering hidden relics and solving Veil-related puzzles.
  - **Using Fade Sight**: Equip Fade Sight to a quick slot, then press the button to activate it. Use it in Veilguard zones to reveal hidden paths or interactable symbols that may lead to relics and artifacts.
- **Veil Shield**
  - **Description**: Veil Shield creates a temporary barrier that absorbs a portion of all incoming magical and physical damage. It's an excellent choice for prolonged encounters in Veil-heavy areas.
  - **Activating Veil Shield**: Assign Veil Shield to a quick slot. During combat, press the assigned button to activate it. The shield lasts for a limited time, absorbing damage and giving you a chance to heal or reposition.

4. Offensive Veil Abilities for Maximum Impact

- **Veil Pulse**

- **Description**: Veil Pulse emits a burst of Fade energy, damaging all enemies in a radius around you. This ability is highly effective for crowd control, especially when facing groups of low-health enemies.
- **How to Equip and Use**: Equip Veil Pulse in your quick slots, then press the button during battle to release a shockwave. Position yourself in the center of enemy groups for maximum impact.

- **Rift Slash**
  - **Description**: Rift Slash is a heavy melee strike that disrupts enemy defenses and deals increased damage to magical foes. This ability is particularly powerful against Veil creatures, helping to break down their barriers and resistances.
  - **Using Rift Slash**: Assign Rift Slash to a quick slot. Use it against powerful Fade creatures, especially those with high defenses. This ability is best used on tougher enemies that require high-damage attacks.

5. Enhancements to Veilguard Abilities

- **Fade-Infused Weaponry**
  - **Description**: Fade-infused weaponry grants a passive enhancement to your weapon, imbuing it with Veil energy that deals bonus damage to Fade creatures.
  - **Unlocking Fade-Infused Weapons**: Fade-infused weaponry can be unlocked by collecting certain Veilguard relics or completing key Veilguard quests. After unlocking, the bonus damage is automatically applied to your weapon.
  - **Using in Combat**: These weapons deal additional damage to demons and spirits, making them invaluable in Veilguard zones.
- **Corruption Resistance**
  - **Description**: Corruption Resistance reduces the effects of Veil corruption, preventing stamina or mana drain when exposed to corrupting magic.
  - **How to Acquire**: This enhancement is granted by specific artifacts found in Veilguard zones. Once acquired, Corruption Resistance becomes a passive ability, automatically reducing the impact of Fade corruption.

6. Strategic Use of Veil Abilities in Combat

- **Combining Abilities for Maximum Effectiveness**:
  - Use **Veil Strike** to stagger an enemy, then follow up with **Rift Slash** for high damage against weakened foes.
  - Activate **Spirit Ward** when surrounded by multiple Fade creatures, reducing incoming damage while you and your companions target high-priority enemies.
- **Positioning with Fade Shroud**: Fade Shroud is ideal for repositioning in tight spaces. Activate it to phase through enemies and avoid attacks, then reappear in a more advantageous location.

- ○ **How to Reposition**: Equip Fade Shroud in a quick slot, and activate it when enemies close in. Move to a safer position while invisible, then deactivate to re-engage in combat.

7. Veilguard Enhancements and Team Synergy

- **Supporting Companions with Veil Abilities**:
  - ○ **Spirit Ward** can protect the entire team from magical attacks, making it ideal for battles with multiple magic-using enemies. Activate it when you're near your companions to maximize the area of effect.
  - ○ **Veil Pulse** can be used to interrupt enemy casters or knock back approaching enemies, giving ranged companions like Rylan or Elara more room to attack.
- **Enhancing Companion Abilities**: Veilguard enhancements often increase the effectiveness of companion skills. For example, Taryn's anti-magic attacks are stronger when used in tandem with **Veil Strike**, while Mira's healing becomes more efficient under **Spirit Ward**'s protection.

8. Customizing and Upgrading Veilguard Abilities

- **Skill Tree Upgrades**: Veilguard abilities can often be upgraded in your skill tree, adding new effects or increasing their power.
  - ○ **Accessing Skill Tree**: Open your character menu by pressing "C" (PC), "Options" (PlayStation), or "Menu" (Xbox), then navigate to the Veilguard skill tree. Invest skill points to unlock upgrades like increased range for **Veil Pulse** or longer duration for **Fade Shroud**.
- **Examples of Upgrades**:
  - ○ **Veil Strike – Enhanced Disruption**: Increases the duration of stagger, allowing more time for follow-up attacks.
  - ○ **Fade Shroud – Extended Phase**: Lengthens the duration of invisibility and increases stamina regeneration while active.

9. Using Veilguard Abilities in Puzzle and Exploration Scenarios

- **Unlocking Hidden Paths with Fade Sight**: In addition to revealing hidden paths, Fade Sight can highlight puzzle elements in Veilguard zones. Use it in exploration areas to locate Veil rifts or clues.
- **Bypassing Obstacles with Fade Shroud**: Certain barriers can be phased through with Fade Shroud. Activate Fade Shroud by pressing its quick slot button to pass through, accessing otherwise unreachable areas or shortcuts.
- **Solving Veil-Based Puzzles**: Veilguard abilities are also essential for solving puzzles. Use **Veil Strike** to activate ancient runes or **Veil Pulse** to power mystical structures, unlocking doors or triggering hidden mechanisms.

10. Mastering Veilguard Abilities for Boss Fights

- **Using Veilguard Abilities Against Bosses**: Many Veilguard zone bosses are vulnerable to specific abilities, like **Rift Slash** or **Spirit Ward**. Experiment with different abilities to identify which are most effective against each boss.
  - **Example Boss Strategy**:
    - **Fade Titan**: Use **Veil Strike** to weaken its defenses, then follow up with **Rift Slash** for massive damage.
    - **Corrupted Spirit Lord**: Activate **Spirit Ward** to protect against its magic, and use **Veil Pulse** to disrupt its spellcasting.
- **Timing Abilities for Maximum Impact**: Many Veilguard abilities have cooldowns, so use them strategically. Apply **Spirit Ward** at the start of battle, and follow up with **Veil Pulse** once enemies are grouped around you.

Summary of Veilguard-Exclusive Abilities and Enhancements

- **Unlock and Equip Veil Abilities**: Gain access to Veil abilities by completing quests, collecting relics, and progressing in the Veilguard storyline.
- **Use Core Abilities for Combat and Defense**: Abilities like **Veil Strike**, **Fade Shroud**, and **Spirit Ward** provide essential offensive and defensive options.
- **Enhance and Customize Abilities**: Invest in skill tree upgrades to increase ability potency, duration, and effects.
- **Utilize Abilities in Exploration and Boss Fights**: Apply Veil abilities in puzzle-solving and major encounters to unlock areas, defeat bosses, and enhance your journey in Veilguard zones.

With a mastery of Veilguard-exclusive abilities and enhancements, you'll be well-equipped to face the challenges of the Fade, counter powerful enemies, and unlock hidden secrets. Embrace the power of the Veil and enjoy the depth it brings to your adventure through Thedas!

CHAPTER 9

Crafting and Resource Gathering

In this chapter, you'll learn the essential skills for crafting and gathering resources in *Dragon Age: The Veilguard*. Discover where to find key materials across Thedas, along with tips on crafting powerful weapons, armor, and potions. You'll also explore how to enhance your equipment with special runes and techniques for farming rare materials. Whether you're looking to strengthen your gear or create unique elixirs, this guide provides everything you need to master the art of crafting and resource gathering.

Materials and Their Locations

In *Dragon Age: The Veilguard*, gathering materials is essential for crafting weapons, armor, potions, and enhancing gear with runes. Each region in Thedas offers unique resources, and knowing where to find them is crucial for creating powerful equipment. This guide will help you identify key materials, locate them efficiently, and maximize your crafting potential.

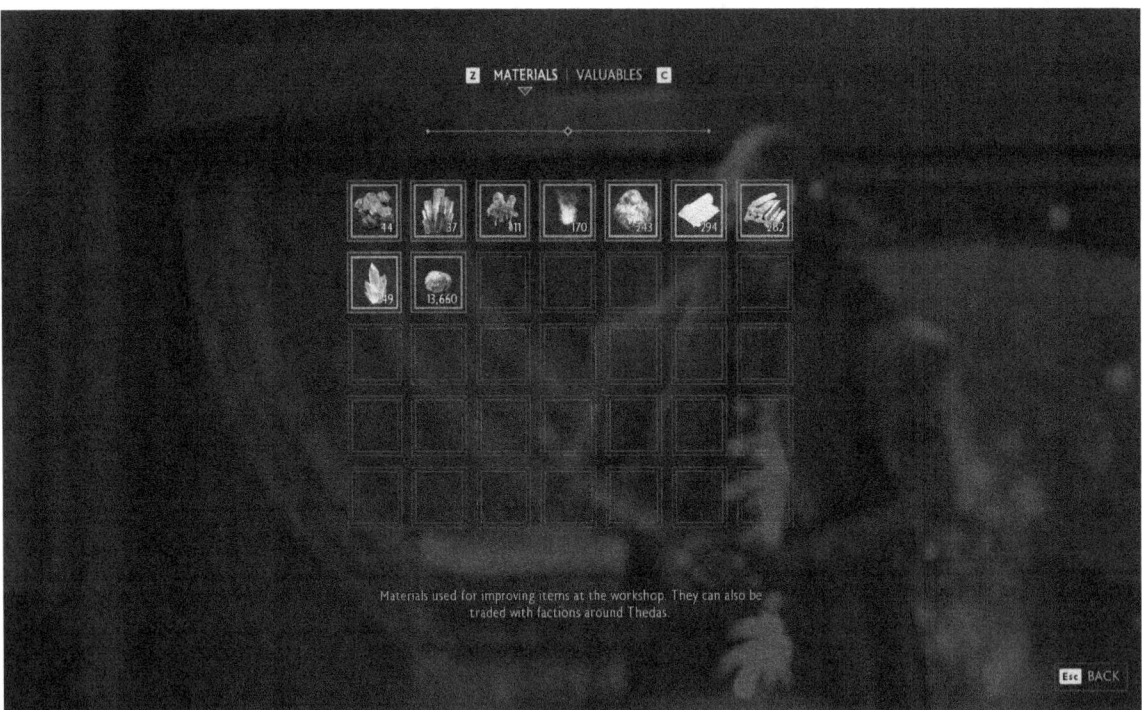

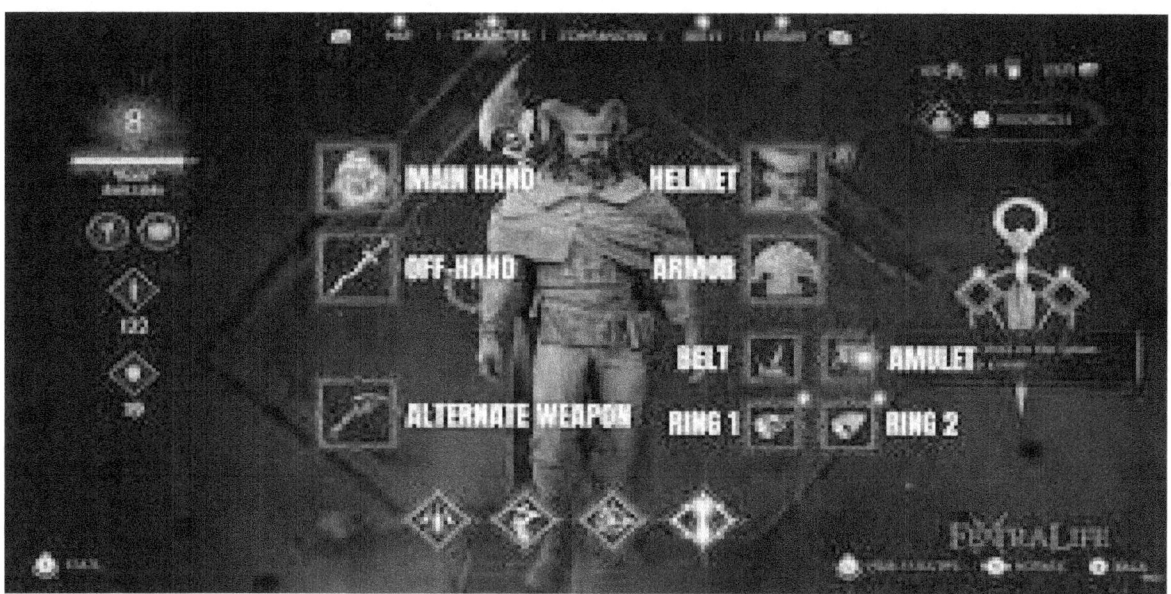

1. Basic Materials and Common Gathering Locations

- **Iron**: A fundamental crafting metal, used for basic weapons and armor.
  - **Where to Find**: Iron deposits are commonly found in **Stormguard Plains** and **Brightfall Forest**.
  - **How to Gather**: Approach an iron deposit and press "X" (PlayStation), "A" (Xbox), or "E" (PC) to gather. Iron deposits respawn after a certain period, so revisit these areas as needed.
- **Leather**: Used in crafting light armor, leather is gathered from animal hides.
  - **Where to Find**: Found by hunting animals in **Westport Meadows** and **Greenwood Thicket**.
  - **How to Gather**: Defeat animals like wolves and deer, then approach their bodies to gather leather. Press "X" (PlayStation), "A" (Xbox), or "E" (PC) when prompted.

2. Intermediate Materials for Advanced Crafting

- **Silverite**: A higher-quality metal used for crafting enhanced armor and weapons.
  - **Where to Find**: Silverite veins are found in the **Misty Peaks** and **Ironwood Outpost** areas.
  - **How to Gather**: Locate silverite veins marked by a silver hue. Approach and press "X" (PlayStation), "A" (Xbox), or "E" (PC) to collect. Silverite is rarer than iron, so keep an eye out for respawn points.
- **Blood Lotus**: A key herb for crafting powerful health potions and elixirs.
  - **Where to Find**: Found near water sources in **Veiled Shore** and **Shaded Lake**.
  - **How to Gather**: Look for bright red flowers near water and approach them. Press "X" (PlayStation), "A" (Xbox), or "E" (PC) to gather. Blood Lotus is fragile, so gather it quickly and in larger quantities.

3. Rare Materials and Exclusive Locations

- **Dragonbone**: Used for the most powerful weapons, dragonbone is extremely rare and often guarded by dragons.
  - **Where to Find**: Found in **Dragon's Den** and **Ashen Crag** regions. Some dragonbone can also be acquired by defeating dragons in specific areas.
  - **How to Gather**: Approach dragonbone deposits after defeating dragons or find loose dragonbone in dragon nests. Press "X" (PlayStation), "A" (Xbox), or "E" (PC) to collect.
- **Fade-Touched Materials**: These enchanted materials add magical effects to crafted items.
  - **Where to Find**: Collected from spirits or demons in **Veilguard zones**. Fade-touched iron, leather, and other materials are dropped by powerful Fade creatures.
  - **How to Gather**: Defeat spirits or demons, then approach the drop location to collect. Press "X" (PlayStation), "A" (Xbox), or "E" (PC) to acquire. These materials are rare, so gather them whenever you encounter Veil creatures.

4. Region-Specific Resources and Unique Uses

- **Elfroot**: An herb used in most healing potions and medicinal items.
  - **Where to Find**: Found abundantly in **Greenwood Thicket** and **Shaded Lake** regions.
  - **How to Gather**: Look for small green plants along forest paths and near rocks. Approach them and press "X" (PlayStation), "A" (Xbox), or "E" (PC) to collect.
- **Obsidian**: A dark mineral used to craft durable armor with high defense against physical damage.
  - **Where to Find**: Found in volcanic areas like **Ashen Crag** and **Charred Pass**.
  - **How to Gather**: Look for black, glassy stones along rocky areas. Approach and press "X" (PlayStation), "A" (Xbox), or "E" (PC) to gather. Obsidian is durable, making it ideal for heavy armor crafting.

5. Exotic and Magical Materials in Veilguard Zones

- **Veil Quartz**: A crystal imbued with Fade energy, useful for crafting magical enhancements.
  - **Where to Find**: Found in Veilguard zones, particularly near Veil rifts in areas like **Veiled Shore** and **Shattered Vale**.
  - **How to Gather**: Approach Veil quartz clusters emitting a faint glow and press "X" (PlayStation), "A" (Xbox), or "E" (PC) to gather. Veil quartz is valuable for crafting items that resist magic.
- **Spirit Essence**: Extracted from defeated spirits, this essence adds powerful enchantments to weapons and armor.
  - **Where to Find**: Dropped by defeated spirits in Veilguard zones like **Fade-Worn Woods** and **Silvered Spire**.

- How to Gather: Defeat spirits, then approach the drop and press "X" (PlayStation), "A" (Xbox), or "E" (PC) to collect. Spirit essence enhances crafted items with unique magical effects, such as increased mana regeneration.

6. Tracking and Marking Resource Locations

- **Using the Map for Resource Tracking**: Many regions will highlight resource-rich areas on your map. These appear as icons representing the material type, such as a herb icon for plants or a pickaxe for metals.
  - **Accessing the Map**: Open your map by pressing "M" on PC, the touchpad on PlayStation, or "View" on Xbox. Resource locations are marked, allowing you to set waypoints to reach them more easily.
- **Setting Waypoints for Efficiency**: Once you identify a resource location, set a waypoint to mark your destination.
  - **How to Set Waypoints**: Select a resource icon on the map, then press "X" (PlayStation), "A" (Xbox), or right-click (PC) to set a waypoint. This will guide you directly to the resource location.

7. Tips for Efficient Material Gathering

- **Plan Resource Runs**: Combine material gathering with other quests in the same area to save time. For example, if a quest takes you near Greenwood Thicket, gather elfroot and leather while completing it.
- **Use Companions for Assistance**: Certain companions may provide bonuses to gathering rates or improve your chances of finding rare items. Lyra, for instance, has a Veil sense ability that highlights magical resources in Veilguard zones.
  - **Activating Companion Abilities**: If a companion offers gathering bonuses, bring them along and let them assist in Veilguard zones or resource-rich areas. Their abilities activate automatically as you gather.

8. Special Gathering Conditions in Veilguard Zones

- **Corruption Effects**: Gathering materials in Veilguard zones exposes you to Fade corruption, which drains stamina or mana over time.
  - **Using Veil Wards**: Protect yourself by activating Veil Wards from your inventory. Open your inventory, select a Veil Ward, and press "X" (PlayStation), "A" (Xbox), or left-click (PC) to apply the protection.
- **Timed Gathering Windows**: Some materials only appear at certain times or under specific conditions, like night or during Veil disturbances.
  - **Observing Conditions**: Pay attention to environmental cues, such as a change in lighting or magical auras, which indicate the presence of rare resources.

Summary of Materials and Their Locations

- **Basic Materials**: Iron and leather are common resources for early crafting and found in accessible areas like Stormguard Plains and Greenwood Thicket.
- **Intermediate Resources**: Silverite and Blood Lotus are valuable materials found in locations like Misty Peaks and Shaded Lake.
- **Rare and Exotic Materials**: Dragonbone, Fade-touched materials, and Spirit Essence are rarer, collected from challenging areas like Dragon's Den or Veilguard zones.
- **Efficient Gathering**: Use your map, set waypoints, and combine gathering with quests to save time and gather materials effectively.

With this guide to gathering materials, you'll be well-prepared to collect resources across Thedas, craft powerful items, and enhance your journey in *The Veilguard*. Enjoy exploring, gathering, and making the most of what Thedas has to offer!

Crafting Weapons and Armor

In *Dragon Age: The Veilguard*, crafting powerful weapons and armor can give you a significant edge in battle. Crafting allows you to customize your equipment to suit your playstyle, enhancing your offensive and defensive capabilities with the materials you gather across Thedas. Here's a complete guide on crafting weapons and armor, from selecting materials to enhancing your gear for maximum effectiveness.

1. Accessing the Crafting Station

- **Locating Crafting Stations**: Crafting stations are typically found in main hubs, such as **Stormguard Keep** and **Brightfall Village**, as well as in some smaller outposts.
  - **How to Interact**: Approach the crafting station and press "X" (PlayStation), "A" (Xbox), or "E" (PC) to begin crafting.
- **Navigating the Crafting Menu**: Once you interact with the station, a menu will open with options to craft weapons, armor, and accessories.
  - **Selecting a Category**: Use the directional pad (PlayStation/Xbox) or mouse (PC) to navigate to the "Weapons" or "Armor" tab and select the item type you want to craft.

2. Choosing a Weapon or Armor Blueprint

- **Understanding Blueprints**: Each weapon or armor piece requires a blueprint, which dictates the base stats and material requirements for crafting.
  - **Finding Blueprints**: Blueprints can be purchased from merchants, found in chests, or rewarded through quests. Some high-tier blueprints are only available in Veilguard zones.

- **How to Equip a Blueprint**: In the crafting menu, navigate to "Blueprints," select your preferred weapon or armor blueprint, and press "X" (PlayStation), "A" (Xbox), or left-click (PC) to equip it.
- **Choosing the Right Blueprint**: Blueprints vary by material requirements, base stats, and additional effects. For example, a "Heavy Armor" blueprint may require obsidian and iron, while a "Mage Staff" blueprint requires magical materials like spirit essence.
  - **Matching Playstyle**: Choose blueprints based on your character's role (e.g., warrior, mage, or rogue) to maximize the effectiveness of crafted gear.

3. Selecting Materials for Crafting

- **Understanding Material Slots**: Each blueprint has material slots with specific categories, such as metal, leather, or essence. The material you use in each slot affects the item's stats.
- **Primary Material**: This material dictates the core attributes of your item, such as damage for weapons or armor rating for defensive gear.
  - **Example**: Using **Dragonbone** as a primary material provides high attack power for weapons, while **Silverite** boosts armor rating.
  - **How to Assign**: Highlight the primary material slot, then select a material from your inventory and press "X" (PlayStation), "A" (Xbox), or left-click (PC) to assign it.
- **Secondary Materials**: These slots allow for additional attributes, such as elemental resistances or critical hit chances.
  - **Example**: Adding **Fade-Touched Leather** to a weapon can grant bonus critical hit rate, while **Veil Quartz** in armor can add magic resistance.
  - **Assigning Secondary Materials**: Highlight a secondary slot, choose a material, and press the appropriate button to apply it. Try different combinations to create gear suited to your combat needs.

4. Crafting Weapons: Key Considerations

- **Choosing the Right Weapon Type**:
  - **Warriors**: Use heavy, damage-focused weapons like greatswords or hammers.
  - **Mages**: Opt for staves that boost spell damage and mana regeneration.
  - **Rogues**: Choose daggers or bows, which prioritize speed, critical hits, and stealth.
  - **How to Select a Weapon**: In the crafting menu, navigate to the weapon type you prefer and select it by pressing "X" (PlayStation), "A" (Xbox), or left-click (PC).
- **Customizing Weapon Attributes**:
  - **Boosting Damage**: Use high-quality metals like **Silverite** or **Dragonbone** to increase weapon damage.

- **Adding Elemental Effects**: Certain materials, like **Veil Quartz** or **Blood Lotus Essence**, add elemental damage to weapons. For example, a staff crafted with **Blood Lotus Essence** may deal additional fire damage.
- **Adding Critical Hit Bonuses**: Using materials like **Fade-Touched Iron** can increase the weapon's critical hit chance, making it ideal for rogues or fast attackers.
- **How to Add Bonuses**: Choose a material with the desired bonus and assign it to the relevant slot during crafting.

5. Crafting Armor: Important Tips

- **Selecting Armor Type**:
  - **Heavy Armor**: Provides high physical defense and is ideal for warriors and tanks.
  - **Light Armor**: Prioritizes mobility and is best suited for rogues.
  - **Mage Robes**: Offer elemental resistances and mana regeneration, ideal for mages.
  - **Choosing Armor Type**: In the crafting menu, go to the "Armor" tab and select the type you want to craft by pressing "X" (PlayStation), "A" (Xbox), or left-click (PC).
- **Maximizing Armor Bonuses**:
  - **Increasing Defense**: Use **Obsidian** or **Iron** to maximize armor rating for tank characters.
  - **Adding Magical Resistances**: Materials like **Veil Quartz** or **Spirit Essence** grant magic resistance, making them ideal for mage or mixed-magic zones.
  - **Adding Stamina or Mana Boosts**: Adding **Elfroot Essence** or **Blood Lotus** can enhance stamina or mana regeneration, making these materials useful for characters that rely on heavy spellcasting or combat skills.
- **Equipping Extra Effects**: Some materials provide unique effects, like reducing damage from specific enemy types or boosting health regeneration.
  - **Example**: Use **Spirit Essence** to reduce damage from Fade creatures or **Dragon Scales** for increased health recovery.

6. Finalizing and Crafting the Item

- **Reviewing Material Choices**: Once you've assigned all materials to a blueprint, review the projected stats and effects to ensure they match your requirements.
  - **How to Review Stats**: In the crafting menu, scroll to the bottom of the blueprint to see the final stats. Adjust materials as needed to reach your desired outcome.
- **Crafting the Item**: When satisfied with the materials and stats, confirm your crafting choice.
  - **Crafting Confirmation**: Press "X" (PlayStation), "A" (Xbox), or "E" (PC) to confirm. The item will be added to your inventory.
- **Equipping the New Item**: After crafting, go to your inventory to equip the item.

- **How to Equip**: Open your inventory by pressing "I" (PC), "Options" (PlayStation), or "Menu" (Xbox), then select the item and press "X" (PlayStation), "A" (Xbox), or left-click (PC) to equip.

7. Enhancing Crafted Gear with Runes

- **Using Runes to Add Effects**: Runes grant additional effects to crafted weapons and armor, such as elemental damage or resistances.
- **Acquiring Runes**: Runes are often found as loot, rewards for quests, or can be crafted with rare materials in Veilguard zones.
- **Applying Runes**: To add a rune to a crafted item, access the "Rune" tab in the crafting menu. Select a rune, then apply it to an eligible item by pressing "X" (PlayStation), "A" (Xbox), or left-click (PC).
- **Examples of Rune Effects**:
    - **Fire Rune**: Adds fire damage to weapons, ideal against frost-based enemies.
    - **Frost Rune**: Adds cold resistance to armor, useful in areas with fire-based foes.

8. Crafting Tips for Optimal Results

- **Combine Materials for Synergy**: Use a mix of materials that boost each other's effects. For example, pairing **Fade-Touched Iron** with **Blood Lotus** can create gear with high critical hit rate and elemental damage.
- **Prioritize High-Quality Materials**: Rare materials, like **Dragonbone** or **Veil Quartz**, provide the highest bonuses, so save these for top-tier gear.
- **Craft for Specific Challenges**: Craft gear tailored to specific regions or enemies. For Veilguard zones, prioritize magic resistance and Veil-imbued materials to counter Fade creatures effectively.

Summary of Crafting Weapons and Armor

- **Access Crafting Stations**: Locate stations in major hubs to begin crafting, and gather materials from each region for variety.
- **Choose Blueprints and Materials**: Select blueprints that suit your role and gather appropriate materials to maximize your item's effectiveness.
- **Customize Attributes**: Use primary and secondary materials to boost damage, add resistances, or increase critical hit rates.
- **Enhance with Runes**: Add runes for extra elemental effects and resistances to further customize your gear.

Mastering weapon and armor crafting in *The Veilguard* allows you to create equipment tailored to your playstyle, giving you the advantage in battle and exploration. Enjoy building powerful, customized gear that enhances your journey through Thedas!

Creating Potions and Elixirs

Potions and elixirs are essential in *Dragon Age: The Veilguard*, providing healing, stamina regeneration, and various boosts that enhance your combat effectiveness. Crafting these items allows you to tailor your potion supply to meet the challenges of each mission and Veilguard zone. This guide covers everything you need to know about crafting potions and elixirs, including ingredient gathering, recipes, and the best uses for each type of potion.

1. Accessing the Potion Crafting Station

- **Locating Alchemy Stations**: Potion crafting stations are available in main hubs, such as **Stormguard Keep** and **Brightfall Village**, and are sometimes found in camps in exploration zones.
    - **How to Interact**: Approach the alchemy station and press "X" (PlayStation), "A" (Xbox), or "E" (PC) to open the crafting menu.
- **Navigating the Crafting Menu**: Once the menu is open, you'll see tabs for various types of potions, elixirs, and tonics.
    - **Selecting a Category**: Use the directional pad (PlayStation/Xbox) or mouse (PC) to navigate to the "Potions" or "Elixirs" tab and select the item type you want to craft.

2. Gathering Key Ingredients for Potions and Elixirs

- **Basic Ingredients**:
    - **Elfroot**: Essential for crafting basic healing potions, Elfroot is commonly found in forested regions like **Greenwood Thicket**.
        - **How to Gather**: Look for green plants along forest paths, approach, and press "X" (PlayStation), "A" (Xbox), or "E" (PC) to collect.
    - **Blood Lotus**: Used in stamina-restoring potions and some elixirs, Blood Lotus grows near water sources in **Shaded Lake** and **Veiled Shore**.
        - **How to Gather**: Approach the bright red flowers and press "X" (PlayStation), "A" (Xbox), or "E" (PC) to gather.
- **Advanced Ingredients**:
    - **Spindleweed**: Found in swampy areas, Spindleweed is used for crafting potent health and resistance potions.
        - **Where to Find**: Look for it in **Misty Marshes** and along riversides. Press "X" (PlayStation), "A" (Xbox), or "E" (PC) to collect.
    - **Fade-Touched Materials**: Rare, enchanted ingredients like Fade-touched elfroot or lotus are essential for Veilguard-exclusive elixirs, which provide magical effects.

- **Where to Find**: Defeat spirits and demons in Veilguard zones, then gather from the drops by pressing the interact button.

3. Crafting Healing Potions

- **Basic Healing Potion**:
  - **Ingredients**: Elfroot (1-2 units)
  - **Description**: Restores a portion of your health, making it a must-have for all characters.
  - **How to Craft**: In the potion crafting menu, select the "Basic Healing Potion" option and press "X" (PlayStation), "A" (Xbox), or "E" (PC) to craft. Once crafted, the potion will appear in your inventory.
  - **Usage**: Equip healing potions in the quick slot for easy access during combat. Press the quick slot button to use when needed.
- **Enhanced Healing Potion**:
  - **Ingredients**: Elfroot (2 units) and Spindleweed (1 unit)
  - **Description**: Restores a larger amount of health, ideal for tougher encounters.
  - **How to Craft**: Select the "Enhanced Healing Potion" option in the crafting menu and press the interact button to craft. Equip it as you would a basic healing potion.

4. Stamina and Mana Regeneration Elixirs

- **Stamina Potion**:
  - **Ingredients**: Blood Lotus (1-2 units)
  - **Description**: Restores stamina, allowing warriors and rogues to use abilities more frequently.
  - **How to Craft**: Navigate to the stamina potion option, select it, and press the crafting button. Equip the potion for quick use during combat.
  - **Usage**: Press the quick slot button to restore stamina instantly, keeping your combat abilities active during extended fights.
- **Mana Elixir**:
  - **Ingredients**: Fade-touched elfroot (1 unit) and Blood Lotus (1 unit)
  - **Description**: Restores mana, ideal for mages who need a steady supply of magical energy.
  - **How to Craft**: Select "Mana Elixir" in the elixirs tab and press the interact button to craft. Equip for quick access in your inventory.
  - **Usage**: Keep this elixir equipped in Veilguard zones where magic demand is high, and press the quick slot button to replenish mana.

5. Resistance Tonics for Elemental Protection

- **Fire Resistance Tonic**:
  - **Ingredients**: Spindleweed (1 unit) and Fade-Touched Leather (1 unit)
  - **Description**: Reduces fire damage, helpful in areas with fire-based enemies or spells.

- **How to Craft**: Find the "Fire Resistance Tonic" in the crafting menu, select it, and press the interact button.
- **Usage**: Equip this tonic before entering fire-heavy areas or battling fire-wielding enemies, and use it just before combat.

- **Cold Resistance Tonic**:
  - **Ingredients**: Blood Lotus (1 unit) and Elfroot Essence (1 unit)
  - **Description**: Grants cold resistance, protecting against frost-based attacks.
  - **How to Craft**: Navigate to the "Cold Resistance Tonic," select, and craft it using the interact button.
  - **Usage**: Ideal for frost-heavy regions or icy caves, use the tonic before facing frost-enchanted enemies for maximum protection.

6. Veilguard-Exclusive Elixirs for Enhanced Abilities

- **Veil Sight Elixir**:
  - **Ingredients**: Veil Quartz (1 unit) and Fade-touched elfroot (1 unit)
  - **Description**: Temporarily allows you to see hidden Veil paths and rifts, essential for exploration in Veilguard zones.
  - **How to Craft**: Select "Veil Sight Elixir" from the Veilguard elixirs tab and craft it with the interact button.
  - **Usage**: Equip the elixir when exploring Veilguard zones, press the quick slot button to activate, and reveal hidden elements in your surroundings.

- **Spirit Ward Tonic**:
  - **Ingredients**: Spirit Essence (1 unit) and Spindleweed (1 unit)
  - **Description**: Reduces damage from spirits and demons, ideal for long sessions in Veilguard zones.
  - **How to Craft**: Find "Spirit Ward Tonic" in the Veilguard elixirs tab, select, and craft it.
  - **Usage**: Equip before entering heavily infested Veilguard zones and use before engaging multiple spirits or demons.

7. Customizing and Enhancing Potions

- **Upgrading Potions**: After crafting, some potions and elixirs can be upgraded using rare materials, enhancing their effects or increasing the duration.
  - **Example**: An enhanced healing potion crafted with additional Spindleweed and Fade-touched materials might restore even more health or provide a regeneration effect.
- **Finding Upgrades**: Certain upgrades become available as you progress in Veilguard quests or upon finding rare materials.
  - **How to Upgrade**: Select an existing potion in the crafting menu, choose "Upgrade" if the option appears, and apply additional materials.

8. Organizing Potions and Elixirs for Quick Access

- **Using the Quick Slot Menu**: Potions and elixirs can be assigned to quick slots, making them accessible during combat without opening the inventory.
  - **How to Equip in Quick Slots**: Open the inventory menu, highlight the desired potion, and press "X" (PlayStation), "A" (Xbox), or right-click (PC) to assign it to a quick slot.
- **Rotating Potions for Different Situations**: Adjust your quick slot items based on your mission. For example, equip healing and stamina potions for general exploration, and swap in resistance tonics for elemental-heavy areas.
- **Checking Status and Refill**: After combat or exploration, check your potion stock and refill at the alchemy station before continuing your journey.

9. Tips for Efficient Potion Crafting and Management

- **Stock Up on Common Ingredients**: Collect common ingredients like Elfroot and Blood Lotus in bulk whenever possible, as they're essential for basic potions and health supplies.
- **Prioritize Veilguard-Exclusive Elixirs in Veil Zones**: Bring Veil Sight Elixirs and Spirit Ward Tonics when exploring Veilguard zones, as these areas often contain hidden paths, rifts, and dangerous spirits.
- **Save Rare Ingredients for High-Tier Potions**: Use rare materials like Fade-touched elfroot and Veil Quartz selectively, as they enhance your most powerful potions and elixirs.
- **Plan Potion Usage for Longer Missions**: For extended missions, prioritize crafting and equipping a mix of healing potions, stamina potions, and elemental resistance tonics to cover all potential needs.

Summary of Creating Potions and Elixirs

- **Access Alchemy Stations**: Use crafting stations in main hubs to start potion-making, and gather ingredients throughout Thedas.
- **Craft Essential Potions**: Start with basic healing and stamina potions, then craft resistance tonics and Veilguard-exclusive elixirs as you gather more ingredients.
- **Upgrade Potions for Greater Effectiveness**: Enhance potions with rare ingredients, boosting their power and making them more effective in challenging zones.
- **Organize and Equip**: Assign potions to quick slots based on mission needs, ensuring you're ready for any situation in combat or exploration.

Crafting and using potions effectively in *The Veilguard* gives you a crucial advantage in combat, exploration, and survival. With a well-stocked potion supply and knowledge of each potion's best use, you're prepared to face any challenge Thedas throws your way. Enjoy creating and using these powerful elixirs to enhance your journey!

Enh4ancing Equipment with Runes

Runes are powerful enhancements in *Dragon Age: The Veilguard* that add unique effects to weapons and armor, such as elemental damage, resistance boosts, and other magical properties. Applying runes allows you to tailor your gear to better suit specific enemies, environments, or playstyles. This guide covers everything you need to know about finding, crafting, and equipping runes to maximize the effectiveness of your equipment.

1. Finding and Acquiring Runes

- **Collecting Runes as Loot**: Runes are often found in chests, as loot from enemies, or rewarded through quests.
  - **Exploration Tips**: Check high-level dungeons, Veilguard zones, and hidden chests in dangerous areas, as these locations frequently yield runes.
  - **How to Collect Runes**: When you find a rune, approach it and press "X" (PlayStation), "A" (Xbox), or "E" (PC) to collect.
- **Purchasing Runes from Merchants**: Certain merchants in major hubs, like **Stormguard Keep** and **Brightfall Village**, sell basic runes.
  - **Finding Rune Merchants**: Look for blacksmiths and specialty traders in town centers. Speak with them by pressing "X" (PlayStation), "A" (Xbox), or "E" (PC) to browse their inventory.
- **Crafting Runes at the Enchanter's Table**: Higher-level or unique runes can be crafted with specific materials, often found in Veilguard zones.
  - **How to Craft**: Visit an Enchanter's Table in main hubs. Approach the table and press the interact button to open the rune-crafting menu, where you can see available recipes and material requirements.

2. Types of Runes and Their Effects

- **Elemental Runes**:
  - **Fire Rune**: Adds fire damage to weapons, making it effective against ice-based enemies.
  - **Frost Rune**: Adds cold damage, useful for battles with fire-based creatures.
  - **Electric Rune**: Adds lightning damage, causing extra harm to water-based enemies or armor-wearing foes.
  - **How to Equip Elemental Runes**: In the crafting menu, select an elemental rune, then apply it to a weapon by pressing "X" (PlayStation), "A" (Xbox), or left-click (PC).

- **Resistance Runes**:
  - ○ **Fire Resistance Rune**: Reduces incoming fire damage, ideal for armor in fire-heavy zones.
  - ○ **Frost Resistance Rune**: Lowers the impact of frost attacks, helping in icy regions.
  - ○ **Spirit Resistance Rune**: Protects against Fade-based magic and spirit damage, essential for Veilguard zones.
  - ○ **Applying Resistance Runes**: Open the armor enhancement menu, select the rune type, and apply it to your armor to gain the resistance.
- **Utility Runes**:
  - ○ **Lifedrain Rune**: Allows weapons to steal a small amount of health on hit, perfect for prolonged fights.
  - ○ **Stagger Rune**: Adds a chance to stagger enemies on hit, useful against heavily armored foes.
  - ○ **Critical Rune**: Increases the critical hit chance, making it ideal for high-DPS builds.
  - ○ **How to Apply Utility Runes**: Equip these on weapons to gain their effects, which are particularly helpful for rogues and high-damage classes.

3. Rune Crafting and Upgrading

- **Crafting Runes**: If you have the right materials, you can craft runes at the Enchanter's Table.
  - ○ **Required Materials**: Some runes require specific items, like **Veil Quartz** or **Spirit Essence**, found in Veilguard zones. These materials give runes additional properties.
  - ○ **How to Craft**: Open the crafting menu at the Enchanter's Table, select the rune you wish to create, and press the interact button. If you have enough materials, the rune will be crafted and added to your inventory.
- **Upgrading Existing Runes**: Certain runes can be upgraded to enhance their effects, such as boosting elemental damage or increasing resistance levels.
  - ○ **Finding Upgrades**: Upgrades are unlocked through special quests or rare items. Visit the Enchanter's Table after acquiring an upgrade to apply it.
  - ○ **How to Upgrade**: Select the rune you wish to upgrade in the crafting menu, choose the "Upgrade" option, and confirm.

4. Applying Runes to Weapons and Armor

- **Accessing the Rune Slot**: Most high-quality weapons and armor have rune slots, which are visible in the item's description. Weapons can typically hold elemental or utility runes, while armor can hold resistance runes.
  - ○ **Viewing Available Rune Slots**: Open your inventory by pressing "I" (PC), "Options" (PlayStation), or "Menu" (Xbox), then select the item to see available rune slots.
- **Installing a Rune**:
  - ○ **Select the Item**: In the inventory, highlight the weapon or armor piece with an open rune slot and select it.

- **Choosing a Rune**: In the rune selection menu, pick a rune from your inventory and press "X" (PlayStation), "A" (Xbox), or left-click (PC) to apply it.
- **Finalizing the Installation**: Confirm your choice to embed the rune. Once installed, the rune's effect is permanently applied until it's replaced or removed.

5. Strategically Choosing Runes for Specific Challenges

- **Preparing for Elemental Zones**:
  - **Fire Zones**: Equip a **Fire Resistance Rune** on armor and a **Frost Rune** on weapons when facing enemies in lava caves or fire-infused regions.
  - **Ice Zones**: Use a **Frost Resistance Rune** and a **Fire Rune** to counter icy environments.
- **Fighting Against Fade Creatures and Spirits**:
  - **Spirit Damage**: Use **Spirit Resistance Runes** on armor in Veilguard zones, as these areas are filled with Fade creatures that deal spirit damage.
  - **Anti-Spirit Weaponry**: Apply **Spirit Damage Runes** to weapons for extra power against Veil creatures.
- **Maximizing Survivability**:
  - **Lifedrain Runes**: For longer battles, especially against tough bosses, a **Lifedrain Rune** can be invaluable for regenerating health.
  - **Stagger and Critical Runes**: Equip **Stagger Runes** to control crowds and **Critical Runes** to enhance damage, particularly for rogues or fast-attack builds.

6. Removing and Replacing Runes

- **Swapping Out Runes**: You may want to switch out runes based on changing mission requirements.
  - **How to Remove a Rune**: In the inventory, select the weapon or armor piece with the rune you wish to replace. Choose the "Remove Rune" option and confirm.
  - **Adding a New Rune**: Once the old rune is removed, you can select a new rune to add, following the same steps to finalize installation.
- **Keeping Runes for Reuse**: Removed runes return to your inventory and can be reused on other items, allowing flexibility without the need to craft duplicates.

7. Upgrading and Enhancing Rune Effects

- **Advanced Rune Upgrades**: Some runes can be upgraded with Veilguard materials, increasing their potency or adding new effects.
  - **Example**: A **Basic Fire Rune** can be upgraded to a **Greater Fire Rune** with higher damage output.
  - **How to Upgrade**: Access the rune crafting menu, select the rune, and press the interact button to apply the upgrade if you have the required materials.

- **Adding Multi-Effect Runes**: Certain high-tier runes provide dual effects, like combining elemental damage with a critical hit bonus.
  - **How to Craft Multi-Effect Runes**: Multi-effect runes require rare materials found in high-level Veilguard zones. Once crafted, they can be applied just like standard runes.

8. Tips for Efficient Rune Usage

- **Prioritize High-Impact Runes**: Save powerful runes, like elemental or lifedrain runes, for your primary weapon or best armor to maximize their impact.
- **Rotate Runes Based on Foes**: Adjust your runes for upcoming missions or based on specific enemies. For example, equip Spirit Resistance Runes for Veilguard missions and Fire Runes for regions with ice-based enemies.
- **Experiment with Combinations**: Different runes can create unique effects when paired with certain materials or abilities. Test different rune combinations on spare gear to find the best setup.

Summary of Enhancing Equipment with Runes

- **Acquire Runes Through Exploration and Crafting**: Find runes in chests, buy them from merchants, or craft them at the Enchanter's Table with Veilguard materials.
- **Choose Runes Based on Playstyle**: Equip elemental runes for offensive boosts, resistance runes for defense, and utility runes for special effects.
- **Apply Runes Strategically**: Install runes in weapons and armor to counter specific threats, boost survivability, or increase damage output.
- **Upgrade and Replace as Needed**: Swap runes as required, upgrading high-impact runes to enhance their effects for more challenging missions.

With these strategies, enhancing your gear with runes in *The Veilguard* will make your character more powerful and adaptable. From adding elemental damage to bolstering defenses, rune enhancements give you the edge you need to face the diverse threats across Thedas. Enjoy experimenting and finding the best combinations for your journey!

Farming for Rare Materials

In *Dragon Age: The Veilguard*, rare materials are essential for crafting high-tier weapons, armor, potions, and runes. These materials provide powerful enhancements and effects, making them highly sought after. Farming rare materials efficiently requires knowing where to find them, how to gather them safely, and the best strategies for maximizing your time and resources. This guide offers all the details you need to efficiently farm rare materials across Thedas.

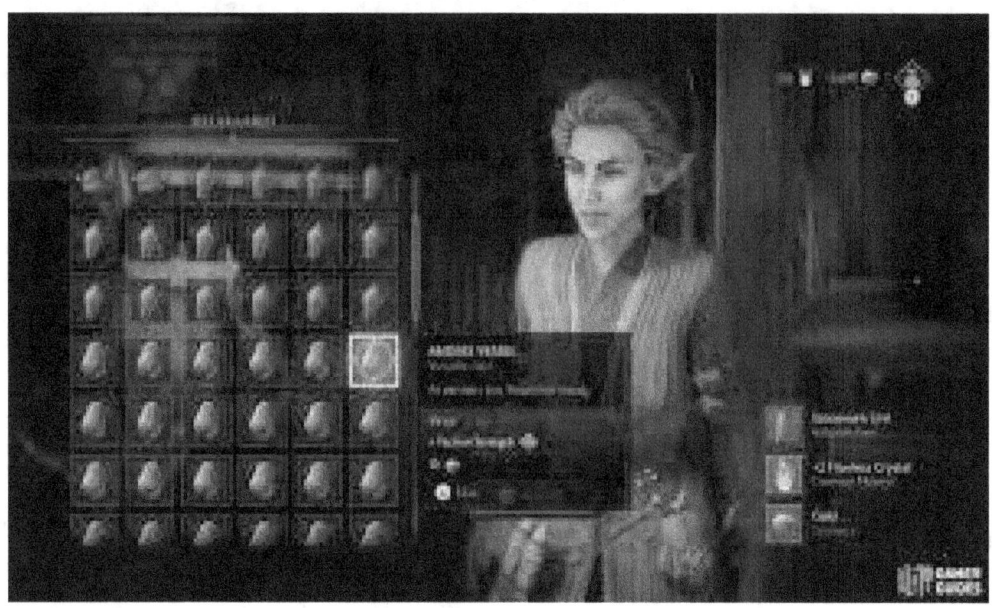

1. Understanding Rare Materials and Their Uses

- **Dragonbone**: Used for crafting the most powerful weapons, granting high attack power and durability.
- **Veil Quartz**: A crystal infused with Fade energy, ideal for enhancing magical equipment and crafting Veilguard-exclusive potions.
- **Fade-Touched Materials**: These enchanted materials, like Fade-touched iron and leather, add unique effects like critical hit bonuses to crafted gear.
- **Spirit Essence**: Gathered from defeated Fade creatures, Spirit Essence is used in potions, elixirs, and magical weaponry.

2. Best Locations for Farming Rare Materials

- **Dragonbone**:
  - **Location**: Primarily found in dragon lairs, such as **Dragon's Den** and **Ashen Crag**.
  - **How to Farm**: Defeat dragons in these regions to find dragonbone around their lairs. Press "X" (PlayStation), "A" (Xbox), or "E" (PC) to collect dragonbone from deposits or dragon remains after battle.
  - **Respawn Tips**: Dragons take time to respawn, so alternate between lairs or return after a game reset to maximize dragonbone collection.
- **Veil Quartz**:
  - **Location**: Veilguard zones like **Veiled Shore** and **Shattered Vale** have clusters of Veil Quartz near rifts.
  - **How to Farm**: Look for clusters emitting a faint glow around rift locations. Approach them and press the interact button to gather Veil Quartz.

- - **Maximizing Yield**: Equip a companion with Veil-related abilities, like Lyra, who can highlight nearby magical resources, making it easier to locate these clusters.
- **Fade-Touched Materials**:
  - **Location**: Commonly dropped by spirits and demons in Veilguard zones, particularly in **Silvered Spire** and **Fade-Worn Woods**.
  - **How to Farm**: Defeat enemies in these zones and loot the drops. Some powerful Fade creatures have a higher chance of dropping Fade-touched materials, so target these for efficient farming.
  - **Optimizing Drops**: Use abilities that increase loot drops or bring companions with bonuses to farming, like Rylan, who has a talent for gathering more items from defeated enemies.
- **Spirit Essence**:
  - **Location**: Found in Veilguard zones, typically dropped by powerful spirit enemies.
  - **How to Farm**: Look for high-level spirit enemies around rifts or in dense Fade creature clusters. Defeat them and press "X" (PlayStation), "A" (Xbox), or "E" (PC) to collect Spirit Essence from drops.

3. Efficient Farming Techniques

- **Cycle Between High-Yield Areas**: Rotate through areas like **Dragon's Den**, **Veiled Shore**, and **Silvered Spire** to gather different types of rare materials without waiting for respawns.
- **Use Game Resets for Faster Respawns**: Some rare resources respawn after a game reset. Save and reload your game in high-yield areas to make the most of this feature.
- **Combine Resource Runs with Side Quests**: Plan your farming around nearby quests to make the most of your time. For example, complete a quest in Shattered Vale while gathering Veil Quartz and Spirit Essence.

4. Using Companion Abilities to Boost Material Collection

- **Lyra's Veil Sense**: Highlights nearby magical resources, making it easier to spot Veil Quartz and Spirit Essence in Veilguard zones.
  - **Activating Veil Sense**: Bring Lyra into your party when farming magical materials. Her ability activates automatically, revealing nearby magical items on your mini-map.
- **Rylan's Loot Bonus**: Increases the chance of finding additional items from defeated enemies.
  - **Optimizing Rylan's Bonus**: Use Rylan's loot bonus in areas with lots of enemies to maximize Fade-touched material drops. His presence can be especially valuable in Fade-Worn Woods or other dense areas.

5. Timing and Special Conditions for Rare Material Respawns

- **Timed Respawns**: Some materials, like Veil Quartz and Spirit Essence, have timed respawn rates in Veilguard zones.

- **Tracking Respawns**: Keep track of the last time you collected from an area, as resources typically respawn after a set period (e.g., every 20 minutes).
- **Weather and Time of Day**: Certain materials, such as Spirit Essence and Fade-touched leather, may have better drop rates at night or during specific weather conditions.
  - **Farming Under Ideal Conditions**: If possible, farm Spirit Essence at night, when spirits are more likely to appear in Veilguard zones, increasing your chances of finding high-level enemies and rare drops.

6. Dealing with Corruption and Fade Effects in Veilguard Zones

- **Protecting Against Corruption**: Prolonged exposure in Veilguard zones can cause Fade corruption, draining stamina or mana over time.
  - **Using Veil Wards**: Before farming in these areas, activate Veil Wards from your inventory to reduce corruption effects. Open your inventory, select the Veil Ward, and press "X" (PlayStation), "A" (Xbox), or left-click (PC) to apply.
- **Managing Corruption Levels**: Monitor your stamina and mana while gathering, as corruption builds up the longer you stay in Veilguard zones. Leave the area temporarily if necessary to recover.

7. Enhancing Drop Rates with Potions and Elixirs

- **Using Drop-Boosting Elixirs**: Certain elixirs, like **Treasure Finder Elixir**, increase the drop rate of rare materials.
  - **Crafting and Using Drop-Boosting Elixirs**: Craft Treasure Finder Elixirs at the alchemy station with ingredients like Blood Lotus and Elfroot. Equip the elixir in a quick slot and activate it before battles in high-drop areas.
- **Pairing with Stamina and Mana Potions**: Stamina potions can be helpful in prolonged farming sessions, allowing you to use abilities frequently without running out of resources.
  - **Using Potions**: Equip stamina or mana potions in quick slots, press the quick slot button during combat, and stay longer in farming areas by keeping your abilities active.

8. Maximizing Veilguard-Exclusive Material Farming

- **Targeting Veilguard Creatures**: Defeating high-level Fade creatures like Veil Wraiths or Spirit Lords increases the likelihood of obtaining rare Veilguard materials, such as Spirit Essence and Veil Quartz.
  - **High-Value Farming Zones**: Veilguard-exclusive creatures are most common in **Shattered Vale** and **Silvered Spire**. Focus on these areas for efficient farming of Veilguard materials.
- **Equipping Veil-Specific Runes and Abilities**: Runes like **Spirit Damage** or abilities like **Veil Strike** can improve your damage output against Veilguard creatures, speeding up farming.
  - **How to Equip**: Add Spirit Damage Runes to your weapons or use Veil abilities in quick slots to increase effectiveness against Fade creatures.

9. Organizing and Storing Rare Materials for Crafting

- **Inventory Management**: Regularly check your inventory space when farming rare materials to avoid running out of room mid-session.
  - **Clearing Inventory**: Open your inventory and discard or sell less valuable items to make room for rare materials.
- **Storing Materials in Base Camps**: Some main hubs have storage chests where you can deposit rare materials.
  - **Using Storage**: In hubs like Stormguard Keep, approach the storage chest and press "X" (PlayStation), "A" (Xbox), or "E" (PC) to open. Transfer rare materials you don't currently need, freeing up space for further farming.

10. Tips for Consistent Rare Material Farming

- **Stay Prepared with Essential Potions and Gear**: Always bring healing potions, Veil Wards, and stamina elixirs when farming in high-risk areas to manage health and stamina effectively.
- **Set Up Efficient Farming Routes**: Create a farming route that covers multiple areas with high-value materials. For example, start at Dragon's Den for Dragonbone, move to Veiled Shore for Veil Quartz, and finish in Silvered Spire for Spirit Essence.
- **Farm During Peak Enemy Spawn Times**: Nighttime or magical disturbances in Veilguard zones increase enemy spawns, creating more opportunities to gather rare drops.

Summary of Farming for Rare Materials

- **Locate High-Yield Zones**: Identify zones rich in specific materials, like Dragon's Den for Dragonbone or Shattered Vale for Veil Quartz.
- **Equip Abilities and Gear for Efficiency**: Use companions' abilities, Veil Wards, and drop-boosting elixirs to improve yield and reduce time spent farming.
- **Manage Corruption and Resource Use**: Protect yourself from Fade corruption and use stamina potions to maintain abilities in prolonged farming sessions.
- **Organize Your Inventory**: Keep your inventory clear and store rare materials at base camps to maximize efficiency on farming runs.

By following these strategies, you'll be able to farm rare materials effectively, enabling you to craft powerful gear and potions for your adventures in *The Veilguard*. Enjoy collecting these valuable resources and upgrading your equipment to tackle the toughest challenges in Thedas!

CHAPTER 10

Enemies and Bosses

In this chapter, you'll gain essential knowledge on the various enemies and powerful bosses you'll encounter in *Dragon Age: The Veilguard*. Learn about the different types of enemies found in Veilguard zones, their strengths and weaknesses, and strategies for overcoming them. This guide also includes tips for tackling challenging bosses, information on legendary encounters, and specific tactics for dealing with Veilguard-exclusive monsters. Prepare yourself to face the most formidable foes with the right strategies and insights to emerge victorious.

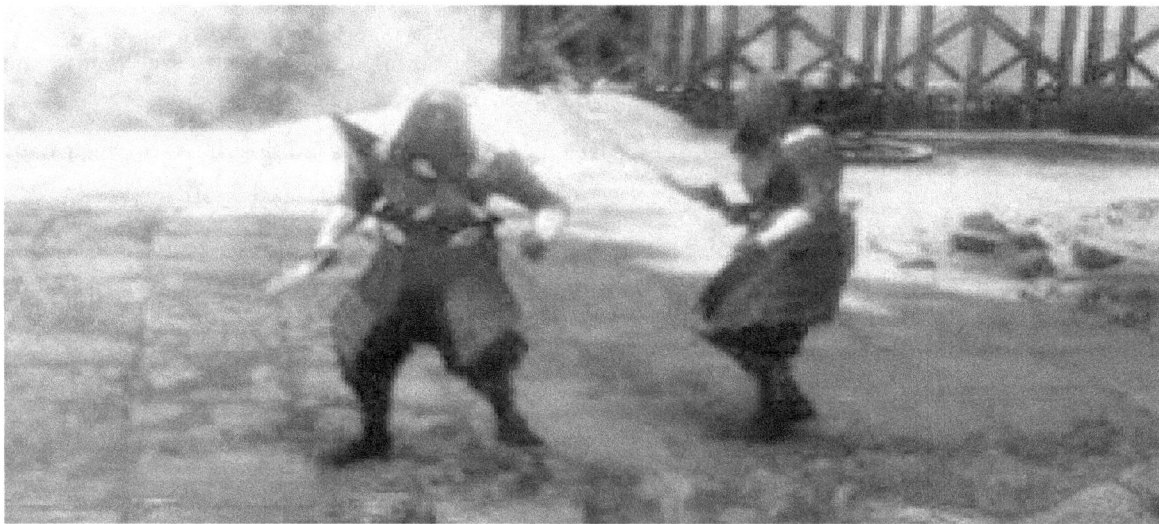

Types of Enemies in Veilguard

Dragon Age: The Veilguard introduces a diverse array of enemies, each with unique characteristics, strengths, and weaknesses. Understanding these enemy types and learning how to approach them effectively is crucial for surviving the game's most challenging zones. Here's a comprehensive guide to the types of enemies you'll encounter in Veilguard and strategies for dealing with each one.

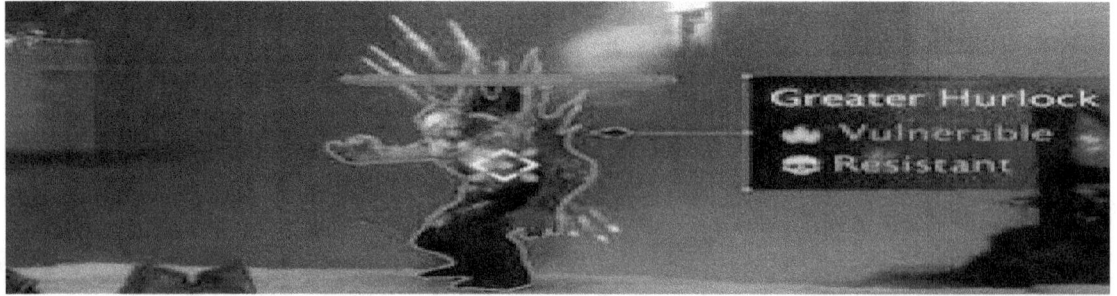

1. Basic Veil Creatures

- **Veil Wraiths**:
  - **Description**: Ghostly entities that linger in Veilguard zones, Veil Wraiths are swift and can phase through physical attacks. They primarily use magic-based attacks.
  - **Weakness**: Vulnerable to spirit and holy magic.
  - **Best Approach**: Use ranged attacks or spirit damage abilities like **Veil Strike** or **Spirit Ward** to weaken them.
  - **How to Engage**: Equip **Spirit Damage** Runes on weapons to deal extra damage to Wraiths. Use ranged attacks by pressing "R2" (PlayStation), "RT" (Xbox), or left-click (PC) to avoid their close-range retaliation.
- **Shade Wolves**:
  - **Description**: These shadowy wolves hunt in packs and use hit-and-run tactics. They're quick and tend to ambush players.
  - **Weakness**: Physical attacks, particularly slashing and piercing.
  - **Best Approach**: Equip weapons with high attack speed or critical chance to deal with their mobility. Take them down one by one to reduce pack strength.
  - **How to Engage**: Use a fast weapon like dual daggers. Press "X" (PlayStation), "A" (Xbox), or "E" (PC) to lock on and attack individual wolves, focusing on reducing their numbers.

2. Elemental Beasts

- **Frostbound Behemoths**:
  - **Description**: Massive creatures imbued with ice magic, Frostbound Behemoths are slow but deal heavy cold damage.
  - **Weakness**: Fire damage and ranged attacks.
  - **Best Approach**: Equip fire-based weapons or spells and keep your distance. Using a fire rune on your weapon increases effectiveness.
  - **How to Engage**: Stay at range and use fire attacks. Equip fire-based abilities in quick slots and press the assigned button to activate during combat.
- **Flame Serpents**:
  - **Description**: Serpentine creatures that slither through lava pools and spit fire at their enemies. They are immune to fire and resistant to physical attacks.
  - **Weakness**: Cold and water-based attacks.
  - **Best Approach**: Use frost abilities or weapons with frost runes. Maintain distance to avoid their fire-based attacks.
  - **How to Engage**: Equip a **Frost Rune** on your weapon and use frost abilities by pressing their respective quick slot buttons. Keep moving to dodge fire attacks.

3. Fade Beasts

- **Nightmare Stalkers**:
  - **Description**: These creatures emerge from nightmares and use fear-based abilities to weaken players.
  - **Weakness**: Holy and spirit damage.
  - **Best Approach**: Equip spirit runes or use abilities that counter fear effects, such as **Spirit Ward**.
  - **How to Engage**: Approach with caution. Activate **Spirit Ward** by pressing its assigned button when close to prevent fear effects from disrupting your attacks.

- **Veil Aberrants**:
  - **Description**: Twisted manifestations of magic, Veil Aberrants are volatile creatures that explode upon death, dealing area-of-effect damage.
  - **Weakness**: Ranged attacks, particularly magic.
  - **Best Approach**: Attack from a distance and be prepared to retreat when they're about to explode.
  - **How to Engage**: Use ranged attacks or spells, keeping a safe distance. When their health is low, move back to avoid the explosion.

4. Corrupted Spirits and Demons

- **Desire Demons**:
  - **Description**: Demons that use charm and illusion to manipulate players, Desire Demons are adept at controlling and weakening minds.
  - **Weakness**: High-damage physical attacks or holy magic.
  - **Best Approach**: Use abilities that resist charm or bring companions who can disrupt illusions.
  - **How to Engage**: Equip high-damage weapons and attack aggressively to prevent them from casting illusions. Press "X" (PlayStation), "A" (Xbox), or "E" (PC) to lock onto and attack.

- **Pride Demons**:
  - **Description**: Massive demons with high defenses and devastating magic attacks, Pride Demons are some of the most challenging enemies in Veilguard.
  - **Weakness**: Holy and spirit damage, particularly from Veilguard-exclusive abilities.
  - **Best Approach**: Bring companions with high defensive abilities, like tanks, and use spirit-damage runes.
  - **How to Engage**: Use spirit-damage abilities like **Veil Strike** to penetrate their defenses. Press the quick slot button assigned to Veil Strike when within range.

5. Veilguard-Exclusive Monsters

- **Ethereal Reavers**:
  - **Description**: These powerful creatures phase between the Veil and physical world, making them hard to track and even harder to kill.
  - **Weakness**: Veilguard-exclusive abilities, such as **Fade Shroud** and **Veil Pulse**.
  - **Best Approach**: Use Veil abilities to disrupt their phasing, keeping them in the physical world long enough to attack.
  - **How to Engage**: Equip **Fade Shroud** in a quick slot and activate it when the Reaver phases out. This will pull them back into the physical realm temporarily.

- **Spectral Giants**:
  - **Description**: Towering spirits bound by the Veil, Spectral Giants are both incredibly strong and highly resistant to physical damage.
  - **Weakness**: Magic, particularly spirit-based attacks.
  - **Best Approach**: Use spirit-based abilities, such as **Spirit Ward**, and keep moving to avoid their heavy attacks.
  - **How to Engage**: Equip spirit-damage abilities and press their respective quick slot buttons when near the Spectral Giant. Move consistently to dodge its slower, but powerful, attacks.

6. Environmental Hazards

- **Veil Rifts**:
  - **Description**: Though not enemies themselves, Veil Rifts continually summon spirits and demons until they are closed, making them hazardous.
  - **Weakness**: Veilguard-exclusive abilities that disrupt the rift, such as **Veil Strike**.
  - **Best Approach**: Prioritize closing the rift first, then eliminate the summoned creatures.
  - **How to Close**: Approach the rift and press "X" (PlayStation), "A" (Xbox), or "E" (PC) to initiate closure. Defeat waves of enemies to seal the rift permanently.

Summary of Types of Enemies in Veilguard

- **Basic Veil Creatures**: Common enemies like Veil Wraiths and Shade Wolves that use physical and magic attacks.
- **Elemental Beasts**: Creatures imbued with elemental powers, such as Frostbound Behemoths and Flame Serpents, which require specific elemental counters.
- **Fade Beasts**: Creatures born from the Fade, like Nightmare Stalkers and Veil Aberrants, which use fear and explosive tactics.
- **Corrupted Spirits and Demons**: Powerful demons like Desire and Pride Demons, with a focus on manipulation and defense.

- **Veilguard-Exclusive Monsters**: Rare, highly challenging enemies that demand the use of Veilguard-exclusive abilities to overcome.
- **Environmental Hazards**: Veil Rifts that summon continuous waves of enemies until closed, adding an extra layer of danger to certain zones.

With this guide, you'll have the knowledge needed to tackle the various enemy types in *The Veilguard*. By understanding their strengths and weaknesses, you can develop strategies for each encounter and make the most of your Veilguard abilities, runes, and tactics. Enjoy mastering the challenges these enemies bring to your journey through Thedas!

Weaknesses and Strengths of Different Enemy Types

In *Dragon Age: The Veilguard*, each enemy type has distinct weaknesses and strengths, making it essential to adapt your tactics and gear to counter them effectively. This guide provides an in-depth look at various enemy types, detailing their strengths and vulnerabilities, as well as recommendations on how to exploit these weaknesses for a successful battle.

1. Veil Creatures

- **Veil Wraiths**
  - **Strengths**: High mobility, resistant to physical attacks, and can phase in and out of visibility.
  - **Weaknesses**: Vulnerable to spirit damage and holy magic.
  - **Best Tactics**: Equip **Spirit Damage** Runes on weapons for increased effectiveness. Use ranged spirit-based attacks or abilities like **Veil Strike** to deal maximum damage.
  - **How to Engage**: Target the Wraith from a distance by pressing "R2" (PlayStation), "RT" (Xbox), or left-click (PC) with spirit-enhanced weapons or abilities.
- **Shade Wolves**
  - **Strengths**: Fast, agile, and tend to attack in packs, making them hard to isolate.
  - **Weaknesses**: Physical attacks, especially slashing weapons.
  - **Best Tactics**: Use high-speed weapons like daggers or swords to deal with their mobility. Focus on reducing the pack size quickly to avoid being overwhelmed.
  - **How to Engage**: Lock onto individual Shade Wolves using "X" (PlayStation), "A" (Xbox), or "E" (PC) and attack quickly with melee weapons.

2. Elemental Beasts

- **Frostbound Behemoths**
  - **Strengths**: High health and powerful ice attacks, immune to frost damage.
  - **Weaknesses**: Vulnerable to fire-based attacks and ranged damage.

- **Best Tactics**: Equip a **Fire Rune** on your weapon or use fire-based spells to exploit their weakness. Keep your distance, as their melee attacks are slow but powerful.
- **How to Engage**: Use ranged fire attacks or fire-enhanced weapons by pressing their assigned quick slot button. Keep moving to avoid their frost attacks.
- **Flame Serpents**
    - **Strengths**: Resistant to physical attacks, immune to fire, and have fire-based ranged attacks.
    - **Weaknesses**: Vulnerable to cold and water-based damage.
    - **Best Tactics**: Equip a **Frost Rune** on your weapon or use ice-based abilities to maximize damage. Stay at a safe distance to avoid their fire breath.
    - **How to Engage**: Use frost abilities by pressing the respective quick slot button or equip frost-enhanced weapons to counter their fire resistance.

3. Fade Beasts

- **Nightmare Stalkers**
    - **Strengths**: Use fear-based abilities that can disrupt or weaken players, resistant to physical damage.
    - **Weaknesses**: Holy and spirit-based attacks.
    - **Best Tactics**: Equip holy or spirit-based runes, or bring companions with fear-resistance abilities. **Spirit Ward** can help counteract their fear effects.
    - **How to Engage**: Activate **Spirit Ward** from the quick slot to protect against fear, then use holy or spirit-based attacks by pressing the corresponding ability button.
- **Veil Aberrants**
    - **Strengths**: High volatility; they explode upon death, dealing significant area damage.
    - **Weaknesses**: Vulnerable to ranged attacks, especially magical ones.
    - **Best Tactics**: Use ranged attacks to avoid their explosion upon death. Equip ranged spirit abilities or spells to maintain distance.
    - **How to Engage**: Attack from a distance with spells or ranged attacks, and step back as their health depletes to avoid the explosion.

4. Corrupted Spirits and Demons

- **Desire Demons**
    - **Strengths**: Specialize in charm and illusion, resistant to magical attacks.
    - **Weaknesses**: High-damage physical attacks, particularly melee.
    - **Best Tactics**: Bring companions who resist charm effects and use powerful physical attacks. Focus on dealing continuous damage to prevent them from casting illusions.

- **How to Engage**: Equip high-damage melee weapons, lock on with "X" (PlayStation), "A" (Xbox), or "E" (PC), and attack aggressively to interrupt their illusions.
- **Pride Demons**
  - **Strengths**: Very high defense, capable of devastating area-of-effect magic attacks.
  - **Weaknesses**: Spirit damage, holy magic, and Veilguard-exclusive abilities.
  - **Best Tactics**: Use **Veil Strike** or **Spirit Ward** to reduce their defenses. Attack from a distance if possible, as their magic attacks cover wide areas.
  - **How to Engage**: Use **Veil Strike** by pressing the assigned quick slot button to weaken their defenses, then follow up with spirit-based attacks.

5. Veilguard-Exclusive Monsters

- **Ethereal Reavers**
  - **Strengths**: They can phase in and out of the Veil, making them hard to track and target.
  - **Weaknesses**: Veilguard-exclusive abilities, particularly **Fade Shroud** and **Veil Pulse**.
  - **Best Tactics**: Use Veil abilities to disrupt their phasing, keeping them in the physical realm long enough to attack.
  - **How to Engage**: Activate **Fade Shroud** from the quick slot to keep them visible, then use melee attacks to maximize damage.
- **Spectral Giants**
  - **Strengths**: High health, resistant to physical damage, and capable of powerful area attacks.
  - **Weaknesses**: Vulnerable to magic, particularly spirit damage.
  - **Best Tactics**: Equip **Spirit Damage** Runes and use magic-based attacks from a distance to avoid their heavy melee attacks.
  - **How to Engage**: Equip spirit-based abilities in quick slots, press the assigned button to activate, and maintain distance to avoid melee damage.

6. Environmental Hazards

- **Veil Rifts**
  - **Strengths**: Continually spawn spirits and demons until closed, making the area increasingly dangerous over time.
  - **Weaknesses**: Veilguard-exclusive abilities that can disrupt or close the rift.
  - **Best Tactics**: Focus on closing the rift first to stop enemy spawns. Use **Veil Strike** to disrupt it, then eliminate spawned enemies.
  - **How to Close**: Approach the rift and press "X" (PlayStation), "A" (Xbox), or "E" (PC) to initiate closure. Defeat any remaining creatures to seal the rift.

Summary of Weaknesses and Strengths of Different Enemy Types

- **Veil Creatures**: Veil Wraiths are vulnerable to spirit attacks, while Shade Wolves are weak to physical attacks.
- **Elemental Beasts**: Frostbound Behemoths are susceptible to fire, and Flame Serpents can be defeated with frost attacks.
- **Fade Beasts**: Nightmare Stalkers are weak to holy damage, and Veil Aberrants are best dealt with from a distance due to their explosive nature.
- **Corrupted Spirits and Demons**: Desire Demons are weak to physical attacks, while Pride Demons can be countered with spirit and Veilguard abilities.
- **Veilguard-Exclusive Monsters**: Ethereal Reavers can be held in the physical realm with Veil abilities, and Spectral Giants are vulnerable to magic, especially spirit damage.
- **Environmental Hazards**: Veil Rifts should be closed quickly using Veilguard abilities to prevent continuous enemy spawns.

By understanding each enemy's strengths and weaknesses, you'll be able to tailor your approach in *The Veilguard*, using the right weapons, abilities, and companions to exploit vulnerabilities. Prepare for each battle with the appropriate gear and strategies to efficiently counter these foes and conquer the dangers of Veilguard zones.

Tips for Beating Difficult Bosses

Difficult bosses in *Dragon Age: The Veilguard* require strategic planning, quick reflexes, and optimal use of your abilities and gear. Each boss has specific attack patterns, strengths, and weaknesses that can be exploited to maximize your chances of victory. Here's a detailed guide to help you prepare for, engage, and defeat these challenging foes with practical tips and tactics.

1. Preparation and Gear Selection

- **Equip High-Damage and Elemental Runes**: Review the boss's known weaknesses and equip your weapons with the appropriate runes. For example, if the boss is weak to fire, equip a **Fire Rune** to increase your damage output.
    - **How to Equip**: Open your inventory, select the weapon, and press "X" (PlayStation), "A" (Xbox), or left-click (PC) to add the appropriate rune.
- **Bring the Right Companions**: Choose companions who complement your strategy. For instance, if the boss uses magic, bring a tank like Lorian to draw its attention while you focus on dealing damage from a distance.

○ **Selecting Companions**: At your camp, interact with the party selection point, press "X" (PlayStation), "A" (Xbox), or "E" (PC) to switch companions.

- **Stock Up on Potions and Elixirs**: Make sure you have health potions, stamina potions, and resistance elixirs (such as fire or frost resistance) tailored to the boss's elemental type.
  ○ **How to Equip Potions**: Access the potion menu, select the potion or elixir you want, and assign it to a quick slot by pressing "X" (PlayStation), "A" (Xbox), or left-click (PC).

2. Understanding Boss Attack Patterns

- **Watch for Openings**: Many bosses have predictable attack patterns. Observe their movements for a few seconds at the start of the fight to identify their attack rhythm and watch for pauses after large attacks, which often create windows for counterattacks.
  ○ **Best Time to Attack**: Wait for the boss to finish a heavy attack, which usually leaves them open for a brief moment. Move in and press "R2" (PlayStation), "RT" (Xbox), or left-click (PC) to attack.
- **Avoid Area of Effect (AoE) Attacks**: Bosses often have AoE attacks that cover large areas and can cause significant damage. Learn the visual or audio cues before these attacks to dodge effectively.
  ○ **Dodging AoE**: When you see the boss winding up an AoE attack, press "Circle" (PlayStation), "B" (Xbox), or "Space" (PC) to dodge and reposition yourself away from the impact zone.

3. Using Veilguard Abilities for an Advantage

- **Veil Strike for High Damage**: Veil Strike is an effective ability for disrupting bosses that rely on magical defenses or powerful attacks. Use it to stagger bosses and create an opportunity for follow-up hits.
  ○ **How to Use Veil Strike**: Assign Veil Strike to a quick slot, then press the corresponding button during combat to activate it against the boss.
- **Fade Shroud for Quick Repositioning**: If you're facing a particularly aggressive boss, Fade Shroud lets you phase out of the physical realm temporarily, allowing you to reposition without taking damage.
  ○ **Activating Fade Shroud**: Equip Fade Shroud in your quick slot and press the corresponding button to activate it, then move to a safer spot or attack from behind while the boss is unaware.

4. Effective Use of Companion Abilities

- **Set Up Companion Abilities Strategically**: Some companion abilities can stun, weaken, or distract the boss, allowing you to focus on dealing damage. For example, Mira's healing ability can keep your team sustained, while Taryn's anti-magic abilities can weaken a spellcasting boss.
  ○ **How to Use Companion Abilities**: In tactical mode, direct your companions by pressing the touchpad (PlayStation), "View" (Xbox), or "T" (PC) to use specific abilities on the boss. Assign them to focus on defense or attack as needed.

- **Command Companions to Attack Weak Points**: If the boss has a weak spot (like a glowing area), direct your companions to attack it, as coordinated attacks can increase the damage dealt.
  - **How to Target Weak Points**: In tactical mode, hover over the weak spot, then press "X" (PlayStation), "A" (Xbox), or left-click (PC) to direct your companions to focus on it.

5. Managing Health and Stamina Carefully

- **Use Potions at the Right Time**: Don't wait until your health is critically low to heal. Use health potions when you're around half health, especially if the boss's attacks deal high damage.
  - **How to Use Potions**: Press the assigned quick slot button for health potions during combat to regain health.
- **Monitor Stamina**: Stamina is essential for using abilities and dodging attacks. Keep an eye on your stamina bar and avoid overusing it, especially when the boss is preparing a major attack.
  - **Replenishing Stamina**: Use stamina potions if your stamina is low. Equip them in quick slots and press the respective button to restore stamina.

6. Exploiting Environmental Hazards and Terrain

- **Use Obstacles as Cover**: Some bosses have ranged or magic attacks that can be blocked by obstacles. Use natural barriers to avoid damage while waiting for a chance to counterattack.
  - **Positioning Behind Obstacles**: Move behind obstacles by pressing the directional stick or WASD keys, using the terrain to block incoming attacks.
- **Leverage Height Differences**: If the boss's attacks have limited range or aim, use ledges or elevated areas to attack from above or evade lower attacks.
  - **Climbing or Moving to High Ground**: Press "X" (PlayStation), "A" (Xbox), or "E" (PC) to climb or jump to higher areas. This positioning can give you an advantage when dealing with slow-moving bosses.

7. Breaking Through Boss Defenses

- **Use High-Damage Combos**: Some bosses have strong defenses that can be broken through with high-damage combos. Use abilities that increase your critical hit rate or enhance your weapon damage.
  - **Activating Combos**: Combine abilities like **Rage Slash** or **Critical Strike** with Veilguard powers to break down defenses. Press the respective quick slot button to activate each ability in sequence.
- **Target Weak Spots**: Many bosses have weak spots that, when hit, cause them to stagger or take additional damage. Look for glowing areas or distinct markings on the boss.
  - **How to Target**: Lock onto the weak spot using "X" (PlayStation), "A" (Xbox), or "E" (PC) and attack directly to maximize damage.

8. Staying Calm and Adapting Mid-Fight

- **Adapt to Changing Attack Patterns**: As bosses lose health, they often change their attack patterns or increase the intensity of their moves. Be ready to adapt your strategy as the fight progresses.
  - **Observing Changes**: Keep a close watch on the boss's movements and shift to a defensive approach when new attack patterns emerge.
- **Take Breaks to Regroup**: In some boss fights, you can create distance or use abilities like Fade Shroud to take a brief break and assess your resources, especially if the battle is lengthy.
  - **Using Fade Shroud to Reset**: Activate Fade Shroud from a quick slot to give yourself time to recover, use a potion, or reposition.

9. Final Tactics for Defeating Difficult Bosses

- **Use Burst Damage Abilities Near the End**: When the boss is low on health, focus on burst damage abilities to finish them off before they unleash any final, devastating attacks.
  - **Activating Burst Abilities**: Assign high-damage abilities like **Veil Pulse** or **Blade Flurry** to your quick slots, and press the corresponding button for a powerful finishing move.
- **Coordinate with Companions for a Strong Finish**: Use companion abilities in tandem to deal maximum damage. For instance, combine Mira's healing with Rylan's critical hit ability to sustain and finish off the boss.
  - **How to Coordinate**: Use tactical mode to direct each companion to unleash their highest-damage abilities simultaneously for a coordinated attack.

Summary of Tips for Beating Difficult Bosses

- **Prepare Wisely**: Equip runes, companions, potions, and abilities tailored to the boss's weaknesses.
- **Study Attack Patterns**: Watch for openings after heavy attacks and avoid AoE attacks by dodging.
- **Utilize Veilguard Abilities**: Use abilities like **Veil Strike** and **Fade Shroud** to counter boss defenses and reposition.
- **Manage Health and Stamina**: Use potions wisely, and monitor stamina to ensure you can dodge when needed.
- **Adapt and Persist**: Adjust to changing attack patterns and keep up the pressure with burst damage near the end.

With these strategies, you'll be well-prepared to face any boss in *The Veilguard*. Focus on exploiting their weaknesses, managing your resources, and adapting mid-fight to ensure your victory. Enjoy the thrill of conquering these powerful foes and mastering the challenges of the game!

Legendary Boss Encounters

In *Dragon Age: The Veilguard*, legendary bosses are the pinnacle of challenging encounters, offering intense battles, complex mechanics, and unique rewards. These bosses require careful preparation, strategic use of abilities, and a deep understanding of their patterns and weaknesses. This guide provides essential tips for each phase of these encounters, helping you take down these formidable foes with confidence.

1. Preparing for Legendary Boss Fights

- **Optimize Gear with High-Damage and Resistance Runes**: Legendary bosses often have elemental or magic-based attacks. Equip resistance runes (like **Fire Resistance** or **Spirit Resistance**) on armor, and high-damage runes (such as **Fire** or **Frost Runes**) on weapons to maximize both offense and defense.
  - **How to Equip Runes**: Open your inventory, select your weapon or armor, and press "X" (PlayStation), "A" (Xbox), or left-click (PC) to add runes.
- **Select Companions with Complementary Abilities**: Choose companions that cover your weaknesses. For example, bring a healer like Mira for sustained fights, or a tank like Lorian to draw boss attention while you attack from a distance.
  - **Choosing Companions**: Interact with the party selection point in camp and press "X" (PlayStation), "A" (Xbox), or "E" (PC) to switch companions.
- **Stock Up on Essential Potions**: Health potions, stamina elixirs, and resistance tonics tailored to the boss's elemental strengths are must-haves. Equip a mix of potions in quick slots for quick access.
  - **Assigning Potions**: In the potion menu, select the desired potion and press "X" (PlayStation), "A" (Xbox), or left-click (PC) to assign it to a quick slot.

2. Recognizing Phases and Attack Patterns

- **Understanding Multi-Phase Boss Fights**: Legendary bosses typically have multiple phases, each with distinct attack patterns and sometimes different vulnerabilities. Pay attention to the boss's health bar, as phases usually change at specific points (e.g., 75%, 50%, and 25% health).
  - **Adjusting Strategy for New Phases**: At each phase transition, the boss may unleash new attacks or become resistant to certain damage types. Be ready to adapt by switching to different attacks or adjusting your positioning.
- **Watch for Visual and Audio Cues**: Legendary bosses often have visual or audio signals before launching powerful moves. For example, a glowing aura or a roar might signal an upcoming area-of-effect (AoE) attack.
  - **Dodging Cues**: When you notice these cues, press "Circle" (PlayStation), "B" (Xbox), or "Space" (PC) to dodge and reposition yourself away from the attack's impact zone.

3. Using Veilguard Abilities for Maximum Impact

- **Veil Strike for Staggering Bosses**: Veil Strike is particularly effective against legendary bosses with high defenses. It briefly staggers the boss, creating an opening for heavy damage.
  - **Activating Veil Strike**: Equip Veil Strike in a quick slot and press the assigned button when close to the boss to interrupt their attack.
- **Fade Shroud for Tactical Repositioning**: Fade Shroud allows you to become invisible temporarily, ideal for dodging heavy attacks or moving behind the boss for a surprise assault.
  - **How to Use Fade Shroud**: Equip Fade Shroud in a quick slot, press the button when the boss winds up a heavy attack, and use this time to get to a safer or more advantageous position.
- **Veil Pulse for AoE Damage**: Some legendary bosses summon minions or create multiple targets that require crowd control. Veil Pulse deals area damage, making it ideal for these situations.
  - **Using Veil Pulse**: Activate Veil Pulse by pressing its quick slot button when multiple enemies or minions are around. This will help control the battlefield, allowing you to focus on the boss.

4. Positioning and Terrain Usage

- **Use Environmental Cover to Block Ranged Attacks**: Some legendary bosses have powerful ranged attacks or AoE spells. Use natural barriers, like rocks or pillars, to block these attacks.
  - **Finding Cover**: Move behind obstacles by pressing the directional stick or WASD keys, using the environment to shield yourself from the boss's ranged abilities.
- **Exploit High Ground for Attacks**: In some arenas, elevated platforms can be used to attack the boss from above, especially if they lack ranged attacks or have limited reach.
  - **Moving to High Ground**: Press "X" (PlayStation), "A" (Xbox), or "E" (PC) to jump or climb to higher ground. From there, use ranged attacks to hit the boss without taking direct hits.

5. Managing Health, Stamina, and Mana

- **Using Health Potions Strategically**: Legendary bosses deal heavy damage, so don't wait until your health is critically low. Use health potions when around half health to avoid being one-shot by powerful attacks.
  - **Activating Potions**: Press the assigned quick slot button for health potions during combat to restore health quickly.
- **Monitor Stamina and Mana**: Stamina is essential for dodging and using abilities, while mana is necessary for casting spells. Keep an eye on these resources and use stamina or mana potions as needed.
  - **Restoring Stamina or Mana**: Equip stamina or mana potions in quick slots, pressing the respective button to restore these resources mid-fight.

6. Utilizing Companion Abilities in Key Moments

- **Direct Companions to Support Roles**: Assign companions to focus on healing, tanking, or dealing damage based on your needs. For instance, Mira's healing ability is invaluable for long fights, while Taryn's anti-magic abilities are useful for bosses that rely on spells.
    - **Setting Companion Roles**: In tactical mode, press the touchpad (PlayStation), "View" (Xbox), or "T" (PC) to instruct companions to prioritize specific roles.
- **Coordinate Attacks on Weak Spots**: Some legendary bosses have weak spots that require coordinated attacks. Target these areas with your companions for bonus damage.
    - **Directing Weak Spot Attacks**: Hover over the weak spot in tactical mode and press "X" (PlayStation), "A" (Xbox), or left-click (PC) to instruct your companions to focus their attacks there.

7. Breaking Down Boss Defenses

- **Use High-Damage Combos to Crack Shields**: Some legendary bosses have shields that reduce incoming damage. Use abilities that deal heavy damage in quick succession to break down these shields.
    - **Combining High-Damage Abilities**: Equip abilities like **Veil Strike** or **Blade Flurry** in quick slots, and press the assigned buttons in sequence to maximize damage.
- **Exploit Elemental Weaknesses**: Check the boss's elemental affinities and use corresponding weaknesses to your advantage. For example, if the boss is weak to frost, use frost-based abilities and runes to maximize damage.
    - **Equipping Elemental Abilities**: Equip the necessary elemental ability or rune, then press the respective quick slot button to activate it.

8. Exploiting Weaknesses and Vulnerabilities

- **Target Glowing Weak Points**: Many legendary bosses have specific areas on their body that are vulnerable to attacks. Look for glowing or distinctive markings and focus attacks there to deal extra damage.
    - **How to Lock Onto Weak Points**: Press "X" (PlayStation), "A" (Xbox), or "E" (PC) to lock onto the weak point, then attack for increased damage.
- **Use Debuffing Abilities**: Some Veilguard abilities and companion skills can lower the boss's defenses, speed, or attack power, making them more manageable.
    - **Activating Debuffs**: Equip debuff abilities like **Veil Disruption** or **Spirit Ward** and press the quick slot button to apply them during combat.

9. Finishing the Fight with Burst Damage

- **Save High-Burst Abilities for the End**: As the boss nears low health, switch to burst damage abilities to finish them off quickly before they enter a more dangerous phase or use desperate attacks.

- **Using Burst Abilities**: Equip abilities like **Veil Pulse** or **Critical Strike** in quick slots, pressing the assigned buttons to unleash powerful finishing moves.
- **Coordinate a Final Assault with Companions**: Use tactical mode to have all companions unleash their highest-damage abilities simultaneously to deliver a strong final blow.
  - **Directing Companion Attacks**: In tactical mode, assign each companion's strongest ability to activate at once by pressing their assigned buttons, overwhelming the boss with combined force.

Summary of Strategies for Legendary Boss Encounters

- **Prepare and Equip Strategically**: Optimize your gear and bring the right companions and potions for each boss's specific strengths and weaknesses.
- **Recognize and Adapt to Phases**: Watch for cues and adjust your tactics as the boss moves through different phases.
- **Leverage Veilguard Abilities**: Use Veilguard abilities like **Veil Strike** and **Fade Shroud** to exploit weaknesses and reposition.
- **Use the Environment to Your Advantage**: Find cover and use high ground to evade attacks, maximizing the arena's layout.
- **Manage Resources Wisely**: Keep an eye on health, stamina, and mana, and use potions and companion support to sustain through the fight.
- **Finish Strong with Coordinated Bursts**: Use high-burst abilities and coordinate with companions for a powerful final strike.

With these tactics, you'll be well-prepared to tackle the toughest legendary bosses in *The Veilguard*. By understanding their patterns, exploiting their weaknesses, and using your abilities strategically, you can conquer even the most challenging encounters and claim the unique rewards they offer. Enjoy the thrill of these epic battles and the rewards that come with victory!

Veilguard-Exclusive Monsters and Tactics

Dragon Age: The Veilguard introduces exclusive monsters that present unique challenges, requiring specific tactics and strategies to overcome. These creatures are infused with the power of the Fade and often have abilities that demand quick reflexes, smart positioning, and mastery of Veilguard abilities. This guide covers each type of Veilguard-exclusive monster, their strengths and weaknesses, and the best tactics for defeating them.

1. Ethereal Reavers

- **Description**: Ethereal Reavers are fast, powerful creatures that phase between the Fade and physical world, making them difficult to target. They deal heavy damage and can evade attacks by phasing out temporarily.

- **Strengths**: High mobility, resistance to physical attacks, and the ability to phase out of the physical realm.
- **Weaknesses**: Vulnerable to Veilguard-exclusive abilities, particularly **Fade Shroud** and **Veil Strike**, which can disrupt their phasing.
- **Best Tactics**:
    - **Disrupt Phasing with Veil Strike**: Veil Strike is particularly effective at pulling Reavers back into the physical realm. Equip it in a quick slot and press the assigned button when the Reaver begins to phase out.
    - **Use Fade Shroud for Positioning**: Use Fade Shroud to phase alongside the Reaver, allowing you to maintain contact and anticipate its next movement. Activate Fade Shroud from the quick slot when the Reaver starts to evade, keeping you in range for a follow-up attack.
    - **Stay Mobile**: Ethereal Reavers have quick, heavy-hitting attacks. Keep moving to avoid their strikes and use dodge by pressing "Circle" (PlayStation), "B" (Xbox), or "Space" (PC).

2. Spectral Giants

- **Description**: Towering spirits bound by Veil magic, Spectral Giants wield immense power and have extremely high health, making them one of the toughest Veilguard-exclusive enemies.
- **Strengths**: High health and defense, heavy melee attacks, resistant to physical damage.
- **Weaknesses**: Vulnerable to spirit-based and magical attacks, especially those boosted by Veilguard abilities.
- **Best Tactics**:
    - **Use Spirit Damage and Magic Attacks**: Physical attacks are less effective against Spectral Giants. Equip spirit-damage runes on your weapon and focus on magic-based abilities. Press the respective quick slot button for spirit abilities like **Veil Pulse** to maximize damage.
    - **Target from a Distance**: Spectral Giants have slow, powerful melee swings, so staying at range can reduce your risk of getting hit. Use ranged spirit abilities and spells to chip away at their health from a safe distance.
    - **Dodge Their Heavy Attacks**: Spectral Giants often telegraph their attacks with a wind-up. When you see them preparing a swing, press "Circle" (PlayStation), "B" (Xbox), or "Space" (PC) to dodge and reposition.

3. Veil Terrors

- **Description**: Veil Terrors are monstrous entities that consume Fade energy to grow stronger. They're capable of unleashing devastating AoE attacks and have a tendency to summon lesser Fade creatures during battle.
- **Strengths**: High AoE damage, ability to summon minions, absorbs Fade energy to heal over time.
- **Weaknesses**: Weak to holy magic and Veil disruption abilities.
- **Best Tactics**:

- **Interrupt Healing with Veil Disruption**: When Veil Terrors begin absorbing energy from the Fade, use **Veil Disruption** to interrupt the process and stop them from healing. Assign Veil Disruption to a quick slot and press the button when the Terror begins to heal.
- **Deal with Summoned Minions First**: Veil Terrors often summon smaller Fade creatures. Focus on eliminating these minions quickly to avoid getting overwhelmed. Use AoE abilities like **Veil Pulse** to clear them efficiently.
- **Stay Clear of AoE Attacks**: Veil Terrors have powerful AoE moves that are telegraphed by a glow or aura around them. When you see the aura, move out of the area and use ranged attacks until it's safe to approach again.

4. Corrupted Guardians

- **Description**: Once protectors of the Veil, these beings have been corrupted and turned hostile. They are heavily armored and possess potent defensive abilities, often using shields and barriers to protect themselves.
- **Strengths**: High defense, physical resistance, and the ability to generate protective barriers.
- **Weaknesses**: Vulnerable to Veilguard abilities that bypass defenses, such as **Veil Strike**.
- **Best Tactics**:
    - **Break Through Barriers with Veil Strike**: Corrupted Guardians frequently shield themselves with barriers. Veil Strike can penetrate these barriers, making it an essential ability for this encounter. Equip it in a quick slot and press the assigned button when the Guardian raises its shield.
    - **Focus on Magic and Elemental Attacks**: Physical attacks are often ineffective. Use magic abilities or elemental attacks (such as fire or frost) to weaken their defenses.
    - **Wait for Openings**: Guardians often have a pattern of raising and lowering their defenses. Wait for moments when they're vulnerable to attack, and press "R2" (PlayStation), "RT" (Xbox), or left-click (PC) to strike.

5. Void Hounds

- **Description**: These spectral beasts are agile, capable of teleporting short distances to evade attacks or close the distance to strike quickly. Void Hounds can unleash a barrage of fast, magical attacks.
- **Strengths**: High speed, teleportation abilities, resistant to most physical damage.
- **Weaknesses**: Weak to Veilguard-exclusive abilities, particularly those that prevent teleportation, such as **Fade Shackles**.
- **Best Tactics**:
    - **Use Fade Shackles to Limit Mobility**: Fade Shackles can prevent Void Hounds from teleporting, making it easier to land hits. Equip it in a quick slot and press the assigned button when the Hound begins to teleport.

- **Maintain Range**: Void Hounds are most dangerous up close. Use ranged attacks and spirit-damage abilities to weaken them from a distance.
- **Dodge Their Fast Attacks**: Void Hounds often use rapid-fire magic attacks. Watch for their telltale movement and press "Circle" (PlayStation), "B" (Xbox), or "Space" (PC) to dodge.

6. Veilbound Archons

- **Description**: These ancient beings wield immense magical power and can control elements within the Veil. Veilbound Archons often summon storms, fire, or ice, creating an ever-changing battlefield.
- **Strengths**: High magical damage, elemental control, and ability to alter the environment.
- **Weaknesses**: Vulnerable to coordinated physical and magical attacks, especially those boosted by Veilguard abilities.
- **Best Tactics**:
    - **Use Elemental Resistance Runes**: Veilbound Archons frequently switch between elemental attacks. Equip **Fire Resistance** or **Frost Resistance Runes** based on the Archon's attacks. Open your inventory, select your armor, and apply the appropriate rune.
    - **Stay on the Move**: Archons create elemental hazards around the battlefield. Keep moving to avoid taking consistent damage from fire, ice, or lightning.
    - **Coordinate with Companions for High-Damage Bursts**: Veilbound Archons have short windows of vulnerability. Instruct companions to unleash their strongest abilities at the same time for maximum damage. Press the touchpad (PlayStation), "View" (Xbox), or "T" (PC) to enter tactical mode and direct companion attacks.

Summary of Veilguard-Exclusive Monsters and Tactics

- **Ethereal Reavers**: Counter their phasing with **Veil Strike** and use **Fade Shroud** to stay close.
- **Spectral Giants**: Use spirit-based attacks from a distance and dodge their slow, powerful swings.
- **Veil Terrors**: Interrupt healing with **Veil Disruption** and eliminate summoned minions with AoE abilities.
- **Corrupted Guardians**: Break through barriers with **Veil Strike** and wait for moments when defenses are down.
- **Void Hounds**: Prevent teleportation with **Fade Shackles** and maintain range to avoid close-combat attacks.
- **Veilbound Archons**: Equip elemental resistance runes, stay mobile to avoid environmental hazards, and coordinate burst attacks.

With these tactics, you'll be well-equipped to face and defeat the Veilguard-exclusive monsters that inhabit *The Veilguard*. By understanding their strengths and weaknesses and leveraging your Veilguard abilities, you can conquer these formidable foes and claim the unique rewards they offer. Enjoy the thrill of the battle and the satisfaction of overcoming these challenging creatures in your journey through Thedas!

CHAPTER 11

Special Features and Secrets

In this chapter, you'll uncover the hidden wonders of *Dragon Age: The Veilguard*. From unlocking powerful, hidden skills and abilities to discovering secret locations and treasure hunts, this guide reveals the game's most exciting secrets. Learn about easter eggs and lore references that enrich the Dragon Age universe, rare events, and timed quests that offer unique rewards. Finally, get a comprehensive achievement guide tailored for completionists who want to experience everything *The Veilguard* has to offer. This chapter is your ultimate resource for finding all the game's hidden content and special features.

Unlocking Hidden Skills and Abilities

In *Dragon Age: The Veilguard*, hidden skills and abilities provide a significant advantage, offering unique powers that can only be unlocked through specific quests, challenges, or hidden locations. Unlocking these abilities requires exploration, solving puzzles, and sometimes meeting special requirements. This guide will walk you through how to find and unlock these powerful skills and abilities, including where to go, what to press, and tips to maximize their potential.

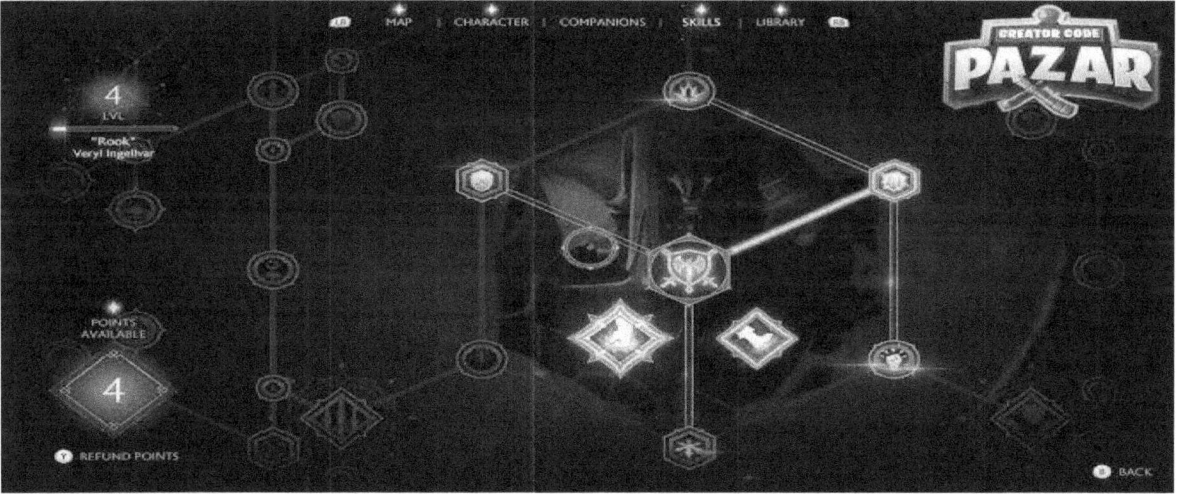

1. Finding Hidden Skill Trainers

- **Mysterious Trainers in Veilguard Zones**: Some hidden skills can only be unlocked by finding specific NPCs or "trainers" located in remote or Veilguard-specific areas.

- **Common Trainer Locations**: Trainers often appear in high-level zones like **Shattered Vale** or **Fade-Worn Woods**. Look for unmarked buildings or areas with distinct landmarks like ancient stones or glowing crystals.
- **How to Interact**: Approach the trainer and press "X" (PlayStation), "A" (Xbox), or "E" (PC) to initiate dialogue. After completing their challenges or quests, the trainer will grant you access to new skills.
- **Meeting Skill Prerequisites**: Some hidden skills require certain skill levels or previous abilities to be unlocked.
  - **How to Check Requirements**: Open the skills menu by pressing "Options" (PlayStation), "Menu" (Xbox), or "C" (PC). Navigate to the hidden skill to see any prerequisites, such as specific skill levels or completed quests.

2. Completing Special Quests for Abilities

- **Veil Trials**:
  - **Description**: These trials are challenging quests found in Veilguard zones, designed to test players in various combat and puzzle-solving scenarios. Successfully completing a Veil Trial often unlocks exclusive Veil abilities.
  - **Where to Find**: Look for **Veil Trial Shrines** in areas like **Veiled Shore** and **Silvered Spire**. These shrines usually emit a faint glow and are surrounded by Veil energy.
  - **How to Start the Trial**: Approach the shrine and press "X" (PlayStation), "A" (Xbox), or "E" (PC) to initiate the trial. You'll need to complete objectives like defeating waves of enemies or solving puzzles to unlock the ability.
- **Guardian Challenges**:
  - **Description**: These are rare, optional boss fights that reward players with unique abilities if they are victorious.
  - **Where to Find**: Guardian bosses are hidden in remote parts of **Dragon's Den** and **Ashen Crag**. Look for entrances marked with ancient runes or symbols.
  - **How to Engage**: Approach the marked area and press "X" (PlayStation), "A" (Xbox), or "E" (PC) to begin the encounter. Successfully defeating the Guardian will grant you a hidden ability tailored to your character's class.

3. Unlocking Abilities through Secret Interactions

- **Ancient Relics and Artifacts**:
  - **Description**: Interacting with specific relics or artifacts across Veilguard zones can unlock unique abilities, especially those that improve your resistance to Fade corruption or enhance your Veilguard skills.
  - **Where to Find**: Look for relics in **Fade-Worn Woods** and **Shattered Vale**. These artifacts often have a unique glow or are found in secluded spots.

- **How to Unlock**: Approach a relic and press "X" (PlayStation), "A" (Xbox), or "E" (PC) to interact. Some relics may require solving a puzzle or defeating nearby enemies before they can be activated.
- **Veil Anomalies**:
  - **Description**: Veil anomalies are hidden disturbances in the Fade that can be found in Veilguard zones. Interacting with these anomalies grants abilities related to Fade manipulation, such as improved mana regeneration or reduced corruption.
  - **Where to Find**: Anomalies are often located near Veil Rifts or Fade-heavy areas like **Silvered Spire**.
  - **How to Access**: Approach an anomaly and press "X" (PlayStation), "A" (Xbox), or "E" (PC) to interact. Some anomalies require specific Veilguard abilities, like **Fade Shroud**, to be active before interaction.

4. Gaining Skills from Ancient Tomes

- **Finding Tomes in Hidden Locations**:
  - **Description**: Ancient tomes are scattered throughout Thedas and contain powerful skills or ability enhancements. Reading these tomes unlocks new abilities or boosts existing ones.
  - **Common Locations**: Tomes can be found in abandoned libraries or ruins like those in **Ashen Crag** and **Stormguard Keep**.
  - **How to Read**: Approach a tome and press "X" (PlayStation), "A" (Xbox), or "E" (PC) to read. Some tomes may be guarded by puzzles or enemies, requiring completion before reading.
- **Meeting Tome Requirements**: Some tomes are locked by skill level or class restrictions.
  - **Checking Requirements**: Hover over the tome's description after interacting to see any restrictions, such as class type or experience level.

5. Unlocking Class-Specific Hidden Abilities

- **Warrior - Veilbound Rage**:
  - **Description**: This ability grants the warrior a temporary boost in strength, making them nearly unstoppable for a short period.
  - **How to Unlock**: Complete a Guardian Challenge in **Dragon's Den** to unlock. After finishing the challenge, speak with the warrior trainer who appears.
  - **Using Veilbound Rage**: Equip it in your abilities menu and press the quick slot button during combat to activate, increasing attack power temporarily.
- **Mage - Fade's Touch**:
  - **Description**: A powerful spell that increases mana regeneration and grants a chance to deal spirit damage to all nearby enemies.
  - **How to Unlock**: Find the mage-specific tome in **Silvered Spire** and interact with it to unlock Fade's Touch.

- **Using Fade's Touch**: Equip in your abilities menu and activate by pressing the assigned quick slot button when surrounded by enemies for maximum effect.
- **Rogue - Shadow's Embrace**:
  - **Description**: This skill allows the rogue to become invisible for a short time, boosting their critical hit chance on the next attack.
  - **How to Unlock**: Complete a Veil Trial at **Veiled Shore** and select the reward for rogues.
  - **Using Shadow's Embrace**: Equip the ability in a quick slot and press it during combat to activate invisibility and prepare a critical strike.

6. Unlocking Group Abilities for Companions

- **Coordinated Assault**:
  - **Description**: This group ability boosts the team's damage for a short period when activated, making it useful for tough battles.
  - **How to Unlock**: Complete the "Unity in Battle" quest found in **Stormguard Keep** and interact with the shrine at the end of the quest.
  - **How to Use**: Equip it in the team abilities menu, then press the assigned quick slot button during a group encounter for a powerful team boost.
- **Protective Aura**:
  - **Description**: Creates a shield that reduces incoming damage for all nearby allies.
  - **How to Unlock**: Speak to the healer NPC in **Brightfall Village** after completing three Veil Trials. She will grant you access to the Protective Aura ability.
  - **How to Use**: Equip it in the abilities menu, then press the assigned button during combat to protect your team from high-damage attacks.

Summary of Unlocking Hidden Skills and Abilities

- **Find Skill Trainers in Veilguard Zones**: Look for hidden NPCs who can train you in special abilities.
- **Complete Veil Trials and Guardian Challenges**: These quests reward powerful abilities that improve your character's effectiveness.
- **Interact with Relics, Artifacts, and Anomalies**: Veilguard zones are filled with items that unlock unique skills when activated.
- **Locate Ancient Tomes**: Hidden tomes provide new abilities or enhancements and are often guarded or locked.
- **Gain Class-Specific Skills**: Warriors, mages, and rogues each have unique hidden abilities accessible through specific trials and locations.
- **Unlock Group Abilities for Companion Synergy**: Group abilities can be unlocked for powerful team-based effects during challenging battles.

By following these steps, you'll unlock the hidden skills and abilities that give you an edge in *The Veilguard*. These skills not only enhance your combat effectiveness but also open up new strategies and opportunities for exploration. Enjoy discovering and mastering these powerful secrets to become a true force in Thedas!

Secret Locations and Treasure Hunts

In *Dragon Age: The Veilguard*, secret locations and treasure hunts add an exciting layer of exploration, rewarding players with rare loot, hidden abilities, and valuable lore. These secret spots are often tucked away in obscure corners of the map, concealed by puzzles, or guarded by challenging enemies. Here's a detailed guide to help you locate and unlock these hidden treasures, including what to look for, where to go, and how to overcome any obstacles along the way.

1. Locating Hidden Caves and Ruins

- **Veiled Hollow (Veilguard Zone)**:
  - **Description**: A mysterious cave in **Veiled Shore** known to contain rare artifacts and high-tier loot.
  - **How to Find**: Head to the northern cliffs of Veiled Shore. Look for a small path marked by faded symbols on nearby rocks. Follow the path until you reach a hidden cave entrance.
  - **How to Enter**: Approach the entrance and press "X" (PlayStation), "A" (Xbox), or "E" (PC) to enter. Be prepared to face high-level enemies inside, so bring powerful weapons and healing potions.
- **Sunken Sanctum (Ashen Crag)**:
  - **Description**: This hidden ruin is submerged partially underwater and contains treasures from an ancient civilization.
  - **How to Find**: In the **Ashen Crag** region, locate a small waterfall. Behind it, you'll find an entrance partially hidden by rocks.
  - **How to Access**: Press "X" (PlayStation), "A" (Xbox), or "E" (PC) to enter. Be cautious of traps inside, and look for levers to unlock deeper sections of the ruin.

2. Navigating Puzzle-Based Treasure Hunts

- **The Crystal Path Puzzle (Shattered Vale)**:
  - **Description**: This treasure hunt involves a puzzle where you must activate crystals in the correct order to open a hidden chamber.
  - **How to Solve**: In **Shattered Vale**, find an arrangement of colored crystals on the ground. Observe their color patterns and activate them in the sequence of blue, green, red, and yellow. Each crystal is activated by pressing "X" (PlayStation), "A" (Xbox), or "E" (PC).

○ **Reward**: Completing the puzzle opens a hidden chamber containing rare Veilguard artifacts and an exclusive weapon upgrade.

- **Veilguard Monoliths (Fade-Worn Woods)**:
  ○ **Description**: Scattered monoliths contain inscriptions that reveal clues to treasure locations. Each monolith offers a piece of a riddle or map.
  ○ **How to Follow Clues**: Activate each monolith by pressing "X" (PlayStation), "A" (Xbox), or "E" (PC) to view its clue. Follow the directions to a hidden area where you'll find a buried chest.
  ○ **Reward**: A unique accessory that boosts Veilguard abilities, enhancing your power when facing Veil creatures.

3. Exploring Secret Shrines and Altars

- **Altar of the Forgotten (Stormguard Keep)**:
  ○ **Description**: This hidden shrine grants powerful blessings and rare items but requires solving a riddle to access.
  ○ **How to Find**: In **Stormguard Keep**, locate the northeast courtyard. You'll see an unmarked path leading to a concealed door. Approach the altar and press "X" (PlayStation), "A" (Xbox), or "E" (PC) to interact.
  ○ **Riddle Solution**: The altar asks a riddle related to the elements of earth, fire, water, and air. Select options in this order: **earth, fire, water, air**. Successfully solving it opens a hidden compartment with a powerful amulet and a unique weapon.
- **Veil's Embrace (Silvered Spire)**:
  ○ **Description**: A shrine that enhances your Veil abilities and unlocks a hidden skill.
  ○ **How to Access**: Near the top of the **Silvered Spire**, find an inconspicuous staircase leading to a small room with an altar. Press "X" (PlayStation), "A" (Xbox), or "E" (PC) to interact.
  ○ **How to Activate**: Place three unique items—such as spirit essence, a fragment of Veil quartz, and a rare herb—on the altar. Completing the offering grants you a skill that improves your resistance to corruption in Veilguard zones.

4. Treasure Maps and Clues for Hidden Chests

- **Map of the Hidden Lagoon**:
  ○ **Description**: A treasure map found in **Greenwood Thicket** that leads to a hidden lagoon filled with valuable loot.
  ○ **How to Acquire**: The map is hidden in a chest guarded by Shade Wolves in **Greenwood Thicket**. Defeat the wolves, open the chest, and take the map.
  ○ **How to Follow**: The map shows a path from Greenwood Thicket to a lagoon with a rock shaped like an arch. Once at the location, press "X" (PlayStation), "A" (Xbox), or "E" (PC) to dig and unearth a chest containing rare gems and potions.

- **Veilguard Cartographer's Map**:
  - **Description**: This map provides clues to a hidden cache of Veilguard artifacts buried in **Fade-Worn Woods**.
  - **How to Acquire**: Find the map on a defeated spirit mage in **Silvered Spire**.
  - **How to Use**: Follow the map's directions to a clearing in Fade-Worn Woods, near an unusual tree formation. Press "X" (PlayStation), "A" (Xbox), or "E" (PC) to dig, revealing a chest with Veilguard artifacts and a powerful Veil-infused weapon.

5. Collecting Hidden Relics for Rewards

- **Relics of the Ancients (Shattered Vale)**:
  - **Description**: Collect five ancient relics scattered across Shattered Vale to unlock a hidden skill and a rare piece of armor.
  - **How to Find**: Look for relics inside hidden caves, guarded ruins, and abandoned structures in Shattered Vale. Each relic emits a faint blue glow.
  - **How to Collect**: Approach each relic and press "X" (PlayStation), "A" (Xbox), or "E" (PC) to add it to your collection.
  - **Reward**: After gathering all five relics, a prompt will appear to return to **Stormguard Keep**. Speak with the historian NPC to receive a Veilguard skill and a unique armor set.
- **The Seven Sigils of Power (Veilguard Zones)**:
  - **Description**: Seven sigils are hidden in Veilguard zones, each enhancing a different Veilguard ability.
  - **How to Locate**: These sigils are scattered throughout Veilguard zones like **Veiled Shore** and **Fade-Worn Woods**, often in hard-to-reach locations or guarded by powerful enemies.
  - **How to Collect**: Approach each sigil and press "X" (PlayStation), "A" (Xbox), or "E" (PC) to claim it.
  - **Reward**: Collecting all seven sigils unlocks the "Master of the Veil" title, a special ability, and boosts to all Veilguard skills.

6. Timed Treasure Hunts and Rare Events

- **The Lunar Eclipse Hunt**:
  - **Description**: A treasure hunt available only during a rare in-game lunar eclipse event, which spawns a unique boss and grants valuable loot.
  - **How to Participate**: Check the in-game calendar to find the date of the next lunar eclipse. Travel to **Veiled Shore** during the eclipse and look for a glowing portal.
  - **How to Enter**: Approach the portal and press "X" (PlayStation), "A" (Xbox), or "E" (PC) to begin the hunt. Defeat the boss to earn exclusive items, including a legendary weapon.
- **Veil Rift Surge**:

- ○ **Description**: During certain times, Veil Rifts in **Silvered Spire** grow unstable, revealing hidden treasures and enhanced enemies.
- ○ **How to Participate**: Visit **Silvered Spire** during a Veil Rift Surge event, which will be marked on your map. Engage with the rifts by pressing "X" (PlayStation), "A" (Xbox), or "E" (PC).
- ○ **Reward**: Each rift defeated during a surge rewards you with rare Veilguard materials and a unique enchantment for your equipment.

Summary of Secret Locations and Treasure Hunts

- **Explore Hidden Caves and Ruins**: Find secluded spots like Veiled Hollow and Sunken Sanctum for valuable loot.
- **Solve Puzzle-Based Treasure Hunts**: Engage with the Crystal Path and Veilguard Monoliths to unlock hidden chambers.
- **Activate Secret Shrines and Altars**: Places like the Altar of the Forgotten and Veil's Embrace grant powerful items and abilities.
- **Follow Treasure Maps and Clues**: Use maps to uncover buried chests and special artifacts in locations like Greenwood Thicket and Fade-Worn Woods.
- **Collect Relics for Powerful Rewards**: Relics in Shattered Vale and sigils in Veilguard zones unlock skills and rare gear.
- **Participate in Timed Events and Rare Hunts**: Events like the Lunar Eclipse Hunt and Veil Rift Surge offer exclusive loot during limited windows.

By following this guide, you'll be able to locate and unlock the hidden treasures scattered throughout *The Veilguard*. These secret locations and treasure hunts add an extra layer of excitement, giving you access to powerful items, skills, and lore that enhance your adventure through Thedas. Enjoy the thrill of the hunt and the rewards that await!

Easter Eggs and Lore References

In *Dragon Age: The Veilguard*, there are numerous hidden details, nods to the series' rich history, and clever easter eggs that longtime fans will appreciate. These hidden elements range from references to past characters and events to amusing nods to pop culture. This guide explores where to find these easter eggs and lore references, how to unlock them, and what each one means in the larger Dragon Age universe.

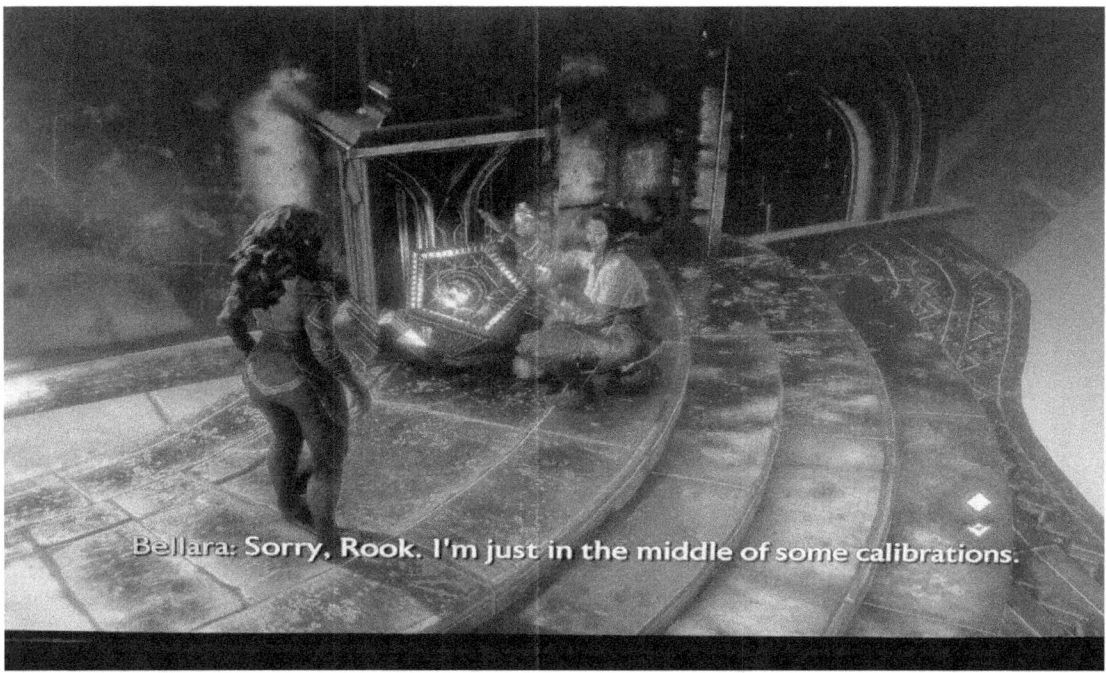

Bellara: Sorry, Rook. I'm just in the middle of some calibrations.

1. Character References from Previous Games

- **The Grey Warden's Sword (Shattered Vale)**:
  - **Description**: This hidden item is a reference to the legendary Grey Wardens and their fight against the Blight.
  - **Where to Find**: In **Shattered Vale**, search near the broken ruins in the southwest. You'll find a sword embedded in the ground, bearing the Grey Warden insignia.
  - **How to Interact**: Approach the sword and press "X" (PlayStation), "A" (Xbox), or "E" (PC) to interact. Doing so unlocks a short dialogue referencing the Wardens' role in protecting Thedas.
- **Anders' Clinic Sign (Stormguard Keep)**:
  - **Description**: A small sign labeled "Anders' Clinic" is a nod to the healer and former Grey Warden from *Dragon Age II*.
  - **Where to Find**: At **Stormguard Keep**, look near the healer's quarters to find a small sign tucked into a corner.
  - **How to Interact**: Press "X" (PlayStation), "A" (Xbox), or "E" (PC) to read the sign, triggering a brief message about Anders' dedication to helping the less fortunate.

2. Hidden Lore Books and Journals

- **The Tale of Flemeth (Ashen Crag)**:
  - **Description**: This lore book tells the story of Flemeth, the enigmatic sorceress who has played a pivotal role throughout the Dragon Age series.

- **Where to Find**: In **Ashen Crag**, near a deserted camp, you'll find an old, worn book with faded text.
- **How to Read**: Approach the book and press "X" (PlayStation), "A" (Xbox), or "E" (PC) to read it. The book contains details about Flemeth's past, hinting at her ancient origins and influence.

- **The Chant of Andraste (Fade-Worn Woods)**:
  - **Description**: This collection of verses from the Chant of Light, Andraste's teachings, is hidden in the Fade-Worn Woods.
  - **Where to Find**: Look for a small shrine near a waterfall in Fade-Worn Woods. The Chant is inscribed on a stone tablet beside the shrine.
  - **How to Interact**: Press "X" (PlayStation), "A" (Xbox), or "E" (PC) to read the Chant, gaining insight into Andraste's philosophy and the religious foundation of Thedas.

3. Pop Culture References

- **The "Griffon's Nest" (Silvered Spire)**:
  - **Description**: A subtle nod to *Game of Thrones*, this area includes a nest with a broken egg labeled "House Griffon."
  - **Where to Find**: Near the top of **Silvered Spire**, you'll find a small nest with a griffon's egg.
  - **How to Interact**: Approach the nest and press "X" (PlayStation), "A" (Xbox), or "E" (PC) to examine it, triggering a humorous dialogue about "winter approaching" and the strength of House Griffon.

- **The "Lost Ring of Invisibility" (Brightfall Village)**:
  - **Description**: A clever nod to *The Lord of the Rings*, this tiny, near-invisible ring has been "lost" by its former owner.
  - **Where to Find**: Near the fountain in **Brightfall Village**, look closely at the ground to find a small, glimmering ring.
  - **How to Interact**: Press "X" (PlayStation), "A" (Xbox), or "E" (PC) to pick up the ring. A brief description will pop up, referencing its ability to make its wearer invisible "at a terrible cost."

4. References to Key Events in Thedas' History

- **The First Blight Plaque (Dragon's Den)**:
  - **Description**: This plaque commemorates the First Blight and the Grey Wardens' role in ending it.
  - **Where to Find**: In **Dragon's Den**, look for a stone plaque near the main entrance, inscribed with text honoring the Wardens.
  - **How to Read**: Approach the plaque and press "X" (PlayStation), "A" (Xbox), or "E" (PC) to read it, uncovering lore about the ancient struggle against the Darkspawn.

- **The Lost Templar Helm (Veiled Shore):**
  - ○ **Description**: A rusted Templar helm that recalls the conflicts between mages and Templars throughout Thedas' history.
  - ○ **Where to Find**: Near the cliffs in **Veiled Shore**, look for a helm partially buried in the sand.
  - ○ **How to Interact**: Press "X" (PlayStation), "A" (Xbox), or "E" (PC) to pick up the helm. A description appears, noting its connection to the Mage-Templar wars and the long-lost Templar who once wore it.

5. Veilguard-Exclusive Easter Eggs

- **Veilwalker's Mirror (Veiled Shore):**
  - ○ **Description**: This enchanted mirror allows a brief glimpse into the Veil, showing spirits and past events.
  - ○ **Where to Find**: Located in a hidden alcove on **Veiled Shore**, near an old, crumbling tower.
  - ○ **How to Use**: Approach the mirror and press "X" (PlayStation), "A" (Xbox), or "E" (PC) to gaze into it. The mirror will display spectral images of past Veilguard mages, offering hints about lost spells and abilities.
- **The Phantom Locket (Fade-Worn Woods):**
  - ○ **Description**: This locket is a Veilguard-exclusive item with the power to reveal hidden paths and doors in Veilguard zones.
  - ○ **Where to Find**: Hidden in a hollow tree in **Fade-Worn Woods**, the locket is guarded by a Shade Wolf.
  - ○ **How to Unlock**: Defeat the Shade Wolf and approach the locket, pressing "X" (PlayStation), "A" (Xbox), or "E" (PC) to collect it. Wearing the locket highlights hidden paths in Veilguard zones, leading to secret areas.

6. Dialogue-Based Lore References

- **Varric's Lost Manuscript (Stormguard Keep):**
  - ○ **Description**: This unfinished manuscript is a nod to Varric's novel series from previous games.
  - ○ **Where to Find**: In **Stormguard Keep**, search the barracks. On a small table, you'll find a manuscript with Varric's name on it.
  - ○ **How to Read**: Approach and press "X" (PlayStation), "A" (Xbox), or "E" (PC) to read the unfinished pages, revealing humorous excerpts and characters reminiscent of Varric's stories.
- **Morrigan's Grimoire Reference (Ashen Crag):**
  - ○ **Description**: A page from Morrigan's grimoire contains spells and hints about her journey after the events of *Dragon Age: Inquisition*.
  - ○ **Where to Find**: In **Ashen Crag**, find a small, unlit campfire near a cliff. A weathered page lies beside it.

    ○ **How to Interact**: Press "X" (PlayStation), "A" (Xbox), or "E" (PC) to pick up the page, which hints at Morrigan's continued research into ancient magic.

Summary of Easter Eggs and Lore References

- **Find References to Past Characters**: Explore Shattered Vale and Stormguard Keep for items that recall the Grey Wardens, Anders, and other beloved characters.
- **Discover Hidden Lore Books and Journals**: Collect books like *The Tale of Flemeth* and *The Chant of Andraste* to deepen your understanding of Thedas' history.
- **Enjoy Pop Culture Nods**: Locate items like the Griffon's Nest and the "Lost Ring of Invisibility" for light-hearted, fun references to fantasy classics.
- **Uncover Historical Plaques and Memorials**: Examine the First Blight Plaque in Dragon's Den and the Templar Helm in Veiled Shore for insights into key events in Thedas.
- **Interact with Veilguard-Exclusive Items**: Use items like the Veilwalker's Mirror and Phantom Locket to explore hidden paths and gain new perspectives on the Veil.
- **Read Dialogue-Based References**: Look for dialogue items such as Varric's Manuscript and Morrigan's Grimoire page to revisit stories of iconic Dragon Age characters.

By following this guide, you'll uncover all the hidden easter eggs and lore references throughout *The Veilguard*. These secrets add depth to your journey, paying homage to past adventures and providing insights into the wider world of Thedas. Enjoy discovering these hidden gems as you explore!

Rare Events and Timed Quests

Dragon Age: The Veilguard offers unique rare events and timed quests that challenge players to engage in limited-time content for exclusive rewards, powerful abilities, and lore insights. Participating in these events requires attention to the in-game calendar and environmental cues, as these quests are only accessible during specific times or conditions. This guide provides details on how to access and complete these rare events, including tips for maximizing your rewards.

1. Lunar Eclipse Hunt

- **Description**: The Lunar Eclipse Hunt is a limited-time event where players can face a unique boss that appears only during an in-game lunar eclipse. This powerful creature drops rare loot and Veilguard-exclusive gear.

- **When It Occurs**: Check the in-game calendar to find the next lunar eclipse. These occur periodically, so planning ahead is essential.
- **Where to Find**: During the lunar eclipse, travel to **Veiled Shore** and look for a glowing blue portal near the water's edge.
- **How to Enter**: Approach the portal and press "X" (PlayStation), "A" (Xbox), or "E" (PC) to enter. You'll be transported to a special arena to face the lunar eclipse boss.
- **Tips for Success**:
  - **Equip High-Resilience Gear**: The boss deals shadow and spirit damage, so equip armor with spirit resistance.
  - **Bring Companions with Veil Abilities**: Abilities like **Veil Strike** and **Fade Shroud** can disrupt the boss's attacks and give you an edge.
- **Rewards**: Successfully defeating the boss yields exclusive lunar-themed weapons, a rare Veilguard amulet, and materials to enhance your Veilguard abilities.

2. Veil Rift Surge

- **Description**: Veil Rift Surges occur when the Veil becomes highly unstable, causing rifts to appear with enhanced enemies and rare loot. These events allow players to earn valuable rewards, Veilguard relics, and magical upgrades.
- **When It Occurs**: Veil Rift Surges happen sporadically and are marked on your in-game map with a flashing purple icon.
- **Where to Go**: Travel to **Silvered Spire** during a Veil Rift Surge and locate the marked rifts. Multiple rifts may appear simultaneously, so be prepared to clear them all.
- **How to Start**: Approach each rift and press "X" (PlayStation), "A" (Xbox), or "E" (PC) to initiate the encounter. Defeat waves of enemies to stabilize the rift.
- **Tips for Success**:
  - **Focus on Clearing Minions First**: Rift surges spawn multiple enemies at once. Eliminate smaller foes quickly to avoid being overwhelmed.
  - **Use Veilguard Abilities for Crowd Control**: **Veil Pulse** and **Spirit Ward** are particularly effective for managing large groups.
- **Rewards**: Each stabilized rift rewards you with rare Veilguard relics, powerful enchantments, and experience boosts. Completing all rifts in the event grants a special Veilguard charm.

3. Celestial Convergence Event

- **Description**: During a celestial convergence, constellations in the sky align, opening up portals to hidden locations with exclusive lore and treasures.

- **When It Occurs**: Celestial convergence happens once a month in-game. Look for a message in the journal about unusual celestial activity.
- **Where to Go**: Head to **Stormguard Keep** and find the central observatory. A new portal will appear under the main telescope.
- **How to Access**: Approach the portal and press "X" (PlayStation), "A" (Xbox), or "E" (PC) to enter a hidden star-lit zone.
- **Tips for Success**:
    - **Prepare for Puzzle Solving**: The celestial zone includes puzzles based on constellation patterns. Pay close attention to the sky and nearby clues.
    - **Use Light-Based Abilities**: Certain puzzles require abilities like **Fade Light** to illuminate hidden paths.
- **Rewards**: Completing the convergence zone rewards you with starlit armor, a unique weapon with celestial buffs, and lore items that reveal insights about the ancient mages of the Veil.

4. Seasonal Festival Quests

- **Description**: Seasonal festivals in *The Veilguard* introduce timed quests with festive themes, mini-games, and event-specific items. These quests are only available during specific times of the year, like the Winter Solstice or Harvest Festival.
- **When They Occur**: Each festival lasts about a week in real-time and aligns with real-world seasons.
- **Where to Participate**: Visit **Brightfall Village** during festival periods. Look for event NPCs who offer unique festival quests and activities.
- **How to Start Quests**: Approach any NPC with a seasonal icon above their head and press "X" (PlayStation), "A" (Xbox), or "E" (PC) to speak with them and start the quest.
- **Tips for Success**:
    - **Try the Mini-Games**: Festival events often include mini-games like archery or races, which reward extra points and seasonal items.
    - **Collect Festival Tokens**: Complete quests to earn tokens, which can be exchanged for event-exclusive items.
- **Rewards**: Festival events reward you with themed clothing, decorations for your camp, and limited-edition potions or charms.

5. Spirit Hunter's Moon

- **Description**: The Spirit Hunter's Moon is a special event where spirits become more active, making it an ideal time for Veilguard mages to hunt them and gather rare resources.
- **When It Occurs**: This event takes place on the full moon every few in-game months, making spirits and Veil creatures more aggressive.
- **Where to Go**: Head to **Fade-Worn Woods** during the full moon. Enemies will be marked with a green aura, signifying increased difficulty and enhanced loot.

- **How to Engage**: Approach marked enemies and press "X" (PlayStation), "A" (Xbox), or "E" (PC) to initiate combat.
- **Tips for Success**:
  - **Equip Spirit Resistance Runes**: Since spirits are stronger during the full moon, spirit resistance runes are helpful for mitigating damage.
  - **Use Veilguard Abilities for Damage Boosts**: Abilities like **Veil Strike** and **Spirit Ward** become more powerful during this event.
- **Rewards**: Successfully defeating marked spirits grants Veilguard-exclusive materials, such as Spirit Essence and Fade Crystal, used for high-level crafting.

6. The Enchanter's Eclipse

- **Description**: The Enchanter's Eclipse is a rare event where the Veil weakens, allowing access to a hidden area known as the **Enchanter's Sanctum**. Here, players can find ancient scrolls and rare enchantments.
- **When It Occurs**: This event happens during certain eclipses in-game. Check the in-game journal for "Veil Disturbances" to see when it's active.
- **Where to Access**: Travel to **Ashen Crag** during the eclipse, where a portal to the Enchanter's Sanctum will appear near the cliffside.
- **How to Enter**: Approach the portal and press "X" (PlayStation), "A" (Xbox), or "E" (PC) to enter. You'll need to solve enchantment-based puzzles inside the sanctum.
- **Tips for Success**:
  - **Bring High-Level Enchanting Materials**: Some puzzles require you to place enchantment runes on pedestals to unlock doors.
  - **Avoid Traps**: The Enchanter's Sanctum is filled with traps. Move carefully and look for signs of pressure plates on the floor.
- **Rewards**: Completing the sanctum rewards you with powerful enchantments, rare materials, and an exclusive Veilguard skill for enhancing magical abilities.

Summary of Rare Events and Timed Quests

- **Lunar Eclipse Hunt**: A powerful boss battle in Veiled Shore, granting exclusive lunar-themed gear.
- **Veil Rift Surge**: Stabilize multiple rifts in Silvered Spire for Veilguard relics and magical upgrades.
- **Celestial Convergence**: Solve constellation-based puzzles in Stormguard Keep for starlit armor and celestial-themed rewards.
- **Seasonal Festival Quests**: Participate in Brightfall Village's seasonal events for limited-time items, mini-games, and rewards.
- **Spirit Hunter's Moon**: Hunt enhanced spirits in Fade-Worn Woods during a full moon for Veilguard crafting materials.

- **The Enchanter's Eclipse**: Enter the Enchanter's Sanctum in Ashen Crag during a Veil eclipse for ancient enchantments and Veilguard-exclusive skills.

By participating in these rare events and timed quests, you'll unlock unique rewards, powerful abilities, and insights into the rich lore of *The Veilguard*. These events offer a fresh and challenging experience, rewarding players who seek out rare opportunities and complete them with strategy and skill. Enjoy discovering all the unique content these events bring to your adventure!

Achievement Guide for Completionists

In *Dragon Age: The Veilguard*, achievements not only provide a sense of accomplishment but also offer rewards, unlock exclusive abilities, and add a deeper understanding of the game's lore. This guide covers the key achievements in *The Veilguard* that completionists will want to pursue, including tips on where to go, what to do, and how to maximize your progress toward completing each one.

1. Master of the Veil

- **Description**: Unlock all Veilguard abilities and reach the highest level in each skill.
- **Requirements**: Fully upgrade each Veilguard ability by completing Veilguard quests, defeating high-level Veil creatures, and gathering rare materials.
- **Where to Start**: Begin by visiting **Brightfall Village** and speaking with the Veilguard mentor NPC, who provides access to ability quests.
- **Tips for Completion**:
  - **Collect Veil Essence**: Veil Essence is necessary to upgrade abilities. Farm it by defeating high-level Veil creatures in **Veiled Shore** and **Fade-Worn Woods**.
  - **Use Veil Trials**: Completing Veil Trials in **Silvered Spire** rewards Veil Essence and ability points, which are essential for full upgrades.
- **Reward**: Unlocking this achievement grants you the title "Master of the Veil" and an exclusive Veilguard cloak with a bonus to Veil abilities.

2. Legendary Slayer

- **Description**: Defeat all legendary bosses in *The Veilguard*.
- **Requirements**: Track down and defeat each legendary boss, some of which only appear during rare events or in specific locations.
- **Where to Find Bosses**:
  - **Lunar Eclipse Boss**: Found in **Veiled Shore** during the Lunar Eclipse Hunt event.
  - **Spectral Giant**: Found in **Fade-Worn Woods**.

- Veilguard Archmage: Located in **Silvered Spire** during a Veil Rift Surge.
- **Tips for Completion**:
  - **Bring Elemental Resistance Gear**: Many bosses use elemental attacks, so prepare with appropriate resistances.
  - **Coordinate with Companions**: Some legendary bosses have multiple phases. Use tactical mode (touchpad on PlayStation, "View" on Xbox, or "T" on PC) to direct your companions for strategic attacks.
- **Reward**: Completing this achievement grants you a unique weapon, "The Veil's Edge," with special bonuses against Veil creatures.

3. Collector of Relics

- **Description**: Find and collect all ancient relics scattered throughout Thedas.
- **Requirements**: Locate and collect all relics, including Veilguard sigils, ancient tomes, and unique artifacts.
- **Where to Look**:
  - **Shattered Vale**: Five relics are scattered around the ruins.
  - **Stormguard Keep**: Look for sigils and artifacts in hidden rooms and behind guarded doors.
  - **Veiled Shore**: Check near cliffside paths and in hidden caves.
- **Tips for Completion**:
  - **Use a Companion with Tracking Skills**: Some companions have abilities that highlight hidden items nearby, making relic-hunting easier.
  - **Complete Related Quests**: Certain relics are only accessible through specific side quests. Check your quest log regularly to ensure you haven't missed any.
- **Reward**: Completing this achievement unlocks a rare relic display for your camp, enhancing stats while in Veilguard zones.

4. Lore Keeper

- **Description**: Collect every lore book, journal, and artifact to uncover the history and secrets of Thedas.
- **Requirements**: Find all lore entries across the map, many of which are hidden in hard-to-reach places or guarded by enemies.
- **Where to Find Lore Items**:
  - **Ashen Crag**: The Tale of Flemeth can be found in a remote camp.
  - **Fade-Worn Woods**: Chant of Andraste inscriptions near the waterfalls.
  - **Silvered Spire**: Rare scrolls and journals in the hidden rooms.
- **Tips for Completion**:
  - **Explore Thoroughly**: Lore items are often hidden in unmarked locations. Search every corner and abandoned area.

        o **Check with NPCs**: Some lore items are unlocked by speaking with certain characters who reveal locations or give hints.
- **Reward**: Completing this achievement unlocks the "Lore Keeper" title and a unique lore compendium in your inventory.

5. Completionist's Heart

- **Description**: Complete every side quest, timed event, and hidden task in *The Veilguard*.
- **Requirements**: Finish all main and side quests, participate in each seasonal festival, complete Veilguard-specific challenges, and find all hidden tasks.
- **Tips for Completion**:
    o **Participate in Events**: Track rare events and participate in seasonal quests. Use the in-game calendar to stay on top of timed events.
    o **Keep an Updated Quest Log**: Use the journal to monitor quest progress, ensuring no side quests are missed.
    o **Talk to NPCs in Each Location**: NPCs in villages and outposts may offer additional tasks or clues to hidden quests.
- **Reward**: Unlocking this achievement grants the "Completionist's Heart" medal and a rare accessory that boosts all primary stats.

6. Veilguard Explorer

- **Description**: Discover all secret locations, hidden caves, and Veilguard-exclusive zones.
- **Requirements**: Explore every hidden area, from the Sunken Sanctum to the Veiled Hollow, and locate all secret shrines and altars.
- **Where to Explore**:
    o **Veiled Shore**: Find hidden caves like Veiled Hollow and locate the Veilwalker's Mirror.
    o **Stormguard Keep**: Access secret rooms in the observatory during the Celestial Convergence event.
    o **Ashen Crag**: Discover the Sunken Sanctum behind the waterfall.
- **Tips for Completion**:
    o **Use Veilguard Abilities**: Certain hidden paths are only accessible with Veilguard abilities like **Fade Shroud** or **Veil Pulse**.
    o **Look for Unmarked Trails**: Follow unmarked paths and check behind natural formations like waterfalls or cliffs.
- **Reward**: Completing this achievement grants the "Veilguard Explorer" title and a special map showing the locations of future events and hidden areas.

7. The Unseen Path

- **Description**: Successfully complete all stealth-based challenges and hidden objectives.
- **Requirements**: Perform stealth takedowns, infiltrate high-security zones, and complete quests without being detected.
- **Where to Go**:
    - **Fade-Worn Woods**: Several quests require stealth to avoid Veil creatures.
    - **Stormguard Keep**: Infiltrate restricted areas undetected during specific quests.
- **Tips for Completion**:
    - **Equip Stealth Gear**: Items that reduce sound or boost stealth capabilities are essential.
    - **Use Shadow's Embrace**: If you're a rogue, activate **Shadow's Embrace** to remain hidden and increase critical hit chance.
- **Reward**: Unlocks a stealth-exclusive weapon and the title "The Shadowed One."

8. Champion of Thedas

- **Description**: Earn this title by completing the main storyline, all legendary boss battles, and every timed event and rare quest.
- **Requirements**: This achievement is one of the most challenging, requiring you to complete every main and side objective, including event-based content.
- **Where to Focus**:
    - **Complete Main and Side Quests**: Finish the main storyline and every available side quest.
    - **Defeat All Bosses and Participate in Rare Events**: Track down all legendary bosses and attend every event, from Lunar Eclipse Hunts to seasonal festivals.
- **Tips for Completion**:
    - **Use Completionist Checklists**: Track all main and side quest objectives, boss battles, and event participation to ensure you don't miss anything.
    - **Prepare for High-Level Content**: Equip the best available gear, and bring companions with a range of abilities to handle varied challenges.
- **Reward**: The "Champion of Thedas" title, a rare armor set, and a unique Veilguard relic that boosts all Veil abilities and resistances.

Summary of Key Achievements for Completionists

- **Master of the Veil**: Fully upgrade all Veilguard abilities by completing ability quests and collecting Veil Essence.
- **Legendary Slayer**: Defeat all legendary bosses in *The Veilguard* for the ultimate weapon.
- **Collector of Relics**: Collect all ancient relics for an exclusive display and bonuses in Veilguard zones.
- **Lore Keeper**: Find every lore entry for insights into Thedas' history and an in-game lore compendium.
- **Completionist's Heart**: Finish all quests and events for a powerful accessory that boosts all stats.

- **Veilguard Explorer**: Discover every secret location and earn a special map for future events.
- **The Unseen Path**: Complete all stealth challenges for a stealth-exclusive weapon.
- **Champion of Thedas**: Achieve the highest honor by completing all game content, including boss battles and rare events, to unlock unique armor and a Veilguard relic.

CHAPTER 12

Game Modes and Multiplayer

This chapter introduces the various game modes in *Dragon Age: The Veilguard*, from solo campaigns to cooperative multiplayer. You'll learn about each mode's unique features, the challenges they bring, and how to best team up with other players in multiplayer. Discover strategies for maximizing your success, whether playing solo, with friends, or joining forces with new allies online. This guide provides tips on coordinating with others, managing team roles, and making the most of your skills in both competitive and cooperative environments.

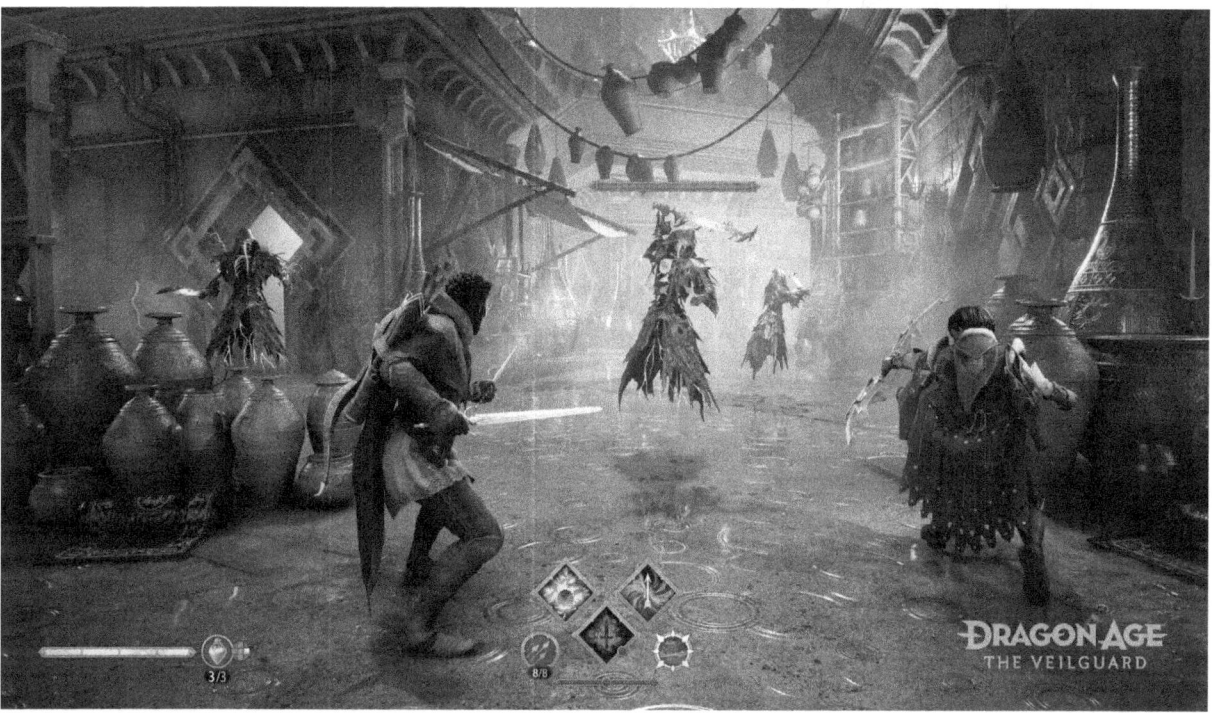

Veilguard Multiplayer Features

Dragon Age: The Veilguard offers a rich multiplayer experience that combines cooperative team play with strategic depth, allowing you to tackle challenging quests, explore exclusive multiplayer dungeons, and unlock unique rewards with friends or new allies online. This guide covers everything you need to know about the multiplayer features in *The Veilguard*, including how to set up a session, coordinate with teammates, and make the most of multiplayer-only content.

1. Setting Up a Multiplayer Session

- **Creating a Lobby**: To start a multiplayer session, head to the main menu and select **Multiplayer**. From here, you can either create a private lobby for friends or join a public game.
  - **How to Create a Lobby**: Select **Create Lobby** and press "X" (PlayStation), "A" (Xbox), or click on **Create** (PC). You'll have the option to invite friends from your platform or set the lobby to public for open matchmaking.
- **Inviting Friends**: Once your lobby is created, you can invite friends to join.
  - **How to Invite Friends**: Open your friends list from the multiplayer lobby, select the friend you want to invite, and press "X" (PlayStation), "A" (Xbox), or click **Invite** (PC) to send an invitation.
- **Joining an Existing Lobby**: To join a public lobby, select **Quick Match** from the multiplayer menu, and the game will find an open session based on your level and preferred game mode.
  - **How to Join**: Press "X" (PlayStation), "A" (Xbox), or click **Quick Match** (PC) to be placed in a session with other players.

2. Game Modes in Multiplayer

- **Cooperative Campaign**: In this mode, you can team up with other players to complete story-driven quests and missions that expand on *The Veilguard* storyline. Cooperative Campaign offers tougher enemies and requires strong teamwork and communication.
  - **How to Access**: Select **Cooperative Campaign** from the multiplayer menu and choose your preferred mission or story arc. Press "X" (PlayStation), "A" (Xbox), or click **Start** (PC) to begin.
  - **Tips**:
    - **Coordinate Abilities**: Assign roles for damage dealing, healing, and crowd control among teammates.
    - **Use Communication**: Use voice chat or the in-game ping system to mark enemies, items, or points of interest.
- **Multiplayer Dungeons**: These exclusive, high-difficulty dungeons require a team to succeed. Each dungeon is filled with challenging enemies, puzzles, and hidden rewards.
  - **How to Start**: Choose **Multiplayer Dungeon** from the multiplayer menu, then select your desired dungeon. Press "X" (PlayStation), "A" (Xbox), or click **Start** (PC) to begin.
  - **Tips**:
    - **Assign Roles**: Designate roles (e.g., tank, healer, damage dealer) to maximize efficiency.
    - **Focus on Puzzle Solving**: Certain areas require coordinated efforts to solve puzzles. Designate a teammate for each section to streamline progress.
- **Timed Events**: Multiplayer includes special timed events that offer unique rewards and achievements for completing specific objectives within a set time.

- **How to Access**: Check the multiplayer menu for active timed events. Select the event, then press "X" (PlayStation), "A" (Xbox), or click **Start** (PC).
- **Tips**:
  - **Prioritize Objectives**: Focus on event goals first to ensure you complete them in time.
  - **Bring Balanced Teams**: Timed events often require fast action and diverse abilities. Make sure your team covers a range of skills.

3. Character and Role Management

- **Choosing Your Multiplayer Character**: Each player can select a unique character class in multiplayer, allowing for balanced team compositions and synergy.
  - **How to Choose**: Before starting a match, select **Character Setup** from the multiplayer menu. Choose a class that complements your team and press "X" (PlayStation), "A" (Xbox), or click **Confirm** (PC).
- **Balancing Team Roles**: Multiplayer success relies on balanced roles. Consider having at least one player in each of these roles:
  - **Tank**: Absorbs damage and keeps enemies focused on them.
  - **Damage Dealer (DPS)**: Focuses on dealing high damage to enemies.
  - **Support/Healer**: Heals teammates and provides buffs to enhance the team's performance.
- **Coordinating Abilities**: Each class has unique abilities that can complement others. For example:
  - **Warriors**: Can use abilities like **Shield Wall** to protect teammates.
  - **Mages**: Offer powerful area-of-effect spells and support with abilities like **Fade Barrier**.
  - **Rogues**: Provide high single-target damage and stealth for ambushing key targets.

4. Loot and Rewards in Multiplayer

- **Exclusive Multiplayer Gear**: Multiplayer features exclusive gear sets, items, and Veilguard-enhanced weapons that can only be earned by participating in multiplayer modes.
  - **Where to Check Rewards**: After completing a mission, press "Options" (PlayStation), "Menu" (Xbox), or "Tab" (PC) to open your rewards screen and view loot obtained.
- **Sharing and Trading Items**: You can share certain items with teammates, allowing players to trade gear that benefits each other.
  - **How to Trade**: Open the inventory during a multiplayer session, select an item, and press "X" (PlayStation), "A" (Xbox), or right-click (PC) to offer it to another player.
- **Multiplayer-Only Currency**: Multiplayer missions award special currency that can be used to purchase exclusive items.
  - **How to Spend Multiplayer Currency**: Visit the multiplayer vendor in **Brightfall Village** or **Stormguard Keep**. Select items from the vendor's shop and press "X" (PlayStation), "A" (Xbox), or click **Purchase** (PC).

5. Communication Tools and Team Coordination

- **Voice Chat and Ping System**: Use voice chat for real-time coordination or the ping system to highlight locations, enemies, and objectives.
  - **Using Voice Chat**: Plug in a headset or microphone, then enable voice chat in the settings menu to communicate with teammates.
  - **Using Pings**: Press "R1" (PlayStation), "RB" (Xbox), or "Alt" (PC) to bring up the ping wheel and select a marker to indicate an area or target.
- **Tactical Mode for Real-Time Strategy**: Use tactical mode for complex fights or coordinating abilities against powerful enemies.
  - **How to Access**: Press the touchpad (PlayStation), "View" (Xbox), or "T" (PC) to enter tactical mode. Assign targets, use abilities, and direct companions from this view.
- **Setting Objectives for the Team**: Designate objectives for each player, such as handling enemies, focusing on specific tasks, or completing puzzle sections.
  - **How to Mark Objectives**: Use the ping system to mark specific points of interest and direct teammates to those locations.

6. Multiplayer-Exclusive Challenges and Achievements

- **Completing Team-Based Achievements**: Multiplayer offers special achievements for team coordination, completing dungeons, or achieving high scores in timed events.
  - **Tracking Achievements**: Access the **Achievements** section from the multiplayer menu to view specific multiplayer objectives.
- **Daily and Weekly Challenges**: Each week, new challenges provide rewards and experience for completing specific tasks, such as defeating bosses, clearing dungeons, or performing team-based actions.
  - **Where to Access**: Open the **Challenges** tab in the multiplayer menu to view active daily and weekly challenges.
- **Tips for Success**:
  - **Check Challenge Requirements**: Before starting, read the challenge descriptions to understand requirements, such as minimum score thresholds or specific abilities.
  - **Complete Challenges with Friends**: Teaming up with regular players increases coordination, making it easier to achieve high scores or meet complex objectives.

7. Multiplayer Progression and Ranking

- **Earning Multiplayer Experience**: Gain multiplayer experience points (MP XP) for completing missions, killing enemies, and achieving objectives. Higher levels unlock better gear and special abilities.
  - **Where to Check XP**: After each mission, view your earned MP XP on the post-game screen.

- **Ranking System**: Multiplayer has a ranking system based on performance and experience, rewarding players with titles, gear, and access to higher-level missions.
  - **Checking Your Rank**: Visit the **Ranking** section in the multiplayer menu to track your current rank and upcoming rewards.
- **Progression Rewards**: Higher ranks grant access to more difficult missions, exclusive armor, and enhanced abilities.
  - **Tips for Ranking Up**:
    - **Focus on High-Score Runs**: Earn bonus XP for completing missions with a high score, achieved by finishing objectives quickly and efficiently.
    - **Complete Weekly Challenges**: These provide large XP boosts that help with ranking progression.

Summary of Veilguard Multiplayer Features

- **Set Up Multiplayer Sessions**: Create private lobbies, invite friends, or join public matches for co-op play.
- **Explore Game Modes**: Enjoy Cooperative Campaigns, Multiplayer Dungeons, and Timed Events for unique multiplayer experiences.
- **Coordinate Roles and Abilities**: Assign roles and coordinate abilities to maximize team efficiency in combat and puzzle-solving.
- **Earn Exclusive Multiplayer Loot**: Collect unique gear, trade items, and spend multiplayer currency at special vendors.
- **Use Communication Tools**: Use voice chat, pings, and tactical mode for effective team coordination.
- **Progress in Multiplayer Ranking**: Complete daily challenges, level up, and earn ranks for access to higher-level missions and exclusive rewards.

With these multiplayer features, *The Veilguard* offers a rich, collaborative experience. Whether you're joining friends for story-driven quests or tackling high-stakes dungeons with new allies, mastering these tools and tactics will make your multiplayer journey enjoyable and rewarding. Enjoy the camaraderie, challenges, and unique content that only multiplayer can provide!

Co-op Strategies for Dungeons

In *Dragon Age: The Veilguard*, multiplayer dungeons are designed to challenge teams with complex combat, strategic puzzles, and formidable bosses. Success in these dungeons requires coordinated teamwork, effective role assignments, and smart ability use. This guide provides essential co-op strategies to help you and your team conquer the most difficult dungeons, including where to position, how to approach each phase, and specific tips for maximizing each team member's strengths.

1. Role Assignment and Team Composition

- **Roles in the Team**:
    - **Tank**: Absorbs damage, keeps enemy attention, and shields teammates from high-damage attacks.
    - **Damage Dealer (DPS)**: Focuses on dealing high damage to enemies, especially bosses and elite foes.
    - **Support/Healer**: Heals teammates, applies buffs, and helps with crowd control to manage large enemy groups.
- **Building a Balanced Team**: A successful dungeon run often requires a balanced team with each role represented. Before starting, discuss your team's composition and make sure each role is covered.
    - **How to Assign Roles**: In the lobby, discuss with teammates which roles they will take, considering each player's strengths and character class.
- **Tips for Each Role**:
    - **Tanks** should focus on positioning to protect DPS and support players.
    - **DPS** players should stay near the tank for protection while dealing damage.
    - **Support/Healers** should stay mobile to avoid enemy focus and prioritize healing and buffing.

2. Coordinating Abilities for Maximum Impact

- **Combo Attacks and Buffs**:
    - **Using Combo Attacks**: Some abilities create powerful combos when used in sequence. For example, mages can freeze enemies, allowing rogues to land critical strikes.
    - **How to Coordinate Combos**: Communicate with your team to time abilities. For example, if the mage announces a freeze spell, rogues can prepare their critical attacks to maximize damage.
- **Timing Buffs and Heals**:
    - **Buff Before Boss Fights**: Before a boss encounter, have support characters apply buffs (such as shields or damage boosts) to the team.
    - **Using Heals Efficiently**: Avoid overusing heals by waiting until players are below 50% health unless facing high-damage attacks.

○ **How to Use Abilities Together**: In tactical mode, press the touchpad (PlayStation), "View" (Xbox), or "T" (PC) to direct your team to use abilities in the right order, or communicate verbally to synchronize timing.

3. Positioning and Managing Enemy Waves

- **Tank Positioning**:
  - ○ **Draw Enemy Attention**: Tanks should position themselves between enemies and DPS/support players, drawing enemy focus to keep teammates safe.
  - ○ **How to Hold Position**: Press "L1" (PlayStation), "LB" (Xbox), or "Alt" (PC) to defend or taunt enemies, keeping their focus on the tank.
- **DPS and Support Positioning**:
  - ○ **Keep Distance from Enemies**: DPS players should stay slightly behind the tank, focusing on dealing damage while avoiding direct enemy attacks.
  - ○ **Stay Mobile as Support**: Support players should keep moving to avoid enemy targeting, prioritizing safety over staying in one spot.
- **Controlling Enemy Waves**:
  - ○ **Use Crowd Control Abilities**: Abilities like **Veil Pulse** (for mages) or **Entangling Roots** (for rangers) can help control enemy waves by slowing or stunning them.
  - ○ **Assign Specific Enemies**: Assign each team member to specific enemies or groups, helping to manage enemy numbers effectively and avoid overwhelming any one player.

4. Puzzle Solving in Multiplayer Dungeons

- **Assign Puzzle Roles**:
  - ○ **Divide and Conquer**: Many dungeons contain puzzles that require players to activate switches, solve riddles, or interact with items. Divide these tasks based on player positions and character abilities.
  - ○ **Using the Ping System for Coordination**: Use the ping system to highlight puzzle elements. Press "R1" (PlayStation), "RB" (Xbox), or "Alt" (PC) to mark items or areas for teammates to focus on.
- **Communicate During Puzzles**:
  - ○ **Avoid Cluttered Areas**: Keep certain players back if a puzzle room becomes crowded. Tanks can stand by to protect the team, while other players focus on the puzzle.
  - ○ **Direct Communication**: Use voice chat or text chat to update teammates on puzzle progress, ensuring all elements are activated at the right time.

5. Boss Strategies and Phase Management

- **Understanding Boss Phases**:

- **Watch for Phase Cues**: Many dungeon bosses have multiple phases, each with unique attack patterns. Watch for visual or audio cues signaling phase changes.
- **Plan for High-Damage Phases**: Some phases include high-damage or area-of-effect attacks. Tanks should move in close to keep the boss's focus while DPS and support players stay at a safe distance.
- **Focus on Weak Spots**:
  - **Identify Boss Weak Points**: Some bosses have weak points (such as a glowing area) that deal extra damage when targeted.
  - **Assign DPS to Weak Spots**: DPS players should focus on these points while tanks keep the boss occupied.
  - **Using Tactical Mode for Boss Weaknesses**: In tactical mode, assign specific players to target weak points by hovering over them and pressing "X" (PlayStation), "A" (Xbox), or left-click (PC).
- **Using Burst Damage at Critical Moments**:
  - **Save Burst Abilities**: Coordinate high-damage abilities for the boss's final phase or to interrupt powerful attacks.
  - **Communicate When Using Burst**: Have one player call out when to use burst damage, ensuring the team coordinates their abilities for maximum effect.

6. Managing Health, Stamina, and Resources

- **Effective Use of Health Potions**:
  - **Save Potions for Emergencies**: Avoid using health potions too early. Wait until health drops below 50% or during high-damage phases to conserve resources.
  - **Share Potions When Possible**: Some items can be shared among teammates. Open the inventory, select the item, and press "X" (PlayStation), "A" (Xbox), or right-click (PC) to share.
- **Managing Stamina and Mana**:
  - **Conserve Abilities for Key Moments**: Avoid using high-stamina or high-mana abilities on weaker enemies. Reserve them for bosses or larger waves.
  - **Use Stamina/Mana Potions as Needed**: Assign stamina or mana potions to quick slots for easy access and press the assigned button when resources are low.
- **Support Resource Management**:
  - **Coordinate Heals and Buffs**: Support players should alternate between healing and buffing to avoid depleting mana or potions. Timing these abilities correctly can be critical during boss fights or intense waves.

7. Resurrection and Reviving Teammates

- **Prioritize Revives in Safe Moments**:
  - **Only Revive When Safe**: Attempt revives during moments of reduced enemy aggression. Tanks should draw enemy focus while support or DPS players handle revives.
  - **How to Revive Teammates**: Approach the fallen player and press "X" (PlayStation), "A" (Xbox), or "E" (PC) to initiate the revive process.
- **Coordinate Team Protection for Revives**:
  - **Create a Protective Barrier**: Use abilities like **Shield Wall** (warrior skill) to create a safe space around the fallen teammate while another player revives.
  - **Assign Roles for Reviving**: Assign one player as the primary reviver and have others focus on creating a safe space.

8. Advanced Tips for High-Level Dungeons

- **Set Up a Pre-Battle Plan**:
  - **Discuss Strategy Beforehand**: Review dungeon layout, potential enemies, and boss phases with the team. Decide on each player's role and the approach for each phase.
- **Communicate Constantly**:
  - **Provide Real-Time Updates**: Keep communication open during the dungeon run. Announce when abilities are ready, call out enemy reinforcements, and update teammates on boss health or phase changes.
- **Maximize Damage During Down Phases**:
  - **Use High-Damage Abilities During Boss Pauses**: Some bosses have down phases where they are vulnerable. Use this time to unleash your strongest abilities and deal maximum damage.
  - **Coordinate with the Team**: Make sure all players attack together during down phases to push through as much damage as possible.

Summary of Co-op Strategies for Dungeons

- **Assign Clear Roles**: Designate each player as tank, DPS, or support for a balanced team composition.
- **Coordinate Abilities and Combos**: Use abilities in synergy for powerful combos and maximize buffs and heals during critical moments.
- **Position Effectively**: Keep tanks between enemies and teammates, with DPS and support staying mobile and at a safe distance.
- **Solve Puzzles Together**: Divide tasks based on abilities, and use the ping system to highlight objectives.
- **Manage Boss Phases and Weak Points**: Watch for phase cues, target weak spots, and save burst damage for critical moments.

- **Conserve Health and Resources**: Use potions only when necessary, and manage stamina and mana carefully.
- **Coordinate Revives**: Only revive teammates when safe, with tanks providing cover.

By following these strategies, your team will be well-prepared to face even the most challenging dungeons in *The Veilguard*. With clear communication, effective role management, and strategic use of abilities, you'll conquer these complex co-op experiences and earn valuable rewards. Enjoy the teamwork and the thrill of victory!

PvP Tips and Team Dynamics

The PvP (Player vs. Player) mode in *Dragon Age: The Veilguard* brings intense battles where strategic teamwork and fast reflexes are crucial for victory. PvP matches test your ability to cooperate, adapt, and outmaneuver opponents in dynamic and competitive environments. This guide provides essential PvP tips and team dynamics strategies to help you and your team achieve success, covering class roles, effective team compositions, and tactics for both individual and group play.

1. Understanding PvP Team Roles

- **Roles in PvP**:
  - **Tank**: Absorbs damage, protects teammates, and disrupts opponents by drawing their focus.
  - **Damage Dealer (DPS)**: Deals high damage to opponents, particularly squishy support characters or isolated players.
  - **Support/Healer**: Heals and buffs allies, often staying back to avoid direct attacks while keeping the team sustained.
- **Choosing Your Role Based on Class**:
  - **Warriors**: Make effective tanks with high defense and crowd-control abilities.
  - **Mages**: Typically DPS or support, using ranged attacks and buffs to assist teammates.
  - **Rogues**: Often act as DPS, with high burst damage and stealth abilities to ambush opponents.
- **How to Set Roles in the Lobby**: Before a PvP match, discuss roles with your team to ensure balanced composition. Access the **Character Setup** screen to finalize your role, pressing "X" (PlayStation), "A" (Xbox), or **Confirm** (PC) when ready.

2. Team Composition and Balance

- **Balanced Team Compositions**:
  - **Tank + DPS + Support**: A classic composition that balances defense, offense, and support. The tank can protect the DPS and support players while focusing on drawing opponents' attacks.

- **Double DPS + Support**: Useful in fast-paced matches where quick kills are crucial. This setup relies on high burst damage and support for healing, making it more vulnerable but deadly if coordinated.
- **Tips for Effective Composition**:
  - **Counter Enemy Team Composition**: If the opposing team has two tanks, consider two DPS to overpower them quickly.
  - **Adapt to the Map**: Some maps favor specific compositions. Tight spaces benefit tanks and melee DPS, while open maps allow ranged DPS to shine.
- **Where to Set Up Roles**: In the **Character Setup** screen before a match, finalize your role and composition strategy with your teammates.

3. Positioning and Map Awareness

- **Using Cover and High Ground**:
  - **Stay Out of Line of Sight**: Use natural cover like walls, rocks, and structures to avoid ranged attacks, positioning yourself to ambush or evade enemies.
  - **Gain High Ground for Better Visibility**: Position yourself on elevated areas to get a clearer view of the battlefield, allowing you to spot enemies and plan attacks.
- **Control Key Areas on the Map**:
  - **Secure Health and Resource Spawns**: Many PvP maps have health or resource pickups. Keeping control of these points can give your team a significant advantage.
  - **How to Use the Ping System**: Press "R1" (PlayStation), "RB" (Xbox), or "Alt" (PC) to mark key areas or targets for teammates, making it easier to coordinate moves.
- **Rotating Between Objectives**:
  - **Move as a Team**: Avoid wandering alone; stick with at least one teammate for support and to prevent easy kills for the opposing team.
  - **Coordinate Movement Using Pings**: Mark objectives or points of interest to signal teammates where to go, making rotations more efficient.

4. Coordinating Attacks and Combos

- **Focus Fire on Key Opponents**:
  - **Target High-Priority Players**: Aim to eliminate enemy support or DPS first to reduce their overall effectiveness.
  - **Use Pings to Mark Targets**: Ping high-priority opponents for your team to focus on, ensuring they are taken down quickly.
- **Chaining Abilities for Maximum Impact**:
  - **Coordinate Burst Damage Abilities**: Combine abilities like a mage's **Firestorm** with a rogue's **Shadow Strike** for lethal combos that overwhelm enemies.

- **Using Crowd Control in Sync**: Have tanks or support characters use crowd control abilities (like stuns or roots) while DPS players unleash burst damage on incapacitated enemies.
- **Using Tactical Mode for Coordination**: In tactical mode, press the touchpad (PlayStation), "View" (Xbox), or "T" (PC) to assign specific targets for each player, creating a synchronized attack plan.

5. Effective Use of Abilities and Resources

- **Cooldown Management**:
  - **Save Key Abilities for Critical Moments**: Reserve abilities like **Shield Wall** or **Healing Aura** for times when your team is under heavy pressure.
  - **Rotate Abilities Among Team Members**: Stagger the use of powerful abilities to ensure the team always has a skill ready for emergencies.
- **Using Potions and Buffs**:
  - **Health and Stamina Potions**: Assign potions to quick slots and use them as soon as health or stamina drops below 50%.
  - **Apply Buffs Before Engagements**: Buffs like **Veilguard's Blessing** or **Spirit Shield** can give you an edge before entering a fight.
  - **Quick Slot Usage**: Equip health potions and buffs in your quick slots for easy access by pressing the assigned button when resources run low.

6. Playing to Each Class's Strengths

- **Tank Strategies**:
  - **Absorb Damage and Disrupt Enemies**: Tanks should use taunts and crowd-control abilities to keep enemies focused on them and away from the DPS and support players.
  - **How to Taunt Enemies**: Use abilities like **Defensive Shout** by pressing the respective quick slot button, drawing attention away from your teammates.
- **DPS Strategies**:
  - **Prioritize Target Elimination**: Focus on taking out high-value targets like enemy support or DPS. Use stealth abilities to ambush these players whenever possible.
  - **Using Stealth Abilities**: If you're a rogue, activate **Shadow's Embrace** to sneak up on opponents, positioning yourself for critical strikes.
- **Support Strategies**:
  - **Stay at a Safe Distance**: Avoid engaging directly with the enemy. Focus on keeping the tank and DPS players buffed and healed.
  - **Use Buffs and Heals Continuously**: Keep an eye on teammate health bars, using abilities like **Heal Pulse** to sustain them during fights.

7. Adapting to the Opposing Team's Strategy

- **Countering Strong Opponents**:
  - **Identify Key Players**: Notice if any enemy player is particularly effective. Coordinate with your team to focus them or disrupt their strategy.
  - **Adapt Tactics Based on Their Composition**: If the opposing team relies heavily on DPS, prioritize targeting them quickly. If they have strong tanks, try to isolate and eliminate support characters.
- **Switching Roles Mid-Game**:
  - **Adapt to Team Needs**: Sometimes, a DPS player might need to take on a more defensive role, or support might need to assist with offense. Communicate any role adjustments based on the flow of the match.

8. Communication and Team Dynamics

- **Real-Time Communication**:
  - **Use Voice Chat for Quick Coordination**: Real-time communication is critical in PvP. Use voice chat to call out enemy positions, alert teammates of incoming attacks, or request support.
  - **Using Tactical Markers**: Use the ping system to mark enemies, objectives, or strategic points in real-time.
- **Supporting Teammates**:
  - **Back Up Team Members Under Attack**: If a teammate is targeted, tanks should intercept, support should heal, and DPS should focus on disrupting the enemy.
  - **Use Resurrections Smartly**: Only attempt to revive teammates if the area is secure. Approach the fallen player and press "X" (PlayStation), "A" (Xbox), or "E" (PC) to revive.
- **Stay Together as a Team**: Avoid separating from the group, as solo players are often easier targets. Stick with the team to maximize support and protection.

9. Advanced PvP Tips for High-Level Matches

- **Observe Opponent Patterns**:
  - **Identify Repeated Behaviors**: Some players rely on specific abilities or patterns. Use this knowledge to predict their moves and counter effectively.
- **Baiting Opponents**:
  - **Use Decoy Tactics**: Have one player bait opponents into vulnerable positions while the rest of the team prepares an ambush.
  - **Feign Weakness**: Sometimes, pretending to retreat can lure opponents into a trap. Communicate this strategy with teammates for coordinated counters.

Summary of PvP Tips and Team Dynamics

- **Establish Clear Team Roles**: Designate tank, DPS, and support roles to create a balanced team.
- **Position and Map Control**: Use cover, control key areas, and mark objectives for strategic advantage.
- **Coordinate Attacks and Combos**: Target high-priority players, chain abilities, and maximize crowd control.
- **Manage Cooldowns and Resources**: Reserve abilities for critical moments and use potions or buffs effectively.
- **Adapt to the Opposing Team's Tactics**: Counter strong opponents and adjust roles as needed.
- **Communicate Constantly**: Use voice chat, pings, and real-time updates to coordinate effectively.
- **Stay Together as a Team**: Maintain group cohesion to avoid solo vulnerability.

By mastering these PvP tips and team dynamics, you'll enhance your competitive edge in *The Veilguard*. Effective communication, team cohesion, and the ability to adapt to your opponents will set your team apart in PvP matches. Good luck, and enjoy the thrill of competition!

Rewards and Unlockables in Multiplayer

Dragon Age: The Veilguard offers a variety of rewards and unlockables in multiplayer mode, including exclusive gear, powerful abilities, unique currency, and special achievements. These rewards not only enhance your character's capabilities but also make the multiplayer experience richer and more engaging. This guide provides a detailed overview of the types of rewards available, how to earn them, and where to access them in the game.

1. Multiplayer-Exclusive Gear and Armor Sets

- **Unique Gear Sets**: Multiplayer offers exclusive gear sets tailored to each class, enhancing abilities and providing unique stat boosts.
    - **Types of Gear**:
        - **Veilguard Set**: Increases Veil-based abilities and resistance.
        - **Arcane Battle Mage Armor**: Boosts magical abilities and mana regeneration.
        - **Shadow Stalker Outfit**: Grants stealth bonuses for rogues, increasing critical damage.
    - **How to Obtain**: These sets are typically rewarded for completing high-level multiplayer dungeons or timed events.
    - **Where to Equip**: Access the inventory menu after a match, select the gear you've unlocked, and press "X" (PlayStation), "A" (Xbox), or click **Equip** (PC).
- **Loot Drops from Bosses**: Defeating bosses in multiplayer dungeons and timed events may yield powerful, multiplayer-exclusive items.

○ **How to Collect Boss Loot**: After defeating a boss, approach the loot drop and press "X" (PlayStation), "A" (Xbox), or left-click (PC) to collect it. Check your inventory after the match to equip any new items.

2. Veilguard Enchantments and Runes

- **Veilguard-Specific Enchantments**: Multiplayer offers unique enchantments that enhance Veilguard abilities, such as increased duration for Veil abilities or faster mana regeneration.
  - ○ **How to Unlock**: Earn Veilguard enchantments by completing specific dungeon challenges or participating in rare events like the **Celestial Convergence**.
  - ○ **How to Apply Enchantments**: Open your inventory, select the gear you want to enhance, and press "X" (PlayStation), "A" (Xbox), or right-click (PC) to apply the enchantment.
- **Multiplayer Runes**: These runes provide additional bonuses for multiplayer, such as extra stamina, mana, or Veilguard power boosts.
  - ○ **How to Acquire Runes**: Runes are rewarded for completing daily and weekly multiplayer challenges. You can also buy them using multiplayer currency from vendors.
  - ○ **Equipping Runes**: Select a weapon in your inventory, press "X" (PlayStation), "A" (Xbox), or right-click (PC) to open the rune menu, then equip your chosen rune.

3. Multiplayer Currency and Vendors

- **Multiplayer Currency**: Multiplayer mode features its own currency, which can be spent on exclusive items and upgrades.
  - ○ **How to Earn**: Earn multiplayer currency by completing dungeons, winning PvP matches, and finishing timed events or weekly challenges.
  - ○ **Where to Check Currency Balance**: Open the multiplayer menu or inventory screen, where your current multiplayer currency balance will be displayed.
- **Special Multiplayer Vendors**:
  - ○ **Vendor Locations**: Multiplayer vendors can be found in **Brightfall Village** and **Stormguard Keep**.
  - ○ **Purchasing Items**: Interact with the vendor by pressing "X" (PlayStation), "A" (Xbox), or "E" (PC), then browse available items. Select an item and press **Purchase** to add it to your inventory.
  - ○ **Items Available**: Vendors offer exclusive armor sets, enchantments, runes, and potions that boost Veilguard powers and multiplayer stats.

4. Exclusive Multiplayer Abilities

- **Multiplayer-Only Abilities**: Certain abilities are only available in multiplayer mode, enhancing team play and providing unique ways to support your allies.
  - ○ **Examples of Multiplayer Abilities**:

- **Guardian's Blessing**: Grants a temporary shield to all nearby teammates.
- **Veil Surge**: Increases mana regeneration and boosts damage for Veilguard abilities in a set radius.
- **Revitalizing Aura**: Heals all allies over time within a specific range.
  - **How to Unlock**: These abilities are unlocked by achieving high ranks in multiplayer, completing specific PvP matches, or purchasing them with multiplayer currency.
  - **How to Equip**: Go to the **Abilities** menu, select the multiplayer ability, and assign it to a quick slot by pressing "X" (PlayStation), "A" (Xbox), or dragging it to the slot (PC).

5. Achievements and Titles

- **Multiplayer Achievements**: Multiplayer mode offers unique achievements that reward you for reaching milestones, such as defeating a set number of players in PvP, completing all multiplayer dungeons, or winning timed events.
  - **Viewing Achievements**: Access the **Achievements** menu from the main screen to see a list of multiplayer-specific achievements.
  - **How to Earn**: Complete tasks like "Legendary Slayer" (defeat all legendary bosses) or "Veilguard Master" (fully upgrade all Veilguard abilities) to unlock rewards.
- **Exclusive Titles**: Titles are awarded for completing major achievements in multiplayer mode, allowing you to display your expertise and dedication.
  - **Examples of Titles**:
    - **Champion of Thedas**: Awarded for reaching the highest rank in PvP.
    - **Master of the Veil**: Earned by completing all Veilguard dungeons.
  - **How to Equip Titles**: Open the **Profile** menu, select **Titles**, and choose the title you want to display.

6. Timed Event Rewards

- **Unique Event-Based Items**: Timed events in multiplayer, such as **Lunar Eclipse Hunts** and **Spirit Hunter's Moon**, offer special items and exclusive gear that can only be earned during the event.
  - **Event Rewards**: Each event offers its own rewards, which may include unique armor pieces, Veilguard weapons, or enchanted accessories.
  - **How to Participate in Events**: Check the multiplayer menu for active events, select the event, and press "X" (PlayStation), "A" (Xbox), or **Start** (PC) to join.
- **Event Currency**: Some events award special currency that can be spent exclusively during the event.
  - **How to Spend Event Currency**: Visit the event vendor (often located near major multiplayer hubs) and select items available for purchase during the event window.

7. Daily and Weekly Challenges

- **Challenge Rewards**: Daily and weekly challenges offer rewards for completing specific tasks in multiplayer, such as winning a set number of PvP matches, defeating a certain number of bosses, or collecting specific items.
    - **Examples of Challenges**:
        - **Daily**: "Defeat 20 Enemies in Multiplayer Dungeons" for a small currency boost.
        - **Weekly**: "Complete 5 PvP Matches" for Veilguard runes and multiplayer currency.
    - **How to Access Challenges**: Open the **Challenges** tab in the multiplayer menu to see active challenges and track your progress.
- **Exclusive Challenge Rewards**: Completing all challenges within a week often grants an additional reward, such as a special weapon or piece of armor.
    - **How to Claim Rewards**: Once a challenge is completed, a notification will appear. Open the **Challenges** tab, select the completed challenge, and press "X" (PlayStation), "A" (Xbox), or click **Claim** (PC) to collect your reward.

8. Ranking Rewards and Progression

- **Earning Ranks in Multiplayer**: Gain ranks in PvP and co-op modes by winning matches, completing challenges, and earning high scores in dungeons.
    - **Benefits of Higher Ranks**: Higher ranks unlock access to exclusive dungeons, powerful abilities, and enhanced gear sets.
    - **Where to Track Rank Progress**: Open the **Rank** section in the multiplayer menu to view your current rank, points, and upcoming rewards.
- **Progression Rewards**: Each rank offers unique rewards, including exclusive armor, titles, and access to advanced missions.
    - **How to Receive Rank Rewards**: After ranking up, go to the **Rewards** tab in the multiplayer menu to collect your new items and abilities.

Summary of Multiplayer Rewards and Unlockables

- **Multiplayer Gear Sets and Armor**: Earn exclusive armor sets tailored to your class by completing high-level dungeons and events.
- **Veilguard Enchantments and Runes**: Acquire powerful runes and enchantments for Veilguard abilities through dungeons and challenges.
- **Multiplayer Currency and Vendors**: Spend earned currency on exclusive items at multiplayer vendors in Brightfall Village and Stormguard Keep.
- **Exclusive Abilities**: Unlock multiplayer-only abilities like **Guardian's Blessing** and **Veil Surge** to support your team.

- **Achievements and Titles**: Complete achievements for unique rewards and equip titles to show off your multiplayer skills.
- **Timed Event Rewards**: Participate in events for special items and event-based currency.
- **Daily and Weekly Challenges**: Complete regular challenges to earn rewards like currency boosts and exclusive items.
- **Ranking Rewards**: Rank up in multiplayer for access to advanced missions and powerful gear.

With these rewards and unlockables, *The Veilguard*'s multiplayer mode offers a range of exciting incentives for completing challenges, ranking up, and participating in timed events. By mastering these aspects, you'll unlock valuable items and abilities to enhance your character and stand out in the multiplayer community. Enjoy exploring the rewards and building your character to its full potential!

Community Challenges and Special Events

In *Dragon Age: The Veilguard*, Community Challenges and Special Events bring the player community together to complete shared goals and earn exclusive rewards. These challenges often involve large-scale objectives, such as defeating a set number of enemies or gathering rare resources, which all players contribute to collectively. Special Events introduce unique, time-limited content, including rare encounters, themed quests, and exclusive rewards. This guide provides a detailed overview of Community Challenges and Special Events, how to participate, and what rewards you can earn.

1. Community Challenges Overview

- **What are Community Challenges?**
    - Community Challenges are large-scale goals set by the game developers that all players work on collectively. These challenges usually last for a limited period and may include tasks like defeating a certain number of Veil creatures or collecting rare items.
    - **Examples of Community Challenges**:
        - **Veilguard Monster Hunt**: All players work together to defeat a set number of Veil creatures across all game modes.
        - **Resource Gathering**: Collect a specified amount of rare resources (e.g., Veil Essence) from different regions.
    - **Where to View Active Challenges**: Check the Community Challenges board in **Brightfall Village** or **Stormguard Keep**. You can also access current challenges from the multiplayer menu by selecting **Community Challenges**.
- **How to Participate**:
    - **Engage in Activities that Contribute**: Simply playing the game and completing activities related to the challenge will automatically contribute to the community goal.

- - **Where to Check Contribution Progress**: Open the **Community Challenges** menu to view your personal contribution and the community's overall progress.
  - **Rewards for Community Challenges**:
    - **Milestone Rewards**: As the community reaches certain milestones, everyone who contributed receives rewards. These may include exclusive gear, special runes, or unique potions.
    - **How to Claim Rewards**: When a milestone is reached, a notification appears. Go to the **Community Challenges** menu, select the completed challenge, and press "X" (PlayStation), "A" (Xbox), or click **Claim** (PC) to collect your reward.

2. Special Events Overview

- **Types of Special Events**:
  - Special Events introduce time-limited content that enhances the gameplay experience. These events often include unique storylines, themed dungeons, or rare encounters and typically last from a few days to a week.
  - **Examples of Special Events**:
    - **Lunar Eclipse Hunt**: A rare event where powerful enemies appear in Veilguard zones, dropping exclusive loot and event currency.
    - **Festival of the Veil**: A seasonal event that introduces themed quests, mini-games, and unique cosmetic rewards.
  - **Where to Find Event Details**: Check the **Events** board in **Brightfall Village** or **Stormguard Keep**. The multiplayer menu also provides an **Events** section for ongoing and upcoming special events.
- **Joining a Special Event**:
  - **Select the Event in the Menu**: Open the **Events** menu, select the active event, and press "X" (PlayStation), "A" (Xbox), or click **Join** (PC) to begin.
  - **Participate in Event-Specific Activities**: Complete event-related tasks, like fighting event-exclusive monsters or participating in special mini-games, to earn event rewards.
  - **Event Progression and Challenges**: Some events include challenges or milestones, rewarding players who complete them. Check the **Event Progress** tab to track your achievements.
- **Rewards for Special Events**:
  - **Event-Specific Gear and Items**: Special Events offer exclusive items, such as themed armor, decorative items for your camp, and unique potions.
  - **Event Currency**: Many events feature their own currency, which can be exchanged at event vendors for unique items.
  - **How to Claim Rewards**: At the end of each event task, you'll be prompted to claim rewards from the **Events** menu or by visiting the event vendor.

3. Event Vendors and Special Shops

- **Accessing Event Vendors**:
  - ○ **Vendor Locations**: Event vendors are typically located in **Brightfall Village** or near **Stormguard Keep**. Look for NPCs with an event icon above their head.
  - ○ **Browsing Items**: Approach the vendor and press "X" (PlayStation), "A" (Xbox), or "E" (PC) to view their special inventory.

- **Spending Event Currency**:
  - ○ **Earning Event Currency**: Complete tasks and challenges during Special Events to earn currency, such as Festival Coins or Eclipse Shards.
  - ○ **Purchasing Items**: Use event currency to purchase unique items like themed armor, weapons, and cosmetic upgrades. Select an item from the vendor's menu and press **Purchase** to add it to your inventory.

- **Types of Items Available**:
  - ○ **Event-Themed Gear**: Cosmetic and functional items tailored to the event's theme.
  - ○ **Consumables**: Potions and elixirs specific to the event that offer temporary boosts.
  - ○ **Unique Enchantments**: Some events offer enchantments or runes that are exclusive to that event and cannot be found elsewhere.

4. Timed Challenges and Exclusive Milestones

- **Timed Challenges**:
  - ○ **What Are Timed Challenges?** Timed challenges are short-term goals within Special Events that require quick completion, often with rare rewards as incentives. Examples include defeating a certain number of enemies within an hour or completing a specific dungeon without using potions.
  - ○ **Where to Access Timed Challenges**: Timed challenges appear in the **Events** menu. Select the timed challenge and press **Join** to start.

- **Milestone Rewards**:
  - ○ **Reaching Event Milestones**: As players complete event challenges, milestone rewards unlock for all participants. Milestones might include community-wide objectives, such as reaching a collective damage goal or completing a set number of event dungeons.
  - ○ **How to Claim Milestone Rewards**: Milestone rewards are claimed from the **Events** menu. Select the milestone and press "X" (PlayStation), "A" (Xbox), or **Claim** (PC) to collect.

5. Leaderboard Competitions and Prestige Rewards

- **Event Leaderboards**:
  - **Competitive Element**: Many Special Events feature leaderboards that rank players based on performance, such as the number of enemies defeated, fastest dungeon completion times, or highest score in a mini-game.
  - **Accessing the Leaderboard**: Open the **Events** menu and select **Leaderboard** to see your ranking and compare it to other players.
- **Prestige Rewards for Top Performers**:
  - **Rewards for High Rankings**: Players who rank high on the leaderboard earn prestige rewards, such as exclusive titles, high-level gear, and rare enchantments.
  - **Examples of Prestige Rewards**:
    - **Titles**: Unique titles like "Veil Conqueror" or "Celestial Champion" that showcase your achievement.
    - **Legendary Gear**: High-level armor or weapons only accessible through top leaderboard performance.
  - **How to Claim Prestige Rewards**: At the end of the event, top players receive a notification to claim rewards. Access them in the **Rewards** tab of the **Events** menu.

6. Strategies for Maximizing Rewards in Community Challenges and Events

- **Focus on High-Yield Activities**:
  - **Target Key Objectives**: Complete activities that yield high event currency or progression points, such as defeating event bosses or completing exclusive dungeons.
  - **Prioritize Community Challenges with Milestone Rewards**: Contribute to challenges with milestone rewards to earn bonuses as the community reaches each goal.
- **Coordinate with Teammates**:
  - **Form Parties for Efficient Farming**: Join friends or other players to tackle challenges faster, particularly in multiplayer dungeons and timed events.
  - **Use Voice Chat for Real-Time Coordination**: Keep communication open to quickly complete tasks and manage resources effectively.
- **Track Your Progress and Adjust Strategy**:
  - **Regularly Check Progress in the Menu**: Open the **Events** or **Community Challenges** menu to track your contributions and view the community's progress.
  - **Adjust Based on Event Rewards**: Focus on tasks that bring you closer to desired rewards, whether it's a specific piece of gear or a high leaderboard rank.

Summary of Community Challenges and Special Events

- **Community Challenges**: Complete large-scale goals as a community for milestone rewards, contributing by playing relevant activities.
- **Special Events**: Participate in time-limited events for unique quests, rare encounters, and event-specific rewards.
- **Event Vendors and Currency**: Earn event currency to spend on exclusive items and gear at special vendors.
- **Timed Challenges and Milestones**: Complete quick tasks and reach milestones to earn rare rewards, available only during the event.
- **Leaderboards and Prestige Rewards**: Compete for top leaderboard positions for prestigious titles, legendary gear, and high-level enchantments.
- **Strategies for Maximizing Rewards**: Target high-yield activities, coordinate with teammates, and track your progress to ensure you maximize rewards.

With Community Challenges and Special Events, *The Veilguard* creates a dynamic, rewarding multiplayer experience that encourages players to collaborate and compete. These events add depth to the game by offering time-limited rewards, exclusive encounters, and prestigious achievements, giving you plenty of reasons to engage and earn alongside other players. Enjoy the thrill of contributing to the community and claiming unique rewards in these exciting events!

Chapter 13

Mods and Customization Options

This chapter introduces you to the world of modding in *Dragon Age: The Veilguard*, providing guidance on how to enhance your gameplay experience with community-created mods. Learn about popular mods that improve visuals, add new features, and expand customization options. You'll find step-by-step instructions for installing and managing mods, as well as tips for troubleshooting compatibility issues. Whether you're looking to tweak game mechanics, customize character appearances, or enrich the world with new content, this chapter will help you navigate the options available and personalize *The Veilguard* to suit your playstyle.

Introduction to Modding in Dragon Age

Modding in *Dragon Age: The Veilguard* opens up a world of possibilities, allowing players to enhance visuals, customize characters, add new content, and even tweak gameplay mechanics. This guide introduces you to the basics of modding, including what mods are, where to find them, and how they can improve your *Dragon Age* experience. With careful selection and installation, mods can tailor *The Veilguard* to your preferences and keep the game fresh with new content and enhancements.

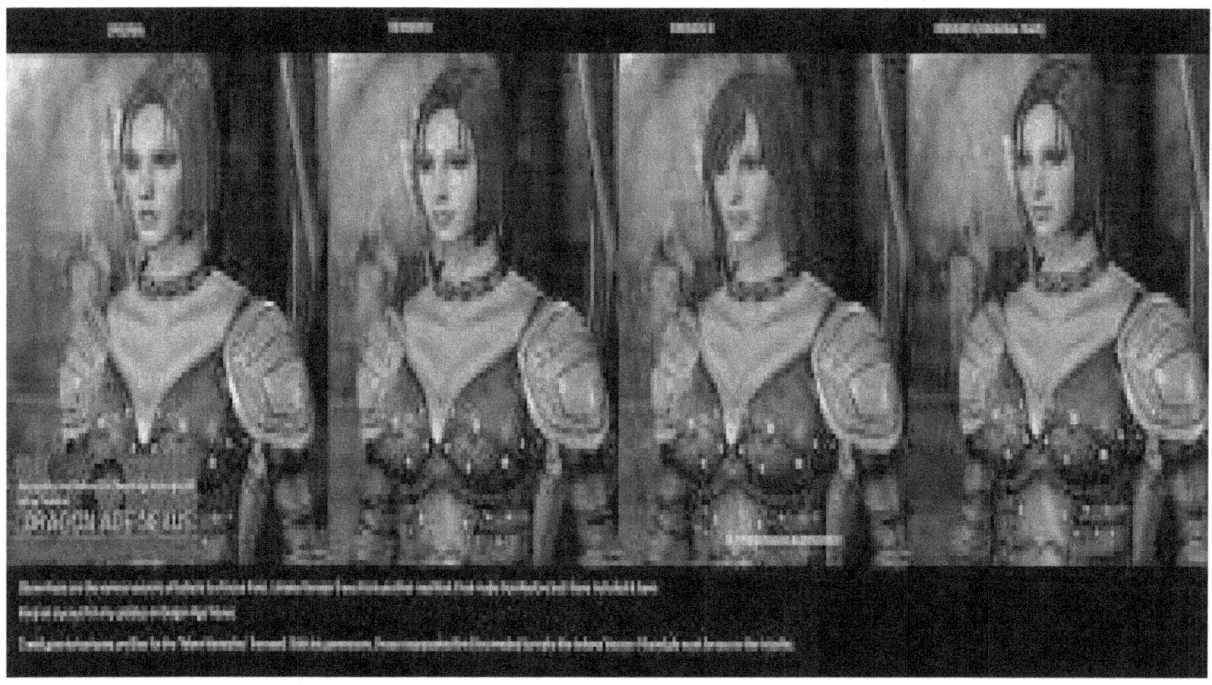

1. What is Modding?

- **Definition of Mods**:
  - Mods (short for modifications) are community-created add-ons or changes to the original game files that enhance, alter, or expand the game in various ways.
  - Common types of mods include:
    - **Visual Enhancements**: Improved textures, lighting adjustments, and reshades.
    - **Gameplay Tweaks**: Adjustments to combat mechanics, difficulty settings, or AI behavior.
    - **Custom Content**: New quests, areas, weapons, and items.
    - **Quality of Life Mods**: UI improvements, inventory management tweaks, and fast-travel enhancements.
- **Why Use Mods?**:
  - Mods allow you to personalize *Dragon Age: The Veilguard*, fix minor issues, enhance graphics, and explore new content created by the modding community. They add replayability, variety, and customization, making the game feel unique to each player.

2. Where to Find Mods for *Dragon Age: The Veilguard*

- **Popular Modding Platforms**:
  - **Nexus Mods**: Nexus Mods is one of the most popular sites for *Dragon Age* mods, offering thousands of mods created by fans. Here, you'll find a wide variety of mods, from simple visual tweaks to complex gameplay changes.
    - **How to Access**: Go to NexusMods.com and search for *Dragon Age: The Veilguard*.
    - **Account Requirement**: You'll need a free Nexus Mods account to download mods.
  - **ModDB**: ModDB is another great platform for game mods, featuring user-created mods and modding tools.
    - **How to Access**: Visit ModDB.com and search for *Dragon Age: The Veilguard*.
- **Community Forums and Discord**:
  - Join *Dragon Age* modding communities, such as Discord servers or forums, where modders share updates and release exclusive mods. These communities are great for finding niche mods or connecting with mod creators.

3. Types of Mods and What They Do

- **Visual Mods**:
  - **Texture Packs**: Improve the quality of textures for characters, landscapes, and buildings.
  - **Lighting and Shader Mods**: Enhance lighting effects, shadows, and color balance to make the game more visually appealing.

- ○ **Character Customization Mods**: Offer new hairstyles, facial features, and armor sets for characters.
- **Gameplay Mods**:
  - ○ **Difficulty Adjustments**: Modify enemy strength, AI, or combat mechanics to make the game easier or harder.
  - ○ **Skill and Ability Tweaks**: Alter the effects of specific abilities or add new skills to customize your playstyle further.
  - ○ **New Quests and Locations**: Some mods introduce entire quests, dungeons, or storylines to expand *The Veilguard*'s world.
- **Quality of Life Mods**:
  - ○ **UI Enhancements**: Improve the user interface by making it more accessible or informative.
  - ○ **Inventory Management**: Mods like increased inventory space or improved sorting help streamline gameplay.
  - ○ **Fast Travel and Map Adjustments**: Enable more fast-travel options or add markers to the map for ease of navigation.

4. Safety and Compatibility Considerations

- **Backing Up Game Files**:
  - ○ Before installing any mods, it's a good idea to back up your game files. This allows you to restore the original files in case a mod causes issues.
    - ■ **How to Backup**: Go to your *Dragon Age: The Veilguard* installation folder, select the game files, and copy them to a backup folder on your computer.
- **Checking Compatibility**:
  - ○ **Mod Compatibility**: Some mods may conflict with each other, especially if they modify similar files. Check each mod's description for compatibility information and avoid installing conflicting mods.
  - ○ **Game Version Compatibility**: Mods are often updated for specific game versions. Make sure the mod version matches your game version to avoid issues.
- **Using Mod Loaders and Managers**:
  - ○ **Mod Managers**: Tools like Vortex (from Nexus Mods) or DA Mod Manager help you install, organize, and manage mods, reducing the risk of compatibility issues.
    - ■ **How to Use Vortex**: Download Vortex from Nexus Mods, install it, and add *Dragon Age: The Veilguard* to your games list. You can then use Vortex to download and activate mods directly.

5. Tips for a Smooth Modding Experience

- **Start with Essential Mods**: Begin with quality-of-life mods or minor visual improvements to get comfortable with the modding process before moving on to more complex mods.

- **Read Mod Descriptions Carefully**: Mod creators often include important installation instructions, compatibility notes, and requirements in the mod's description.
- **Use the Comments Section**: Other users often leave feedback on mod compatibility, known issues, and workarounds in the comments. Check these comments for insights before installing.
- **Limit Multiple Mods at Once**: Try installing one or two mods at a time and testing the game. This way, if an issue arises, you can easily identify the problematic mod.

With these insights, you'll be ready to start your journey into modding *Dragon Age: The Veilguard*, opening the door to a truly personalized gameplay experience. Whether you're looking to improve visuals, enhance gameplay, or add new content, mods allow you to shape *The Veilguard* to suit your preferences. Enjoy exploring the rich variety of mods created by the community and customizing the game in ways that make it uniquely yours!

Recommended Mods for *Dragon Age: The Veilguard*

Modding in *Dragon Age: The Veilguard* enhances gameplay, adds new features, and customizes the game to your preferences. Here's a guide to some of the most popular and recommended mods, categorized by type and functionality, to improve graphics, gameplay mechanics, and quality of life. Each mod includes a description, installation tips, and information on where to access its features in-game.

1. Visual Enhancement Mods

- **High-Resolution Texture Pack**
    - **Description**: This mod replaces the game's default textures with high-resolution versions, providing sharper details for characters, landscapes, and environments.
    - **Where to Find**: Available on Nexus Mods.
    - **Installation Tips**: Download through Vortex (or manually) and install it into the game's texture folder.
    - **How to Activate**: Once installed, the textures automatically apply when you load the game, improving the visual quality of models, terrain, and more.
- **Enhanced Lighting and Shadows**
    - **Description**: This mod improves lighting effects, shadows, and color grading, giving the game a more immersive, realistic look.
    - **Where to Find**: Available on Nexus Mods.
    - **Installation Tips**: Follow the instructions carefully, as some lighting mods require specific shaders or graphical settings to work correctly.
    - **How to Adjust Settings**: Many lighting mods offer settings in the options menu where you can adjust brightness, contrast, and other visual effects.

- **Character Customization Overhaul**
  - ○ **Description**: This mod adds new hairstyles, facial features, and armor options for character customization, allowing you to create a more unique appearance.
  - ○ **Where to Find**: Nexus Mods.
  - ○ **Installation Tips**: Install through a mod manager, and follow any additional setup instructions in the mod's description.
  - ○ **How to Use**: In the character creation screen, new customization options will appear under hairstyles, armor, and face options.

2. Gameplay Enhancement Mods

- **Advanced Combat Mechanics**
  - ○ **Description**: This mod rebalances combat, adding depth to the AI, improving enemy tactics, and introducing more complex skill trees for each class.
  - ○ **Where to Find**: Available on Nexus Mods or ModDB.
  - ○ **Installation Tips**: Download and install through a mod manager. Some skill trees or features might require manual activation in the settings menu.
  - ○ **Where to Access New Mechanics**: Changes are applied automatically, but new skill trees can be found in the **Skills** menu.
- **Expanded Inventory and Loot Management**
  - ○ **Description**: Increases inventory capacity, adds better item sorting options, and allows you to tag favorite items for quick access.
  - ○ **Where to Find**: Nexus Mods.
  - ○ **Installation Tips**: Install with a mod manager, and make sure to check compatibility with other inventory-related mods.
  - ○ **How to Use**: Open your inventory menu to find new sorting options. Additional item slots will be automatically added.
- **Enhanced Enemy AI**
  - ○ **Description**: This mod increases the difficulty by improving enemy AI, making them more strategic in combat and adding new enemy abilities.
  - ○ **Where to Find**: Nexus Mods.
  - ○ **Installation Tips**: Install using a mod manager. Some AI mods require a high-performance setup, so ensure your PC meets recommended specs.
  - ○ **Where to See Changes**: You'll notice changes in enemy behavior during combat, particularly with higher-level enemies and bosses.

3. Quality of Life Mods

- **Fast Travel Everywhere**
  - **Description**: Enables fast travel to any location from the map screen, saving you time when navigating the world.
  - **Where to Find**: Nexus Mods.
  - **Installation Tips**: Download and install through a mod manager.
  - **How to Use**: Open your map and select any point of interest to fast travel there directly, rather than using pre-set fast travel points.

- **UI Overhaul and Improved Map Markers**
  - **Description**: Enhances the user interface, making menus more organized and adding detailed markers to the map for quests, collectibles, and fast-travel points.
  - **Where to Find**: Nexus Mods.
  - **Installation Tips**: Install with a mod manager and restart the game to activate UI changes.
  - **How to Access New Map Markers**: Open the map, where new markers will highlight points of interest, making it easier to locate quests, vendors, and landmarks.

- **Auto Loot and Inventory Sorting**
  - **Description**: Automatically loots items from defeated enemies and organizes your inventory, eliminating the need for manual sorting.
  - **Where to Find**: Nexus Mods.
  - **Installation Tips**: Install through a mod manager, ensuring compatibility with other inventory-related mods.
  - **How to Enable**: This mod runs automatically during gameplay, looting items upon enemy defeat and sorting inventory items based on their type and rarity.

4. Content Expansion Mods

- **New Questlines and Story Content**
  - **Description**: Adds entire new questlines and story content that blend with the main narrative, often with voice acting and custom environments.
  - **Where to Find**: Nexus Mods or ModDB.
  - **Installation Tips**: Install through a mod manager and follow any specific instructions for activation, as some mods require additional files or settings.
  - **How to Access New Quests**: The new quests will appear as new icons on the map or from specific NPCs in populated areas like **Brightfall Village** or **Stormguard Keep**.

- **Player Housing and Customizable Camp**
  - **Description**: This mod allows you to customize a player house or camp with furniture, storage options, and crafting stations, creating a personalized space in the game world.
  - **Where to Find**: Nexus Mods.

- **Installation Tips**: Install via a mod manager and read the instructions for adding furniture or using crafting stations.
- **How to Access Your House or Camp**: After installing, travel to the specified area (often marked on the map) to enter your customizable house or camp.

- **Expanded Romance Options**
  - **Description**: Unlocks new romance options with existing characters or adds new romanceable characters with branching dialogue and storylines.
  - **Where to Find**: Nexus Mods.
  - **Installation Tips**: Install with a mod manager and follow any mod-specific instructions for compatibility with existing save files.
  - **How to Begin a New Romance**: Once installed, the new romance dialogue options will appear naturally in conversations with eligible characters.

5. Performance and Optimization Mods

- **FPS Boost and Optimization Pack**
  - **Description**: Optimizes the game for higher frame rates and smoother gameplay, often by adjusting background processes and resource usage.
  - **Where to Find**: Nexus Mods.
  - **Installation Tips**: Follow the installation guide closely, as some performance mods may require manual tweaks to graphics settings.
  - **How to Adjust Settings**: Some mods include an options menu, allowing you to adjust settings for optimal performance based on your system.

- **Reduced Texture Load for Lower-End PCs**
  - **Description**: Lowers the resolution of background textures to improve performance on lower-spec PCs, maintaining visual quality while reducing lag.
  - **Where to Find**: Nexus Mods.
  - **Installation Tips**: Install through a mod manager or manually place files in the game's texture folder.
  - **How to Activate**: The lower texture load is automatically applied, optimizing performance on systems that struggle with the game's default settings.

Tips for Using and Managing Mods

- **Start with Essential Mods**: Begin with mods that improve quality of life and performance before adding more complex mods like new content or gameplay tweaks.
- **Check Compatibility**: Read each mod's description to ensure compatibility with your version of *Dragon Age: The Veilguard* and other mods.
- **Test Mods Gradually**: Add one or two mods at a time and test the game to make sure they work properly, preventing issues with conflicting mods.

- **Use Mod Loaders**: Use Vortex or DA Mod Manager to simplify mod installation, keep mods organized, and reduce the risk of compatibility issues.

With these recommended mods, you can enrich your *Dragon Age: The Veilguard* experience by enhancing graphics, adding fresh gameplay features, and improving overall quality of life. Whether you're looking to customize your character, streamline gameplay, or dive into new stories, these mods provide exciting ways to make the game truly your own. Enjoy exploring the creative work of the *Dragon Age* modding community and tailoring *The Veilguard* to suit your unique playstyle!

Installing and Managing Mods

Modding *Dragon Age: The Veilguard* can greatly enhance your gameplay experience, but it's important to know how to install and manage mods safely. This guide walks you through the steps for installing mods, using mod managers, and ensuring compatibility to keep your game stable. With the right approach, you'll be able to customize and expand the game without running into issues.

1. Preparing for Modding: Back Up Your Game Files

- **Why Backups Are Important**:
  - Modding can sometimes cause conflicts or crashes, so backing up your game files ensures you can restore them if needed.
  - **How to Backup Game Files**:
    - Locate the *Dragon Age: The Veilguard* installation folder, typically in **Program Files > Steam (or Origin) > Dragon Age: The Veilguard**.
    - Copy the entire game folder to a new location on your computer, such as **Documents > Game Backups**.

2. Choosing a Mod Manager

- **Recommended Mod Managers**:
  - **Vortex (Nexus Mods)**: Vortex is a popular mod manager that simplifies downloading, installing, and organizing mods.
  - **DA Mod Manager**: Specifically designed for *Dragon Age* games, DA Mod Manager allows advanced options for managing mods and resolving conflicts.
  - **How to Download Vortex**:
    - Go to NexusMods.com and search for Vortex. Download and install the mod manager.
  - **How to Set Up Vortex**:

■ Launch Vortex, log in with your Nexus Mods account, and add *Dragon Age: The Veilguard* to the list of managed games. Vortex will automatically detect the installation folder and prepare for modding.

3. Finding Mods and Downloading Them

- **Accessing Mods on Nexus Mods or ModDB**:
  - Go to NexusMods.com or ModDB.com and search for *Dragon Age: The Veilguard* mods.
  - **Filter Mods by Category**: Use filters to browse categories like graphics, gameplay, and quality-of-life improvements.
- **Downloading Mods**:
  - For Vortex Users: Select **Download with Vortex** on the mod page. Vortex will automatically download and prepare the mod for installation.
  - For Manual Downloads: Click **Manual Download** to save the mod files to your computer. This is often required for mods not hosted on Nexus.

4. Installing Mods with Vortex

- **Automatic Installation with Vortex**:
  - Once the mod is downloaded, open Vortex and go to the **Mods** tab. You'll see the downloaded mods listed here.
  - Select the mod you want to install, then click **Enable**. Vortex will handle the installation and manage the necessary files.
  - **Checking Load Order**: Some mods require a specific load order to function properly. You can adjust this in Vortex by dragging mods up or down in the **Load Order** list.
- **Manual Installation for Non-Nexus Mods**:
  - Download the mod manually and extract the files using software like WinRAR or 7-Zip.
  - Locate the *Dragon Age: The Veilguard* installation folder, and find the **Mods** or **Override** folder within.
  - Place the extracted mod files into the **Mods** or **Override** folder.
  - **Verifying Installation**: Launch the game and check if the mod has been applied. Some mods may require an in-game activation in the settings menu.

5. Organizing Mods for Compatibility

- **Understanding Load Order**:
  - Load order refers to the order in which mods are loaded into the game. Mods that modify similar files need a specific order to work correctly.
  - **How to Manage Load Order in Vortex**:
    - ■ Go to the **Mods** tab, where you can see each mod's load order. For mods that specify a load order, drag them up or down to set their priority.

- **Handling Conflicts**:
  - **Conflict Notifications**: Vortex will alert you if two mods conflict with each other. These conflicts occur when two mods attempt to modify the same files or resources.
  - **Resolving Conflicts**: Vortex allows you to set load order rules to resolve conflicts. Right-click on the conflicting mod, select **Manage Rules**, and choose which mod should load first.
  - **Using Patch Mods**: Some mod authors release compatibility patches to ensure their mod works well with others. Always check the mod description to see if a compatibility patch is available.

6. Testing Mods in the Game

- **Launching the Game**:
  - After installing and organizing mods, launch *Dragon Age: The Veilguard* to ensure everything is working smoothly.
  - **Starting a New Save**: It's often best to start a new save file when testing new mods, especially mods that change gameplay mechanics or add new quests.
- **Checking for Errors or Conflicts**:
  - Load into the game and test the modded content. If you encounter any issues (e.g., crashes, missing textures, or glitches), the mod may be incompatible or require further adjustments.
  - **Returning to Vortex for Adjustments**: If a mod isn't working as expected, return to Vortex to adjust the load order or disable the mod temporarily.

7. Updating and Uninstalling Mods

- **Updating Mods**:
  - **Checking for Updates**: Periodically, mod creators release updates to fix bugs or add new features. Check the mod's page on Nexus Mods or ModDB for updates.
  - **Updating Through Vortex**: If a mod update is available, Vortex will notify you. Select **Update** to download the latest version and apply it.
  - **Manual Update**: For manually installed mods, download the updated files, delete the old files from the **Mods** folder, and replace them with the new ones.
- **Uninstalling Mods**:
  - **Uninstall with Vortex**: In Vortex, go to the **Mods** tab, select the mod, and click **Disable** or **Uninstall**. This will remove the mod files from the game directory.
  - **Manual Uninstallation**: For manually installed mods, go to the **Mods** folder in the game directory and delete the specific mod files.

8. Troubleshooting Common Mod Issues

- **Game Crashes on Startup**:
  - **Cause**: Incompatible mods or incorrect load order.

- **Solution**: Disable recently installed mods, one at a time, to identify the problem. Adjust the load order if necessary.
- **Missing Textures or Glitches**:
  - **Cause**: Conflicting visual mods or outdated mod files.
  - **Solution**: Check for mod updates or reinstall visual mods. Ensure texture mods are compatible with each other.
- **Mod Not Appearing in Game**:
  - **Cause**: Incorrect installation path or disabled mod.
  - **Solution**: Verify the mod is enabled in Vortex or correctly placed in the **Mods** folder for manual installations.

9. Best Practices for Mod Management

- **Keep Mods Organized**:
  - Use Vortex or DA Mod Manager to keep your mods organized, avoid conflicts, and enable quick adjustments.
- **Install Mods Gradually**:
  - Install one or two mods at a time and test your game. This way, if an issue arises, you can identify the problematic mod quickly.
- **Check Mod Descriptions and Compatibility**:
  - Always read mod descriptions and compatibility notes before installing. Many issues arise from incompatible mods, so take time to review details.

By following these steps, you'll be well-prepared to install, manage, and troubleshoot mods in *Dragon Age: The Veilguard*. Modding enhances your game, adds variety, and allows you to enjoy a customized experience. With careful management, you'll enjoy a smooth and stable gameplay experience, bringing a new level of personalization to your journey in *The Veilguard*. Enjoy exploring the world of mods!

Customizing Your Gameplay Experience

Dragon Age: The Veilguard offers a rich foundation for players who want to shape the game according to their preferences. Customizing your gameplay can range from adjusting difficulty and visual settings to installing mods that change combat mechanics or add new content. This guide provides a comprehensive overview of ways to tailor your experience, including in-game options and external modding tools.

1. Adjusting In-Game Settings

- **Difficulty Options**:
    - **Description**: *Dragon Age: The Veilguard* allows you to choose from multiple difficulty levels that adjust enemy strength, AI tactics, and resource availability.
    - **How to Change Difficulty**: Go to **Options** in the main menu, then select **Gameplay**. From there, you can choose between difficulties like Easy, Normal, Hard, and Nightmare.
    - **Tips for Customizing Difficulty**:
        - **Easy Mode**: Ideal for story-focused players, with reduced enemy health and simpler AI.
        - **Nightmare Mode**: For those seeking a challenge, Nightmare increases enemy damage, adds advanced AI tactics, and tests your combat skills.
- **Visual Settings**:
    - **Graphics and Resolution**: Customize the game's resolution, texture quality, and effects.
    - **How to Adjust Graphics Settings**: In the **Options** menu, go to **Graphics**. Here, you can set resolution, adjust texture quality, and enable or disable features like shadows, anti-aliasing, and post-processing effects.
    - **Field of View (FOV)**: Adjusting the FOV can help players who prefer a wider view of the surroundings. This setting is often found in the **Advanced Graphics** options.
- **Sound and Control Customization**:
    - **Adjusting Sound**: In **Options** > **Audio**, you can customize music, voice, and sound effects volumes to suit your preference.
    - **Control Mapping**: If you prefer a custom control layout, you can rebind controls in **Options** > **Controls**, assigning specific actions to different keys or buttons.

2. Using Character Customization Options

- **Character Creation**:
    - **Appearance Options**: *The Veilguard* provides a range of customization options for creating a unique character, from face shape and skin tone to hairstyles and eye color.
    - **How to Access Character Creation**: Start a new game and go through the character creation process, where you can make adjustments to various physical features.
    - **Tips for a Distinctive Character**: Experiment with hairstyles, facial details, and armor colors to make a character that reflects your style.
- **Class and Skill Specialization**:
    - **Choosing a Class**: Select from Warrior, Mage, Rogue, or the Veil Warden, each offering a distinct playstyle and abilities.
    - **How to Assign Skill Points**: As you level up, access the **Skills** menu to assign points to abilities, choose specializations, and unlock powerful skills.
    - **Customizing Your Playstyle**:

- **Warrior**: Opt for tanking or melee DPS by choosing skills that increase defense or critical damage.
- **Mage**: Mix offensive spells and healing abilities to control the battlefield.
- **Rogue**: Specialize in stealth and critical strikes for a high-risk, high-reward approach.

3. Adding Mods for Enhanced Customization

- **Visual Enhancement Mods**:
  - **Description**: Mods can enhance textures, lighting, and character appearances, making the game more immersive.
  - **Popular Mods**:
    - **High-Resolution Texture Pack**: Sharpens textures for a more detailed environment.
    - **Enhanced Lighting**: Adds realistic lighting and shadow effects for a visually rich experience.
  - **How to Install**: Download from Nexus Mods or ModDB and install through a mod manager like Vortex.
- **Gameplay Mods**:
  - **Combat Mods**: Modify enemy AI, add new abilities, or change damage mechanics to customize combat difficulty and strategy.
  - **Role-Playing Enhancements**: Mods like expanded dialogue options or romance options let you experience a deeper role-playing aspect.
  - **How to Access Mods in the Game**: Once installed, these mods automatically apply, though some mods may include settings accessible via **Options** or specific menus like **Skills**.
- **Quality of Life Mods**:
  - **UI Overhauls**: Improve the user interface, making it easier to access inventory, quests, and map features.
  - **Inventory and Loot Mods**: Expand inventory space, improve loot sorting, and add auto-looting options.
  - **How to Enable Mods**: After installing through a mod manager, mods should be ready when you launch the game. Quality of life mods usually integrate seamlessly without additional setup.

4. Tweaking Game Mechanics with Advanced Settings

- **Enemy Scaling and Leveling Adjustments**:
  - **Description**: Adjusting how enemies scale to your level can balance difficulty and enhance immersion.
  - **How to Adjust Scaling**: Use gameplay mods that include level scaling features, or adjust difficulty settings in the **Options** menu.
  - **Recommended Settings**:

- **Increased Scaling**: For a challenging experience, set enemy levels close to or above yours.
- **Reduced Scaling**: If you prefer exploring areas without intense combat, lower the scaling.

- **Skill and Ability Customization**:
  - **Expanding Skill Trees**: Some mods introduce additional skills or alter skill effects, providing more options for character builds.
  - **Accessing New Skills**: After installing relevant mods, go to the **Skills** menu and explore new abilities or expanded skill paths.
  - **Suggestions for Balanced Builds**:
    - For balanced combat, mix offensive and defensive skills.
    - Allocate points to one specialization for a focused, powerful build.

5. Personalizing Your Environment and Base of Operations

- **Player Housing Mods**:
  - **Description**: Many mods allow you to customize a home or base, adding storage, crafting stations, and decorative items.
  - **Popular Mods**:
    - **Customizable Camp Mod**: Set up a personal camp with options for storage, crafting, and upgrading items.
    - **Player Housing Mod**: Choose from various styles of player homes and customize with furniture and decor.
  - **How to Access Your Customized Space**: Travel to your home or camp by using the map and select **Enter Base** to start customizing.
- **Crafting and Resource Gathering**:
  - **Crafting Customization**: Some mods enhance crafting mechanics, add new items, or expand resources, allowing you to create unique armor, potions, and weapons.
  - **How to Craft and Upgrade**: Access crafting stations at your base or camp, then select **Craft** or **Upgrade** to improve items and make new gear.
  - **Suggestions for Unique Builds**:
    - Craft armor with high elemental resistances for specific battles.
    - Create potions that boost mana or health for long dungeons.

6. Exploring New Content with Expansion Mods

- **Questline and Story Mods**:
  - **Description**: Mods like these add new quests, story arcs, and characters, expanding *The Veilguard*'s world and lore.

- - **How to Access New Quests**: New quests typically appear on the map or can be initiated by talking to NPCs in major locations like **Brightfall Village** or **Stormguard Keep**.
  - **Recommended Quest Mods**:
    - **The Lost Veil**: A mod that introduces a mysterious storyline involving Veilguard relics.
    - **Guardian's Path**: Adds a challenging questline with powerful rewards and lore-based content.
- **Companion and Romance Options**:
  - **Expanded Companions**: Certain mods allow for new companion interactions, adding depth to your team's relationships.
  - **Where to Find New Companions**: New companions often appear at key locations or join you after completing specific quests.
  - **How to Initiate Romance**: Expanded romance options appear as new dialogue choices with eligible characters, allowing for a richer role-playing experience.

7. Managing Mods and Customization for a Smooth Experience

- **Using Mod Managers**:
  - **Vortex and DA Mod Manager**: These tools simplify the installation and organization of mods, helping you avoid conflicts and ensuring that your customized setup runs smoothly.
  - **How to Install Mods**: Use Vortex or DA Mod Manager to install mods by selecting **Download with Vortex** or **Add Mod**, ensuring mods are enabled and in the correct load order.
- **Checking for Mod Updates**:
  - **Updating Mods**: Periodically check for updates to mods you've installed, as mod authors often release bug fixes, improvements, and new features.
  - **Accessing Update Notifications**: Vortex will notify you of available updates, or you can visit the mod page to download the latest version manually.
- **Troubleshooting Compatibility**:
  - **Common Issues**: If the game crashes or experiences glitches, it may be due to mod conflicts. Check the load order or disable mods to identify the issue.
  - **Community Support**: Use Nexus Mods forums or Discord groups for advice from other players who may have encountered similar issues.

Summary of Customizing Your Gameplay Experience

- **Adjust In-Game Settings**: Tweak difficulty, visual settings, and control options to set a comfortable base.
- **Explore Character Customization**: Make your character unique with appearance options, skill specializations, and custom playstyles.

- **Install Mods for Enhanced Customization**: Use visual, gameplay, and quality-of-life mods to expand and improve the game.
- **Tweak Game Mechanics**: Adjust scaling, skill builds, and combat difficulty for a personalized experience.
- **Add New Content**: Expand the game world with questline mods, companion options, and story expansions.
- **Manage Mods Effectively**: Keep mods organized with a mod manager, update regularly, and troubleshoot conflicts for smooth gameplay.

With these tools and techniques, you'll have everything you need to tailor *Dragon Age: The Veilguard* to your unique style, making every playthrough an experience that reflects your preferences and creativity. Enjoy the journey, knowing that you've crafted a gameplay experience that's all your own!

Troubleshooting Mod Compatibility

Modding *Dragon Age: The Veilguard* can greatly enhance your gameplay, but compatibility issues between mods can occasionally cause crashes, glitches, or other gameplay problems. This guide walks you through common compatibility issues, how to identify and resolve conflicts, and tips for managing mods to ensure a smooth experience. With the right approach, you can enjoy a customized game without the headaches of mod incompatibility.

1. Identifying Mod Conflicts

- **Common Signs of Mod Conflicts**:
    - **Game Crashes on Launch**: If your game crashes immediately after starting, it's likely due to an incompatible or conflicting mod.
    - **Graphical Glitches**: Missing textures, distorted visuals, or character model errors often indicate visual mod conflicts.
    - **Broken Gameplay Mechanics**: Issues like unresponsive abilities, missing dialogue options, or bugged quests can be caused by overlapping gameplay mods.
- **Using Mod Managers to Spot Conflicts**:
    - **Vortex and DA Mod Manager**: These tools can identify and highlight potential conflicts. Vortex, in particular, will notify you if two mods are trying to modify the same files.
        - **How to Check for Conflicts in Vortex**: Go to the **Mods** tab, and look for conflict notifications. Conflicting mods will be highlighted, with options to set load order rules.

- **How to Check for Conflicts in DA Mod Manager**: DA Mod Manager will show any errors or conflicts when loading mods. Double-check for any alerts or warnings when launching your mod list.

2. Managing Load Order

- **Understanding Load Order**:
  - Load order determines the sequence in which mods are loaded by the game, which affects how overlapping files interact. Incorrect load order can cause one mod to override another, leading to conflicts.
- **Setting Load Order in Vortex**:
  - **Drag and Drop**: Go to the **Mods** tab in Vortex. Drag mods up or down to set the desired load order. Typically, mods that make major changes to gameplay or visuals should load first, while minor mods load afterward.
  - **Creating Load Order Rules**: Right-click on a mod, select **Manage Rules**, and specify whether the mod should load before or after another mod.
- **Load Order Tips**:
  - **Visual Mods First**: Load visual enhancement mods (e.g., texture packs, reshades) before gameplay-altering mods.
  - **Game Mechanics Mods Next**: Mods that change abilities, skills, or AI should load after visual mods to ensure they apply properly.
  - **Minor or Quality-of-Life Mods Last**: Mods that don't drastically alter the game (e.g., inventory expansions, UI improvements) can load last.

3. Disabling and Testing Mods

- **Testing Mods One at a Time**:
  - If you're experiencing issues, disable mods one at a time to identify the problematic mod.
  - **How to Disable Mods in Vortex**: In the **Mods** tab, toggle the switch next to each mod to disable it. Launch the game after disabling each mod to see if the issue persists.
- **Creating a Test Profile**:
  - Use a separate profile for testing mods, especially when adding several new ones.
  - **How to Create a Profile in Vortex**: Go to **Profiles**, select **Create Profile**, and name it something like "Testing Profile." Install a few mods at a time, testing after each batch to ensure compatibility.
- **Starting with Essential Mods**:
  - Begin by enabling essential mods that you know are compatible, then gradually add others to reduce the chances of conflicts.

4. Using Compatibility Patches

- **What are Compatibility Patches?**
  - Compatibility patches are small mods created to bridge conflicts between two mods. For example, if two mods alter the same texture or gameplay mechanic, a patch can ensure they work together smoothly.
- **Finding Compatibility Patches**:
  - Check the description on each mod's page for mentions of required patches. Popular mods often have compatibility patches for other well-known mods.
  - **How to Install Compatibility Patches**: Download and install patches like any other mod, ensuring they load after the conflicting mods.
- **Keeping Track of Patches**:
  - **Use Vortex**: Vortex helps keep track of which patches you've installed, so you don't accidentally disable them. Always double-check that patches are enabled and correctly ordered in the load order.

5. Updating Mods for Compatibility

- **Why Update Mods?**:
  - Mod creators often release updates to fix bugs, improve features, and ensure compatibility with other popular mods. An outdated mod might be incompatible with the latest version of the game or other mods.
- **Checking for Updates in Vortex**:
  - **Automatic Update Notifications**: Vortex will alert you if an update is available. Go to the **Mods** tab and select **Update** next to the mod in question.
- **Updating Manually Installed Mods**:
  - For manually installed mods, visit the mod's page on Nexus Mods or ModDB to download the latest version. Replace the old files in the game's mod folder with the new files.

6. Troubleshooting Specific Issues

- **Game Freezes or Stutters**:
  - **Cause**: Large mods or incompatible visual mods can cause performance issues.
  - **Solution**: Lower graphical settings, reduce the number of visual mods, or check for mod updates that improve performance.
- **Missing Textures or Models**:
  - **Cause**: Conflicting visual mods, or mods installed in the wrong folder.
  - **Solution**: Ensure all visual mods are compatible and check that files are in the correct **Mods** or **Override** folder.
- **Quests or Dialogue Not Appearing**:

- **Cause**: Quest or NPC mods may conflict with other content mods.
    - **Solution**: Adjust load order so quest mods load after other gameplay mods, or look for a compatibility patch.
- **Skills or Abilities Not Working**:
    - **Cause**: Mods altering skills or abilities may conflict with one another.
    - **Solution**: Disable conflicting mods or check for updates that improve skill compatibility.

7. Using the Community for Support

- **Mod Comments and Forums**:
    - Mod authors and users often provide solutions to common issues in the comments section of a mod's page. Check here for insights or fixes if you're experiencing issues.
- **Discord and Community Servers**:
    - Many *Dragon Age* modding communities have Discord servers where users can share advice and troubleshooting tips.
    - **How to Find Support**: Look for a link to the modding community or Discord server on the mod's page or search for *Dragon Age* modding servers on Discord.
- **Nexus Mods Support Forum**:
    - Nexus Mods has a general support forum where players can discuss mod compatibility issues and get help. Join the forum to connect with other players who may have encountered similar problems.

8. Best Practices for Mod Compatibility

- **Limit the Number of Mods**:
    - Using too many mods, especially those that change core gameplay mechanics, increases the chance of conflicts. Start with a smaller selection of essential mods.
- **Install Mods Gradually**:
    - Add new mods in small batches, testing between each group. This approach helps you quickly identify any mod causing issues.
- **Read Mod Descriptions Carefully**:
    - Mod creators usually specify compatibility requirements or known conflicts in the description. Make sure to read these details before installing.
- **Keep Mods Updated**:
    - Always check for updates, as mod authors regularly release fixes and compatibility improvements.
- **Organize Your Load Order**:
    - A clear load order, with major mods loaded first and minor ones last, will reduce the chances of conflict.

Summary of Troubleshooting Mod Compatibility

- **Identify Conflicts**: Watch for crashes, graphical issues, or broken mechanics as signs of compatibility issues.
- **Manage Load Order**: Adjust load order to ensure major mods load first, followed by minor mods and quality-of-life improvements.
- **Disable and Test Mods Individually**: Narrow down conflicts by disabling mods one at a time.
- **Use Compatibility Patches**: Install patches to bridge conflicts between popular mods.
- **Update Mods Regularly**: Keep mods up to date to reduce the risk of compatibility issues.
- **Seek Community Support**: Join forums, Discord, or mod comments for advice from other users.

By following these steps, you can enjoy a customized and modded experience in *Dragon Age: The Veilguard* with minimal issues. Proper mod management and troubleshooting will help you get the most out of the game's modding potential while avoiding common pitfalls. Enjoy exploring a personalized version of *The Veilguard*!

Chapter 14

Trophy and Achievement Guide

This chapter serves as a comprehensive guide to unlocking all trophies and achievements in *Dragon Age: The Veilguard*. Whether you're a completionist aiming for 100% or just looking to earn specific milestones, this guide details the requirements for each achievement, with tips on how to tackle challenging objectives. From story-based trophies to combat achievements and hidden tasks, you'll find clear instructions and strategies to help you maximize your accomplishment in *The Veilguard*. Prepare to explore every corner, conquer every enemy, and achieve every goal!

List of All Trophies and Achievements

Dragon Age: The Veilguard features a variety of trophies and achievements that reward players for exploring, mastering combat, and completing story milestones. This guide provides a comprehensive list of all trophies and achievements, including tips on how to earn each one and where to press if specific actions are needed.

1. Story Progression Achievements

These achievements are awarded as you progress through the main storyline. They cannot be missed if you complete the game.

- **The First Step**
  - **Description**: Complete the introductory quest and join the Veilguard.
  - **How to Unlock**: Finish the opening questline by following the main objectives.
  - **Where to Press**: Press **Options** (PlayStation), **Menu** (Xbox), or **M** (PC) to open the quest journal and check the main storyline progress.
- **Champion of Brightfall**
  - **Description**: Complete the quests in Brightfall Village and secure the town.
  - **How to Unlock**: Finish all main quests related to Brightfall Village.
  - **Tips**: Make sure to talk to every NPC marked with a quest marker in Brightfall to avoid missing any objectives.
- **Keeper of the Veil**
  - **Description**: Defeat the Guardian of the Veil in the main storyline.
  - **How to Unlock**: This is a major story milestone and is achieved by following the main storyline.

○ **Where to Press**: During the fight, press **L2** (PlayStation), **LT** (Xbox), or **Ctrl** (PC) to lock onto the Guardian for easier targeting.

2. Combat Achievements

These trophies reward players for mastering combat mechanics, defeating enemies, and using specific strategies in battle.

- **First Blood**
  - **Description**: Defeat your first enemy.
  - **How to Unlock**: Earned automatically after your first combat encounter.
- **Unstoppable**
  - **Description**: Defeat 100 enemies.
  - **Tips**: Revisit enemy-heavy areas or use multiplayer dungeons to rack up kills quickly.
- **Elemental Fury**
  - **Description**: Defeat 20 enemies with elemental abilities.
  - **How to Unlock**: Use abilities like **Firestorm** or **Frost Bolt** to kill enemies with elemental effects.
  - **Where to Press**: Open the **Abilities** menu by pressing **Options** (PlayStation), **Menu** (Xbox), or **K** (PC) to equip elemental skills.
- **Master of Combos**
  - **Description**: Perform 50 successful ability combos in combat.
  - **Tips**: Pair skills from different classes, such as a mage's freeze spell followed by a rogue's critical hit.

3. Exploration Achievements

Explore the world of Thedas to earn these achievements. They encourage discovering hidden areas, interacting with landmarks, and collecting valuable items.

- **The Explorer**
  - **Description**: Discover all major locations in *The Veilguard*.
  - **Tips**: Check the map for undiscovered areas and use fast travel to explore remote regions.
  - **Where to Press**: Press **Map** on the touchpad (PlayStation), **View** (Xbox), or **M** (PC) to track discovered locations.
- **Treasure Hunter**
  - **Description**: Open 50 treasure chests.
  - **Tips**: Look for treasure chests in dungeons, hidden caves, and enemy camps. Some require lockpicking skills.

- **Where to Press**: Approach a chest and press **X** (PlayStation), **A** (Xbox), or **E** (PC) to open it.
- **Veil Secrets**
  - **Description**: Discover all hidden Veilguard relics and artifacts.
  - **Tips**: Use the **Veil Pulse** ability (activated in the Skills menu) to highlight nearby relics.

4. Companion and Relationship Achievements

These achievements are earned by building relationships with companions and making specific dialogue choices.

- **True Companions**
  - **Description**: Build a strong relationship with at least three companions.
  - **Tips**: Talk to companions regularly and complete their loyalty missions.
  - **Where to Press**: Open the **Party** menu by pressing **Options** (PlayStation), **Menu** (Xbox), or **P** (PC) to manage companions and check relationship status.
- **Romantic at Heart**
  - **Description**: Start a romance with a companion.
  - **How to Unlock**: Select romance dialogue options with eligible companions.
  - **Tips**: Choose supportive and kind responses to increase relationship affinity.
- **Loyalty Above All**
  - **Description**: Complete all loyalty missions for your companions.
  - **Where to Press**: Track loyalty missions in the quest journal by pressing **Options** (PlayStation), **Menu** (Xbox), or **J** (PC).

5. Crafting and Resource Achievements

These achievements focus on resource gathering, crafting equipment, and enhancing your character's gear.

- **Master Crafter**
  - **Description**: Craft 10 unique items at a crafting station.
  - **How to Unlock**: Gather resources like iron, wood, and herbs, then go to a crafting station.
  - **Where to Press**: At a crafting station, press **X** (PlayStation), **A** (Xbox), or **E** (PC) to open the crafting menu.
- **Herbalist**
  - **Description**: Gather 100 herbs from various locations.
  - **Tips**: Herbs respawn over time, so revisit previously explored areas to collect more.
- **Enhancer**
  - **Description**: Apply an enchantment to any piece of gear.
  - **How to Unlock**: Enchantments can be crafted and applied at your base or any enchanted station.
  - **Where to Press**: Select the item you wish to enchant and press **X** (PlayStation), **A** (Xbox), or **E** (PC) to apply the enchantment.

6. Multiplayer and Co-op Achievements

These achievements reward players for participating in multiplayer modes, completing co-op challenges, and supporting teammates.

- **Team Player**
  - **Description**: Complete your first multiplayer dungeon.
  - **How to Unlock**: Join a multiplayer session from the main menu and complete a dungeon with other players.
- **Veilguard Savior**
  - **Description**: Revive a teammate during a co-op match.
  - **How to Unlock**: Approach a fallen teammate and press **X** (PlayStation), **A** (Xbox), or **E** (PC) to revive them.
- **Multiplayer Champion**
  - **Description**: Reach the highest rank in multiplayer.
  - **Tips**: Focus on completing multiplayer challenges and high-difficulty dungeons to earn points for ranking up.

7. Hidden and Special Achievements

Some achievements are hidden or have special conditions. These achievements reward unique exploration, role-playing choices, and completing rare tasks.

- **The Chosen Path**
  - **Description**: Make a decision that significantly changes the course of the story.
  - **Tips**: At certain moments, you'll be given multiple choices that impact the narrative. Choose carefully to earn this achievement.
- **Unseen Guardian**
  - **Description**: Find and defeat a hidden Veil creature in the depths of the Fade.
  - **How to Unlock**: Look for hidden pathways in Fade locations and prepare for a challenging encounter.
  - **Where to Press**: In tactical mode, press the touchpad (PlayStation), **View** (Xbox), or **T** (PC) to direct your team in combat.
- **Legacy of the Veilguard**
  - **Description**: Complete all achievements in *The Veilguard*.
  - **Tips**: This is the ultimate completionist achievement, awarded when all other achievements are unlocked.

Summary of Trophies and Achievements

This list provides a thorough overview of the trophies and achievements available in *Dragon Age: The Veilguard*, from story-based goals and exploration challenges to multiplayer accomplishments and hidden achievements. By following these guidelines and knowing where to press for specific actions, you'll be well on your way to unlocking each one and showcasing your mastery of *The Veilguard*.

Tips for Earning Difficult Achievements

In *Dragon Age: The Veilguard*, some achievements are particularly challenging, requiring skill, strategy, and sometimes patience to unlock. This guide offers tips for earning the game's most difficult achievements, covering everything from complex combat feats to hidden exploration goals. With these strategies, you'll be better prepared to tackle even the toughest challenges and earn every reward.

1. Combat Achievements

These achievements require mastery of combat mechanics, strategic use of abilities, and effective enemy management.

- **Unstoppable Force**
  - **Description**: Complete a dungeon without taking any damage.
  - **Tips**:
    - **Use Defensive Abilities**: Equip abilities like **Shield Wall** (Warrior) or **Veil Barrier** (Mage) to minimize the chance of taking damage.
    - **Take Advantage of Ranged Attacks**: For ranged classes, keep your distance from enemies to avoid melee attacks.
    - **Team Up in Co-op**: In multiplayer, let your teammates take the lead while you focus on avoiding damage.
    - **Where to Press**: Open the **Abilities** menu with **Options** (PlayStation), **Menu** (Xbox), or **K** (PC) to ensure defensive skills are equipped.
- **Elemental Mastery**
  - **Description**: Defeat 50 enemies using each elemental type (fire, ice, lightning).
  - **Tips**:
    - **Rotate Elemental Abilities**: Equip fire, ice, and lightning abilities and switch between them during combat.
    - **Target Weak Enemies**: Use elemental abilities on weaker enemies to quickly increase your count.

- **Where to Press**: In the **Skills** menu, press **X** (PlayStation), **A** (Xbox), or **E** (PC) to assign elemental abilities to your hotbar.
- **One vs. Many**
  - **Description**: Defeat 10 or more enemies in a single battle without any assistance.
  - **Tips**:
    - **Choose Enemy-Dense Areas**: Find areas with lots of weak enemies, such as bandit camps or Veil-infested caves.
    - **Use Area-of-Effect Skills**: Equip abilities like **Firestorm** (Mage) or **Whirlwind** (Warrior) to damage multiple enemies at once.
    - **Stock Up on Potions**: Have health and mana potions ready, as solo fights can be taxing.
    - **Where to Press**: Use tactical mode by pressing the touchpad (PlayStation), **View** (Xbox), or **T** (PC) to plan and execute crowd-control strategies.

2. Exploration Achievements

These achievements involve finding hidden areas, rare items, and secrets across Thedas.

- **Secrets of the Veil**
  - **Description**: Discover all hidden Veilguard relics scattered throughout the world.
  - **Tips**:
    - **Use Veil Pulse**: Equip the **Veil Pulse** ability, which highlights nearby relics.
    - **Check Every Nook and Cranny**: Explore caves, ruins, and side paths off the main roads.
    - **Review the Map Regularly**: Look for any unexplored regions or icons indicating hidden areas.
    - **Where to Press**: Activate Veil Pulse by pressing **L1** (PlayStation), **LB** (Xbox), or **Q** (PC).
- **Ultimate Explorer**
  - **Description**: Visit every major and minor location in *The Veilguard*.
  - **Tips**:
    - **Fast Travel Helps**: Use fast travel to reach distant or missed locations.
    - **Follow Quest Lines**: Many quest lines will naturally guide you to undiscovered locations.
    - **Check Your Map**: Open the map frequently to track which areas you've visited.
    - **Where to Press**: Open the map with **Options** (PlayStation), **Menu** (Xbox), or **M** (PC) to check progress.
- **Hunter's Reward**
  - **Description**: Find and loot every unique treasure chest.
  - **Tips**:

- **Mark Special Chests**: Some chests have unique appearances or are in hidden areas, so mark their locations on the map if possible.
- **Use the Thief's Tools Ability**: Some chests require a high lockpicking skill, available for rogues or via thief companions.
- **Return to Areas After Progressing**: Some treasure chests only become accessible after certain story milestones.
- **Where to Press**: Open the **Skills** menu with **Options** (PlayStation), **Menu** (Xbox), or **K** (PC) to ensure you have Thief's Tools equipped.

3. Companion and Relationship Achievements

These achievements require building relationships with companions through specific dialogue choices and completing loyalty missions.

- **True Friend**
  - **Description**: Max out friendship with three companions.
  - **Tips**:
    - **Choose Positive Dialogue**: Always select dialogue options that align with each companion's values.
    - **Complete Loyalty Missions**: Each companion has a personal quest that strengthens your bond with them.
    - **Gift Unique Items**: Some companions respond well to gifts found throughout the game.
    - **Where to Press**: Check friendship status by opening the **Party** menu with **Options** (PlayStation), **Menu** (Xbox), or **P** (PC).
- **Romantic Journey**
  - **Description**: Start and complete a romance with a companion.
  - **Tips**:
    - **Be Consistent**: Choose romantic dialogue options consistently to build a romantic relationship.
    - **Complete Companion's Side Quests**: Romanceable companions often require completion of their quests for romance options to appear.
    - **Spend Time in Camp**: Visit your companion in camp frequently, as some romantic dialogue only appears there.

4. Crafting and Resource Achievements

These achievements focus on gathering resources and creating high-quality equipment.

- **Grandmaster Crafter**
  - **Description**: Craft a legendary weapon.

- Tips:
  - **Collect Rare Materials**: Materials like Veilstone and Elemental Shards are required for legendary items. Look for these in high-level dungeons.
  - **Use Crafting Perks**: Some crafting perks improve the quality of crafted items.
  - **Where to Press**: Access a crafting station, press **X** (PlayStation), **A** (Xbox), or **E** (PC), and select the legendary weapon recipe.

- **Resourceful Gatherer**
  - **Description**: Gather 1,000 units of various resources.
  - **Tips**:
    - **Revisit Resource-Rich Areas**: Locations with dense foliage and caves often respawn resources over time.
    - **Trade for Resources**: Vendors often sell basic resources, so use in-game currency to supplement your collection.
    - **Where to Press**: Track your resources in the inventory by pressing **Options** (PlayStation), **Menu** (Xbox), or **I** (PC).

5. Multiplayer and Co-op Achievements

These achievements are designed for multiplayer mode, rewarding teamwork and cooperative success.

- **Resilient Ally**
  - **Description**: Revive fallen teammates 20 times.
  - **Tips**:
    - **Play Support Roles**: Roles like healer or support make it easier to stay back and assist teammates.
    - **Coordinate with Friends**: Play with friends and let them know you're working on this achievement.
    - **Where to Press**: Approach a downed teammate and press **X** (PlayStation), **A** (Xbox), or **E** (PC) to revive.

- **Dungeon Master**
  - **Description**: Complete all multiplayer dungeons on the highest difficulty.
  - **Tips**:
    - **Team Up with High-Level Players**: Strong teammates will make this achievement easier.
    - **Equip High-Level Gear**: Ensure you have the best possible gear for each class role.
    - **Where to Press**: Open the multiplayer menu and select a dungeon at the highest difficulty level.

6. Hidden and Special Achievements

These achievements are often based on hidden objectives or require specific actions during gameplay.

- **Veilwalker**
  - **Description**: Enter the Veil 10 times.
  - **Tips**:
    - **Look for Veil Rifts**: Enter rifts in areas marked by purple glow or distortion effects.
    - **Stock Up on Potions**: Encounters in the Veil can be intense, so bring potions to heal.
    - **Where to Press**: Approach a Veil Rift and press **X** (PlayStation), **A** (Xbox), or **E** (PC) to enter.
- **Legacy of the Hero**
  - **Description**: Complete the game on Nightmare difficulty.
  - **Tips**:
    - **Prioritize Defensive Abilities**: Choose skills that reduce damage and increase healing.
    - **Plan Battles Carefully**: Use tactical mode frequently to control the battlefield.
    - **Stockpile Resources**: Gather plenty of potions and focus on armor upgrades.
    - **Where to Press**: Press the touchpad (PlayStation), **View** (Xbox), or **T** (PC) to enter tactical mode, allowing for strategic planning during combat.

Summary of Tips for Earning Difficult Achievements

To unlock *Dragon Age: The Veilguard*'s most challenging achievements, focus on mastering combat, exploring thoroughly, and managing relationships with companions. Equip defensive abilities, stock up on essential resources, and plan your strategies carefully, especially in high-difficulty battles and multiplayer dungeons. By following these tips, you'll be well-equipped to conquer every challenge and earn every trophy and achievement in the game. Good luck, and enjoy your journey through Thedas!

Completionist Checklist for *Dragon Age: The Veilguard*

Achieving 100% completion in *Dragon Age: The Veilguard* is a rewarding journey that requires thorough exploration, mastering combat, and completing every side quest, achievement, and collectible. This checklist provides a step-by-step guide for completionists, with all key objectives broken down by category. Follow this guide to track your progress, avoid missing anything, and fully experience everything *The Veilguard* has to offer.

1. Main Storyline Completion

- **Complete All Main Quests**: Ensure every main storyline quest is completed. These quests unlock as you progress and cannot be missed if you follow the story.

- **Where to Press**: Track main story quests in the **Quest Journal** by pressing **Options** (PlayStation), **Menu** (Xbox), or **J** (PC).
- **Major Boss Battles**: Finish each main story boss battle, as these are key to progression.
  - **Tips**: Use tactical mode (touchpad on PlayStation, **View** on Xbox, or **T** on PC) to plan your attacks during difficult fights.

2. Side Quests and Companion Missions

- **Complete All Side Quests**:
  - Side quests are found in each region, often marked by NPCs or icons on the map.
  - **Where to Press**: View all active and completed side quests in the **Quest Journal** to ensure none are missed.
- **Complete Companion Loyalty Missions**:
  - Each companion has a unique loyalty mission. Completing these missions deepens relationships and unlocks achievements.
  - **Where to Press**: Open the **Party** menu (Options on PlayStation, **Menu** on Xbox, **P** on PC) to check companion missions.
- **Special Encounters and Event-Based Quests**:
  - Some quests are triggered by events or special locations, often hidden off the beaten path.
  - **Tips**: Explore thoroughly and talk to all NPCs to uncover these quests.

3. Exploration and Collectibles

- **Discover All Locations**:
  - Visit every marked and unmarked location, including towns, dungeons, and hidden areas.
  - **Where to Press**: Open the map (touchpad on PlayStation, **View** on Xbox, **M** on PC) to track undiscovered areas.
- **Find All Veilguard Relics**:
  - Use the **Veil Pulse** ability to locate hidden relics scattered throughout the game world.
  - **Where to Press**: Activate Veil Pulse by pressing **L1** (PlayStation), **LB** (Xbox), or **Q** (PC) near relic sites.
- **Collect All Treasure Chests**:
  - Treasure chests are hidden in dungeons, caves, and other remote areas. Some may require a lockpicking skill.
  - **Where to Press**: Open a chest by pressing **X** (PlayStation), **A** (Xbox), or **E** (PC).
- **Harvest Resources from Every Region**:
  - Resources like herbs and ores are found in specific regions. Gather all available types.
  - **Tips**: Check areas frequently, as some resources respawn over time.

4. Trophies and Achievements

- **Story Achievements**:
  - Complete each main story arc and milestone to unlock story-related achievements.
- **Combat Achievements**:
  - Achievements include defeating enemies with specific abilities, completing dungeons without taking damage, and performing ability combos.
  - **Tips**: Check the list of achievements on your console or Steam to track which combat feats are still needed.
- **Exploration Achievements**:
  - These achievements often involve finding hidden areas, collecting all Veilguard relics, and completing every side quest.
  - **Tips**: Use the map and quest journal to ensure all objectives are complete.
- **Multiplayer Achievements**:
  - Multiplayer achievements include completing co-op dungeons, reviving teammates, and ranking up in multiplayer mode.
  - **Where to Press**: Access the multiplayer menu from the main menu to start a co-op session.
- **Hidden Achievements**:
  - Some achievements are hidden and unlock based on specific in-game choices or secret tasks.
  - **Tips**: Check guides or the community forums for hidden achievement details if you're having trouble locating them.

5. Character Development

- **Reach Max Level**:
  - Level up your character to the maximum level by completing quests, defeating enemies, and using experience-enhancing items.
  - **Tips**: Prioritize high-XP activities like dungeons and boss fights to reach the level cap quickly.
- **Unlock All Skill Trees and Specializations**:
  - Explore every skill tree and unlock each specialization option for your class.
  - **Where to Press**: Open the **Skills** menu with **Options** (PlayStation), **Menu** (Xbox), or **K** (PC) to assign skill points.
- **Complete All Companion Skill Trees**:
  - Level up your companions and assign points to unlock all abilities in their skill trees.
  - **Tips**: Bring companions on side quests and battles to earn experience and reach their full potential.

6. Crafting and Resource Gathering

- **Craft All Unique Weapons and Armor**:
  - Craft each unique item at a crafting station. Some recipes require rare resources.
  - **Where to Press**: Open the crafting menu at a crafting station by pressing **X** (PlayStation), **A** (Xbox), or **E** (PC).
- **Apply All Enchantments**:
  - Enchant gear with various enchantments to complete the enchantment list.
  - **Tips**: Collect Veil essence and rare materials to craft powerful enchantments.
- **Gather All Types of Resources**:
  - Ensure you've gathered each type of herb, ore, and essence. Some are unique to specific regions.
  - **Where to Track Resources**: Check your inventory (Options on PlayStation, **Menu** on Xbox, **I** on PC) to verify collected resources.

7. Relationship and Romance

- **Maximize Relationships with All Companions**:
  - Build strong bonds with each companion by engaging in their dialogue, completing loyalty missions, and choosing supportive responses.
- **Complete All Possible Romances**:
  - Romance eligible companions by choosing romantic dialogue options and completing their storylines.
  - **Where to Track Relationships**: Open the **Party** menu to view relationship status with companions.

8. Multiplayer Goals

- **Complete Every Multiplayer Dungeon**:
  - Finish each multiplayer dungeon on all available difficulty levels.
- **Rank Up to Max Multiplayer Rank**:
  - Gain multiplayer experience by completing dungeons and challenges to reach the highest rank.
- **Earn All Multiplayer Exclusive Rewards**:
  - Collect special items, gear, and abilities available only in multiplayer mode.
  - **Where to Press**: Check your progress in the multiplayer menu to see exclusive multiplayer rewards.

9. Special Events and Community Challenges

- **Participate in Community Challenges**:
  - Complete objectives that contribute to community goals. These may involve defeating a set number of enemies or gathering resources.
- **Finish All Special Event Quests**:
  - Special events often introduce new quests or challenges with unique rewards. Complete these during the event period.
  - **Where to Press**: Check the **Events** board in Brightfall Village or the multiplayer menu for current challenges.

Summary of Completionist Checklist

This checklist provides a roadmap to achieving 100% completion in *Dragon Age: The Veilguard*, covering story progression, side quests, achievements, crafting, relationships, multiplayer, and more. With this guide, you'll be able to track every objective and unlock every achievement, making the most of your journey through Thedas. Enjoy the satisfaction of becoming a true Veilguard completionist!

Special Veilguard Achievements and Rewards

In *Dragon Age: The Veilguard*, special achievements unlock exclusive rewards such as rare gear, unique abilities, and powerful items. These achievements often require dedication, skill, and exploration, making them some of the most coveted accomplishments in the game. This guide outlines the special Veilguard achievements, the steps to earn them, and the rewards they grant, helping you make the most of your gameplay.

1. Veil Mastery Achievements

These achievements focus on mastering the powers of the Veil, from uncovering relics to confronting hidden foes within the Veil.

- **Veilwalker**
  - **Description**: Enter the Veil 15 times across different locations.
  - **Reward**: Unlocks the **Veilwalker Cloak**, a unique piece of armor that increases mana regeneration within the Veil.
  - **Tips**:
    - **Where to Press**: Use **Veil Pulse** by pressing **L1** (PlayStation), **LB** (Xbox), or **Q** (PC) when near Veil Rifts to locate entry points.
    - Revisit known Veil locations in dungeons and quest areas to complete this achievement.
- **Guardian of Secrets**
  - **Description**: Collect all Veilguard relics scattered across the world.
  - **Reward**: Grants **Ancient Veilguard Staff**, an exclusive weapon with enhanced elemental damage.
  - **Tips**:

- **Activate Veil Pulse** in locations like caves and ruins to locate hidden relics.
- Check your **Quest Journal** for clues about relic locations.

- **Veil's Chosen**
  - **Description**: Defeat all major Veil creatures hidden throughout the Veilguard.
  - **Reward**: Unlocks **Veilguard Amulet**, which increases resistance to Veil-based attacks and adds a temporary shield when entering combat.
  - **Tips**:
    - Look for powerful creatures marked by a purple glow or distortion effect.
    - **Use Tactical Mode** (touchpad on PlayStation, **View** on Xbox, or **T** on PC) to plan your approach before engaging these challenging enemies.

2. Combat Mastery Achievements

Earn these achievements by mastering combat techniques, achieving kill milestones, and successfully executing powerful combos.

- **Combo Conqueror**
  - **Description**: Execute 100 successful ability combos with your companions.
  - **Reward**: Unlocks the **Veilguard Ring of Precision**, which increases combo damage and critical hit chance.
  - **Tips**:
    - Use abilities like **Freeze** (Mage) followed by **Backstab** (Rogue) to create combos.
    - Press **L1** (PlayStation), **LB** (Xbox), or **Ctrl** (PC) to command companions in tactical mode for precise combo execution.

- **Unbreakable Defense**
  - **Description**: Block or dodge 500 attacks without taking damage.
  - **Reward**: Grants the **Shield of the Veil**, which reduces damage from all attacks by 15%.
  - **Tips**:
    - Equip a shield as a Warrior or use defensive abilities like **Veil Barrier**.
    - **Where to Press**: Hold **L2** (PlayStation), **LT** (Xbox), or **Right Click** (PC) to block during combat.

- **The Veil's Wrath**
  - **Description**: Defeat 100 enemies using Veil-enhanced abilities.
  - **Reward**: Unlocks the **Veilguard's Fury**, a powerful skill that deals massive AoE damage to all enemies nearby.
  - **Tips**:
    - Equip Veil-based abilities, such as **Veil Strike** or **Shadow Pulse**, for a greater impact.
    - **Where to Press**: Open **Abilities** (Options on PlayStation, **Menu** on Xbox, **K** on PC) to assign Veil-enhanced skills to your hotbar.

3. Exploration and Discovery Achievements

These achievements encourage players to explore every part of Thedas, discovering hidden locations, lore, and treasure along the way.

- **Master of the Wilds**
    - **Description**: Discover all hidden areas in each region.
    - **Reward**: Unlocks **Wanderer's Boots**, which increase movement speed and reduce fall damage.
    - **Tips**:
        - **Where to Press**: Open the map (touchpad on PlayStation, **View** on Xbox, **M** on PC) and look for any greyed-out regions to track undiscovered areas.
        - Search forests, cliffs, and underground passages for hidden entrances.
- **Ancient Scholar**
    - **Description**: Find and read every lore book hidden in The Veilguard.
    - **Reward**: Grants **Wisdom of the Veil**, a passive bonus that boosts mana regeneration and decreases spell cooldown.
    - **Tips**:
        - Lore books are often found in temples, libraries, and Veil rifts. Use **Veil Pulse** to highlight hidden books.
        - Check all bookcases and libraries in towns for any lore entries you may have missed.
- **Treasure Seeker**
    - **Description**: Open all unique treasure chests across the game.
    - **Reward**: Unlocks **Bag of Holding**, an item that expands your inventory capacity.
    - **Tips**:
        - Certain treasure chests may require lockpicking. Assign points to **Thief's Tools** if you're a rogue or bring a companion with that skill.
        - **Where to Press**: Press **X** (PlayStation), **A** (Xbox), or **E** (PC) to open chests.

4. Crafting and Resource Achievements

These achievements focus on gathering resources, crafting unique items, and enhancing equipment through enchantments and upgrades.

- **Artisan of The Veil**
    - **Description**: Craft 20 unique items at a crafting station.
    - **Reward**: Unlocks the **Craftsman's Belt**, which reduces crafting resource costs by 10%.
    - **Tips**:
        - Gather resources like iron, herbs, and essence from each region.

- **Where to Press**: Open the crafting menu at any crafting station (press **X** on PlayStation, **A** on Xbox, **E** on PC) to create items.
- **Master Enchanter**
  - **Description**: Apply every type of enchantment to a piece of equipment.
  - **Reward**: Grants the **Veilguard's Focus**, an amulet that boosts mana by 20% and improves enchantment effects.
  - **Tips**:
    - Explore dungeons and gather materials to create enchantments at your base.
    - Enchantments can be applied to armor and weapons by visiting an enchantment station, usually found in major cities or your camp.
- **Alchemist Supreme**
  - **Description**: Brew every type of potion available.
  - **Reward**: Unlocks the **Potion Master's Satchel**, which increases potion capacity.
  - **Tips**:
    - Collect ingredients like herbs, essence, and Veil-based materials.
    - **Where to Press**: Access the alchemy station (Options on PlayStation, **Menu** on Xbox, **K** on PC) to view available potions and brew recipes.

5. Multiplayer and Co-op Achievements

These achievements are for those who engage in multiplayer mode, offering unique rewards for cooperative play.

- **Veilguard Veteran**
  - **Description**: Complete 50 multiplayer dungeons.
  - **Reward**: Unlocks the **Veteran's Sigil**, which boosts health regeneration and increases resilience in multiplayer mode.
  - **Tips**:
    - **Where to Press**: Start a multiplayer dungeon by accessing the multiplayer menu from the main screen.
    - Team up with players at similar levels to increase efficiency and make dungeon runs faster.
- **Battle Medic**
  - **Description**: Revive 50 teammates during multiplayer matches.
  - **Reward**: Grants the **Healer's Charm**, a necklace that increases healing speed and improves potion effectiveness.
  - **Tips**:
    - Play as a support class or bring extra health potions to sustain yourself while reviving teammates.
    - **Where to Press**: Approach downed teammates and press **X** (PlayStation), **A** (Xbox), or **E** (PC) to revive.

- **Ultimate Strategist**
  - **Description**: Win 20 PvP matches in multiplayer mode.
  - **Reward**: Unlocks the **Champion's Medallion**, which enhances damage and resistance in PvP battles.
  - **Tips**:
    - **Where to Press**: Select PvP mode from the multiplayer menu to join a match.
    - Focus on team coordination and balance to outmaneuver the opposing team.

Summary of Special Veilguard Achievements and Rewards

This guide provides an overview of the special Veilguard achievements, offering tips and highlighting the unique rewards you can earn. From exploring the Veil's mysteries to mastering combat and crafting, these achievements challenge you to fully engage with all aspects of *Dragon Age: The Veilguard*. By completing each one, you'll unlock powerful equipment, enhance your abilities, and gain prestige as a true Veilguard master. Good luck on your journey, and enjoy the satisfaction of uncovering all that Thedas has to offer!

CHAPTER 15

Advanced Tips and Tricks

This chapter provides in-depth strategies to help players optimize their gameplay in *Dragon Age: The Veilguard*. From min-maxing character builds to mastering efficient leveling and skill progression, these tips and tricks are designed for players looking to take their game to the next level. You'll also find techniques for exploiting the environment in battles, adapting strategies for different playstyles, and tackling the most challenging endgame content. With these advanced insights, you'll be prepared to face anything Thedas throws your way and achieve mastery in *The Veilguard*.

Min-maxing Character Builds in *Dragon Age: The Veilguard*

Min-maxing is the process of maximizing your character's strengths while minimizing weaknesses to create the most efficient build possible. In *Dragon Age: The Veilguard*, each class has unique abilities, attributes, and equipment that can be optimized to enhance performance in combat and quests. This guide offers in-depth advice on min-maxing each character class, including which stats to prioritize, how to assign skill points, and tips for selecting the best gear. Follow these tips to create a powerful character tailored to your playstyle.

1. Understanding Core Attributes for Each Class

- **Warrior**:
  - **Primary Attributes**: Strength (for melee damage) and Constitution (for health and defense).
  - **Attribute Focus**:
    - **Strength**: Increases melee attack power and ability to wear heavy armor.
    - **Constitution**: Boosts health and improves survivability, essential for tanking.
  - **Where to Press**: Open the **Character** menu by pressing **Options** (PlayStation), **Menu** (Xbox), or **I** (PC) and assign points to Strength and Constitution as you level up.
- **Mage**:
  - **Primary Attributes**: Magic (for spell power) and Willpower (for mana and mana regeneration).
  - **Attribute Focus**:

- **Magic**: Boosts the effectiveness of spells, especially damage-dealing abilities.
        - **Willpower**: Increases mana capacity and improves spellcasting efficiency.
    - ○ **Where to Press**: Use the **Character** menu to prioritize Magic and Willpower points for powerful spells and consistent casting.
- **Rogue**:
    - ○ **Primary Attributes**: Dexterity (for critical hit chance) and Cunning (for critical damage and stealth).
    - ○ **Attribute Focus**:
        - **Dexterity**: Increases accuracy, critical hit rate, and evasion, key for stealthy, high-damage attacks.
        - **Cunning**: Boosts damage output on critical hits and enhances abilities like lockpicking.
    - ○ **Where to Press**: Access the **Character** menu and allocate points to Dexterity and Cunning to maximize critical damage output.

2. Choosing and Developing Skill Trees

- **Warrior Skill Trees**:
    - ○ **Offensive Build**: Focus on **Two-Handed Weapon Skills** to boost melee damage. Skills like **Whirlwind** and **Mighty Blow** provide area damage and heavy strikes.
    - ○ **Defensive Build**: Use **Sword and Shield Skills** for tanking, prioritizing abilities like **Shield Wall** and **Defensive Shout** to absorb damage and protect teammates.
    - ○ **Where to Press**: Open the **Skills** menu with **Options** (PlayStation), **Menu** (Xbox), or **K** (PC), then allocate points to either Two-Handed or Sword and Shield based on your role.
- **Mage Skill Trees**:
    - ○ **Damage Focus**: Develop the **Elemental Skill Tree** for high-damage spells like **Firestorm** and **Ice Shard**.
    - ○ **Support and Control Focus**: The **Spirit and Arcane Skill Trees** provide healing, mana regeneration, and crowd control. Abilities like **Barrier** and **Mind Control** keep enemies in check and assist teammates.
    - ○ **Where to Press**: In the **Skills** menu, choose Elemental spells for damage or Spirit spells for support to enhance your chosen playstyle.
- **Rogue Skill Trees**:
    - ○ **Stealth and Crit Build**: Invest in the **Subterfuge Tree** for abilities like **Shadow Strike** and **Poison Dagger** to increase critical hit damage and stealth options.
    - ○ **Ranged DPS Build**: Develop the **Archery Tree** for long-range abilities, including **Long Shot** and **Pinning Shot**.
    - ○ **Where to Press**: Access **Skills** in the menu and select Subterfuge for stealth or Archery for a ranged build.

3. Optimizing Gear and Equipment

- **Warrior**:
  - **Weapons**: For offense, prioritize two-handed weapons with high damage output. For defense, choose a sword and shield combination.
  - **Armor**: Select heavy armor with bonuses to Strength and Constitution, boosting survivability and melee power.
  - **Where to Press**: Access the **Inventory** menu (Options on PlayStation, **Menu** on Xbox, **I** on PC) to equip weapons and armor that align with your Strength and Constitution priorities.
- **Mage**:
  - **Weapons**: Equip staves that enhance Magic and Willpower, boosting spell power and mana capacity.
  - **Armor**: Opt for robes with mana regeneration and magic boosts to improve casting efficiency.
  - **Where to Press**: In the **Inventory** menu, select gear that maximizes your Magic and Willpower, ensuring high spellcasting potential.
- **Rogue**:
  - **Weapons**: For melee, use daggers with high critical damage. For ranged builds, bows with Dexterity and Cunning bonuses are ideal.
  - **Armor**: Light armor with bonuses to Dexterity and Cunning enhances critical hit chances and evasion.
  - **Where to Press**: In **Inventory**, select daggers or bows, and equip light armor that supports Dexterity and Cunning.

4. Using Advanced Min-maxing Techniques

- **Skill Synergy**:
  - Combine abilities from different skill trees to maximize impact. For example, a Mage using **Ice Shard** followed by **Firestorm** creates a powerful elemental combo.
  - **Where to Press**: Assign abilities in the **Abilities** menu for easy access during battles, and experiment with combinations.
- **Stat-Boosting Potions and Enchantments**:
  - Use potions to temporarily boost primary attributes before a challenging fight. Enchant gear to enhance key stats, such as critical hit rate for Rogues or mana regeneration for Mages.
  - **Where to Press**: Visit crafting stations (press **X** on PlayStation, **A** on Xbox, **E** on PC) to create potions and apply enchantments.
- **Choosing Specialization Classes**:
  - As you level up, specialization classes become available. Each class has unique abilities that further enhance your build.
  - **Warrior Specializations**: Berserker (boosts damage), Templar (magic resistance), Champion (tank abilities).

- **Mage Specializations**: Blood Mage (life-draining spells), Arcane Warrior (melee combat), Spirit Healer (healing and support).
- **Rogue Specializations**: Assassin (high crit damage), Duelist (evasion and melee), Ranger (summoning animals).
- **Where to Press**: Access specialization options in the **Skills** menu once available, and select a specialization that complements your playstyle.

5. Tips for Each Class's Min-maxing Playstyle

- **Warrior**:
  - **Offensive Warriors**: Equip two-handed weapons and focus on high-damage skills like **Mighty Blow**. Keep an eye on Strength to increase raw power.
  - **Defensive Warriors**: Use a sword and shield setup, focusing on Constitution to improve defense. Skills like **Shield Wall** and **Taunt** help control the battlefield.
  - **Strategy**: In battles, use **L2** (PlayStation), **LT** (Xbox), or **Right Click** (PC) to block when playing defensively. Position yourself between enemies and teammates to absorb damage.
- **Mage**:
  - **Damage Mages**: Use high-damage spells and prioritize Magic to enhance spell power. Maintain distance from enemies and use **Veil Pulse** to spot vulnerable foes.
  - **Support Mages**: Equip mana-regeneration gear and focus on healing or crowd-control spells. Willpower boosts allow for more frequent casting.
  - **Strategy**: Use the **L1** (PlayStation), **LB** (Xbox), or **Q** (PC) key to activate **Veil Pulse** for spotting opportunities and healing teammates in critical moments.
- **Rogue**:
  - **Stealth Rogues**: Equip daggers and focus on Dexterity and Cunning to maximize critical damage. Skills like **Shadow Strike** and **Poison Dagger** are key.
  - **Ranged Rogues**: Use bows and boost Dexterity to improve accuracy and damage output from a distance.
  - **Strategy**: Enter **Stealth Mode** by pressing **R3** (PlayStation), **Right Stick** (Xbox), or **Shift** (PC), then approach enemies from behind for critical strikes.

Summary of Min-maxing Character Builds

To create an optimized character in *Dragon Age: The Veilguard*, focus on the primary attributes for your class, choose complementary skills, and select gear that enhances your strengths. Through skill synergy, strategic use of potions and enchantments, and specialization classes, you'll develop a powerful build suited to your playstyle. Follow these tips to make the most of your character's abilities, mastering every challenge in Thedas.

Efficient Leveling and Skill Progression in *Dragon Age: The Veilguard*

Leveling up efficiently and progressing through skills strategically is crucial for maximizing your character's potential in *Dragon Age: The Veilguard*. This guide provides techniques to gain experience quickly, allocate skill points wisely, and unlock abilities that enhance your effectiveness in combat and exploration. By following these tips, you'll ensure a smooth journey to higher levels and a powerful skill set to tackle the game's toughest challenges.

1. Maximize Experience Gain

- **Complete Quests Efficiently**:
  - **Focus on Main and Side Quests**: Quests are the fastest way to earn experience. Prioritize the main storyline for substantial XP gains, then tackle side quests for additional rewards.
  - **Where to Press**: Track active quests in the **Quest Journal** by pressing **Options** (PlayStation), **Menu** (Xbox), or **J** (PC) to ensure you're completing as many as possible.
- **Engage in Combat Regularly**:
  - **Clear Enemy Camps and Dungeons**: Defeating enemies grants experience, so clear out enemy camps and dungeons as you explore.
  - **Revisit High-XP Areas**: Some areas, such as caves and ruins, have respawning enemies, providing a steady source of XP.
  - **Where to Press**: Enter tactical mode (touchpad on PlayStation, **View** on Xbox, **T** on PC) to analyze enemies and plan effective combat strategies.
- **Utilize Multiplayer Dungeons**:
  - **Multiplayer XP Boosts**: Multiplayer dungeons offer higher XP rewards. Team up with other players to clear challenging areas faster and accumulate more experience.
  - **Where to Press**: Access the multiplayer menu from the main screen to join dungeons with friends or other players.

2. Choosing the Right Skills Early On

- **Warrior Skill Progression**:
  - **Early Skills for Survivability**: For warriors, start by unlocking **Shield Wall** (if playing as a tank) or **Mighty Blow** (for two-handed builds). These abilities will help you control battles and survive early-game encounters.
  - **Intermediate Skills**: As you level up, prioritize abilities like **Taunt** (for tanks) or **Whirlwind** (for DPS) to control the battlefield and deal area damage.
  - **Where to Press**: Open the **Skills** menu by pressing **Options** (PlayStation), **Menu** (Xbox), or **K** (PC) to assign points to Shield Wall, Taunt, or Whirlwind.
- **Mage Skill Progression**:
  - **Early Skills for Damage or Support**: Start with **Fireball** for offensive builds or **Barrier** for support builds. These core skills provide strong area damage or protection.

- Intermediate Skills: Unlock **Ice Shard** or **Veilguard** abilities to expand your elemental or support options.
- Where to Press: In the **Skills** menu, assign early points to Fireball (damage) or Barrier (support), then invest in additional elemental or healing skills as you level.

- **Rogue Skill Progression**:
  - **Early Skills for Critical Damage**: Begin with **Backstab** for melee rogues or **Long Shot** for ranged rogues. These skills provide excellent single-target damage.
  - **Intermediate Skills**: Unlock **Poison Dagger** (melee) or **Pinning Shot** (ranged) to expand your tactical options and control enemies.
  - **Where to Press**: Open the **Skills** menu and select Backstab or Long Shot early on. Invest in additional critical or ranged abilities as you gain levels.

3. Efficient Skill Point Allocation

- **Prioritize Core Skills**:
  - Invest in skills that complement your character's role and playstyle. Each class has essential skills that serve as the foundation for effective combat.
  - **Warrior**: Focus on **Shield Wall** and **Taunt** for tanks, or **Mighty Blow** and **Whirlwind** for DPS warriors.
  - **Mage**: Prioritize **Barrier** and **Revive** for support, or **Fireball** and **Ice Shard** for damage.
  - **Rogue**: Focus on **Backstab** and **Poison Dagger** (melee) or **Long Shot** and **Pinning Shot** (ranged).
  - **Where to Press**: Access the **Skills** menu to allocate points as you level up, focusing on core skills first.

- **Unlock Complementary Skills**:
  - Once core skills are established, expand with complementary abilities that boost synergy.
  - **Examples**:
    - **Warrior Tanks**: Invest in **Defensive Shout** for additional control over enemies.
    - **Mage Support**: Add **Mind Control** or **Healing Aura** to enhance party survivability.
    - **Rogue Stealth**: Invest in **Shadow Strike** or **Evasion** to maximize critical hit opportunities.
  - **Where to Press**: In the **Skills** menu, review skill descriptions to find those that enhance your primary skills.

- **Upgrade Key Abilities**:
  - Many skills have upgrades that improve damage, duration, or range. Prioritize upgrades on high-use abilities.
  - **Examples**:
    - **Warriors**: Upgrade **Whirlwind** for increased area damage.
    - **Mages**: Upgrade **Barrier** to extend its duration.

- **Rogues**: Upgrade **Backstab** for higher critical multipliers.
  - ○ **Where to Press**: In the **Skills** menu, click on each skill to view and apply available upgrades.

4. Utilizing Skill Synergies for Maximum Effect

- **Cross-Class Combos**:
  - ○ Pair skills from different classes to create powerful combos.
  - ○ **Examples**:
    - **Mage and Rogue**: Use **Freeze** (Mage) followed by **Backstab** (Rogue) for increased critical damage.
    - **Warrior and Mage**: **Taunt** (Warrior) draws enemies close, then follow up with **Firestorm** (Mage) to deal AoE damage.
  - ○ **Where to Press**: Use tactical mode (touchpad on PlayStation, **View** on Xbox, **T** on PC) to coordinate cross-class abilities effectively.
- **Skill Chains**:
  - ○ Chain abilities within the same class for greater impact.
  - ○ **Examples**:
    - **Warrior**: Use **Mighty Blow** followed by **Whirlwind** for heavy damage output.
    - **Mage**: Cast **Ice Shard** to freeze enemies, then follow up with **Fireball** for elemental synergy.
    - **Rogue**: Use **Shadow Strike** to initiate combat, then follow up with **Poison Dagger** for sustained critical hits.
  - ○ **Where to Press**: In the **Skills** menu, assign these skills to your hotbar and practice chaining them together in combat.

5. Strategies for Efficient Leveling and Progression

- **Focus on High-XP Activities**:
  - ○ Prioritize dungeons, main quests, and boss fights, as these activities grant more XP compared to smaller encounters.
  - ○ **Where to Press**: Use the **Map** (touchpad on PlayStation, **View** on Xbox, **M** on PC) to locate dungeons and high-XP areas.
- **Equip XP-Boosting Gear**:
  - ○ Some items offer XP bonuses. Equip these when grinding or completing quests for faster leveling.
  - ○ **Where to Press**: Check the **Inventory** (Options on PlayStation, **Menu** on Xbox, **I** on PC) and equip any XP-enhancing items you find.
- **Use Potions and Buffs**:
  - ○ Some potions and buffs provide temporary XP boosts. Use these before major encounters for increased rewards.

- **Where to Press**: Visit crafting stations (press **X** on PlayStation, **A** on Xbox, **E** on PC) to create XP-boosting potions.

Summary of Efficient Leveling and Skill Progression

To level up efficiently in *Dragon Age: The Veilguard*, prioritize main and side quests, clear enemy camps and dungeons, and invest skill points in core abilities. Unlock complementary skills, upgrade high-use abilities, and exploit skill synergies for maximum impact. Equip XP-boosting items, use buffs, and focus on high-XP activities to reach higher levels quickly. With these strategies, you'll build a powerful character capable of handling any challenge that Thedas presents. Enjoy mastering your character's progression!

Exploiting the Environment in Battles

In *Dragon Age: The Veilguard*, leveraging the environment can give you a significant advantage in combat. From using high ground to setting traps, these strategies will help you turn the battlefield to your favor, allowing you to control enemy movements, reduce incoming damage, and maximize the effectiveness of your abilities. This guide will walk you through advanced tactics for exploiting the environment in battles, including positioning, terrain advantages, and interactive elements that can improve your combat success.

1. Using High Ground and Line of Sight

- **Gain a Height Advantage**:
  - High ground gives you better visibility and makes it easier to control the flow of battle. Ranged characters, such as Mages and Archers, can use high ground to attack from a safer distance and avoid melee threats.
  - **How to Position**: Move your character to elevated areas like cliffs, rocks, or staircases.
  - **Where to Press**: Use the left joystick or **WASD** keys to move to higher ground, giving you a better view of the battlefield and reducing the risk of melee attacks.
- **Break Line of Sight**:
  - If facing ranged enemies, use obstacles like walls, trees, or rocks to block their line of sight. This forces enemies to reposition, giving you an opportunity to control the pace of combat.
  - **How to Hide**: Position yourself behind cover when not actively engaging enemies.
  - **Where to Press**: Use the left joystick or **WASD** keys to move in and out of cover as needed.

2. Using Environmental Hazards to Your Advantage

- **Luring Enemies into Traps**:

- Some areas have environmental hazards such as fire pits, spiked traps, or unstable ledges. Lure enemies into these hazards to deal extra damage or knock them down.
- **How to Lure Enemies**: Use taunt abilities like **Taunt** (Warrior) or movement-based abilities like **Blink** (Mage) to manipulate enemy positions.
- **Where to Press**: Use tactical mode (touchpad on PlayStation, **View** on Xbox, **T** on PC) to position your character and lure enemies into hazards.

- **Triggering Explosive Barrels**:
    - Some areas have explosive barrels or flammable materials that can be triggered to damage nearby enemies.
    - **How to Trigger**: Use fire-based abilities like **Fireball** (Mage) or shoot the barrels if you're a ranged character.
    - **Where to Press**: Position yourself near an explosive barrel and press **R2** (PlayStation), **RT** (Xbox), or **Left Click** (PC) to target and activate the explosion.

- **Using Water and Electricity**:
    - If there's water on the ground, electric spells or lightning arrows can be used to electrify it, dealing AoE damage to enemies standing in the water.
    - **How to Set Up**: Lead enemies into shallow water areas, then cast an electric spell like **Lightning Bolt**.
    - **Where to Press**: Cast electric spells in water areas by pressing the hotkey assigned to your electric ability (use the **Abilities** menu to assign hotkeys).

3. Positioning for Crowd Control and AOE Attacks

- **Cluster Enemies Together**:
    - Grouping enemies in a tight space makes them more vulnerable to area-of-effect (AOE) attacks. Use narrow spaces like doorways or choke points to control enemy movement.
    - **How to Cluster**: Use skills like **Taunt** (Warrior) or **Mind Control** (Mage) to force enemies to gather in one spot.
    - **Where to Press**: Enter tactical mode to direct your party members and funnel enemies into tight areas, pressing **L2** (PlayStation), **LT** (Xbox), or **Right Click** (PC) to control positioning.

- **AOE and Trap Combos**:
    - Set up traps or use AOE spells when enemies are clustered. For example, a Rogue can plant traps in a choke point, and a Mage can follow up with **Firestorm**.
    - **How to Set Up**: Place traps or cast AOE spells in enemy-heavy areas.
    - **Where to Press**: Select the AOE ability or trap from the **Skills** menu and place it strategically.

4. Using Interactive Objects and Terrain Features

- **Activate Destructible Elements**:
  - Some areas have destructible barriers or crates that can be broken to open new paths or reveal hiding spots.
  - **How to Use**: Destroy these objects to create more space or to uncover resources and additional cover.
  - **Where to Press**: Position your character near destructible objects and press **R2** (PlayStation), **RT** (Xbox), or **Left Click** (PC) to break them.
- **Natural Obstacles for Defense**:
  - Natural obstacles like trees, boulders, or narrow ledges can block enemy movement and funnel them into more controlled paths.
  - **How to Position**: Stand behind large objects to block enemy attacks, especially useful against ranged enemies.
  - **Where to Press**: Move using the left joystick or **WASD** keys to take cover behind natural obstacles.

5. Controlling Enemy Aggression and Pathing

- **Drawing Aggro with Tanks**:
  - Use tank abilities like **Shield Wall** and **Taunt** to draw aggro and control enemy movements, keeping them away from squishy party members.
  - **How to Control Aggro**: Position your tank in front of enemies while using **Taunt** to keep their focus.
  - **Where to Press**: In the **Skills** menu, assign **Taunt** and press it in battle to keep enemies focused on your tank.
- **Kiting and Ranged Attacks**:
  - For ranged characters, keep a safe distance and use the environment to avoid direct confrontations. Move in a circle or figure-eight pattern to keep enemies moving without closing in on you.
  - **How to Kite**: Use narrow paths and high ground to maintain distance from melee attackers.
  - **Where to Press**: Use the left joystick or **WASD** keys to maintain movement, keeping a safe distance from enemies as you fire.

6. Using Environmental Synergy with Abilities

- **Elemental Combos**:
  - Combine environmental effects with class abilities for powerful results. For instance, setting oil or dry grass on fire creates a blaze that damages all nearby enemies.
  - **How to Set Up**: Cast fire spells on flammable surfaces or electric spells in water.

- **Where to Press**: Activate abilities by pressing their hotkeys or select them from the **Abilities** menu to execute these combos.
- **Push and Knockback Effects**:
  - Use abilities that push enemies into environmental hazards, off cliffs, or into traps.
  - **Examples**:
    - **Warriors**: Use **Shield Bash** to knock enemies back.
    - **Mages**: Cast **Gust** to push enemies away.
  - **Where to Press**: In the **Skills** menu, assign abilities with knockback effects and use them near cliffs or hazards to maximize impact.

7. Tactical Mode for Strategic Positioning

- **Pause and Plan**:
  - Tactical mode allows you to pause the action, assess the battlefield, and plan your moves, especially useful when dealing with a challenging environment.
  - **How to Use**: Enter tactical mode to view enemy positions and interactive elements, then position your party accordingly.
  - **Where to Press**: Activate tactical mode with the touchpad (PlayStation), **View** (Xbox), or **T** (PC) to direct your party effectively.
- **Coordinating Party Member Abilities**:
  - Assign each party member to a specific role or position in the environment. For example, keep a Mage on high ground while positioning a Warrior at the front to block enemy advances.
  - **Where to Press**: Use tactical mode to select each party member and place them in advantageous positions for effective combat synergy.

Summary of Exploiting the Environment in Battles

Mastering environmental tactics in *Dragon Age: The Veilguard* can significantly enhance your combat effectiveness. Utilize high ground, break line of sight, lure enemies into hazards, and create synergies with environmental elements to gain the upper hand. With smart positioning, skillful use of interactive objects, and careful control over enemy movement, you can turn every battle into a strategically controlled encounter. Embrace these tactics to become a formidable force in Thedas!

Strategies for Different Playstyles in *Dragon Age: The Veilguard*

Dragon Age: The Veilguard allows players to experience the game through various playstyles, each with its unique approach to combat, exploration, and character development. Whether you prefer a tanky warrior, a powerful mage, or a stealthy rogue, this guide offers effective strategies tailored to different playstyles. By understanding your class strengths and using complementary tactics, you can make the most of your chosen role and adapt to any challenge in Thedas.

1. Tank Playstyle (Warrior)

The Tank Warrior playstyle is designed to absorb damage, control enemy aggression, and protect allies. This build emphasizes high defense, crowd control abilities, and positioning to manage enemy movement and keep threats away from vulnerable teammates.

- **Key Abilities and Skills**:
  - **Shield Wall**: Reduces incoming damage and blocks melee attacks. Essential for surviving intense encounters.
  - **Taunt**: Draws enemies' attention, keeping them focused on you instead of your allies.
  - **Defensive Shout**: Reduces damage taken by nearby allies, increasing their survivability.
  - **Where to Press**: Open the **Skills** menu (Options on PlayStation, **Menu** on Xbox, **K** on PC) to assign defensive abilities like Shield Wall and Taunt.
- **Strategies**:
  - **Positioning for Maximum Defense**: Stand between enemies and your allies, using Shield Wall to block incoming attacks and absorb damage.
  - **Control the Battlefield**: Use Taunt to draw enemies toward you, then position yourself in a chokepoint or narrow area to control enemy movement.
  - **Support Allies**: Use Defensive Shout when allies are low on health, providing a defensive buffer while healers or support mages restore their health.
- **Gear Priorities**:
  - **Heavy Armor**: Prioritize armor that boosts Constitution and Strength for higher health and durability.
  - **Shield and Sword**: Opt for shields that provide extra resistance and swords that enhance blocking effectiveness.
  - **Where to Press**: Access the **Inventory** (Options on PlayStation, **Menu** on Xbox, **I** on PC) to equip gear that supports high defense.

2. DPS (Damage-Per-Second) Playstyle (Warrior, Rogue, or Mage)

The DPS playstyle focuses on dealing maximum damage to enemies, often sacrificing defense for offensive power. Each class has unique ways to play as a DPS, from melee-focused warriors to ranged mages and stealthy rogues.

- **Key Abilities and Skills**:
  - **Warrior**: **Mighty Blow** for single-target damage and **Whirlwind** for crowd control.

- Rogue: **Backstab** for critical hits and **Poison Dagger** for sustained damage over time.
- Mage: **Fireball** for area damage and **Ice Shard** for freezing enemies.
- **Where to Press**: Open the **Skills** menu and assign high-damage abilities based on your class.

- **Strategies**:
  - **Maximize Burst Damage**: Use skills like Backstab (Rogue) or Fireball (Mage) to deal heavy damage quickly, targeting high-priority enemies first.
  - **Keep Moving**: Avoid staying in one place for too long, especially for Rogue and Mage builds with lighter defenses. Constantly reposition to avoid incoming attacks.
  - **Use Tactical Mode for Targeting**: Enter tactical mode to prioritize high-value targets, such as enemy mages or archers, and eliminate them quickly.
  - **Where to Press**: Use tactical mode (touchpad on PlayStation, **View** on Xbox, **T** on PC) to plan your moves and choose targets efficiently.

- **Gear Priorities**:
  - **Warrior DPS**: Two-handed weapons with high Strength bonuses.
  - **Rogue DPS**: Light armor that boosts Dexterity and critical damage.
  - **Mage DPS**: Staves with Magic and Willpower enhancements.
  - **Where to Press**: Equip DPS-optimized weapons and armor in the **Inventory** menu to maximize damage output.

3. Support/Healer Playstyle (Mage)

The Support Mage playstyle is essential for keeping the party healthy, providing crowd control, and reducing the damage allies take. Healers prioritize spells that restore health, create shields, and manage enemy movement to protect the party.

- **Key Abilities and Skills**:
  - **Barrier**: Creates a temporary shield around allies, absorbing damage.
  - **Heal**: Restores health to allies, keeping them alive during extended fights.
  - **Mind Control**: Temporarily distracts enemies, redirecting their attacks.
  - **Where to Press**: Open the **Skills** menu to assign spells like Barrier and Heal for continuous support.

- **Strategies**:
  - **Stay at a Safe Distance**: Position yourself at the back of the party to avoid drawing enemy attention.
  - **Maintain Shields on Allies**: Cast Barrier on allies, especially tanks, to absorb damage and buy time for healing spells.
  - **Manage Enemy Behavior**: Use Mind Control on dangerous enemies to divert their attacks away from weaker allies.

- Coordinate Healing with Attacks: Use tactical mode to time your heals and shields during boss attacks or enemy onslaughts, maximizing their effectiveness.

- **Gear Priorities**:
  - **Robes with Mana Regeneration**: Look for robes that enhance Willpower and mana regeneration.
  - **Staves with Magic Boosts**: Equip staves that increase healing power or provide bonus mana.
  - **Where to Press**: Equip mana-efficient gear in the **Inventory** to sustain long battles and continuous support.

4. Stealth/Assassin Playstyle (Rogue)

The Stealth Rogue playstyle relies on stealth, high critical damage, and precision to take down enemies before they can react. This approach is ideal for players who prefer a hit-and-run style, focusing on isolated enemies and using critical strikes to maximize damage.

- **Key Abilities and Skills**:
  - **Backstab**: Deals critical damage from behind, perfect for high-damage stealth attacks.
  - **Shadow Strike**: Increases critical damage and improves stealth abilities.
  - **Evasion**: Reduces the chance of taking damage, improving survivability during close encounters.
  - **Where to Press**: Open the **Skills** menu to select and assign abilities that enhance stealth and critical strikes.

- **Strategies**:
  - **Stay in Stealth as Much as Possible**: Use the environment for cover and approach enemies from behind.
  - **Target Key Enemies First**: Focus on high-priority targets like mages or archers, eliminating them before they become a threat.
  - **Chain Attacks for Sustained Damage**: After attacking from stealth, use abilities like Poison Dagger to maintain damage while retreating to stealth.
  - **Where to Press**: Activate **Stealth Mode** with **R3** (PlayStation), **Right Stick** (Xbox), or **Shift** (PC) to approach targets undetected.

- **Gear Priorities**:
  - **Daggers with High Crit Bonuses**: Equip daggers that boost Dexterity and critical hit chance.
  - **Light Armor with Evasion**: Light armor enhances evasion, making it easier to dodge enemy attacks.
  - **Where to Press**: Equip high-crit gear in the **Inventory** menu to maximize the impact of each stealth strike.

5. Hybrid Playstyle (Multiclass Builds)

The Hybrid playstyle combines elements from two or more roles, allowing for flexibility in combat. For example, a Mage can focus on both support and damage, or a Warrior might combine tanking with DPS capabilities.

- **Key Abilities and Skills**:
  - **Mage Hybrid (Damage + Support)**: Use a mix of **Barrier** for protection and **Fireball** for damage.
  - **Warrior Hybrid (Tank + DPS)**: Combine **Taunt** with **Mighty Blow** for a balanced tank-DPS approach.
  - **Rogue Hybrid (Melee + Ranged)**: Equip both Backstab and Long Shot for versatility in close and ranged combat.
  - **Where to Press**: Use the **Skills** menu to allocate points across multiple skill trees, selecting abilities that enhance both roles.
- **Strategies**:
  - **Adapt to Changing Situations**: Switch between roles as needed, focusing on support or DPS depending on the situation.
  - **Control Enemy Movement**: As a hybrid, you can shift between crowd control and damage, adapting based on the enemy's position.
  - **Manage Resources Efficiently**: Hybrid builds require careful mana or stamina management. Use potions and resource-efficient skills to avoid running out during long fights.
- **Gear Priorities**:
  - **Balanced Equipment**: Look for gear that provides a blend of defensive and offensive stats.
  - **Specialized Weapons**: Equip a staff or weapon that complements your primary skill focus while supporting your secondary role.
  - **Where to Press**: Use the **Inventory** menu to select versatile gear that supports multiple roles.

Summary of Strategies for Different Playstyles

Each playstyle in *Dragon Age: The Veilguard* offers unique strategies and tactics for maximizing character potential. Tanks focus on absorbing damage, DPS builds on delivering high damage, Support builds on healing and shielding, Stealth on critical strikes, and Hybrids on flexibility. By understanding the strengths and strategies of your chosen playstyle, you can effectively navigate battles, support your team, and take full advantage of your character's capabilities. Enjoy mastering the art of combat in Thedas!

Endgame Content and Challenges in *Dragon Age: The Veilguard*

Once you've completed the main storyline of *Dragon Age: The Veilguard*, the game opens up with new, challenging endgame content designed to test your skills, strategy, and character build. Endgame activities include high-level dungeons, elite boss battles, specialized quests, and unique rewards. This guide provides detailed tips on tackling endgame content, where to find these activities, and how to prepare for the toughest challenges in Thedas.

1. High-Level Dungeons

- **Description**: Endgame dungeons are designed with higher-level enemies, intricate puzzles, and valuable loot. These dungeons often feature elite monsters and require advanced strategies.
- **Key Dungeons**:
  - **The Abyssal Depths**: Known for powerful dark magic enemies and rare resources for crafting.
  - **Forgotten Catacombs**: Features undead enemies with resistances to physical damage, requiring a mix of elemental attacks.
- **Where to Access**:
  - **The Abyssal Depths**: Found in the **Shadowed Marshes** region; press **Map** (touchpad on PlayStation, **View** on Xbox, **M** on PC) and locate the dungeon icon.
  - **Forgotten Catacombs**: Accessible from the **Cursed Ruins** area in the northwest part of the map.
- **Strategies**:
  - **Team Composition**: Bring a balanced team, including a tank for damage absorption, a mage for elemental attacks, and a healer for sustain.
  - **Prepare for Status Effects**: Equip gear that grants resistance to poison, fire, and other status effects commonly found in endgame dungeons.
  - **Pace Yourself**: Clear enemies gradually, avoiding the risk of being overwhelmed by large groups.

2. Elite Boss Battles

- **Description**: Elite bosses are the most challenging foes in *The Veilguard*, boasting unique mechanics, high health pools, and devastating attacks. Defeating them unlocks powerful loot and achievements.
- **Notable Elite Bosses**:
  - **The Shadow Revenant**: An undead specter with phase-shifting abilities and immunity to certain attacks.
  - **Veil Serpent**: A massive serpent boss that resides within a Veil Rift, using poison-based attacks and summoning minions.

- **Where to Access**:
    - **Shadow Revenant**: Found in the **Haunted Grove**; press **Map** to locate its icon in the southwest region.
    - **Veil Serpent**: Located in the **Veilguard Rift**; approach the rift and press **X** (PlayStation), **A** (Xbox), or **E** (PC) to enter.
- **Strategies**:
    - **Learn Boss Mechanics**: Each boss has specific mechanics, so observe their attack patterns to dodge or counter effectively.
    - **Use Tactical Mode**: Enter tactical mode (touchpad on PlayStation, **View** on Xbox, **T** on PC) to position your party members strategically and avoid the boss's AoE attacks.
    - **Optimize Elemental Attacks**: Equip weapons or abilities that exploit the boss's elemental weaknesses, such as fire for undead bosses or ice for poison-immune creatures.

3. Legendary Gear and Crafting Materials

- **Description**: Endgame content introduces rare crafting materials and legendary gear with unique bonuses that significantly enhance your character's abilities. Some materials are exclusive to specific endgame dungeons or bosses.
- **Key Materials and Where to Find Them**:
    - **Veil Essence**: A material used to craft Veilguard-exclusive weapons, found in Veil Rifts.
    - **Dragon Scale**: Used for high-defense armor, dropped by draconic bosses like the Veil Serpent.
    - **Ancient Relic Fragments**: Scattered across elite dungeons, required for creating certain legendary weapons.
- **Where to Craft**:
    - Visit the main city's crafting station (e.g., **Brightfall Forge**); press **X** (PlayStation), **A** (Xbox), or **E** (PC) to interact with the crafting table.
- **Strategies**:
    - **Farm Specific Bosses**: Some bosses drop unique materials, so defeat them multiple times if you need specific items.
    - **Equip Resource Boosting Gear**: Certain items increase material drop rates; equip these to collect resources faster.
    - **Upgrade and Enchant**: Use the materials you collect to not only craft gear but also enchant it with elemental resistance or enhanced critical damage.

4. Veilguard Exclusive Questlines

- **Description**: These post-story quests are exclusive to those who have completed the main campaign. They dive into advanced lore and include high-stakes missions that introduce unique characters and lore revelations.
- **Key Quests**:

- ○ **The Secrets of the Veil**: Investigate hidden aspects of the Veil, with quests that span multiple regions and rifts.
  - ○ **The Lost Veilguard**: A story-driven quest that uncovers the fate of a legendary Veilguard warrior.
- **Where to Access**:
  - ○ **The Secrets of the Veil**: Automatically unlocked upon completing the main storyline; found in **Brightfall Village**. Talk to the Veil Scholar to begin.
  - ○ **The Lost Veilguard**: Accessed via a hidden cave in the **Stormguard Mountains**.
- **Strategies**:
  - ○ **Bring a Balanced Party**: These quests often have mixed challenges, from puzzle-solving to intense combat. Prepare for a variety of encounters.
  - ○ **Use Veil Pulse**: To locate hidden quest items, activate Veil Pulse by pressing **L1** (PlayStation), **LB** (Xbox), or **Q** (PC).
  - ○ **Explore Thoroughly**: Veilguard-exclusive quests often have secret areas and lore entries that provide insight into the story.

5. Multiplayer Raids and Co-op Dungeons

- **Description**: Multiplayer endgame content includes raids and co-op dungeons where players team up to take on challenging foes and earn exclusive rewards. These activities require coordination and teamwork.
- **Available Raids**:
  - ○ **The Eternal Veil**: A raid within the deepest rift of the Veil, featuring multiple bosses with intricate mechanics.
  - ○ **Dragon's Wrath**: A co-op dungeon against dragonkin enemies, requiring careful coordination to survive.
- **Where to Access**:
  - ○ Access raids and co-op dungeons from the **Multiplayer Menu** on the main screen. Press **X** (PlayStation), **A** (Xbox), or **E** (PC) to join a multiplayer session.
- **Strategies**:
  - ○ **Assign Roles**: Designate a tank, DPS, and healer to ensure a balanced team for survival.
  - ○ **Coordinate Abilities**: Sync up powerful abilities to maximize damage output during boss encounters.
  - ○ **Use Voice or Text Chat**: Communication is essential in multiplayer; use voice chat or the in-game text chat to coordinate with teammates.

6. Challenge Modes and Timed Events

- **Description**: These modes offer special challenges, such as completing dungeons within a time limit or fighting against waves of elite enemies. Timed events often provide seasonal or limited-time rewards.

- **Key Events**:
  - ○ **Trial of the Ancients**: Complete a dungeon within a set time to earn exclusive rewards.
  - ○ **Veilguard Assault**: Defend against waves of Veil creatures, increasing in difficulty with each wave.
- **Where to Access**:
  - ○ **Trial of the Ancients**: Found in **Brightfall Arena**; talk to the Arena Master to begin.
  - ○ **Veilguard Assault**: Available at Veilguard Outposts; press **X** (PlayStation), **A** (Xbox), or **E** (PC) to initiate the challenge.
- **Strategies**:
  - ○ **Speed Over Caution**: In timed events, prioritize quick attacks over defensive maneuvers to complete objectives faster.
  - ○ **Chain AOE Attacks**: Use area-of-effect abilities to clear waves of enemies quickly in assault challenges.
  - ○ **Equip Event-Specific Gear**: Certain items provide bonuses for timed events, such as increased movement speed or cooldown reduction.

Summary of Endgame Content and Challenges

Endgame content in *Dragon Age: The Veilguard* offers a variety of activities, from high-level dungeons and elite bosses to multiplayer raids and exclusive questlines. Each challenge requires strategic preparation, from selecting the right party composition to equipping the best gear. By taking on these endgame activities, you'll unlock legendary gear, uncover hidden lore, and face the ultimate trials of Thedas. Good luck, and enjoy the thrill of becoming a true Veilguard master!

Appendices

Character Build Examples for Each Class

In *Dragon Age: The Veilguard*, building an optimized character can significantly impact your experience, allowing you to tackle tough enemies, breeze through dungeons, and enhance your role in both solo and multiplayer gameplay. This guide provides detailed build examples for each class: Warrior, Mage, and Rogue, with a focus on creating powerful and effective setups for various playstyles. Each build example includes core skills, suggested attributes, and recommended gear to help you make the most of your character's strengths.

1. Warrior Build Examples

Build A: Tank Warrior

- **Purpose**: Absorbs enemy damage, protects allies, and controls the battlefield.
- **Primary Attributes**:
  - **Constitution**: Boosts health and defense, essential for withstanding enemy attacks.
  - **Strength**: Increases melee power, helping you hold aggro.
- **Key Skills**:
  - **Shield Wall**: Essential for blocking melee attacks and reducing incoming damage.
  - **Taunt**: Draws enemy attention, allowing you to control their focus and protect squishier teammates.
  - **Defensive Shout**: Reduces damage taken by allies within range, providing added protection in challenging fights.
  - **Where to Press**: Access these skills through the **Skills** menu (Options on PlayStation, **Menu** on Xbox, **K** on PC) and assign them to your hotbar.
- **Recommended Gear**:
  - **Shield and Sword**: Look for shields that boost Constitution and swords that add Strength, maximizing defense and damage.
  - **Heavy Armor**: Prioritize armor with Constitution bonuses to increase your survivability.
  - **Where to Press**: Open the **Inventory** (Options on PlayStation, **Menu** on Xbox, **I** on PC) to equip tank-specific gear.

Build B: DPS Warrior

- **Purpose**: Deals high melee damage with a focus on two-handed weapons and powerful attacks.
- **Primary Attributes**:
    - **Strength**: Enhances damage output, critical for heavy melee attacks.
    - **Dexterity**: Improves critical hit chance, helping you land powerful blows.
- **Key Skills**:
    - **Mighty Blow**: High-damage skill, perfect for targeting tough enemies.
    - **Whirlwind**: Area-of-effect ability that deals damage to all nearby enemies, ideal for crowd control.
    - **Rage Strike**: Increases damage output temporarily, helping you maximize burst damage.
    - **Where to Press**: Assign these skills in the **Skills** menu, focusing on DPS-oriented abilities.
- **Recommended Gear**:
    - **Two-Handed Weapons**: Equip axes or swords with high Strength bonuses for maximum damage.
    - **Medium Armor**: Armor that enhances Strength and Dexterity for balanced offense and durability.
    - **Where to Press**: Equip DPS-oriented gear in the **Inventory** to focus on maximizing damage output.

2. Mage Build Examples

Build A: Damage Mage

- **Purpose**: Specializes in high-damage elemental spells, ideal for taking down groups of enemies from a distance.
- **Primary Attributes**:
    - **Magic**: Boosts spell power and effectiveness, critical for a damage-focused Mage.
    - **Willpower**: Increases mana capacity, allowing for more frequent casting.
- **Key Skills**:
    - **Fireball**: High-damage AOE spell that hits multiple enemies, perfect for starting fights.
    - **Ice Shard**: Freezes enemies, increasing vulnerability to fire-based follow-up attacks.
    - **Lightning Bolt**: Deals direct damage and can stun enemies, disrupting their attacks.
    - **Where to Press**: Assign offensive spells like Fireball and Lightning Bolt in the **Skills** menu for easy access.
- **Recommended Gear**:
    - **High-Power Staff**: Choose a staff that enhances Magic and spell damage.
    - **Robes with Mana Regeneration**: Robes that boost Willpower and Magic are ideal for extended casting.
    - **Where to Press**: Equip gear that prioritizes Magic in the **Inventory** to maximize spell damage.

Build B: Support Mage

- **Purpose**: Focuses on healing, shields, and crowd control to support the party.
- **Primary Attributes**:
  - **Willpower**: Increases mana capacity and regeneration, essential for continuous support.
  - **Magic**: Enhances the power of healing and shield spells.
- **Key Skills**:
  - **Barrier**: Provides a shield to allies, absorbing damage and giving them a chance to recover.
  - **Heal**: Directly restores health to teammates, crucial for keeping the party alive.
  - **Mind Control**: Temporarily distracts enemies, taking pressure off the tank and DPS.
  - **Where to Press**: In the **Skills** menu, assign Barrier and Heal to your hotbar for quick access to support abilities.
- **Recommended Gear**:
  - **Staff with Mana Bonuses**: Equip a staff that boosts Willpower for better mana management.
  - **Robes with Cooldown Reduction**: Look for robes that shorten cooldown times on support spells, allowing for frequent casting.
  - **Where to Press**: Select support-boosting gear in the **Inventory** to enhance healing and crowd-control abilities.

3. Rogue Build Examples

Build A: Stealth Assassin

- **Purpose**: Specializes in stealth, critical strikes, and quick elimination of high-priority targets.
- **Primary Attributes**:
  - **Dexterity**: Increases critical hit chance and evasion, ideal for avoiding damage and dealing critical hits.
  - **Cunning**: Boosts critical damage and enhances abilities like lockpicking.
- **Key Skills**:
  - **Backstab**: High-damage attack that deals critical damage from behind, perfect for stealthy attacks.
  - **Poison Dagger**: Applies poison damage over time, useful for sustained DPS.
  - **Evasion**: Reduces the chance of taking damage, improving survivability during stealth engagements.
  - **Where to Press**: In the **Skills** menu, prioritize skills like Backstab and Poison Dagger to maximize stealth efficiency.
- **Recommended Gear**:
  - **Daggers with Crit Bonuses**: Equip daggers that boost Dexterity and critical damage.
  - **Light Armor with Evasion**: Light armor enhances evasion, making it easier to avoid damage.

- **Where to Press**: Equip high-crit gear in the **Inventory** to enhance stealth and assassination effectiveness.

Build B: Ranged Marksman

- **Purpose**: Uses ranged attacks and high mobility to deal consistent damage from a distance.
- **Primary Attributes**:
  - **Dexterity**: Boosts accuracy and critical hit chance, essential for landing ranged shots.
  - **Cunning**: Increases critical damage, making each shot more impactful.
- **Key Skills**:
  - **Long Shot**: Deals high damage to enemies at a distance, perfect for starting combat.
  - **Pinning Shot**: Immobilizes enemies, preventing them from closing in on you.
  - **Rapid Fire**: Increases attack speed, allowing for quick damage output.
  - **Where to Press**: Access the **Skills** menu and assign ranged skills like Long Shot and Rapid Fire to maximize ranged DPS.
- **Recommended Gear**:
  - **Bow with Dexterity Bonuses**: Choose a bow with high Dexterity and Cunning bonuses for increased accuracy and crit damage.
  - **Light Armor with Movement Speed Boost**: Light armor that enhances Dexterity and provides speed boosts, perfect for staying mobile.
  - **Where to Press**: Equip ranged gear in the **Inventory** that prioritizes critical hits and mobility.

4. Hybrid Build Example

Build: Battlemage (Mage + Melee)

- **Purpose**: A versatile hybrid that combines melee strength with spellcasting, allowing for flexible combat both up close and at a distance.
- **Primary Attributes**:
  - **Magic**: Boosts spell damage and effectiveness in combat.
  - **Strength**: Increases melee damage, giving the Battlemage more options in close-range combat.
- **Key Skills**:
  - **Veilguard Slash**: A melee attack infused with magic, providing both physical and elemental damage.
  - **Firestorm**: High-damage AOE spell, perfect for softening enemies before engaging in melee.
  - **Barrier**: Adds a shield for close-combat engagements, increasing survivability.
  - **Where to Press**: In the **Skills** menu, select a mix of melee and spellcasting abilities to create a balanced Battlemage build.
- **Recommended Gear**:

- **Staff or Sword**: Equip a staff with Magic bonuses or a sword that boosts Strength, depending on your preferred range.
- **Hybrid Armor**: Armor that offers a mix of Magic and Strength, allowing for both spellcasting and melee combat.
- **Where to Press**: Open the **Inventory** to equip hybrid gear that supports both melee and magic capabilities.

Summary of Character Build Examples for Each Class

These build examples provide a strong foundation for each class, from Tank Warriors to Stealth Rogues and Damage Mages. By focusing on key attributes, skills, and gear specific to each build, you can create a powerful character tailored to your playstyle. Experiment with these builds to find the perfect balance of strengths for taking on the toughest challenges in *The Veilguard*. Enjoy your journey in Thedas with a character that feels uniquely yours!

Glossary of Terms for *Dragon Age: The Veilguard*

This glossary provides definitions for key terms and concepts in *Dragon Age: The Veilguard*, helping both new and experienced players understand the language of the game. These definitions cover gameplay mechanics, class-specific abilities, lore elements, and common phrases that appear throughout *The Veilguard*.

A

- **Aggro**: Refers to the attention of enemies focused on a particular character, usually the tank, who absorbs damage to protect other party members.
- **AOE (Area of Effect)**: Abilities or attacks that affect multiple enemies within a specified area. Useful for crowd control and damaging groups.

B

- **Barrier**: A magical shield that protects characters by absorbing a certain amount of damage before it breaks. Primarily used by Mages to protect allies.
- **Buff**: A temporary enhancement applied to a character, improving their attributes or abilities. Buffs can increase health, damage, speed, and other stats.

C

- **CC (Crowd Control)**: Abilities that temporarily impair or control enemy actions, such as stuns, freezes, or knockbacks, to reduce the number of active threats.
- **Cooldown**: The period required before an ability or spell can be used again. Managing cooldowns is crucial for sustained combat effectiveness.

D

- **Debuff**: A negative status effect applied to enemies, reducing their effectiveness by lowering their stats, impairing their movement, or dealing damage over time.
- **DOT (Damage Over Time)**: An ability that causes damage gradually over a period rather than all at once. Examples include poison and burn effects.

E

- **Endgame**: High-level content available after completing the main storyline, including elite dungeons, boss battles, and exclusive quests.
- **EXP (Experience Points)**: Points earned from completing quests and defeating enemies, used to level up characters and unlock new abilities.

F

- **Fast Travel**: A feature allowing players to quickly move between locations on the map they've already visited.
- **Flanking**: Attacking an enemy from the side or behind to increase damage or accuracy, especially useful for Rogues and characters with stealth abilities.

G

- **Gear**: Equipment, such as weapons, armor, and accessories, that enhances a character's attributes and abilities. Gear can be crafted, looted, or purchased.
- **Grinding**: Repetitive activities to accumulate resources, experience, or currency. Often done in specific areas with high enemy density.

H

- **HP (Health Points)**: Represents a character's life. When HP reaches zero, the character falls in battle and must be revived or replaced.
- **Hotbar**: A set of slots where players can assign abilities, spells, and items for quick access during combat.

I

- **Inventory**: A storage menu where players can view, equip, and manage items, gear, and resources collected during gameplay.
- **Intelligence**: An attribute that boosts spell power and magical effectiveness for spellcasting classes, especially Mages.

L

- **Line of Sight**: A visual line between a character and a target, required for ranged attacks and certain abilities to hit. Obstacles can block line of sight, preventing attacks.
- **Loot**: Items collected from defeated enemies, chests, or quests. Loot can include gear, resources, currency, and rare items.

M

- **Mana**: A resource used by spellcasters, such as Mages, to cast spells. Mana regenerates over time or can be restored using potions.
- **Mob**: A term for non-player characters (NPCs) or monsters that are enemies, often found in dungeons or open-world areas.

N

- **NPC (Non-Player Character)**: Characters controlled by the game, often quest givers, merchants, or allies.
- **Nerf**: A decrease in the effectiveness of an ability or item, often as part of a game update or balance patch.

P

- **Party**: The group of characters, usually consisting of the player's main character and companions, that work together in battles and quests.
- **Passive Ability**: An ability that provides a continuous effect without needing to be activated, often enhancing attributes like defense or speed.

Q

- **Quest**: Missions or tasks given by NPCs or discovered in the environment. Quests provide rewards, experience points, and items upon completion.
- **Quickslot**: A slot in the hotbar where items or abilities can be placed for quick access, useful for healing potions or frequently used abilities.

R

- **Ranged Attack**: An attack performed from a distance, typically by Archers or Mages. Ranged attacks are useful for staying out of melee range.
- **RPG (Role-Playing Game)**: A genre of game focused on character development, story progression, and interaction with the game world. *Dragon Age* is an RPG.

S

- **Stamina**: A resource used by physical classes, like Warriors and Rogues, for performing special attacks. Like mana, stamina regenerates over time.
- **Status Effect**: A temporary condition affecting a character or enemy, such as burn, poison, or freeze, often applied by abilities or environmental hazards.

T

- **Tactical Mode**: A mode that pauses combat, allowing players to position characters, select abilities, and issue commands with precision. Essential for complex battles.
- **Tank**: A character who draws enemy attacks, protecting allies by absorbing damage and controlling aggro. Typically has high health and defense.

U

- **Ultimate Ability**: A powerful ability, often unlocked at higher levels, that has a long cooldown but deals substantial damage or provides significant benefits.
- **Upgrade**: Improving an item, skill, or ability to enhance its effectiveness, often through crafting or spending resources.

V

- **Veil**: A mystical barrier between the physical world and the Fade, the realm of spirits and demons. The Veil is central to the lore and gameplay of *The Veilguard*.
- **Vendor**: An NPC that sells goods, equipment, or services, allowing players to purchase or sell items.

W

- **Wave**: A group of enemies that spawn in succession, often during defense quests or timed events, where players must survive multiple waves to complete the objective.
- **Weapon Proficiency**: A character's skill with a certain type of weapon, such as swords or bows, which increases damage and effectiveness with that weapon type.

XP

- **XP (Experience Points)**: Points gained through battles, quests, and exploration that contribute to leveling up. Higher levels unlock new abilities and attributes.

Conclusion

This glossary provides a foundation for understanding *Dragon Age: The Veilguard*'s core terminology. Familiarizing yourself with these terms will help you navigate the game's mechanics, communicate effectively with other players, and enhance your overall gameplay experience.

Frequently Asked Questions (FAQ) for *Dragon Age: The Veilguard*

This FAQ section provides answers to common questions players may have while playing *Dragon Age: The Veilguard*. Covering everything from gameplay mechanics to character progression and endgame content, this guide will help new and experienced players find quick solutions and enhance their understanding of the game.

1. What is the Veil in *Dragon Age: The Veilguard*?

- **Answer**: The Veil is a mystical barrier separating the physical world from the Fade, the realm of spirits and demons. In *The Veilguard*, you can interact with the Veil to access hidden areas, encounter unique enemies, and unlock powerful abilities that tap into its magic.

2. How do I choose the best class for my playstyle?

- **Answer**: Each class has unique strengths suited to different playstyles:
  - **Warrior**: Great for tanking and dealing melee damage.
  - **Mage**: Ideal for casting powerful spells and supporting allies.
  - **Rogue**: Specializes in stealth, critical hits, and ranged attacks.
- Consider your preferred combat role (damage, support, or defense) when choosing a class, and feel free to experiment with different builds as you progress.

3. How do I level up quickly?

- **Answer**: To level up efficiently:
  - Complete main and side quests for substantial experience gains.
  - Clear enemy camps and dungeons frequently.

○ Take on high-XP activities like elite dungeons and multiplayer challenges.
- Equip any XP-boosting items you find, and consider teaming up in multiplayer dungeons, as they tend to offer higher XP rewards.

4. Can I respec my character's skills?

- **Answer**: Yes, you can respec (reset) your skills by visiting a Respec Trainer found in major towns or certain safe areas. There may be a fee involved, but it allows you to reallocate skill points to try different builds and abilities.

5. What is Tactical Mode, and when should I use it?

- **Answer**: Tactical Mode is a pause-and-plan feature that allows you to issue commands to your party, assess enemy positions, and strategize. Use Tactical Mode during complex fights, boss battles, or when positioning is key, as it provides greater control over the battlefield.

6. How do I manage my inventory and avoid becoming over-encumbered?

- **Answer**: To manage your inventory effectively:
  ○ Periodically sell or dismantle unwanted gear and items at vendors.
  ○ Store excess items in your stash (available at main camps or towns).
  ○ Use inventory-expanding items, if available, to increase capacity.
- Remember to check your inventory often (Options on PlayStation, **Menu** on Xbox, **I** on PC) and keep only essential items.

7. How do I unlock specializations for my character?

- **Answer**: Specializations unlock at a certain level or after completing specific quests related to your class. Once unlocked, you can choose from advanced skill trees that enhance your character's abilities:
  ○ **Warrior Specializations**: Berserker, Templar, Champion.
  ○ **Mage Specializations**: Blood Mage, Arcane Warrior, Spirit Healer.
  ○ **Rogue Specializations**: Assassin, Duelist, Ranger.
- You can access these options in the **Skills** menu when they become available.

8. What is the best way to earn gold in *The Veilguard*?

- **Answer**: To accumulate gold quickly:
  ○ Complete quests and side missions, as they often reward gold.
  ○ Loot enemies and treasure chests in dungeons.
  ○ Sell items and gear that you don't need.
- Participate in multiplayer challenges and high-level dungeons for additional rewards that can be sold.

9. How do I upgrade and enchant my gear?

- **Answer**: Upgrades and enchantments are available at crafting stations located in major towns and camps.
    - **To upgrade**: Use materials found throughout the world to increase gear stats.
    - **To enchant**: Use rare resources to apply elemental or special effects to weapons and armor.
- Access the crafting table by pressing **X** (PlayStation), **A** (Xbox), or **E** (PC) to start the upgrade or enchantment process.

10. Are there any hidden quests or secret locations in the game?

- **Answer**: Yes, *The Veilguard* is full of hidden quests and secret areas. These can be discovered by:
    - Exploring off the main paths, caves, and abandoned buildings.
    - Using **Veil Pulse** (press **L1** on PlayStation, **LB** on Xbox, **Q** on PC) to reveal hidden objects and paths.
    - Talking to NPCs in towns, as some will provide clues or unlock hidden side quests.

11. What should I know about multiplayer in *The Veilguard*?

- **Answer**: Multiplayer includes co-op dungeons, raids, and PvP modes. To maximize multiplayer success:
    - Coordinate with teammates, as communication is key for tougher dungeons.
    - Assign each player a role (tank, DPS, healer) for a balanced team.
    - Use the **Multiplayer Menu** (accessed from the main screen) to join or create sessions and access exclusive multiplayer rewards.

12. How does the endgame content work, and what can I do after finishing the main story?

- **Answer**: Endgame content offers elite challenges, such as:
    - **High-Level Dungeons**: Filled with powerful enemies and rare loot.
    - **Elite Boss Battles**: Tougher than main-story bosses, providing unique rewards.
    - **Veilguard Questlines**: Exclusive post-story quests that explore additional lore.
    - **Multiplayer Raids**: Large-scale dungeons designed for team play.
- These activities allow you to continue leveling up, upgrade gear, and experience new challenges.

13. Can I romance NPCs or companions in *The Veilguard*?

- **Answer**: Yes, certain NPCs and companions can be romanced. To build a romantic relationship:
    - Choose supportive or kind dialogue options that align with the companion's personality.
    - Complete loyalty missions for companions, which often unlock romance options.
- Visit companions in camps and engage in dialogue regularly to progress these relationships.

14. How do I change or improve my character's appearance?

- **Answer**: Character appearance can be customized at the start of the game and modified using certain items or by visiting a vendor that offers appearance changes in major towns.

15. What's the best way to prepare for boss fights?

- **Answer**: Boss fights can be challenging, so make sure you:
    - **Stock Up on Potions**: Health, mana, and status resistance potions are essential.
    - **Equip the Right Gear**: Use armor and weapons that provide resistance or boost stats relevant to the boss.
    - **Study Boss Patterns**: Many bosses have attack patterns—use Tactical Mode (touchpad on PlayStation, **View** on Xbox, **T** on PC) to observe and plan your strategy.
- Position your party members effectively and be prepared to adjust tactics as the fight progresses.

Index of Important Locations in *Dragon Age: The Veilguard*

The world of *Dragon Age: The Veilguard* is filled with diverse regions, hidden dungeons, and key locations that offer quests, resources, and unique challenges. This guide provides an index of significant places to visit, organized by region, with tips on what to find, explore, and accomplish in each location. For convenience, navigation tips and where to access each location on your map are also included.

1. Brightfall Village

- **Description**: A central hub for quests, merchants, and interactions with NPCs, Brightfall Village is where players can rest, resupply, and gather valuable information for upcoming quests.
- **Key Activities**:
    - **Quest Board**: Check the quest board for side missions and bounties.
    - **Brightfall Forge**: Craft and upgrade weapons, armor, and enchanted items.
    - **Respec Trainer**: Allows players to reallocate skill points for a fee.
- **Where to Press**: Open the **Map** (touchpad on PlayStation, **View** on Xbox, **M** on PC) to find Brightfall Village, marked in the central region.

2. The Shadowed Marshes

- **Description**: A swampy area known for dark magic and Veil rifts. The Shadowed Marshes are filled with dangerous creatures and environmental hazards, requiring caution.
- **Key Locations**:

- **The Abyssal Depths**: A high-level dungeon featuring dark magic enemies and rare crafting materials.
  - **Veil Rifts**: Several Veil Rifts can be found here, containing spirits and Veil-related resources.
- **Where to Press**: Use **Veil Pulse** by pressing **L1** (PlayStation), **LB** (Xbox), or **Q** (PC) to locate hidden objects and paths within the marshes.

3. Stormguard Mountains

- **Description**: A rugged, mountainous area where players encounter strong enemies, as well as breathtaking views and hidden caves.
- **Key Locations**:
  - **The Lost Veilguard Cave**: A hidden cave that unlocks after completing main story quests, revealing lore about a legendary Veilguard warrior.
  - **Dragon's Roost**: Home to dragonkin enemies, this location offers rare materials like Dragon Scales.
- **Where to Press**: Access the **Map** to locate the Stormguard Mountains in the northern part of the world. Approach the dragon's lair cautiously as it contains elite enemies.

4. The Veilguard Rift

- **Description**: A unique area accessible through Veil portals, the Veilguard Rift allows players to interact directly with the Fade, encountering spirits, demons, and powerful enemies.
- **Key Locations**:
  - **Veil Serpent's Lair**: A boss area where players fight the Veil Serpent, a challenging poison-based enemy.
  - **Veilguard Relic Site**: Contains hidden relics that offer lore and exclusive rewards.
- **Where to Press**: Approach the Veilguard Rift portal and press **X** (PlayStation), **A** (Xbox), or **E** (PC) to enter. Use **Veil Pulse** within to locate relics and secrets.

5. Cursed Ruins

- **Description**: These ruins are home to undead enemies and various cursed relics. The Cursed Ruins offer challenging battles and are rich in lore.
- **Key Locations**:
  - **Forgotten Catacombs**: An elite dungeon containing undead enemies and hidden treasures, ideal for high-level players.
  - **Dark Altar**: A cursed altar where players can engage in optional challenges to earn powerful items.
- **Where to Press**: Find the Cursed Ruins in the western part of the map. Open the **Map** and track the dungeon entrance from the nearest fast travel point.

6. Haunted Grove

- **Description**: A mystical forest shrouded in fog and mystery, known for ghostly apparitions and dangerous creatures. Haunted Grove is filled with lore and side quests.
- **Key Locations**:
  - **Shadow Revenant's Shrine**: The area where players face the Shadow Revenant, a high-level spectral boss.
  - **Ancient Relic Sites**: Scattered relics that provide unique story insights and rewards.
- **Where to Press**: Access the **Map** and look for the Haunted Grove marker in the southwest region. Use **Veil Pulse** to locate hidden relics among the trees.

7. Brightfall Arena

- **Description**: A combat arena located within Brightfall Village where players can test their skills in timed challenges and waves of enemies.
- **Key Activities**:
  - **Trial of the Ancients**: A timed event offering exclusive rewards for completing a dungeon under a set time limit.
  - **PvP and Co-op Challenges**: Multiplayer modes that allow players to team up or compete against each other.
- **Where to Press**: In Brightfall Village, talk to the Arena Master near the arena's entrance to start trials or multiplayer challenges.

8. Veilguard Outposts

- **Description**: Located at key points throughout the world, these outposts serve as checkpoints where players can rest, resupply, and engage in defense challenges.
- **Key Activities**:
  - **Veilguard Assault**: Defend the outpost from waves of Veil creatures in a timed challenge.
  - **Merchant Stalls**: Outposts offer basic supplies and items for sale.
- **Where to Press**: Locate outposts on the **Map**, often marked along main travel routes. Engage with the Assault Challenge by approaching the outpost's central post.

9. The Fade Nexus

- **Description**: An ethereal realm only accessible through Veil portals. The Fade Nexus is an abstract, floating environment where players encounter powerful spirit-based enemies and unique lore.
- **Key Locations**:
  - **Ancient Fade Library**: A hidden section containing rare lore books and scrolls that deepen the game's story.

- - **Guardian's Domain**: Home to the Guardian of the Fade, a challenging boss with high resistance to physical damage.
- **Where to Press**: Enter the Fade Nexus through Veil portals located in various regions. Use **Veil Pulse** within the Nexus to reveal hidden objects and pathways.

10. Merchant's Crossing

- **Description**: A bustling trading hub that connects several regions, Merchant's Crossing is filled with vendors offering unique items, resources, and gear.
- **Key Activities**:
  - **Rare Item Vendors**: Shop for unique items and crafting materials not found elsewhere.
  - **Contract Board**: Pick up additional quests or contracts for extra rewards.
- **Where to Press**: Open the **Map** to locate Merchant's Crossing in the eastern region. Vendors are marked with merchant icons within the area.

11. Frostreach Caverns

- **Description**: A snowy, ice-covered cave system home to frost-based enemies and rare materials. Frostreach Caverns require specific gear to handle the cold environment.
- **Key Locations**:
  - **Ice Wraith's Lair**: A mini-boss area with ice-themed enemies that drop cold-resistant gear and frost-based crafting items.
  - **Frozen Veil Shard Site**: Contains Veil shards infused with ice magic, used for crafting unique items.
- **Where to Press**: Locate Frostreach Caverns in the north by following the mountain pass. Equip cold-resistant gear found in the **Inventory** to minimize damage from frost effects.

12. Brightfall Academy

- **Description**: An educational institution in Brightfall Village where players can learn advanced skills, respec, and take on skill challenges.
- **Key Activities**:
  - **Respec Training**: Reset and reallocate skill points.
  - **Skill Challenges**: Test new abilities and practice combos in controlled settings.
- **Where to Press**: Visit Brightfall Academy near the center of Brightfall Village. Interact with instructors to begin training sessions or respec your skills.

Summary of Important Locations

This index of important locations in *Dragon Age: The Veilguard* provides an overview of the areas you'll encounter, highlighting each location's key activities and the resources they offer. By referencing this guide, you can plan your journey, tackle challenging dungeons, and make the most of each region in Thedas. Remember to use the **Map** and **Veil Pulse** to navigate and uncover hidden areas, maximizing your exploration and enhancing your experience in the world of *The Veilguard*.